Focus on Sexuality Research

Series Editor: Marta Meana

For further volumes:
http://www.springer.com/series/10132

Anne A. Lawrence

Men Trapped in Men's Bodies

Narratives of Autogynephilic Transsexualism

Foreword by Ray Blanchard

Springer

Anne A. Lawrence
University of Lethbridge
Lethbridge, Alberta, Canada

ISBN 978-1-4614-5181-5 ISBN 978-1-4614-5182-2 (eBook)
DOI 10.1007/978-1-4614-5182-2
Springer New York Heidelberg Dordrecht London

Library of Congress Control Number: 2012948681

Printed on acid-free paper

Springer is part of Springer Science+Business Media (www.springer.com)

Foreword

One day, around 1987 or 1988, I spent the afternoon in a reference room of the Robarts Library of the University of Toronto. I was trying to find a word—or failing that, to invent one—to denote a phenomenon I had gradually apprehended during clinical interviews with many biologically male patients interested in sex reassignment surgery. That phenomenon was the tendency of certain males to become erotically aroused by the thought or image of themselves as females. The word I finally invented, after fruitless searching through various kinds of dictionaries, was *autogynephilia.* I could scarcely have imagined, on that long-ago day in that quiet room, that I would be writing the Foreword to a complete book on the subject 25 years later.

My early writings on autogynephilia were published in specialty journals with limited circulations. They were intended for a small readership of clinicians who specialized in the assessment and management of gender dysphoric patients. The general availability of the Internet in the home and workplace was still several years away, and access to print journals for people unconnected to major universities was difficult. I therefore had no expectation that the readership of my autogynephilia papers would ever extend beyond the small group I had originally envisioned.

One person who did manage to find and read them was the author of the present volume, Dr. Anne A. Lawrence. She was open to my ideas, which—although actually rooted in eight decades of prior clinical thinking—were bitterly opposed as heretical innovations by the increasingly politicized transgender community and the clinicians who served it. My ideas included the notions that gender identity and sexuality are not separate and unrelated phenomena but rather two sides of the same coin; that there are two major, etiologically and phenomenologically different types of male-to-female transsexualism; and that neither of these types is *sui generis*—rather, one is related to ordinary homosexuality and the other is related to autogynephilia. The contemporary dogma in the transgender and allied health communities was that male-to-female transsexualism is caused by a feminine gender identity—a proposition that is obviously and utterly circular without some auxiliary hypothesis such as neuroanatomic intersexuality. On this orthodox view, gender identity is about one's sex but not about sexuality, and to connect it with an erotic preference like homosexuality or autogynephilia is conceptually (and politically) incorrect. Dr. Lawrence did not merely accept my ideas; she pushed them towards their logical conclusion and, in a 1998 essay published on her Web site, startled even me with the audacious title of her essay, "Men Trapped in Men's Bodies: An Introduction to the Concept of Autogynephilia." And so it was that the word *autogynephilia* began its slow escape from the library.

Challenging the emotionally invested beliefs of any group often has its price, and Dr. Lawrence began receiving hate mail shortly after her views became known. Worse consequences than hate mail awaited J. Michael Bailey, who published a book dealing in large part with autogynephilia in 2003. This book, *The Man Who Would Be Queen*, so enraged some male-to-female transsexuals that a small group of them made a coordinated and sustained effort to get Dr. Bailey fired from his university faculty and ruined professionally. The events of this extraordinary campaign have been documented in a long and meticulously documented essay by medical historian and bioethicist Alice Domurat Dreger.

In light of this history, it is remarkable that Dr. Lawrence has written a book that describes autogynephilic transsexuals in a way that differs in important regards from the way many in this group wish to see themselves or wish to be seen by others. Her motives for completing this project are twofold. First, she is convinced that psychologists, psychiatrists, and other helping professionals can provide better care to autogynephilic gender dysphoric men if they understand the nature and significance of autogynephilia. Second, she believes that there exist many isolated and confused autogynephiles who would be comforted and reassured by the knowledge that there are others in the world like them and that, in the long term, autogynephilic transsexuals would lead mentally healthier lives if they had a self-understanding based on objective reality.

The book with which Dr. Lawrence's volume is most readily compared is Magnus Hirschfeld's 1910 classic work, *Die Transvestiten*. Both books include multiple autobiographies written by persons who might nowadays be grouped under the umbrella term "transgendered," both also include direct clinical observations of transgendered persons by the authors, and both contain substantial sections of theoretical interpretation and conjecture. If I were forced to recommend to someone that he or she read only one of these two books, I would—despite my deep admiration for the great Magnus Hirschfeld—recommend Dr. Lawrence's volume. *Men Trapped in Men's Bodies* is more focused, organized, and clear. It is simply a more efficient and accessible introduction, for modern readers, to the phenomenon of autogynephilic transsexualism. It does not, and does not attempt to, provide an account of homosexual transsexualism in natal males or females—a topic that would properly require a volume of its own.

Some days of one's work life one remembers with a shudder of horror, others with pleasurable memories of satisfaction at a job finally completed. Today, as I sign the Foreword to this excellent book by my friend and colleague Anne Lawrence, is like the long-ago day when I shut the last of the dictionaries and decided simply to invent the word I needed—*autogynephilia*.

Ray Blanchard
Department of Psychiatry
University of Toronto

Acknowledgments

This book could not have been written without the help and support of several colleagues and friends, whose assistance I gratefully acknowledge and to whom I offer my sincere thanks. Marta Meana, editor of the Springer *Focus on Sexuality Research* series, encouraged me to submit the proposal for this book, advocated for its acceptance by the publisher, and helped me find and trust my authorial voice in creating the manuscript. Her comments and suggestions on my chapter drafts and her overall support for the project were invaluable.

Three other colleagues, J. Michael Bailey, Robinn J. Cruz, and Paul L. Vasey, were also kind enough to read portions of the manuscript, share their observations, and propose various improvements. Their analyses, whether congratulatory or skeptical, helped me to proceed with a healthy mixture of caution and enthusiasm.

Although he provided no direct input to the book, Kenneth J. Zucker helped create the conditions that made it possible. He edited and published my earliest academic articles in *Archives of Sexual Behavior*, helped me to believe that I had something valuable to say, and taught me how to say it with greater clarity, precision, and economy.

More than anyone else, Ray Blanchard is responsible for this book's existence. He introduced the concept of autogynephilia and conducted the seminal research from which all further investigations of the topic would proceed. He graciously read and reread my early chapter drafts, gently pointing out areas where changes were needed and praising my more successful efforts. After nearly two decades of reading Dr. Blanchard's elegant prose in his numerous academic publications, I have inevitably absorbed some elements of his style and made them my own; if any parts of my writing ever verge on eloquence, I largely have him to thank.

Anne A. Lawrence

Acknowledgments

Contents

Chapter 1
Men Trapped in Men's Bodies

Two Types of Male-to-Female Transsexuals

Male-to-female (MtF) transsexuals—men who want to have sex reassignment surgery (SRS) and live as women—are often described by themselves and others as "women trapped in men's bodies" (e.g., Benjamin, 1966, p. 34; Person & Ovesey, 1974a, p. 17). This metaphor implies that these transsexuals not only want to look like women and live as women but that they also display the behavioral and psychological traits that are typical of women, their male bodies notwithstanding.

It is doubtful whether any MtF transsexuals can accurately be described as women trapped in men's bodies, but there are two distinctly different types of MtF transsexuals, and the metaphor is much more applicable to one type than to the other. One MtF transsexual type consists of males who have a life-long history of female-typical interests, behaviors, and personality characteristics. From earliest childhood, these individuals behaved like girls, identified with girls, and often proclaimed themselves to *be* girls. Their interests, mannerisms, and preferred toys and activities were female-typical, and girls were their favored playmates. They began cross-dressing openly in early childhood and continued to cross-dress into adulthood, and their cross-dressing was not associated with sexual arousal. Their feminine identifications and behaviors persisted throughout adolescence and into adulthood. They discovered that they were sexually attracted exclusively to men. They usually chose occupations, hobbies, and leisure activities that were female-typical.

If any MtF transsexuals deserve to be thought of as women trapped in men's bodies, these pervasively feminine MtF transsexuals have the best claim. Because MtF transsexuals of this type are exclusively sexually attracted to men and thus homosexual relative to their biological sex, and because they resemble (or, more accurately, *are*) the most feminine of homosexual men, they are usually referred to in the medical and scientific literature as *homosexual* MtF transsexuals.

A.A. Lawrence, *Men Trapped in Men's Bodies: Narratives of Autogynephilic Transsexualism*, Focus on Sexuality Research, DOI 10.1007/978-1-4614-5182-2_1,

There is a second MtF transsexual type, however, consisting of males who bear little resemblance to women trapped in men's bodies. Although they intensely desire to be female, they display few of the interests, behaviors, and psychological traits that are typical of women. In most respects, they closely resemble ordinary non-transsexual men. From earliest childhood, these individuals knew they were boys and behaved like boys, although many of them report that they had secret fantasies about becoming female as far back as they can remember. Their interests, manner-isms, and preferred toys and activities were usually male-typical. In most cases, other boys were their favored playmates, but a few primarily engaged in solitary play. Some began cross-dressing in early childhood, almost always surreptitiously. Nearly all were cross-dressing secretly by the time of puberty, and their cross-dressing was associated with intense sexual arousal. In other respects, however, their masculine interests and behaviors continued to be, at least superficially, unremarkable throughout adolescence and into adulthood. They rarely chose female-typical occupations and usually chose strongly male-typical ones, in fields such as engineering, computer programming, or military service. They discovered that they were either sexually attracted to women or, less commonly, were not strongly attracted to other people of either sex. Many of them fantasized at times about having sex with men, but only when they also fantasized about themselves as female; at other times, they found the idea of sex with men unappealing or repugnant. They also continued to be erotically aroused by cross-dressing and by the fantasy of being female—something traditionally associated with transvestic fetishism, not transsexualism.

Several years ago, I described MtF transsexuals of this second type as "men trapped in men's bodies" (Lawrence, 1998), because in most respects they resemble nontranssexual men, although they genuinely *do* feel trapped in their male bodies and have an intense desire to have female bodies. Because transsexuals of this second type are nonhomosexual relative to their biological sex (i.e., they do not experience exclusive sexual attraction to men), they are usually referred to as *nonhomosexual* MtF transsexuals in the medical and scientific literature, to distinguish them from their exclusively homosexual MtF counterparts. Nonhomosexual MtF transsexuals are also, and more controversially, referred to as *autogynephilic* transsexuals, because some clinicians and theorists have concluded that these transsexuals almost always share an unusual erotic interest called *autogynephilia*—a propensity to be erotically aroused by the thought of being female. This unusual erotic interest, and what transsexuals who experience it have to say about it, is the subject of this book.

Trapped in the Wrong Body

Jay Prosser, a female-to-male (FtM) transsexual, explained that "transsexuals continue to deploy the image of wrong embodiment because being trapped in the wrong body is simply what transsexuality feels like" (Prosser, 1998, p. 69), and I would not disagree with his assessment. But I believe that MtF transsexuals of the second type—nonhomosexual MtF transsexuals—continue to employ the image of being "*women* trapped in men's bodies," not because they believe it is truly accurate, but because it is concise and superficially plausible. Attempting to provide a more accurate explanation would be a lengthy process and would not necessarily result in a more nuanced understanding, because the feelings associated with nonhomosexual MtF transsexualism are very difficult to understand, even for those of us who experience them firsthand. I routinely warn my nonhomosexual MtF transsexual patients: "Some people will accept you; some will support you; some will admire your courage; some will be your advocates; but no one except another transsexual *like yourself* will really understand you, because the feelings you experience are so strange that they defy most people's comprehension."

Homosexual MtF transsexualism is easier to comprehend. Extremely feminine men who are sexually attracted to other men and who dress as women have been observed in essentially all cultures. In some cultures—primarily in Asia, Oceania, and Latin America—such men are sufficiently prevalent that socially sanctioned transgender roles exist to accommodate them (e.g., Bartlett & Vasey, 2006; Nanda, 1994; Teh, 2001; Whitam, 1997; Winter, 2006). Ordinary men and women often seem to find it understandable, even predictable, that extremely feminine homosexual men might want to live full-time or part-time as women. As Levine (1993) observed, "Many people intuitively grasp a relationship between homoeroticism and the persistent intense, but transformed childhood wish to be female." (p. 134). Bloom (2002) similarly noted that "Drag queens (gay cross-dressers) make sense to most of us. There is a congruence of sexual orientation, appearance, and temperament [in] feminine gay men dressing as women" (p. 51).

Nonhomosexual MtF transsexualism, in contrast, seems to make little sense: Why would an apparently masculine man who is attracted to women want to make his body resemble a woman's body and live as a woman? The image of being a woman trapped in a man's body—being a woman mentally and psychologically but a man anatomically—at least begins to suggest something of the pain, frustration, and incomprehension that nonhomosexual MtF transsexuals feel about not having the bodies they want. But it is a misleading metaphor, because it erroneously implies the presence of female-typical attitudes and behaviors, which are rarely present in nonhomosexual MtF transsexuals. It also omits the element that nonhomosexual MtF transsexuals find hardest to talk about: the intense, perplexing, shame-inducing erotic arousal that seems to simultaneously animate and discredit their desires to have female bodies. Sometimes that erotic arousal is center-stage and obvious; sometimes it lurks around the edges of the phenomenon and even briefly seems to disappear. For many affected persons, the arousal feels almost incidental much of the time: merely an unsought physical response that is somehow linked to one's longing to be female and one's distress over one's male embodiment. Yet, for nonhomosexual MtF transsexuals who pay close attention, the sexual arousal that accompanies the desire to be female is difficult to ignore completely.

An Autogynephilic Transsexual's Case History

Although I have suggested that the feelings that accompany nonhomosexual (or autogynephilic) MtF transsexualism defy most people's comprehension, I will nevertheless try to convey some sense of them. Here, then, is a psychosexual autobiography, written from a third-person perspective by a colleague who is an autogynephilic MtF transsexual—a transsexual who recognizes herself to be autogynephilic. I'll refer to her as Ms. Z. Like all brief personal histories, Ms. Z's account necessarily omits many details, but she affirms that, to the best of her knowledge and recollection, it is entirely accurate. I present it here as an illustrative case history; I do not claim that it is typical or representative.

> In most respects, he seemed to be a normal boy. He liked toy cars and airplanes, engaged in rough-and-tumble play, and did not seem to be delicate or effeminate. According to his mother, however, he showed an early interest in women's bodies and clothing: At about age 4, for example, he loved to stroke his mother's legs when she was wearing nylon stockings. His first conscious memory of wanting to wear girls' clothing occurred when he was age 6: A girl who was his regular playmate had a ballerina tutu that he yearned to wear. The fantasy of doing so felt both exciting and shameful. By the age of 8, he fantasized about being a girl and wearing girls' clothing nearly every night as he lay in bed. Whenever he did this, his penis became erect. He didn't understand why this happened, and he didn't like it. He found photographs of women's and girls' clothes in magazines and catalogs; he fantasized about wearing these pretty clothes. He fantasized about having long hair and being treated like a girl and having a girl's name; these fantasies also made his penis become erect. He was ashamed of having a penis and wanted it gone. He fantasized about having an operation to remove his penis; ironically, this also caused his penis to become erect.
>
> When he was age 9, he was sometimes allowed to stay home alone. He used these opportunities to try on his mother's clothing. This felt exciting and shameful. The clothes were too big, but that wasn't important; they were women's clothes. He tried on panties, bras, slips, and dresses. His penis always became erect, and sticky fluid oozed from its tip. He didn't like the erections; they were unpleasant and made the clothes not fit well. Sometimes fluid from his penis got on the clothes. He feared that his cross-dressing would be discovered, but he couldn't make himself stop. His mother eventually did discover his cross-dressing; she confronted him and made him promise to stop. He stopped briefly but soon resumed, trying to be more careful.
>
> His cross-dressing and fantasies of being female continued throughout adolescence. He hated the physical changes that accompanied puberty: facial hair, a deeper voice, genital enlargement. He was attracted to girls but too timid to date them. He envied their clothes and their lovely bodies; he burned with envy. His interests, however, were not notably feminine: His favorite subjects in school were geometry and calculus, and his hobby was programming computers. He read about transvestites and MtF transsexuals but couldn't identify with either category. Transvestites were attracted to women and sexually aroused by cross-dressing, like him; but transvestites valued their penises and didn't want them to be cut off, which was *not* like him. MtF transsexuals wanted female bodies, like him; but they were attracted to men and were never sexually aroused by cross-dressing, which was *not* like him. His feminization fantasies caused a buildup of sexual tension, but his only relief was in wet dreams. He read that boys masturbated by stroking their penises, but he couldn't stand to touch his. At age 18, he finally discovered how to give himself an orgasm by rubbing against the bed sheets; he would masturbate that way for the rest of his life.

When he went away to college, he finally had his own room and could cross-dress in privacy. He bought female clothes and wore them in private and occasionally in public; this was always erotically arousing. He experimented with black market estrogen. He liked the physical effects and found it sexually arousing to develop breasts, but taking estrogen seemed futile: He knew that he couldn't pass as a woman and that he would never be accepted for sex reassignment, because he wasn't attracted to men. He reasoned that if he could learn to like sex with men, he might qualify for sex reassignment. He met gay men and let them penetrate him, but he was simply not attracted to men and couldn't pretend to be. He dated a few women during his final years in college but never had sex with any of them; he was too inhibited. He thought about castrating himself but couldn't find the courage. He wished that he could be normal but feared that he never would be.

After college, he overcame his inhibitions and had sex with a woman for the first time. He loved looking at and touching her naked body. Although her body was exciting, it was not exciting enough that he could ejaculate inside of her. For that, he had to fantasize about being female. He did not fantasize about being female *with her*, just about being female; she was superfluous to his fantasy. He dated over a dozen women during his young adulthood, but he could never ejaculate with any of them except through the fantasy of being female. He tried having sex with very attractive women, hoping they would excite him enough that a fantasy would be unnecessary; this never worked. His female partners observed that he always "went away" immediately before his orgasm. He invariably felt miserable and depressed after orgasm, when he once again had to confront the reality of being male. He continued to cross-dress but found little satisfaction in it: What was the point if his body was male? He discovered erotica written for cross-dressers but could never find precisely what he wanted. Complete, permanent physical feminization, especially genital surgery, was what he found sexually exciting, but this was rarely emphasized. Stories that culminated in sex with men seemed to be the rule, but these were a turn-off for him. His fantasy world would have no men in it. With the exception of occasional nocturnal emissions, he had never experienced an orgasm in his life without a feminization fantasy playing in his head. He felt that some essential element of normal sexuality was missing in him; he felt sexually crippled. His obligatory reliance on feminization fantasies for arousal felt like a mental illness.

He consulted three different psychologists and psychiatrists about his wish to be female at various times in his life, but none was able to offer him any solutions, nor even a diagnosis that made sense to him. Eventually he consulted a therapist who specialized in transgender issues. She told him that he might be able to pass as a woman after all and might even be a candidate for SRS. At last he thought he saw a way forward. He started attending cross-dressing conventions and gradually developed confidence in his ability to pass as a female. He underwent facial hair removal and medically supervised hormone therapy. He grew his hair long, learned makeup skills, and acquired an appropriate feminine wardrobe. He changed his name, started living full-time as a woman, and eventually underwent SRS.

She—a pronoun change is now required—was delighted with the results of SRS. She loved having female genitalia; she liked her body for the first time in her life. She loved living as a woman, too; she adored women and was proud to be one of them at last. She had her first awake orgasm as a woman a few months after SRS, masturbating the same way she had as a man. She still found that feminization fantasies were obligatory to reach orgasm. Her orgasms after SRS were less intense and harder to achieve, but at least she was no longer miserable and depressed after having them: Her body was finally as it should be. She dated lesbian women and other MtF transsexuals and had sex with some of them, but she could never achieve orgasm in their presence. She would have needed to rely on feminization fantasies for this, and she somehow couldn't bring herself to do so. Eventually she resigned herself to celibacy, although she missed the simple comfort of another woman's body pressed against her own. She still has never had an orgasm while awake without a feminization fantasy running in her head. She still regards her obligatory reliance on feminization fantasies for arousal—her autogynephilia—as a mental illness: a profound, disabling defect in her ability to feel genuine sexual love for another person.

The Concept of Autogynephilia

The term *autogynephilia* was introduced in 1989 by psychologist Ray Blanchard (Blanchard, 1989a); it literally means "love of oneself as a woman" (in Greek, *auto* = self, *gynē* = woman, and *philia* = love). Blanchard formally defined autogynephilia as "a male's propensity to be sexually aroused by the thought of himself as a female" (Blanchard, 1989b, p. 616). Blanchard theorized, based on his own research and that of other investigators, that all or almost all nonhomosexual MtF transsexuals have the propensity to be sexually aroused by the thought of themselves as females. He further theorized that these transsexuals' desire for sex reassignment is directly linked to their autogynephilic desire to be female.

Blanchard's theory that "nonhomosexual MtF transsexualism equals autogynephilic transsexualism" was both evolutionary and revolutionary. It was evolutionary in the sense that it could be seen as a logical extension of previous observations about transvestism (i.e., erotic cross-dressing) and MtF transsexualism that had been published in the psychiatric literature, albeit that perhaps were not yet widely appreciated. Clinicians and researchers had observed, for example, that:

- Some cases of MtF transsexualism developed from what originally appeared to be transvestism (Lukianowicz, 1959).
- Transvestites as well as transsexuals experienced a form of cross-gender identity (desire to be the other sex; Stoller, 1968).
- The transvestite's "key fantasy" was "becoming a woman" (Ovesey & Person, 1976, p. 229), not merely dressing as a woman.
- Some MtF transsexuals were homosexual in orientation, whereas others were primarily heterosexual but also had a history of transvestism (Money & Gaskin, 1970/1971).
- MtF transsexualism was (virtually) always accompanied or preceded by one of two anomalous erotic preferences—either homosexuality or erotic arousal associated with cross-dressing or cross-gender fantasy (Freund, Steiner, & Chan, 1982).

To synthesize these observations and derive from them the theory that all or almost all MtF transsexuals who are nonhomosexual in orientation have the propensity to be sexually aroused by the fantasy of themselves as female could be seen, at least in retrospect, as an unremarkable deductive leap.

But Blanchard's theory equating nonhomosexual MtF transsexualism with autogynephilic transsexualism was also revolutionary, in that it emphasized *the erotic fantasy of oneself as a female* as the essential feature underlying this variety of transsexualism. The concept of autogynephilia placed erotic desire at the center of the transsexual experience for nonhomosexual men: It suggested, at least implicitly, that autogynephilic erotic desire, or some closely related derivative of it, could be thought of as the driving or motivating force behind the desire for sex reassignment in nonhomosexual MtF transsexuals. This was a revolutionary challenge to the dominant paradigm, which asserted that transsexualism was entirely about expressing one's "true" gender identity and had nothing whatsoever to do with sexual arousal or erotic desire.

The concept of autogynephilia, then, provided more than just a new and more precise name for a recognized erotic phenomenon—sexual arousal associated with cross-dressing or cross-gender fantasy. It also provided the basis for a proposed typology of MtF transsexualism, in that Blanchard theorized that all or virtually all MtF transsexuals were either exclusively homosexual or were nonhomosexual *and* autogynephilic. Moreover, the concept of autogynephilia at least implicitly provided a theory of motivation for the pursuit of sex reassignment by nonhomosexual men: These autogynephilic men plausibly were motivated to seek sex reassignment because it would allow them to actualize their desires to have female bodies—desires that grew out of their autogynephilic fantasies.

The narrative histories of MtF transsexuals who have experienced autogynephilic arousal are the subject of this book. These transsexuals, whom I have called "men trapped in men's bodies," have important stories to tell—stories that are virtually unknown, both to the professionals who treat transsexual clients and to persons who experience autogynephilic arousal, think about undergoing sex reassignment, and may be searching for narrative histories that will help them better understand themselves. Before considering these narratives of autogynephilic transsexualism, however, it will be helpful to examine the observations and investigations that led Blanchard to develop the concept of autogynephilia and the MtF transsexual typology and implicit theory of transsexual motivation associated with it. It will also be useful to review the limited studies of autogynephilia conducted by other researchers.

Definitions and Terminology

Clarifying some definitions and terminology is a necessary first step. The task is complicated by the fact that definitions of some important terms related to transsexualism have been used inconsistently or have changed over time. Three terms that come up repeatedly are *gender identity*, *cross-gender identity*, and *gender dysphoria*. Briefly, gender identity is "a person's inner conviction of being male or female" (American Psychiatric Association [APA], 2000, p. 823). Cross-gender identity denotes the desire to belong to the opposite sex or gender. Gender dysphoria denotes discomfort with one's biological sex or assigned gender. Cross-gender identity and gender dysphoria are highly correlated phenomena, as one would predict; but the denotations of the two terms are slightly different.

The term *gender identity* has been used in two different ways. Sometimes it denotes the fundamental sense of being male or female that an individual develops during the first 18–30 months of life and that is usually unchangeable thereafter; Stoller (1968) called this *core gender identity*. Nonhomosexual MtF transsexuals do not have female core gender identities: In childhood and adulthood, before and after sex reassignment, they know they are and always will be biologically male. Gender identity, however, can also denote a person's sense of being psychologically male or female (Money, 1986). Ovesey and Person (1973) distinguished between core gender identity and this latter type of gender identity, which "can be defined as an individual's self-evaluation of psychological maleness or femaleness" (p. 54). Docter (1988) described how nonhomosexual MtF transsexuals (and many transvestites) gradually develop strong, persistent female gender identities of this latter type after years or decades of presenting themselves as women. Nonhomosexual MtF transsexuals experience their newly developed female gender identities as incongruent with their core gender identities (Stoller, 1968).

Cross-gender identity (sometimes called *cross-gender identification*) is usually thought of as being aspirational, at least initially: It reflects, in the words of Ovesey and Person (1973), "a wish, not a conviction" (p. 64). Typical symptoms of cross-gender identity or identification include "stated desire to be the other sex [and] desire to live or be treated as the other sex" (APA, 2000, p. 581). In the context of transsexualism, there is usually an assumption, implicit or explicit, that a person's cross-gender identity must be "strong and persistent" (APA, 2000, p. 581) to be clinically significant. When a MtF transsexual's cross-gender identity has become sufficiently strong and persistent, it can supplant her original core gender identity and become her new primary or dominant gender identity (Docter, 1988).

The word *dysphoria* denotes discomfort or discontent; the term *gender dysphoria* is applicable to persons who are "intensely and abidingly uncomfortable in their anatomic and genetic sex and their assigned gender" (Fisk, 1974, p. 10). Fisk also noted, however, that one of the cardinal signs of gender dysphoria is the intense wish to change sex—in other words, cross-gender identity. Blanchard did not always use the term *gender dysphoria* consistently; sometimes he described it exclusively in terms of discontent (e.g., "persistent discontent with the primary or secondary sexual characteristics of one's body"; Blanchard, 1993b, p. 70) and at other times in terms of discontent *and* aspiration (e.g., "discontent with one's biological sex, the desire to possess the body of the opposite sex, and the desire to belong to the opposite sex"; Blanchard, 1993a, p. 301). Gender dysphoria and cross-gender identity seem to operate as two sides of the same coin in many or most patients with longstanding, clinically diagnosed transsexualism. Many autogynephilic men, however, probably experience significant gender dysphoria years or decades before they develop strong, persistent cross-gender identities.

Transsexualism usually denotes either the combination of persistent cross-gender identity (desire to be the other sex) and severe gender dysphoria (APA, 2000, p. 828) or cross-gender identity that is *usually* accompanied by gender dysphoria and the wish for hormonal and surgical sex reassignment (World Health Organization [WHO], 1992, p. 365). Blanchard (1993a) considered transsexualism to be simply severe gender dysphoria. Transsexualism was an official diagnosis in the 1987 edition of the *Diagnostic and Statistical Manual of Mental Disorders* (DSM; APA, 1987), but it was replaced in the 1994 edition by the new diagnosis of *gender identity disorder* (GID; APA, 1994). GID is conceptualized as involving both strong, persistent cross-gender identity and persistent gender dysphoria (APA, 2000, p. 581). The terms transsexualism and GID are often used synonymously (e.g., Selvaggi et al., 2005). Recent studies have demonstrated that most of the symptoms that are associated with GID, transsexualism, and gender dysphoria—for example, cross-gender identification, feelings of similarity to the opposite sex, desire to live as the opposite sex, anatomic dysphoria, and desire for hormonal and surgical sex reassignment—are highly correlated in patients who have been diagnosed with GID (Deogracias et al., 2007; Singh et al., 2010). Accordingly, distinctions between "men with severe gender dysphoria," "men with persistent cross-gender identities," "men with GID," and "MtF transsexuals" are likely to be subtle, if they are meaningful at all.

Sexual orientation refers to the category of persons to whom an individual is sexually attracted (or with whom he or she tends to fall in love). The two terms most commonly used to describe sexual orientation are *homosexual* (sexually attracted to persons of the same sex) and *heterosexual* (sexually attracted to persons of the opposite sex). Because these terms are referenced to biological sex, they do *not* change after sex reassignment. For example, a MtF transsexual who has completed sex reassignment and is attracted to women is considered heterosexual. Alternatively, the terms *androphilic* (sexually attracted to men) and *gynephilic* (sexually attracted to women) can be used to describe sexual orientation without referencing the sex of the person who experiences the attraction.

The latest edition of the DSM describes *paraphilias* as psychosexual disorders "characterized by recurrent, intense sexual urges, fantasies, or behaviors that involve unusual objects, activities, or situations and cause clinically significant distress or impairment in social, occupational, or other important areas of functioning" (APA, 2000, p. 535). Some paraphilic behaviors are illegal or potentially harmful to other people; other paraphilic behaviors are both legal and harmless. Autogynephilia is one of the latter type of paraphilias (Blanchard, 1993a). Other recognized paraphilias that will be mentioned in this book include *pedophilia* (sexual attraction to children), *fetishism* (sexual attraction to specific inanimate objects), *zoophilia* (sexual attraction to nonhuman animals), *transvestic fetishism* (sexual arousal to wearing women's apparel), and *sexual masochism* (sexual arousal to experiencing suffering or humiliation). In some cases, a pattern of sexual attraction can be considered both a paraphilia and a sexual orientation; pedophilia and zoophilia are examples (Miletski, 2005; Seto, 2012). Blanchard (1989a, 1993a) considered autogynephilia to be both a paraphilia and a sexual orientation.

Early Development of the Concept of Autogynephilia

Blanchard developed the concept of autogynephilia in the course of his attempt to create a coherent system or taxonomy for classifying various types of gender dysphoria or GID in men (Blanchard, 2005). Clinicians had recognized for decades that men with gender dysphoria or transsexualism were heterogeneous in their clinical presentations. Many observers hypothesized that there were two or more distinct forms of MtF transsexualism, possibly with entirely different etiologies. Theorists had proposed several different taxonomies and classification schemes for MtF transsexualism (for a review, see Lawrence 2010b). No one taxonomy, however, was generally accepted when Blanchard began his investigations.

Blanchard decided to start with the classification system originally proposed by Magnus Hirschfeld, the pioneering German physician and sex researcher who coined the term *transvestite* in 1910 (Hirschfeld, 1910/1991). Hirschfeld (1918) classified the individuals he called transvestites—a category that included both MtF transsexuals and transvestites, as the terms are used today—into four groups, based on their erotic interest in men, women, both men and women, or neither men nor women. He referenced his classification system to a person's biological sex; consequently, his system categorized a transvestite (or MtF transsexual) attracted to men as homosexual, one attracted to women as heterosexual, and one attracted to both men and women as *bisexual*. Hirschfeld called those transvestites and MtF transsexuals who were attracted to neither men nor women *automonosexual*, a term that is no longer widely used. Nowadays the preferred term for these individuals is *analloerotic*, "not sexually attracted to other people" (Blanchard, 1989a), although the more familiar but less accurate term *asexual* is sometimes substituted.

In an early investigation, Blanchard (1985b) classified 163 MtF transsexual patients using Hirschfeld's four categories and examined the percentage of patients in each group who gave a history of sexual arousal in association with cross-dressing. He discovered that 73% of the patients in the combined heterosexual, bisexual, and asexual/analloerotic groups gave such a history (the three groups were statistically indistinguishable from each other), versus only 15% in the homosexual group—a highly significant difference. Based on this result, Blanchard theorized that there were probably only two basic types of MtF transsexuals: a homosexual type and a "heterosexual" (nonhomosexual) type. His theory was consistent with Freund et al.'s (1982) observation that there existed two distinct types of cross-gender identity among transvestites and MtF transsexuals: one type associated with homosexual orientation and another type associated with what Freund et al. called *cross-gender fetishism*—sexual arousal in connection with cross-dressing or cross-gender fantasy.

Because Blanchard had not yet coined the term autogynephilia, his study (Blanchard, 1985b) also used the term *cross-gender fetishism* to refer to sexual arousal associated with cross-dressing. Freund et al. (1982) had stated that

> cross-gender fetishism is characterized by the subject's fantasizing, during fetishistic activity, that he or she belongs to the opposite sex and that the fetish, always in such cases an object characteristic of the opposite sex, is used to induce or enhance cross-gender identity. (p. 50)

Both Freund et al. and Blanchard realized that the sexual arousal men experienced in association with cross-dressing and other forms of cross-gender fetishism was related to the fantasy of being female—the essential concept in autogynephilia—but this arousal was still linked conceptually to the idea of a fetish object. Blanchard (1985b) expanded the idea of the fetish object to include activities symbolic of femininity; he noted that "the individual's favorite such symbol might not be women's clothing but some aspect of the feminine toilet, such as putting on makeup or shaving the legs" (p. 249). This expanded concept of the fetish object can be seen as laying the foundation for the more encompassing concept of autogynephilia.

Blanchard (1985b) also conceptualized the bisexual and analloerotic subtypes of MtF transsexualism as resulting from the interaction of a fundamentally heterosexual orientation with the yet-unnamed "erotic anomaly" that underlay cross-gender fetishism:

> The differentiation of these subtypes from the heterosexual "parent group" is brought about by two different processes. In asexual [MtF] transsexualism, cross-gender fetishism (or the anomaly underlying it) so overshadows, or competes with, the erotic attraction to females that the individual appears to have little erotic attraction to other persons at all; his heterosexuality is, in a sense, latent. The process believed to account for the apparent existence of bisexual [MtF] transsexuals is somewhat different. In these individuals, the erotic anomaly manifested in cross-gender fetishism also finds expression in the fantasy of having intercourse, as a woman, with a man. The effective erotic stimulus, however, is not the male physique per se, as it is in true homosexual attraction, but rather the thought of being a female, which is symbolized in the fantasy of being penetrated by a male. For these persons, the imagined—occasionally real—male sexual partner serves the same function as women's apparel or makeup, namely, to aid and intensify the fantasy of being a woman. (pp. 249–250)

Four years later, Blanchard would coin a term for the underlying erotic anomaly in cross-gender fetishism: autogynephilia.

Accounting for Departures from Theorized Associations with Sexual Orientation

Astute readers will have noted that the association Blanchard (1985b) observed between cross-gender fetishism and sexual orientation in MtF transsexuals was not a perfect one: About 27% of nonhomosexual MtF transsexuals denied cross-gender fetishism, and about 15% of homosexual MtF transsexuals reported it. These departures from the predictions of Blanchard's theory have not escaped the notice of his theory's critics. Some of them have argued that, because many nonhomosexual MtF transsexuals deny cross-gender fetishism, at least some cases of nonhomosexual MtF transsexualism may be unrelated to cross-gender fetishism or autogynephilia and that these may constitute a putative "third type." Others have argued that, because some homosexual MtF transsexuals report cross-gender fetishism, this (or the erotic anomaly that underlies it) is merely an incidental finding with no particular typological or etiological significance. Subsequent investigations have also found the relationship between MtF transsexual typology and autogynephilia to be strong but not perfect (Blanchard & Clemmensen, 1988; Blanchard, Clemmensen, & Steiner, 1987; Lawrence, 2005; Nuttbrock, Bockting, Mason, et al., 2011). Blanchard conducted two additional studies prior to his introduction of the term autogynephilia that helped put these departures from his theory's predictions into perspective.

Blanchard, Racansky, and Steiner (1986) measured changes in penile blood volume in 37 heterosexual cross-dressing men who listened to audiotaped recordings of narratives describing four scenarios: cross-dressing, sex as a female with a male partner, sex as a male with a female partner, and solitary, nonsexual activity. The participants included transvestites, nonhomosexual MtF transsexuals, and nonhomosexual men with intermediate conditions. The participants were divided into groups, based on whether they claimed they had always, usually, rarely, or never felt sexually aroused when cross-dressing during the previous year. All four groups displayed significantly greater physiological sexual arousal (measured as mean increase in penile volume) in response to the cross-dressing narrative than in response to the neutral, nonsexual narrative; this included the group that denied having felt sexually aroused during cross-dressing. Interestingly, six out of nine members of the latter group claimed that they had *never* been aroused by cross-dressing at *any* time. Blanchard et al. concluded that nonhomosexual cross-dressing men, "even those who deny recent or past erotic arousal in association with cross-dressing or applying makeup, still tend to respond with penile tumescence to fantasies of such activities" (p. 460). In short, many or most nonhomosexual cross-dressing men who deny sexual arousal in association with cross-dressing are not reporting accurately. This result suggested, at least by implication, that many or most of the nonhomosexual MtF transsexuals who deny sexual arousal in association with cross-dressing or autogynephilic fantasy are also not reporting accurately. Blanchard theorized that the misreporting his participants engaged in probably was not intentional, but reflected a genuine lack of awareness of their sexual arousal. This explanation plausibly accounts for many or most instances in which nonhomosexual MtF transsexuals deny having experienced autogynephilic sexual arousal.

An interesting incidental finding of the Blanchard et al. (1986) study was that, for many of the participants—including those who described themselves as sometimes but not always sexually aroused by cross-dressing—the most sexually arousing scenario of the four was the fantasy of being a female having sex with a male. Blanchard had previously argued that sexual arousal in this context reflected the autogynephilic fantasy of enacting the female sexual role, not genuine attraction to the male physique. One could speculate that this pattern of autogynephilic fantasy might eventually lead some heterosexual cross-dressing men, including some nonhomosexual MtF transsexuals, to conclude that their sexual orientation had changed and that they had become exclusively sexually attracted to men. This might account for the existence of supposedly "homosexual" MtF transsexuals who report a history of sexual arousal with cross-dressing or cross-gender fantasy. A recent article that summarized data from four northern

European gender clinics provided additional support for this explanation: It reported that 23 (52%) of 44 male patients with adult-onset gender dysphoria described themselves as exclusively sexually attracted to men, but their treating clinicians believed that only 4 (9%) were genuinely androphilic, based on patient interviews and clinical records (Nieder et al., 2011). There are also several reports of nonhomosexual MtF transsexuals who admitted that they deliberately misrepresented themselves to clinicians as homosexual (Blanchard, Steiner, & Clemmensen, 1985; Walworth, 1997).

In a second important study that is relevant to understanding departures from the predicted relationship between autogynephilia and MtF transsexual typology, Blanchard, Clemmensen, & Steiner (1985) studied the association between a self-favorable or *socially desirable* response style (the tendency to describe oneself in morally excellent or admirable terms) and several aspects of self-reported clinical history in 64 heterosexual male gender patients, about two thirds of whom were MtF transsexuals. Blanchard, Clemmensen, et al. found that a socially desirable response style was strongly correlated with the tendency to describe oneself as a "classic" or "textbook" example of MtF transsexualism: one "who has felt and acted feminine from earliest childhood, has never been sexually aroused by women's apparel, and is romantically inclined toward males" (p. 508). The aspect of clinical history that was most highly correlated with socially desirable responding was absence (or denial) of cross-gender fetishism. It seems plausible, therefore, that some cases in which nonhomosexual MtF transsexuals deny autogynephilic arousal may reflect the influence of self-favorable or socially desirable responding.

Further evidence that persons who experience autogynephilic arousal with cross-dressing often deny such arousal and that denial is associated with socially desirable responding comes from a recent study involving adolescent boys, mean age 14 years, who were referred to a gender identity clinic because of transvestic fetishism (Zucker et al., 2012). Remarkably, 45 (47%) of 96 boys did not admit to sexual arousal associated with cross-dressing on even a single item of a 10-item scale measuring transvestic fetishism, even though this was the very problem for which they were clinically referred. In this study, too, a socially desirable response style was strongly correlated with denial of sexual arousal with cross-dressing.

It is important to recognize that socially desirable responding does not necessarily imply deliberate misrepresentation or lying. Paulhus (1984) observed that socially desirable responding can reflect either *impression management* (conscious misrepresentation) or *self-deceptive enhancement* (self-favorable presentation that is genuinely believed to be true). It is entirely possible that many instances in which Blanchard et al.'s (1986) heterosexual cross-dressing men denied being sexually aroused, despite the fact that they actually were, and many instances in which Zucker et al.'s (2012) adolescent boys denied transvestic fetishism, despite being clinically referred for this, were attributable to self-deceptive enhancement, not deliberate misrepresentation.

Additional Correlates of Sexual Orientation in MtF Transsexualism

In another investigation of MtF transsexual typology, Blanchard et al. (1987) studied 125 gender dysphoric male patients, of whom 52 were classified as homosexual and 73 as heterosexual (i.e., nonhomosexual). About 82% of the nonhomosexual patients had a history of sexual arousal with cross-dressing, compared to roughly 10% of the homosexual patients; this was consistent with previous observations of a statistically strong but not perfect relationship between sexual orientation and cross-gender fetishism (i.e., autogynephilia). The nonhomosexual patients presented for assessment at an older mean age than the homosexual patients, about 34 vs. 26 years. The nonhomosexual and homosexual patients began cross-dressing at about the same mean ages—9.6 and 11.0 years, respectively—but the mean age of first cross-gender wishes was significantly older in the nonhomosexual group, 9.8 vs. 7.7 years. On average, then, the nonhomosexual gender dysphoric men began to have cross-gender wishes around the same time or shortly after they began cross-dressing, whereas the homosexual gender dysphoric men began to have cross-gender wishes more than 3 years before they began cross-dressing. Blanchard et al. concluded that the pattern of the data was "consistent with the view that heterosexual and homosexual gender dysphoria are likely to prove etiologically distinct conditions" (p. 149).

Blanchard (1988) subsequently examined self-reported childhood femininity and age at clinical assessment in 256 MtF transsexuals, whom he divided into homosexual, heterosexual, bisexual, and asexual/analloerotic groups. Comparing equal numbers of participants ($n = 16$) from each of these four groups, Blanchard found that the homosexual participants reported significantly greater childhood femininity and also presented for assessment at a significantly younger mean age than the heterosexual, bisexual, and asexual/analloerotic participants; the three nonhomosexual groups did not differ significantly from each other on either childhood femininity or mean age at assessment. Although this study did not address autogynephilia or cross-gender fetishism directly, it provided further evidence that there are two distinctly different types of MtF transsexualism: one associated with homosexual orientation and greater childhood femininity and another associated with nonhomosexual orientation and less childhood femininity.

In the same year, Blanchard and Clemmensen (1988) investigated the relationship between severity of gender dysphoria and frequency of sexual arousal and masturbation accompanying cross-dressing in 193 nonhomosexual gender dysphoric men. Lacking a specific measure of gender dysphoria, they used persistence of cross-gender identity as a proxy for this—a reasonable strategy, as the latter measure was strongly associated with the likelihood that an individual had an interest in SRS. Blanchard and Clemmensen found that the gender dysphoric men with more persistent cross-gender identities (and by implication, more intense gender dysphoria) reported less frequent sexual arousal and less frequent masturbation with cross-dressing—a relationship that the authors thought might reflect socially desirable responding, at least in part. Nevertheless, more than half of the men with the most intense gender dysphoria reported that they had sometimes been sexually aroused when cross-dressing during the past year, and just under one-half reported that they had at least occasionally masturbated when cross-dressing during the past year. Among the men who acknowledged ever having experienced sexual arousal with cross-dressing—only about 84% of the men did—roughly half reported that they sometimes considered sexual arousal with cross-dressing to be bothersome. This finding was consistent with a previous report by Buhrich (1978) that heterosexual cross-dressing men sometimes experience sexual arousal associated with cross-dressing as unwanted.

Introducing the Term *Autogynephilia*

Blanchard first used the term *autogynephilia* in two articles published in 1989. In the first of these (Blanchard, 1989a), he reviewed his own and earlier attempts to construct meaningful taxonomies of gender dysphoria and gender identity disorders in men. He concluded that "the nonhomosexual gender dysphorias, together with transvestism, constitute a family of related disorders" (p. 322) and that the "erotic (or amatory) propensity" (p. 323) underlying these disorders should be called autogynephilia ("love of oneself as a woman"). As far as I am aware, this was the first article in which Blanchard referred to autogynephilia as a *sexual orientation*, when he theorized that "All gender dysphoric males who are not sexually oriented toward men are instead sexually oriented toward the thought or image of themselves as women." (pp. 322–323). Blanchard would reintroduce the concept of autogynephilia as a sexual orientation 4 years later in a more elaborated form (Blanchard, 1993a).

In a second article published in the same year, Blanchard (1989b) described two newly developed scales for measuring aspects of autogynephilia and one for measuring sexual interest in other persons. He reported on the ability of these scales to distinguish homosexual, heterosexual, bisexual, and asexual/analloerotic subgroups within a sample of 212 MtF transsexuals. Blanchard found that scores on the Core Autogynephilia Scale, a measure of erotic arousal in association with the fantasy of having various features of the nude female form (face, breasts, vulva, etc.) were significantly higher in the three nonhomosexual groups than in the homosexual group. Scores on the Autogynephilic Interpersonal Fantasy Scale, a measure of erotic arousal in association with the fantasy of being admired as a female by another person, were significantly higher in the bisexual group than in the other three groups. Scores on the Alloeroticism Scale, a measure of sexual attraction to other people, were significantly lower in the asexual/analloerotic group than in the other three groups. Two previously developed scales also differed between groups: The homosexual group achieved significantly lower scores on measures of Heterosexual Experience and Cross-Gender Fetishism than the three nonhomosexual groups. Blanchard concluded that his findings supported the theory that "the major types of nonhomosexual gender dysphoria constitute variant forms of one underlying disorder, which may be characterized as autogynephilic gender dysphoria" (p. 616). Among the three nonhomosexual types, bisexual MtF transsexuals achieved significantly higher scores on autogynephilic interpersonal fantasy, suggesting the hypothesis that "bisexual gender dysphorics' interest in male sexual partners is mediated by a particularly strong desire to have their physical attractiveness as women validated by others" (p. 622). Blanchard cautioned, however, that the term "bisexual" should not be interpreted too literally: "This 'bisexual' behavior need not reflect an equal erotic attraction to the male and female physiques (and would perhaps be better characterized as *pseudobisexuality*)" (p. 622).

Blanchard's Proposed Transsexual Typology: Brief Comments

Blanchard's (1989a) proposal that "all gender dysphoric males who are not sexually oriented toward men are instead sexually oriented toward the thought or image of themselves as women" (pp. 322–323) was the first explicit statement of the MtF transsexual typology that would prove to be the most controversial outgrowth of the concept of autogynephilia. Some readers might expect me to discuss this typology in detail, setting forth the evidence pro and con; but I have decided not to do so. The aim of this book is to present and discuss the narratives of transsexuals who report that they have experienced autogynephilia, whereas most of the debate about Blanchard's typology concerns the experiences of nonhomosexual MtF transsexuals who allege that they have *not* experienced autogynephilia and therefore purportedly do not conform to the typology. Consequently, a detailed examination of the arguments for and against Blanchard's typology is really peripheral to the aim of this book.

I would simply like to state for the record that, based on my clinical experience and my reading of the scientific literature, I am firmly convinced that the overwhelming majority—probably 98% or more—of cases of severe gender dysphoria in men arise in connection with either effeminate homosexuality or autogynephilia; most of the rare exceptions probably arise in connection with conditions such as schizophrenia and certain personality disorders. The idea that substantial numbers of MtF transsexuals belong to a putative "third type" that is neither homosexual nor autogynephilic is inconsistent with my clinical experience and is, in my opinion, inconsistent with the best available empirical evidence. It is true that, in several major studies (Blanchard 1985b; Blanchard et al., 1987; Blanchard & Clemmensen, 1988; Lawrence, 2005; Nuttbrock, Bockting, Mason, et al., 2011), between 11% and 27% of nonhomosexual MtF transsexuals or gender dysphoric men denied having experienced autogynephilic arousal; but, based on observations in other studies described earlier (Blanchard et al., 1986; Blanchard, Clemmensen, et al., 1985; Zucker et al., 2012), their denials can easily be accounted for without theorizing the existence of a third major MtF transsexual type. Some clinicians and researchers disagree with my point of view. Arguments against Blanchard's transsexual typology have been presented in recent articles by Moser (2010) and Serano (2010); interested readers may wish to consult these articles.

Exploring the Implications of Autogynephilia

In proposing the concept of autogynephilia, Blanchard took a huge step toward explaining the phenomenon of "men trapped in men's bodies"—men who are not effeminate and are sexually attracted to women but also want to become women. The concept itself was only the beginning, however: Blanchard continued to conduct research on autogynephilia during the early 1990s, further extending and developing the associated theory. Other clinicians and researchers neglected Blanchard's concept for several years, but eventually some of them also began to investigate the clinical manifestations of autogynephilia, the associated MtF transsexual typology, and the implications of these for understanding and treating male gender dysphoria. These developments will be the subject of Chap. 2.

Chapter 2
Theory and Case Histories

Further Research Studies of Autogynephilia in Transsexuals

After Blanchard proposed the concept of autogynephilia and the MtF transsexual typology associated with it (Blanchard, 1989a, 1989b), he continued to conduct research to extend the concept, develop the theory associated with it, and explore its clinical manifestations and therapeutic implications. His work resulted in several important publications in the early 1990s (Blanchard, 1991, 1992, 1993a, 1993b, 1993c; Freund & Blanchard, 1993). Autogynephilia subsequently received little attention for several years. Eventually, however, clinicians and researchers again began to recognize and study autogynephilia in transsexuals and examine the diagnostic and therapeutic implications of the concept of autogynephilia.

Different Types of Autogynephilia

Blanchard (1991) addressed the topic of autogynephilia in a major review article that also introduced new concepts and new data. He observed that there appeared to be four broad, nonexclusive categories of autogynephilic fantasies and behaviors: *physiologic*, involving female physiologic functions (e.g., pregnancy, lactation, or menstruation); *behavioral*, involving engaging in stereotypically feminine behaviors; *anatomic*, involving having female anatomic features; and *transvestic*, involving wearing women's clothing. He noted that "the most common behavioral fantasies of adult autogynephilic men involve the thought of themselves, as women, engaging in sexual intercourse or other erotic activities" (p. 237), especially with male partners. Blanchard then presented an important case history, that of Philip, an autogynephilic man whose favorite erotic fantasy was having a woman's body but who had never cross-dressed as an adult. Philip's case demonstrated that "when a patient's primary sexual object is the thought of himself with a woman's body, there may be little overt paraphilic behavior" (p. 239). The article presented new data

A.A. Lawrence, *Men Trapped in Men's Bodies: Narratives of Autogynephilic Transsexualism*, Focus on Sexuality Research, DOI 10.1007/978-1-4614-5182-2_2,

about the co-occurrence of anatomic autogynephilia, transvestism, and fetishism (sexual attraction to specific inanimate objects): 90% of men with anatomic autogynephilia reported co-occurring transvestism, and 55% reported co-occurring fetishism. These results were consistent with the recognized tendency of paraphilic sexual interests to co-occur or cluster (Abel & Osborn, 1992; Gosselin & Wilson, 1980).

Etiological Conjectures

Blanchard's 1991 review article also contained an important section called "Etiological Conjectures" (pp. 246–248), in which Blanchard theorized about the etiologies of autogynephilia and transsexualism in nonhomosexual men. Regarding the former, Blanchard suggested that anatomic autogynephilia, transvestism, and fetishism for female garments all involved "a kind of error in locating heterosexual targets in the environment" (p. 246). He presented his ideas on this topic in greater detail in an article that appeared 2 years later (Freund & Blanchard, 1993); because his formulation is a complicated one, I will defer a detailed explanation until I discuss that article later in this chapter.

Blanchard (1991) further theorized that nonhomosexual MtF transsexualism has its origin in autogynephilic sexual arousal but can eventually develop a sustaining force of its own, one in which sexual arousal per se plays little or no part. His analysis is important enough to quote at length:

> Any viable theory relating the etiologies of autogynephilia and transsexualism must explain the following well-established observation: Gender dysphoria, in young nonhomosexual males, usually appears along with, or subsequent to, autogynephilia; in later years, however, autogynephilic sexual arousal may diminish or disappear, while the transsexual wish remains or grows even stronger. Such histories are often produced by gender dysphoric patients, but one does not have to rely on self-report to accept that the transsexual motive may attain, or inherently possess, some independence from autogynephilia. The same conclusion is suggested by the fact that surgical castration and estrogen treatment—which decrease libido in gender dysphorics as in other men—usually have no effect on the desire to live as a female or the resolve to remain in that role.
>
> One may speculate that the above developmental sequence reflects the operation, in autogynephilic men, of certain normal heterosexual behaviors. Many men, after years of marriage, are less excited by their wives than they were initially but continue to be deeply attached to them; in other words, pair-bonding, once established, is not necessarily dependent on the continuation of high levels of sexual attraction. It is therefore feasible that the continuing desire to have a female body, after the disappearance of sexual response to that thought, has some analog in the permanent love-bond that may remain between two people after their initial strong sexual attraction has largely disappeared. (p. 248)

Blanchard was making the point that nonhomosexual MtF transsexualism starts out as an erotic phenomenon and remains a sexual phenomenon in the broadest sense. However, the transsexual wish could eventually be sustained by something resembling pair-bonding—a form of attachment—after the erotic elements that characterized its early phase diminished or disappeared, just as a conventional romantic relationship can be sustained by pair-bonding or attachment after the intense erotic attraction of its early phase begins to fade.

Blanchard's idea that nonhomosexual MtF transsexuals could develop something resembling pair-bonded relationships with their idealized images of themselves as female-bodied persons might sound bizarre to anyone who has not experienced autogynephilia firsthand, but Blanchard was not the first investigator to make such a suggestion. Buckner (1970) had previously observed that the typical heterosexual transvestite also "acts toward himself in a way that a normal person acts toward a socio-sexually significant other" (p. 381). Buckner added that

> When a male adopts this pattern [of masturbation with articles of feminine clothing] and elaborates it into an entire feminine identity, he finds it gratifying in both sexual and social ways. When it becomes fixed in his identity, he begins to relate toward himself in some particulars as if he were his own wife. (p. 387)

In other words, a pattern of cross-gender behavior that begins with erotic cross-dressing can evolve to a point at which the heterosexual transvestite seems to be engaged in something resembling a pair-bonded relationship with the feminine aspect of himself.

Buckner's (1970) concept of an elaborated "entire feminine identity" offers another key to understanding this phenomenon. I have previously noted that the term *cross-gender identity* is aspirational, at least as it is often operationally defined: It denotes the gender that the gender dysphoric person *wants* to become, not the gender that he or she already *is*. But with time and lived experience in the opposite gender role, the cross-gender identity of a gender dysphoric man need not remain wholly aspirational: It can become a well-developed, highly valued part of his self-system and can eventually supplant his original male gender identity and become his (or her) dominant gender identity. Both Docter (1988) and Doorn, Poortinga, and Verschoor (1994) conceptualized the development of "secondary" or "late-onset" MtF transsexualism—roughly synonymous with nonhomosexual MtF transsexualism—as reflecting the ascendency of an increasingly powerful and esteemed female gender identity within the self-system of a gender dysphoric man. Whether one prefers to think of the genesis and continuation of nonhomosexual MtF transsexualism in terms of something resembling attachment (or pair-bonding) to the image of one's female-bodied self or in terms of the ascendency of a new, cherished female gender identity within one's self-system is not terribly important. Both represent attempts to put into words something that is hard to understand and adequately describe, even for those of us who have experienced it: the process by which a man's erotic desire to turn his body into a facsimile of a female body eventually gives rise to a strongly held, highly valued cross-gender identity and the process by which that new identity—that image of himself as a female—becomes the focus of his desire, admiration, idealization, attachment, and love—the same emotions that he might experience for an actual female partner.

A few years later, Blanchard (1993c) would express these same ideas slightly differently in his observation that the "behavior and motivation [underlying nonhomosexual MtF transsexualism] is subjectively experienced as a desire for physical union with a feminine self-image" (p. 243) and in his theory that "an autogynephile's desire to unite in the flesh with his feminine self-image corresponds to a heterosexual's desire to unite in marriage with a female partner" (p. 243).

Autogynephilia Competes with Heterosexual Attraction

Blanchard (1992) subsequently examined the relationship between strength of heterosexual attraction and intensity of anatomic autogynephilia in a sample of 427 transvestic or gender dysphoric men. He hypothesized that "autogynephilia arises in association with heterosexuality but also competes with it" (p. 273) and this is exactly what the data revealed: The highest levels of autogynephilia were associated with intermediate levels of heterosexual attraction. Blanchard interpreted these results as consistent with the theory that autogynephilia is a variant form of heterosexuality that also competes with heterosexual interest. Men with little heterosexual attraction evince low levels of autogynephilia, and autogynephilia increases with increasing heterosexual attraction, at least to a point. Then increasing heterosexual attraction becomes associated with slightly but significantly lower levels of autogynephilia as a result of the theorized competition.

Blanchard (1992) further theorized that autogynephilia was competitive with heterosexual attraction in two distinctly different ways. He observed that, although autogynephilia and heterosexual attraction usually coexisted, there were some cases in which autogynephilia was so intense that it effectively replaced heterosexual attraction. Individuals who experienced autogynephilia of this intensity were theoretically heterosexual—they were attracted to female bodies, not male bodies—but they experienced little or no attraction to the female bodies of *other people* (i.e., they were analloerotic). Blanchard believed that the relative intensities of alloerotic heterosexual attraction and autogynephilia were largely determined during psychosexual development, so he called this form of competition between autogynephilia and heterosexual attraction *developmental competition* (p. 275).

But Blanchard (1992) also observed that gender dysphoric men sometimes reported that their autogynephilic fantasies or enactments or their associated feelings of gender dysphoria temporarily became less intense or less compelling when they entered into a new heterosexual relationship or fell in love with a woman. Several case reports of this phenomenon exist in the psychiatric literature (e.g., Marks, Green, & Mataix-Cols, 2000; Shore, 1984; Steiner, 1985). Blanchard referred to this type of competition between autogynephilia and heterosexual attraction as *dynamic competition* (p. 275).

Anatomic Autogynephilia Predicts Gender Dysphoria

In 1993, Blanchard published three investigations addressing the relationship between anatomic autogynephilia and gender dysphoria. In the first of these, Blanchard (1993c) examined the association between the type of cross-gender self-image that cross-dressing men reported to be most strongly associated with sexual arousal—a nude female, a female clothed in underwear or sleepwear, or a fully clothed female—and the intensity of their gender dysphoria. He discovered that the men who were most sexually aroused by the image of themselves as nude women were significantly more gender dysphoric than the others. He concluded that the results supported "the hypothesis that those nonhomosexual men most aroused sexually by the thought of having a woman's body are also those most interested in acquiring a woman's body through some permanent, physical transformation" (p. 241). Blanchard further suggested that "the finding that the specific content of autogynephiles' erotic fantasies relates to their degree of gender dysphoria has potential relevance for practical clinical prognosis" (p. 248). Specifically, he conjectured that the content of an autogynephilic patient's sexual fantasies might prove to be a useful prognostic indicator of the likelihood that the patient would eventually decide to pursue sex reassignment. Unfortunately, no subsequent researchers appear to have investigated this intriguing idea.

In a related study, Blanchard (1993a) investigated differences in the strength of gender dysphoria in autogynephilic men who were or were not sexually aroused by imagining themselves with various specific female anatomic features (breasts, buttocks, legs, genitals, and face). He found that men who reported being sexually aroused by picturing themselves with female genitals—interestingly, only 86% of the autogynephilic individuals so reported—were significantly more gender dysphoric than those who denied such arousal. These results confirmed that "men who are sexually aroused at the thought of having a vulva are more likely to want to be women" (p. 301). Blanchard went on to explain:

> The present study and my previous studies on this topic [Blanchard, 1993b, 1993c] all point to the conclusion that the female attributes a man imagines when sexually aroused are related to the type and degree of feminization that he desires at other times. This simple and rather intuitive observation runs counter to the prevailing view in the clinical field of gender dysphoria. The majority of workers committed to the care of gender-dysphoric patients has maintained the position that paraphilias and gender identity disorders are completely separate entities, against the minority view that these are related, albeit distinguishable, phenomena. The present study supports the latter position and suggests that—in nonhomosexual men—autogynephilia and gender dysphoria are two sides of the same coin. (p. 306)

Thus, in nonhomosexual men, autogynephilia, gender dysphoria, and cross-gender identity are merely different sides of the same paraphilic (or paraphilia-related) phenomenon.

In the same article, Blanchard (1993a) also expanded on his earlier suggestion (Blanchard, 1989a) that autogynephilia can be considered a sexual orientation. He observed that, paraphilic features notwithstanding,

> autogynephilia might be better characterized as an orientation than as a paraphilia. The term *orientation* encompasses behavior, correlated with sexual behavior but distinct from it, that may ultimately have a greater impact on the life of the individual. For heterosexual and homosexual men, such correlated behavior includes courtship, love, and cohabitation with a partner of the preferred sex; for autogynephilic men, it includes the desire to achieve, with clothing, hormones, or surgery, an appearance like the preferred self-image of their erotic fantasies. (p. 306)

In yet another article, Blanchard (1993b) described anatomic autogynephilia and gender dysphoria in men with *partial autogynephilia*—men whose "erotic self-images include a mixture of male and female anatomic features, most often women's breasts and men's genitals" (p. 71). The article included four case studies of partial autogynephiles who wanted to have female breasts but not female genitals; in most cases they were adamant about wanting to retain their male genitals. Blanchard described these partial autogynephiles as experiencing "agonizing levels of gender dysphoria" (p. 75), presumably because they experienced severe discontent with their secondary sex characteristics, albeit no discontent with their primary sex characteristics (i.e., their genitals).

Analogs of Autogynephilia in Men Attracted to Children, Amputees, and Animals

Blanchard coauthored a seminal article (Freund & Blanchard, 1993) that described analogs of transvestic and anatomic autogynephilia in men who were pedophilic (sexually attracted to children). This article also described a man who was sexually attracted to anthropomorphic plush animals, masturbated using them, and fantasized becoming a plush animal himself. Freund and Blanchard proposed that there existed a hitherto unrecognized class of paraphilias in which affected men experienced powerful erotic desires to impersonate or make their bodies resemble the types of persons or things to which they felt sexually attracted. Specifically, they theorized that:

> For every class of sexual object, there will be small subgroups of men who develop the erotic fantasy of being the desired object, and who develop the sustained wish to transform their own bodies into facsimiles of the desired object. (p. 562)

Freund and Blanchard thought that paraphilias of this kind represented *erotic target location errors*. This term reflected their theory that the mental dysfunction underlying these paraphilias involved an error in accurately locating the "target" of one's erotic interest: specifically, erroneously locating that target in or on one's own body, rather than in or on the body of another individual. Readers who would like to learn more about erotic target location errors are invited to consult my review article (Lawrence, 2009a), but an in-depth understanding of the concept is not essential. What is genuinely important is that Freund and Blanchard described pedophilic men who experienced precise analogs of transvestic and anatomic autogynephilia: sexual arousal associated with wearing children's clothing (or replicas thereof) and imagining themselves to be children.

Thirteen years later, I theorized that men who desired to undergo elective amputation of a healthy limb and were often sexually aroused by the idea of doing so—a phenomenon historically conceptualized as a paraphilia called *apotemnophilia* (Money, Jobaris, & Furth, 1977)—likewise experienced something analogous to anatomic autogynephilia (Lawrence, 2006). I observed that data from several published reports suggested that these men were almost always sexually attracted to amputees and were often sexually aroused by impersonating amputees; moreover, they displayed a much higher than expected prevalence of transvestism and GID. I proposed that

> apotemnophilia may represent the intersection of two distinctly different paraphilic aspects or dimensions. One dimension involves an uncommon erotic target preference: attraction

> to amputees. The second dimension involves an erotic target location error, in which the individual desires to turn his body into the desired erotic target (or a facsimile thereof), rather than simply desiring that body configuration in another person. (p. 269)

A few years later, I described additional instances of pedophilic men who displayed analogs of transvestic and anatomic autogynephilia (Lawrence, 2009a). In the same article, I summarized data concerning men who were sexually attracted to anthropomorphic plush animals, liked to costume themselves as plush animals and were sometimes sexually aroused by doing so, and seemed to identify with plush animals or fantasized becoming plush animals. I also presented data about men who were sexually attracted to real animals (i.e., who were *zoophilic*) and identified as real animals and about other men who wished they could become real animals (i.e., who experienced *species dysphoria*—the belief that they were born as the wrong species; see Beetz, 2004).

Thus, there is persuasive evidence for the existence of men who are sexually attracted to children, identify as children, are sexually aroused by dressing as children, and want to turn their bodies into facsimiles of children's bodies; men who are sexually attracted to amputees, identify as amputees, are sexually aroused by impersonating amputees, and want to have surgery to become amputees; men who are sexually attracted to plush animals, seem to identify with plush animals, like to impersonate plush animals and are sometimes sexually aroused by doing so, and probably fantasize about turning their bodies into facsimiles of plush animals; and men who are sexually attracted to real animals, identify as real animals, and may in some cases—although this is speculative—be sexually aroused by the idea of becoming real animals and fantasize about turning their bodies into facsimiles of real animals' bodies.

How does this information help us to understand the phenomenon of men who are sexually attracted to women, identify as women, are sexually aroused by dressing as women, and want to turn their bodies into facsimiles of women's bodies—the phenomenon of autogynephilic transsexualism? I believe that the existence of these analogs of autogynephilic transsexualism calls into question the most influential biological and psychoanalytic theories of nonhomosexual MtF transsexualism, because such theories should also be able to account for these analogous phenomena but cannot easily do so. For example: It is plausible that hormonal abnormalities during prenatal development could result in a male-bodied person with a brain that had developed in a female-typical direction (Swaab, 2007). It is less plausible that a prenatal developmental disturbance could result in a male-bodied person with a brain that had developed like that of an amputee or a plush animal. Turning to psychoanalytic explanations, it is plausible that a boy might attempt to manage unresolved separation anxiety arising in infancy by means of a "reparative fantasy of symbiotic fusion with the mother" (Person & Ovesey, 1974a, p. 5). It is less plausible that a boy might attempt to manage such unresolved separation anxiety through the fantasy of symbiotic fusion with another child, a plush animal, or an amputee.

I consider it more parsimonious to theorize that autogynephilic MtF transsexualism and the analogous conditions that exist in men who are sexually attracted to children, amputees, plush animals, and perhaps real animals, all represent manifestations of an unusual type of paraphilia in which affected men feel sexually aroused by the idea of impersonating or becoming whatever category of person or thing they find sexually attractive. Their paraphilic desires, in turn, often give rise to strongly held, highly valued alternative identities that ultimately become their dominant identities.

Empirical Studies of Autogynephilia Published After 1993

After the publication of Blanchard's 1993 articles, no further empirical investigations of autogynephilia were published for approximately 8 years. Docter and Fleming (2001) were apparently the first to address the topic again after this hiatus. They used a 70-item questionnaire to measure aspects of transgender behavior in 455 self-described transvestites and 61 self-described MtF transsexuals. Large majorities of both groups had been married to women and only small minorities expressed a preference for male partners, so it is reasonable to assume that most, perhaps nearly all, participants were nonhomosexual (and thus putatively autogynephilic). In an initial factor analysis of the participants' responses, Docter and Fleming extracted five factors that characterized the transgender behavior of the participants; they called these factors Transgender Identity, Transgender Role, Transgender Sexual Arousal (in effect, a measure of transvestic autogynephilia), Androallure (interest in affectionate, social, or sexual encounters with men), and Pleasure. The authors then conducted a second-order factor analysis, based on the correlation matrix for the five primary factors; this resulted in two Secondary Factors, I and II. Describing the results of this secondary factor analysis, Docter and Fleming observed:

> The original factor of Sexual Arousal was most heavily loaded on [Secondary] Factor I. The pattern of loadings for the other three [sic] original factors supports the interpretation of this as a Transvestic Autogynephilia factor—that is, experiencing sexual arousal in association with the thought or image of oneself as a woman. For Secondary Factor II, the highest loading (.57) was the primary factor of Androallure with moderate positive loadings for Identity and Role factors, and a very low loading (.17) for Sexual Arousal. We have named this factor Autogynephilic Pseudobisexuality. (p. 266)

In summary, based on a survey of over 500 mostly nonhomosexual (and putatively primarily autogynephilic) transvestite and MtF transsexual participants, Docter and Fleming independently derived a high-order description of transgender behavior involving two main factors, Transvestic Autogynephilia and Autogynephilic Pseudobisexuality. These two factors closely resembled the two major dimensions of autogynephilia that Blanchard (1989b) had described and operationalized in his Core Autogynephilia and Autogynephilic Interpersonal Fantasy scales, which were discussed in Chap. 1; the principal difference was that Docter and Fleming's questionnaire had emphasized transvestic autogynephilia, which was consequently emphasized in their Secondary Factor I. These results from Docter and Fleming can be seen as an independent confirmation of Blanchard's description of the major dimensions of autogynephilia, obtained using a completely different methodology.

In 2003, I published the results of a survey of 232 MtF transsexuals who had undergone SRS with surgeon Toby Meltzer during the period 1994–2000 (Lawrence, 2003). I observed that about 86% of respondents had experienced one or more episodes of autogynephilic arousal before undergoing SRS and 49% had experienced hundreds of episodes or more. Two years later, in a second article based on data from the same survey, I reported that 89% of the respondents classified as nonhomosexual on the basis of their sexual partnership history reported one or more experiences of autogynephilic arousal before undergoing SRS, vs. 40% in the small number of respondents classified as homosexual (Lawrence, 2005); there was evidence that some of these supposedly homosexual participants had misreported their partnership histories and were actually nonhomosexual.

Veale, Clarke, and Lomax (2008) reported the results of a survey of 234 MtF transsexuals and 127 natal women, about 90% of whom completed survey materials online. The survey questionnaire included modified versions of Blanchard's (1989b) Core Autogynephilia and Autogynephilic Interpersonal Fantasy scales. The authors used cluster analysis to partition their MtF transsexual participants into ostensibly autogynephilic and nonautogynephilic groups, but their analytic procedures were questionable, and both groups obtained mean autogynephilia scores that were equal to or higher than the mean scores obtained by Blanchard's (1989b) nonhomosexual (autogynephilic) participants. As J. Michael Bailey and I observed in a Letter to the Editor commenting on these results, "Veale et al.'s cluster analysis really defined an 'autogynephilic' group and an 'even more autogynephilic' group" (Lawrence & Bailey, 2009, p. 174). Consequently, Veale et al.'s claims to have found results that were inconsistent with Blanchard's typology of MtF transsexualism were unconvincing. Perhaps the most interesting finding from the Veale et al. survey was that autogynephilic arousal was extremely common, perhaps almost universal, in the MtF population that the authors recruited. Veale et al. observed that some natal women endorsed items on their modified autogynephilia scales but conceded that "it is unlikely that these biological females actually experience sexual attraction to oneself as a woman in the way that Blanchard conceptualized it" (p. 595).

Moser (2009) conducted a survey of 29 natal women to determine whether any of them had experienced autogynephilic arousal. To this end, he constructed an Autogynephilia Scale for Women, using modified items from Blanchard's scales measuring cross-gender fetishism (Blanchard, 1985a) and autogynephilia (Blanchard, 1989b) and a few items of his own devising. Several of Moser's informants endorsed some of his survey items, but Moser himself conceded that "It is possible that autogynephilia among MTFs and natal women are different phenomena and the present inventories lack the sophistication to distinguish these differences" (p. 544). I subsequently argued that this was indeed the case, because Moser's items "fail to adequately assess the essential element of autogynephilia—sexual arousal simply to the thought of being a female—because they do not emphasize that element" (Lawrence, 2010d, p. 3).

In 2010, I published a study of the relative prevalence of nonhomosexual and homosexual MtF transsexualism across national cultures (Lawrence, 2010c) that had implications for understanding the phenomenon of autogynephilic transsexualism. In this article, I attempted to explain the observation that nearly all MtF transsexuals in Asian cultures are homosexual, whereas most MtF transsexuals in the USA, Canada, and the UK are nonhomosexual. I demonstrated that differences in a measure of *societal individualism*—the degree to which a culture condones its members pursuing personal happiness and self-expression, regardless of the opinions of others—accounted for most of the differences in the relative prevalence of nonhomosexual MtF transsexualism. If one assumes that nonhomosexual MtF transsexualism is equivalent to autogynephilic transsexualism—a justifiable assumption, in my opinion—these results suggest the hypothesis that the *permissible expression of autogynephilia*, rather than the prevalence or severity of autogynephilia, primarily accounts for these cross-cultural differences. Undergoing MtF sex reassignment probably feels far more permissible to autogynephilic men living in individualistic Western cultures than to their counterparts in cultures in which individual self-expression is discouraged.

Nuttbrock, Bockting, Mason, et al. (2011) investigated the lifetime prevalence of one type of autogynephilia, transvestic fetishism (TF), in 571 MtF transgender persons—not all of whom were transsexual—living in New York City. Their findings were similar to those reported by Blanchard (1985b): In their study, 73% of nonhomosexual participants reported a history of TF, compared to only 23% of homosexual participants. Deviations from the predictions of Blanchard's theory could be accounted for by a combination of misreporting or inaccurate assessment of sexual orientation and underreporting of TF by affected persons (see Lawrence, 2010a). Nuttbrock, Bockting, Mason, et al., however, chose to emphasize a few areas in which they claimed their results deviated from the predictions of Blanchard's theory. In particular, they argued—unconvincingly, in my opinion—that age and ethnicity, in addition to sexual orientation, were important predictors of TF. The authors and I debated these issues at length in a series of Letters to the Editor (Lawrence, 2010a, 2011b; Nuttbrock, Bockting, Rosenblum, Mason, & Hwahng, 2010, 2011); interested readers are referred to these letters for further details.

One of the most revealing passages in the article by Nuttbrock, Bockting, Mason, et al. (2011) emphasized that Blanchard's concept of autogynephilia and the MtF transsexual typology derived from it had social and political implications that transcended issues of scientific validity:

> [Blanchard's] findings have sociopolitical implications far beyond scientific circles because they directly contradict basic tenets of the worldwide transgender movement: sex and gender are deemed to be separate, socially constructed dimensions of personal identity characterized by individual variation and social diversity. (p. 249)

Leaving aside the question of whether there is indeed a worldwide transgender movement and, if so, whether its beliefs are monolithic, the implications of the above statement are clear: The authors believed that Blanchard's ideas were politically unacceptable, regardless of their scientific validity.

Reviews, Popular Accounts, and Critiques of Autogynephilia

In addition to the empirical investigations of autogynephilia conducted by Blanchard and other researchers, there have been a few reviews, popular accounts, and critiques of the concept of autogynephilia, its meaning and significance, and the MtF transsexual typology and theory of motivation associated with it. In one review article, Blanchard (2005) summarized the early history of the concept of autogynephilia. I authored four reviews devoted entirely to autogynephilia (Lawrence, 2004, 2007, 2009b, 2011a) and a review of erotic target location errors that contained extensive discussions of transvestic and anatomic autogynephilia (Lawrence, 2009a).

In my review of erotic target location errors (Lawrence, 2009a), I summarized data on the prevalence of autogynephilia. In a national probability survey, 2.8% of Swedish men reported at least one episode of sexual arousal associated with cross-dressing (Långström & Zucker, 2005). Other studies have found prevalence rates between 1% and 18% for sexual arousal with cross-dressing or cross-gender fantasy; all of these studies have methodological limitations, but collectively they suggest that perhaps 2–3% of men have engaged in erotic cross-dressing at times and even more have occasionally experienced erotic arousal in association with cross-gender fantasies. However, clinically significant autogynephilic arousal, manifesting as frequent cross-dressing or habitual cross-gender fantasy during sexual activity, is probably much less prevalent. This more intense form of autogynephilia probably affects fewer than 1% of men and perhaps fewer than 0.1%. Autogynephilia that is sufficiently intense to cause severe gender dysphoria and the persistent desire for sex reassignment—autogynephilic transsexualism—is evidently rarer still.

Only a few studies have produced reliable prevalence estimates for MtF transsexualism and severe gender dysphoria in Western countries. In Scotland, the reported prevalence of severe gender dysphoria in men is about 1 in 7,400 (0.014%; Wilson, Sharp & Carr, 1999). In Belgium, about 1 in 12,900 (0.0078%) adult men has undergone MtF SRS (De Cuypere et al., 2007); in the Netherlands, the figure is about 1 in 11,900 (0.0084%; Bakker, van Kesteren, Gooren, & Bezemer, 1993). In New Zealand, the reported prevalence of MtF transsexualism based on passport data is about 1 in 3,600 (0.028%; Veale, 2008). Roughly one half to two thirds of the MtF transsexuals and gender dysphoric men in these countries would be expected to be nonhomosexual and presumably autogynephilic (see Lawrence, 2010c).

In my recent reviews devoted to autogynephilia (Lawrence, 2007, 2009b, 2011a), I emphasized that autogynephilia is not merely an erotic phenomenon but also involves the same feelings of idealization and attachment that characterize romantic love. Extending Blanchard's (1989a, 1993a) idea that autogynephilia is a sexual orientation as well as a paraphilia, I explained:

> Sexual orientations are characterized by feelings of idealization and attachment in addition to feelings of erotic desire. For example, gynephilic men do not merely lust for women: They also—at least most of the time—idealize them, fall in love with them, derive feelings of comfort and security from them, and seek to establish enduring bonds with them. Autogynephilia is much the same: Like other sexual orientations, autogynephilia potentially involves all the feelings and behaviors we associate with the word *love*, broadly construed.

> Autogynephilic MtF transsexuals are erotically aroused by imagining themselves as female, but they also idealize the thought of being female, experience feelings of comfort and security from their autogynephilic fantasies and behaviors, and usually want to bond permanently with their idealized feminine self-images by completely embodying and enacting them (i.e., by undergoing hormone therapy and sex reassignment surgery). (Lawrence, 2011a, pp. 140–141)

To put this conclusion more succinctly: Autogynephilic MtF transsexuals are men who love women and want to become what they love (Lawrence, 2007).

The best known popular account of autogynephilia and the MtF transsexual typology associated with it appeared in the book *The Man Who Would Be Queen* (Bailey, 2003). The book and its author incurred the wrath of some transgender activists and their allies, who took issue with the opinions and attitudes expressed in the book (Dreger, 2008; Lawrence, 2008). I authored two reviews of autogynephilia (Lawrence, 1998, 2000) that were intended for nonprofessional audiences but were structured as academic articles (e.g., they contained in-text literature citations). Finally, two critiques of autogynephilia have recently been published in second-line academic journals (Moser, 2010; Serano, 2010).

Case Histories of Autogynephilic Transsexualism Are Rare

Although Blanchard's theory that "nonhomosexual MtF transsexualism equals autogynephilic transsexualism" was groundbreaking, and the MtF transsexual typology derived from it and implicit theory of transsexual motivation associated with it had obvious clinical implications, Blanchard's formulation was not immediately influential, and some clinicians still do not accept it. His theory contradicted the conventional wisdom that transsexualism is unrelated to erotic desire and is exclusively about the desire to live in the opposite gender role, and this may be partly responsible for the theory's limited influence and acceptance. But probably Blanchard's theory also simply seemed too *theoretical* to many clinicians. It is important to remember that, with only two exceptions (i.e., Blanchard, Clemmensen, et al., 1985; Blanchard et al., 1986), the theory of autogynephilia and the concepts associated with it were developed and validated almost exclusively from survey data that were routinely collected in the institution where Blanchard worked. Although Blanchard's clinical experience undoubtedly informed his theories, his articles about autogynephilia included few case histories or clinical vignettes to illustrate his ideas. The only notable case history was that of Philip, the anatomic autogynephile who did not cross-dress, which appeared in two early articles and a later one (Blanchard, 1991, 1993b, 2005). There were also a few brief descriptions of anatomic and behavioral autogynephilic fantasies (e.g., Blanchard, 1993c). One article (Blanchard) included four case histories of men with partial autogynephilia, but none of these men was transsexual by usual definitions (i.e., none wanted to undergo SRS). Blanchard also wrote a book chapter (Blanchard, 1990) that contained three detailed case histories illustrating heterosexual, analloerotic, and bisexual MtF transsexualism; although he cited two of his own articles in which he had used the term autogynephilia (Blanchard, 1989a, 1989b), none of the case histories were presented as instances of autogynephilic transsexualism, nor did the word autogynephilia appear anywhere in the chapter.

Only a few subsequent case histories of autogynephilic transsexualism have appeared in the professional literature. Ekins and King (2001) presented the case of Janice, a nonhomosexual MtF transsexual who was aware of Blanchard's theory and who identified as autogynephilic. Janice experienced sexual arousal in association with cross-dressing long before puberty and was gender dysphoric from an early age, but her autogynephilic feelings led her to doubt that she was genuinely transsexual. She used feminization fantasies to facilitate coitus with her wife. She eventually underwent SRS at age 41 and continued to experience autogynephilic arousal thereafter; her fantasies involving anatomic autogynephilia are set forth in detail. I described a 38-year-old nonhomosexual MtF transsexual patient who identified with the concept of autogynephilia and reported a strong interest in having sex with men (Lawrence, 2004). The patient acknowledged that her interest did not represent genuine androphilia but merely reflected "the way in which being with a man sexually made her feel like a desirable woman" (p. 80).

Barrett (2007) presented three brief case histories of men with gender identity concerns and supposed autogynephilia. Barrett, however, considered autogynephilia to be one of the differential diagnoses in MtF transsexualism—that is, one of several "non-transsexual disorders of gender identity" (p. 35) that clinicians needed to differentiate from genuine transsexualism. Perhaps for that reason, none of Barrett's case histories of autogynephilia involved men who intensely desired to undergo sex reassignment and live as women. The first of these histories (SM) was presented as one "in which the autogynaephillic [sic] drive is rather clear" (p. 35), but Barrett never described any of the patient's autogynephilic fantasies, so the basis for this judgment seemed anything but clear. Barrett's other two cases (DW and DM; pp. 36–37) included cursory descriptions of the patients' histories of sexual arousal with cross-dressing, but what Barrett really emphasized was that these patients wanted to have female anatomic features but did not want to live in an unequivocally feminine gender role. Barrett seemed to believe that the hallmark of autogynephilia was the desire for physical feminization accompanied by "a fundamentally unchanged life, in a male gender role" (p. 36)—in short, pure anatomic autogynephilia that was unaccompanied by any significant cross-gender identification. Men who expressed an unequivocal wish to live as women seemingly did not qualify as autogynephilic in Barrett's view, even if they had extensive histories of sexual arousal in association with cross-dressing. Barrett recognized the existence of "heterosexual male secondary transsexuals" (p. 22) with such histories, but his descriptions of them did not mention anything resembling anatomic autogynephilia; perhaps for this reason, Barrett did not characterize nonhomosexual secondary MtF transsexuals as autogynephilic, even when they described evident transvestic autogynephilia.

Finally, there is an unusual case history of "autogynophillia" [sic] in a 44-year-old man who displayed transvestic fetishism and expressed a desire for SRS

(Duisin, Barisić, & Nikolić-Balkoski, 2009). Unfortunately, the authors did not describe the patient's autogynephilic fantasies and behaviors in much detail, limiting the value of this report.

Missing Discourses and Forbidden Narratives

Although "the study of autogynephilia is, more than anything, the study of what people say about their experiences" (Blanchard, 2005, p. 439), hardly any MtF transsexuals themselves have said much about their experiences of autogynephilia, at least until quite recently. As of the mid-1990s, only a few first-person narratives by MtF transsexuals contained descriptions of sexual arousal in association with cross-dressing or the thought or image of having a female body, and none that I am aware of actually used the term autogynephilia. Works of erotic fiction could be seen as exceptions to this pattern: Erotic stories containing explicitly autogynephilic themes and written as first-person narratives are not uncommon, especially on the Internet. But these erotic stories do not purport to be genuinely autobiographical; indeed, many are highly implausible. They can be easily dismissed as fabrications that are designed to satisfy the prurient interests of fetishistic transvestites but are of no significance to "real" MtF transsexuals.

Perhaps the scarcity of first-person descriptions of autogynephilia by MtF transsexuals reflects the belief that experiencing sexual arousal in association with cross-dressing or cross-gender fantasy disqualifies one from being genuinely transsexual. Whatever the explanation, it is almost impossible to find an autobiographical account in which a MtF transsexual explicitly states, "Yes, I was sexually aroused by the idea of having a woman's body, and this was part of the reason that I sought SRS." Thus, first-person descriptions of autogynephilia—especially anatomic autogynephilia—by MtF transsexuals appear to constitute "missing discourses" (cf. Fine, 1988) or "forbidden narratives" (cf. Church, 1995).

This narrative vacuum leaves severely gender dysphoric men who experience autogynephilia without viable MtF transsexual role models. The autobiography of Christine Jorgensen (1967) was a beacon of hope for many MtF transsexuals because it was a story with which they could identify. But gender dysphoric men who experience autogynephilia, especially anatomic autogynephilia, do not yet have a Christine Jorgensen with whose story *they* can identify. At present, they have only a few autobiographical shards that seem at all relevant to their circumstances. Let us briefly consider what these consist of.

Hunt (1978), a nonhomosexual MtF transsexual who had undergone SRS, authored an autobiography in which she explicitly described autogynephilic arousal and its close resemblance to heterosexual desire:

> I was feverishly interested in [girls]. I studied their hair, their clothes, their figures. And I brooded about the increasing differences between us. I seethed with envy while at the same time becoming sexually aroused—I wanted to possess them even as I wanted to become them. In my nighttime fantasies, as I masturbated or floated towards sleep, I combined the two compulsions, dreaming of sex but with myself as the girl. (p. 60)

In an autobiographical essay, Bornstein (1995), a nonhomosexual MtF transsexual who had undergone SRS, repeatedly quoted from erotica written for heterosexual cross-dressers and confided that "I never stopped reading those porno books. I still have a small collection of them." (p. 232). Bornstein also observed that, 7 years after undergoing SRS, she continued to be aroused by the image of herself as a female:

> It's been 7 years, and y'know what? I still get a thrill when I look at myself in the mirror and I see girl not boy. (p. 238)

In a detailed account of her SRS experience, Griggs (1998), another MtF transsexual, discussed her lifelong analloeroticism and obligatory reliance on fantasies of being female to achieve orgasm during masturbation. Based on a subsequent autobiographical work (Griggs, 2004), in which she described one long-term nonsexual relationship with a man and two long-term relationships with women, Griggs' sexual orientation appeared to be nonhomosexual. She wrote:

> When I lived as a man, I had no desire to have intercourse with a woman. I likewise had no inclination for a homosexual relationship with a man. Erotic imagery was invariably contingent on my being female, and even during masturbation, whether the object of my desire was man or woman, I could not reach a climax without imagining that I was female. This is still true. When confronted as a teenager by the reality that I was male, my private experience of sexuality was void, and the resulting appetite, or specifically the lack of it, was vaguely questioned by friends, family, and the women I dated. (Griggs, 1998, p. 50)

Griggs did *not* state, however, that the "object of her desire" during masturbation was her image of herself as a female. Rather, the supposed object of her desire was another "man or woman," despite her report of having felt no desire for either men or women earlier in her life. Thus, her description of what could be interpreted as anatomic autogynephilia is equivocal.

McCloskey (1999), a MtF transsexual whose history is consistent with a nonhomosexual orientation—she was not effeminate in childhood, married a woman and fathered two children, and underwent SRS at age 53—authored an autobiography in which she described her lengthy history of cross-gender fetishism. Prior to gender transition, she had identified as "just a heterosexual cross-dresser" (p. 48), "just a guy who gets off dressing occasionally as a woman" (p. 50). Until about a year before she underwent SRS in 1996, her cross-dressing had routinely been associated with sexual arousal and, presumably, masturbation:

> Until the spring of 1995, each of the five thousand episodes [of cross-dressing] was associated with quick male sex. (p. 16)

McCloskey also offered a third-person description of her preferred erotic materials, which included images of feminized men whose male genitalia were not visible. She implied that this preference reflected her erotic fantasy of undergoing "complete" (i.e., genital) sex reassignment:

> His preoccupation with gender crossing showed up in the pornographic magazines he used. There are two kinds of crossdressing magazines, those that portray men in dresses with private parts showing and those that portray them hidden. He could never get aroused by the ones with private parts showing. His fantasy was of complete transformation. (p. 19)

This impressive candor notwithstanding, McCloskey subsequently stated that she rejected Blanchard's ideas about autogynephilia ("it's a mistaken theory, with no scientific basis"; McCloskey, 2008, p. 467) and claimed that the concept of autogynephilia was inapplicable to her (e.g., she described herself as "exhibiting no 'autogynephilia'"; McCloskey, 2003, para. 26).

Zander (2003), a nonhomosexual MtF transsexual—she identified as lesbian before and after undergoing SRS—discussed her simultaneous feelings of lust and envy toward attractive women in a collection of autobiographical essays. She described experiencing

> a slightly schizophrenic feeling whenever I met an attractive girl. The spontaneous male reflex (don't tell me it's not biological!) "If I could only have sex with her!," instantaneously followed by "and have such a body!". I used to call this my "Have her and be her" fantasy, and for decades it dominated my response to attractive women. (p. 104)

There are also a few examples of narratives by nonhomosexual MtF transsexuals in which erotic arousal associated with cross-dressing is described but is deemphasized or implied to be of little significance. Richards (Richards & Ames, 1983), a nonhomosexual MtF transsexual—she was not effeminate during childhood, married a woman, and fathered a child—described unequivocal erotic arousal associated with cross-dressing between the ages of 6 and 13 (she did not specify her exact age) in her autobiography. She denied, however, that she masturbated while cross-dressed or even that her erotic arousal was related to cross-gender ideation:

> My forays into my sister's wardrobe were happening with greater frequency. It would be natural to think that this cross-dressing must have been associated with some sexual activity. In fact it was not. I would sometimes get an erection as I pulled on some silky underthing, but this was pretty much a response to the soft touch of the fabric. It was not associated with the transformation to a girl. The same thing might happen as I dried myself with a soft towel after a bath. It is peculiar indeed that I could control the desire to masturbate but not the desire to dress in my sister's clothes. I did have wet dreams; so the mechanism was in perfectly good shape. (p. 27)

Cummings (1992), another nonhomosexual MtF transsexual—she was not effeminate as a child, was unambiguously sexually attracted to women, and identified as a heterosexual transvestite for many years—likewise described sexual arousal, erection, and ejaculation in association with cross-dressing. However, she seemed to downplay the significance of these occurrences and portrayed herself as an unwilling victim of her own erotic reflexes:

> Was there a sexual component to this dressing up? Yes and no. I was ambushed by orgasm in a way I found quite antipathetic. Because my routine involved dressing up and standing in front of the mirror while I admired my feminised reflection, I wanted the image to be as female as possible and would, as most transvestites learn to do, pull my genitals back and clamp them between my thighs. Adolescence combined with friction tended to create an erection, quite the reverse of what I wanted and this in turn often resulted in orgasm and ejaculation. Contrary to what one might imagine, this ruined my enjoyment. Of course the moment of orgasm was pleasurable but it *was* only a moment and the consequent ejaculation called an immediate halt to my activity, partly because I had to prevent any semen from soiling my sister's clothes and partly because I disliked intensely the presence of the sticky fluid on my body. I would hastily undress and wash myself. (p. 11)

The narratives by autogynephilic transsexuals that I will introduce in the next chapter were collected with the intention of addressing the scarcity of accounts by MtF transsexuals of their autogynephilic feelings and desires. My goal was to make an anthology of these missing discourses and forbidden narratives available to anyone who might find such accounts valuable: in particular, clinicians seeking to better understand their nonhomosexual MtF transsexual clients and nonhomosexual MtF transsexuals seeking to better understand themselves.

Chapter 3
Narratives by Autogynephilic Transsexuals

Rationale for the Narrative Project

The decision to solicit and publish narratives by autogynephilic transsexuals arose from my observation that personal accounts by transsexuals who acknowledged autogynephilic arousal were scarce and my conviction that they needed to be collected and made available to clinicians and other autogynephilic transsexuals. I had searched almost in vain for personal narratives written by MtF transsexuals who acknowledged that autogynephilia had played an important role in their lives. I believed that such narratives needed to be available to professionals, to provide concrete illustrations of the phenomena Blanchard described, and to autogynephilic men who were struggling with gender dysphoria, to reassure them that they were not alone, not crazy, and not ineligible for sex reassignment.

My decision to collect and publish these narratives was also informed by my own history of gender dysphoria and autogynephilic erotic arousal. Beginning in early childhood, I experienced both the wish to be female and erotic arousal in association with cross-dressing and cross-gender fantasy. These feelings intensified in adolescence and continued throughout my adult life. For many years, I imagined I might be unique in both wanting to be female and being erotically aroused by the fantasy of being female. Although my experience of erotic arousal in association with cross-dressing was suggestive of fetishistic transvestism, I didn't believe that I was simply a transvestite, because I also felt an intense desire to have SRS. That desire led me to suspect that I might be some type of transsexual. But the consensus in the medical literature was that erotic arousal in association with cross-dressing or cross-gender fantasy excluded the diagnosis of transsexualism (see Blanchard & Clemmensen, 1988) and was a contraindication to SRS (e.g., Dolan, 1987; Lundström, Pauly, & Wålinder, 1984; Person & Ovesey, 1974b).

A.A. Lawrence, *Men Trapped in Men's Bodies: Narratives of Autogynephilic Transsexualism*, Focus on Sexuality Research, DOI 10.1007/978-1-4614-5182-2_3,

When I read Blanchard's writings on autogynephilia in 1994, I discovered a theory that seemed to apply to me. Blanchard's concept of autogynephilic transsexualism was consistent with my feelings and history and reassured me that there were others like myself. I later wrote:

> When I first read [Blanchard's work] in 1994, I experienced a kind of epiphany. Certainly it spoke to my own experience like nothing I had ever encountered before. It was enlightening and empowering to discover that someone thought feelings of sexual arousal to the idea of having a woman's body were consistent with genuine transsexualism—and that they provided a logical rationale for seeking sex reassignment. (Lawrence, 1999a)

This discovery still left me feeling isolated, however, because I was unable to locate other clinicians or researchers who accepted Blanchard's ideas and could independently confirm their validity:

> As I discussed Blanchard's theory with colleagues, I discovered two surprising things. First, his theory was not widely known. Second, many of those who did know about it thought it was not so much wrong as heretical. The intensity of their reactions was astonishing. It was as though thinking about transsexualism as a sexual problem involved such a paradigm shift that it frightened people. (Lawrence, 1999a)

I was also unable to find any detailed histories of persons like myself, either in the form of case reports or personal narratives.

After I underwent SRS in 1996, I began to think of myself as a transsexual activist. I created a website, *Transsexual Women's Resources* (now *Dr. Anne Lawrence on Transsexualism and Sexuality*; http://www.annelawrence.com) to provide information to other MtF transsexuals. The site became popular, and I decided to use it to solicit narratives by MtF transsexuals who also experienced autogynephilia. My decision to undertake the project was influenced by the ideas of feminist theologian Carol Christ (1980), who emphasized the importance of personal narratives in the lives of natal women:

> Women's stories have not been told. And without stories there is no articulation of experience. Without stories a woman is lost when she comes to make the important decisions of her life. Without stories she cannot understand herself. (p. 1)

I felt that Christ's ideas might also be relevant to gender dysphoric males whose experiences were like mine: A collection of first-person narratives by MtF transsexuals who experienced autogynephilia might help other gender dysphoric males with similar histories make the important decisions of their lives.

Collecting the Narratives

From October 1998 through October 2011, I collected hundreds of narratives written by autogynephilic transsexuals by means of a solicitation posted on the *Transsexual Women's Resources* website. The exact language of the solicitation varied slightly over the years, but this version from 2005 is representative:

Seeking Personal Histories of Sexual Arousal Associated with Sex Reassignment

I am still seeking narratives concerning sexual feelings and fantasies associated with or centered on the sex reassignment experience. If you identify as transsexual and are willing to share your experiences concerning this topic, please read on. I would particularly like to hear from persons who have either been approved for sex reassignment surgery or are postoperative.

Some transsexual women report that the process of becoming feminized, either in reality or in fantasy, has been or still is sexually arousing. This phenomenon—sexual excitement at the thought or image of oneself as a woman—is called *autogynephilia*. Have you experienced feelings like this?

Transsexual women have sometimes described sexual arousal in connection with doing or fantasizing the following:

- Wearing women's clothing.
- Having or acquiring a woman's body, or aspects such as breasts or a vagina.
- Feminizing one's body by applying cosmetics, shaving one's legs, etc.
- Imagining being pregnant, breast-feeding, or menstruating;
- Engaging in typically feminine activities.
- Being among women where men are not present.

Have thoughts or experiences like these been sexually arousing for you in the past? Have they continued to be arousing after transition or postoperatively? Did sexual desire play any part in your decision to transition? Was the desire to live out fantasies like these part of your reason for transitioning? Did you ever think that you couldn't "really" be transsexual because you had such fantasies? Have you told others (friends, lovers, therapists) about your feelings? What was the outcome? How have your feelings affected your sex life—either during solo sex or with partners? How have your feelings affected your relationships with other people?

If you are willing to share your experience—anonymously—here's how: Simply write (or paste) your narrative into the space below and click the "submit" button. The form will accommodate up to about 2,000 words. This method is completely anonymous—your name and email address WILL NOT be transmitted to me unless you manually enter them somewhere in the space below. Whatever you submit is sent to me automatically by my Internet Service Provider—and its name, not yours, appears in the "From" line of the message I receive.

I may include excerpts from the narratives I receive in published articles or presentations. While you are welcome to include your name or other identifying information if you wish, I will remove or change any such information before publication. Feel free to be as sexually explicit as you wish. If you have either been approved for sex reassignment surgery or are postoperative, please include this information in your statement.

Please note that I am not requesting statements from persons who have never had such feelings or who object to the idea that other people might have them: The world has plenty of such statements already.

As described above, the solicitation was followed by a text box into which informants could write or paste their narratives. Clicking a "submit" button transmitted the contents of the text box to me anonymously, via a cgi-email script. Roughly one third of informants, however, chose to bypass this method of anonymous transmission and emailed narrative material to me directly, usually because they regarded the anonymous method as too limiting or simply unnecessary. The option of emailing narratives to me directly was explicitly mentioned in later versions of the solicitation. Over the 13-year collection period, I received about 470 narratives addressing or purporting to address the topic of autogynephilia.

In addition to the brief description of autogynephilia provided in the solicitation, informants also had access to one or more essays on my website that explained autogynephilia in greater detail. Originally, the essay was "Men trapped in men's bodies: An introduction to the concept of autogynephilia" (Lawrence, 1998). This was replaced in 2000 by "Sexuality and transsexuality: A new introduction to autogynephilia" (Lawrence, 2000) and in 2004 by "Autogynephilia: A paraphilic model of gender identity disorder" (Lawrence, 2004). The last essay was supplemented in 2007 by "Becoming what we love: Autogynephilic transsexualism conceptualized as an expression of romantic love" (Lawrence, 2007). Several informants referenced one or more of these essays in their narratives.

In the final paragraph of the solicitation, I sought to make it clear that I only wanted to hear from MtF transsexuals who had personally experienced autogynephilia, not from anyone who had an opinion on the topic. Some opponents of Blanchard's theory have criticized that paragraph. For example, after I posted on the Internet a few of the earliest narratives I had received (Lawrence, 1999c, 1999d), Barnes (2001) objected that "all she [Lawrence] really did was solicit responses from those sympathetic with her theory" (p. 24). Roughgarden (2004) similarly alleged that "the narratives that Lawrence posted are the ones most likely to be supportive. Lawrence discourages counternarratives" (p. 272). Such criticisms are both misplaced and inaccurate.

My stated intention was to collect narratives from MtF transsexuals who had personally experienced autogynephilia, in order to learn what they had to say about it. It would seem self-evident that MtF transsexuals who had *not* experienced autogynephilia would be unable to provide relevant narratives. If my intention had been different—for example, to conduct a survey of MtF transsexuals' opinions about Blanchard's transsexual typology—then soliciting narratives from persons who had not experienced autogynephilia would have been appropriate. But I was not conducting such a survey. Because Blanchard's MtF transsexual typology is controversial, however, some of its opponents seem to believe that every discussion of autogynephilia must include a debate about that typology—a debate in which they are entitled to participate. I disagree.

Moreover, not every MtF transsexual informant who experienced autogynephilia and submitted a narrative agreed with everything Blanchard theorized. Some informants disagreed with Blanchard (and me) about the meaning and significance of autogynephilia; others challenged Blanchard's transsexual typology or his implicit theory of transsexual motivation. I neither discouraged nor suppressed such dissenting opinions by autogynephilic informants; they are presented in detail in Chap. 10 and occasionally in other chapters as well.

Editing and Analysis

Editing and analysis of the narratives was a multistep process. First, I eliminated any messages that did not describe the informant's personal experience of autogynephilia. I received a few dozen such messages, most of which either condemned the concept of autogynephilia or disagreed with all or part of the associated theory. I also eliminated a handful of narratives—fewer than a dozen—that I believed were fabrications; I will describe these and the reasons I considered them fabrications later in this chapter. From the remaining narratives, I grouped together those that appeared to have been submitted by the same informant. Most informants sent only one narrative, but some sent two or more, up to a maximum of six. There may have been a few instances in which a single individual submitted more than one narrative and I was unable to recognize this. This process resulted in a collection of one or more narrative submissions from 301 different informants.

Although I had solicited narratives only from persons who identified as transsexual, I received several narratives from autogynephilic persons who either denied being transsexual or who did not appear to be transsexual according to usual definitions. I had wanted to emphasize narratives written by informants who were recognizably transsexual, because such narratives were scarce. Moreover, narratives by informants who were not recognizably transsexual could too easily be dismissed as not truly relevant to understanding the phenomenon of autogynephilic transsexualism. Consequently, I divided the 301 autogynephilic informants into those whom I could classify with some confidence as transsexual and those whom I was unable to classify as transsexual or who appeared to be nontranssexual.

Deciding which informants qualified as transsexual and which did not required some subjective judgments. A few informants did not provide enough unambiguous information about gender dysphoria, cross-gender identification, cross-gender expression, formal diagnoses, or treatment history to permit definitive classification. In general, I considered informants to be transsexual if they expressed the wish to have a female body or to live and be recognized as a woman. More specifically, I considered informants to be transsexual if they (a) identified themselves as such or described the severe gender dysphoria (discomfort with anatomic sex or gender role) or pronounced cross-gender identity (desire to be female, live as a woman, or undergo SRS) that are typical of MtF transsexualism; (b) stated that they were using hormones to feminize their bodies (with one exception noted below), were living full-time in female role, or had been approved for SRS (implying both of the former), or (c) stated that they had completed SRS.

Some informants were especially difficult to classify. The largest subgroup of these consisted of individuals who experienced the most prevalent form of *partial autogynephilia* (Blanchard, 1993b): the desire to have female breasts, and often other female anatomic features as well, but without any strong desire to have female genitalia or undergo SRS. Some of these individuals reported that they were using low doses of feminizing hormones to develop breasts or were considering living full-time as women, factors that further complicated the decision process. For the sake of consistency, I eventually decided to classify informants who described partial autogynephilia and did *not* desire to have female genitalia or undergo SRS as nontranssexual, even if they reported that they were using feminizing hormones. Narratives from several informants who conformed to this description are included in Chap. 11.

Even more difficult to classify were a few informants who expressed a wish to have female genitalia—or who had in some cases undergone SRS to acquire female-appearing genitalia—but who claimed they had no desire to live in a traditional female role or had concluded that it was not feasible to do so. Some of these individuals stated that they only wanted female genitalia, others that they wanted female genitalia and breasts but nothing more, and still others that they wanted complete physical feminization. All, however, either claimed they wanted to live as men or stated that living in a male gender role seemed like the best option available to them. Attempting to classify these individuals begs the question: What is the essential feature of MtF transsexualism? Is it the desire to live as a woman? The desire to have something resembling a female body? If the latter, is the desire to have female-appearing genitalia enough? There are no universally satisfactory answers to these questions. I eventually decided to classify any informant who expressed an unequivocal desire to have female genitalia as transsexual. This was partly for the sake of consistency, but it also reflected my clinical experience with a few patients who had told me they wanted SRS but had no desire to live as women: In every case, it eventually became clear that these clients actually did want to live as women (albeit sometimes as rather androgynous women) but had simply concluded that this was unfeasible and had therefore put the idea out of their minds. I suspect (but obviously cannot prove) that many, if not most, autogynephilic men who claim to want only female genitalia actually want both fully feminized bodies and a female-typical social role but cannot bring themselves to admit this. Narratives from several informants in the group described above are included in Chap. 6.

A total of 249 informants met one or more of the inclusion criteria that permitted me to classify them as transsexual: 130 met criterion (a), 91 met criterion (b), and 28 met criterion (c). The Appendix summarizes the highest inclusion criterion satisfied by each informant whom I categorized as transsexual and the specific element(s) in the informant's narrative that led me to conclude that the inclusion criterion had been satisfied. I will subsequently refer to these informants as the "autogynephilic transsexual informants" or "transsexual informants"; this denotes only that they reported having experienced autogynephilic arousal, not necessarily that they considered this arousal to have the same meaning or significance that Blanchard theorized.

There were also 52 narratives by informants who did not meet any of these inclusion criteria, but who nevertheless described autogynephilic feelings; some of these informants were probably transsexual but simply did not provide enough information for me to confidently classify them as such. I felt that many of the narratives by these informants contained information that might contribute to a better understanding of autogynephilic transsexualism; consequently, I decided to devote a separate chapter, Chap. 11, to their accounts. I will subsequently refer to these informants as the "nontranssexual autogynephilic informants" or the "nontranssexual autogynephiles."

The inclusion criteria I used admittedly leave the study open to criticism that some of the informants I categorized as transsexual might not have been "genuinely" transsexual according to more stringent criteria. Most of the informants I considered transsexual would presumably meet criteria for a diagnosis of transsexualism in the *International Classification of Diseases* (ICD-10; WHO, 1992), which requires only the presence of cross-gender identity, usually accompanied by gender dysphoria. But critics could argue that some of my transsexual informants might not have experienced severe enough gender dysphoria or a sufficiently persistent cross-gender identity to satisfy the definition of transsexualism in the most recent edition of the DSM

(APA, 2000, p. 828). Indeed, a few informants who experienced significant gender dysphoria or cross-gender identity chose not to refer to themselves as "transsexual," but used alternative terms, such as "transgendered," to describe themselves. It is important to remember, however, that the symptoms classically associated with transsexualism—gender dysphoria, cross-gender identity, anatomic dysphoria, belief that one's feelings resemble those of the opposite sex, desire to live as a member of the opposite sex, and wish for hormonal and surgical sex reassignment—are highly correlated (Deogracias et al., 2007; Singh et al., 2010). Moreover, autogynephilic transsexualism and less severe autogynephilic conditions (e.g., fetishistic transvestism) are more usefully conceptualized as points on a continuum of symptomatology than as distinct disorders (Benjamin, 1966; Docter, 1988; Lawrence, 2009a, 2009b; Levine, 1993; Person & Ovesey, 1978; Whitam, 1987). Consequently, attempting to draw a definitive line between autogynephilic transsexualism and closely related conditions is probably neither feasible nor crucially important.

I next edited the narratives by the 249 transsexual informants and the 52 nontranssexual informants in the interests of insuring anonymity and improving readability. I redacted any information that might identify the informants and removed material that was peripheral to the topic of autogynephilia (e.g., detailed accounts of family history or educational achievements). I also performed some basic copyediting: correcting misspellings, inserting missing words, expanding abbreviations, reordering some sentences and paragraphs to improve clarity, and condensing excessively prolix passages. The resulting document contained about 128,000 words.

Finally, I conducted a thematic analysis of the narratives. I created a new thematic category for each major theme I identified and placed narrative excerpts pertaining to that theme in the corresponding category. Some of the themes were essentially predetermined and represented fundamental elements or concepts in the theory of autogynephilia (e.g., anatomic autogynephilia); other themes arose directly from the content of the narratives. Whenever I identified a new theme, I reexamined previously analyzed narratives for possible instances of the theme, extracted any relevant narrative excerpts, and placed them in the appropriate category. This process ultimately yielded 30 distinct thematic categories that together contained about 75,000 words of narrative excerpts. All of the narratives by transsexual informants yielded useful excerpts; about two thirds of the narratives by nontranssexual informants did as well. Sometimes I further edited the narrative excerpts for length when I incorporated them into the text of the chapters.

The methodology I employed was similar in many ways to the constant comparative method used in the grounded theory approach to qualitative analysis (Glaser & Strauss, 1967; Strauss & Corbin, 1998). This study was not, however, a grounded theory analysis, because my intention was not to generate a new theoretical model of autogynephilia. A serviceable theory of autogynephilia already existed, and all the informants were aware of it, as evidenced by their decisions to submit narratives. Instead, the intention of this study was primarily descriptive: I wanted to document the feelings and opinions of MtF transsexuals who had experienced autogynephilic arousal, including what they had to say about the role autogynephilia had played in their lives.

Validity Issues

How confident am I that the transsexual and nontranssexual informants represented themselves accurately and reported their feelings and experiences truthfully? For most informants, I cannot claim great confidence, although there were a few cases in which I either knew an informant casually or had some corroborating historical information. Concerns about truthfulness and accuracy are potential issues whenever personal narratives are used as data sources, but are especially pertinent in studies like this one, in which the absence of face-to-face contact with informants precludes the use of nonverbal information to assess probable truthfulness.

Several clinicians who have worked extensively with MtF transsexuals have reported that their clients tend to consciously or unconsciously distort their histories to conform to the picture of "classic" MtF transsexualism. A classic MtF transsexual is one "who has felt and acted feminine from earliest childhood, has never been sexually aroused by women's apparel, and is romantically inclined toward males" (Blanchard, Clemmensen, et al., 1985, p. 508). For example, Lukianowicz (1959) stated that male gender patients often gave inaccurate reports of the early onset of cross-gender wishes:

> A wishful falsification of memory takes place, the patients begin to recall and misinterpret various insignificant incidents in their childhood, till they finally firmly believe that "ever since I can remember, I always wanted to be a woman." (The incessant progress of these emotionally overvalued ideas resembles the relentless development of delusions in paranoia.) (p. 51)

Bancroft (1972) argued that one challenge to understanding the developmental history of MtF transsexualism was that

> transexuals [sic] distort their past histories to fit in to their transexual identity and are therefore more likely to report early transexual urges to support the idea that they are basically female… [One patient] when first seen reported his transexual feelings to be of recent origin; 9 months later he was reporting them as starting much earlier in his life. (p. 62)

Fisk (1974) observed that clients who sought SRS tended to misrepresent their histories—sometimes deliberately but more often unintentionally—to make them conform to accepted ideas about classic transsexualism:

> Slowly, there appeared instances in which the seemingly very pat histories revealed inconsistencies, downright fabrications and blatant distortions. The element of conscious fabrication or manipulation seemed quite secondary to the phenomenon of retrospectively "amending" one's subjective history. Here, the patient quite subtly alters, shades, rationalizes, denies, represses, forgets, etc., in a compelling rush to embrace the diagnosis of transsexualism. (pp. 8–9)

Fisk's phrase "embrace the diagnosis of transsexualism" suggests that he saw these clients as attempting to convince *themselves* as well as others that the diagnosis was applicable to them. Sørensen and Hertoft (1980) similarly noted that MtF transsexuals typically displayed "memory distortion with exclusion of earlier masculine traits" (p. 139). Walworth (1997) reported that the five most common topics about which MtF transsexuals admitted to having misled their therapists were "sexual arousal in response to women's clothing[,] sexual attraction to women[,] preferring girls' games and toys as a child[,] childhood wishes to have been born a girl[, and] identifying with female characters as a child" (p. 359). Taken together, these observations suggest that MtF transsexuals' histories of childhood femininity, childhood cross-gender wishes, absence of erotic arousal with cross-dressing, and sexual attraction to men should not necessarily be taken at face value.

On the other hand, MtF transsexuals' histories that contradict the picture of classic transsexualism can be seen as a form of "reluctant testimony" and are likely to be more credible. In particular, self-reported histories of an absence of femininity or cross-gender wishes in childhood, a lack of sexual attraction to men, or the presence of erotic arousal with cross-dressing or cross-gender fantasy should arouse less suspicion, because there is little reason for informants to consciously or unconsciously misreport these things.

I strongly suspected that one or two people who submitted narratives engaged in less-than-truthful reporting. For example, between February 1999 and November 2001, I received eight separate narratives that dealt with the issue of erotic arousal from the idea of feeling regret following sex reassignment (i.e., being a "man trapped in a woman's body"). These narratives varied in some details (e.g., stated age, whether or not sex reassignment had been completed), but shared certain thematic similarities (e.g., emphasis on the inconvenience of obligatory seated urination), characteristic spelling errors, and unusual syntax. I concluded that these narratives were probably fabrications that had been submitted by a single individual and that described erotic fantasies, not genuine occurrences. Consequently, I decided to exclude these narratives. Even so, many of the thoughts and feelings expressed in them were not terribly different from those found in seemingly more plausible accounts.

Some MtF transsexuals and other persons object to the theory associated with the concept of autogynephilia, and it is possible that a few of them might have attempted to discredit the study or cast doubt on the theory of autogynephilia by submitting false or misleading narratives. What sorts of narratives might advance these goals? A narrative that described bizarre but just barely plausible fantasies or behaviors and was accepted as genuine but subsequently revealed to be a fabrication might discredit the study in the eyes of some. It would be difficult, however, for an individual to prove that he or she was actually the author of any particular narrative, much less that the contents of that narrative were indeed fabricated. In any case, with the exception of the "man trapped in a woman's body" narratives described above, only one other narrative, which I will describe below, contained material of doubtful plausibility. Alternatively, a fabricated narrative that contradicted some general principle derived from or associated with the theory of autogynephilia, if accepted as genuine, might cast doubt on the theory in the eyes of some. A narrative that described both intense autogynephilic arousal and an exclusively homosexual orientation in a MtF transsexual would fall into this category. A narrative describing the absence of autogynephilic arousal in a nonhomosexual MtF transsexual, however, would neither cast much doubt on the theory nor be eligible for inclusion. As I noted in Chap. 1, denial of autogynephilic arousal by nonhomosexual MtF transsexuals is a recognized, reasonably well understood, and not especially interesting phenomenon. Moreover, I stated in my solicitation that I had no interest in receiving narratives from persons who had not experienced autogynephilia.

I received only one narrative that was ostensibly from a MtF transsexual who reported both extensive autogynephilic arousal and an exclusively homosexual orientation. I decided to exclude this narrative, because I suspected it was a fabrication: Some of the history it recounted was internally contradictory, and it was submitted a few months after the publication of the controversial book *The Man Who Would Be Queen* (Bailey, 2003) and contained narrative detail that seemed to have been taken directly from two different case descriptions in that book.

Some evidence for the accuracy and truthfulness of the narratives lies in the fact that, in general, they were remarkably consistent with each other, with existing information concerning autogynephilic fantasies and behaviors (e.g., from transgender erotica), with the clinical histories of the MtF transsexual patients I have seen in my practice, and with the theory of autogynephilia generally. The specific detail and emotional frankness that characterized much of the writing conveyed a strong sense of verisimilitude; the informants frequently expressed amazement at their own candor, offering asides like "I can't believe I'm telling you this" or "This sounds crazy, even to me, but it's true."

Previous Publication of Selected Narratives

In 1999, I published 59 of the narratives I had received to date in two separate documents on my website (Lawrence, 1999c, 1999d). I included excerpts from these 59 narratives in two papers I presented at the Harry Benjamin International Gender Dysphoria Association XVI Biennial Symposium in London in 1999; the texts of these papers were subsequently published on my website (Lawrence, 1999a, 1999b). Selected excerpts from the 59 narratives also appeared in the magazine *Transgender Tapestry* in connection with an article I published there (Lawrence, 2000). Blanchard (2005) quoted excerpts from these 59 narratives as well. Because the current analysis employed more rigorous inclusion criteria than I had used in 1999, only 50 of the original 59 narratives were selected for inclusion in the current study.

Illustrative Examples of Narratives

This section presents seven illustrative examples of narratives submitted by the transsexual informants who acknowledged autogynephilia. Most are presented more or less as I received them, with only minor copyediting; the exceptions are the fourth and sixth examples, which were significantly edited for length. Collectively, they illustrate most of the major themes discussed by the informants. In this and subsequent chapters, three-digit numbers in parentheses following the narrative excerpts will be used to identify individual transsexual informants.

The first example is one of the narratives I first published on my website in 1999 (Lawrence, 1999d):

> I am a 42-year-old male-to-female preoperative transsexual. I have been living full time as female for over a year, have completed a legal name change, and have been on hormone therapy for several years. I have just finished reading your article on autogynephilia and can honestly say that, for the first time ever, I have the feeling "this is me!" Previously, when I've read the literature on transsexualism, I've thought that many, indeed most, of the descriptions applied to me. But there was always something just slightly different from the way I truly felt. It was because of these feelings that I have had doubts about whether I was "really" a transsexual.
>
> My sexual fantasies all include myself in female form, either being forced to become female or voluntarily. Frequently they involve a submissive element on my part: I am either forced to be a woman or forced to behave in a particularly submissive manner. If there was a male involved, it was usually a vague or faceless man with extremely strong and powerful physique. From my very earliest masturbatory experiences, I have exclusively used this type of "becoming female" fantasy for arousal.
>
> My childhood seemed rather typically male from an outside viewpoint. I can still vividly remember an early experience of becoming aroused at the thought of becoming female when I was approximately 9 or 10 years old. I was overweight and I had begun to develop breasts, solely from my weight. I would soap my breasts in the shower and imagine I was really a woman with a real woman's breasts, and I would become extremely aroused.
>
> I lived fairly successfully as a man for most of my 39 years prior to seeking professional help. I was married for approximately 5 years in my early 30s. My sex life was satisfying to an extent, but I would always use feminization fantasies to achieve orgasm. I thought this was a flaw in my nature, felt guilty because of it, and never discussed this with my wife. I always felt envious of my wife's body and would invariably fantasize about being like her or trading places whenever we had sex. I also regularly fantasized about becoming any of a variety of beautiful women, such as popular actresses, models, or centerfolds.
>
> I did not engage in much cross-dressing at an early age. I did sneak occasionally into my mother's room and try on a slip, panties, or a bra, but that was the extent of it. Once I graduated from college and was on my own, I began shaving my legs and would invariably achieve extreme states of arousal, culminating in masturbation. It wasn't until I actually started therapy that I began appearing in public dressed as a female. In the early days, I would become aroused whenever anyone—a sales clerk, a casual stranger—would address me as "Ma'am" or perform some courtesy, such as holding a door for me. This arousal led to a heightened fear of discovery (i.e., that my erection would give me away). After hormone therapy, this became less of a problem and eventually stopped altogether. I thought perhaps it was the initial novelty of the situation that caused my arousal and that this novelty was wearing off as I became accustomed to presenting in the feminine role. But now I realize that I still get that jolt of erotic thrill at being viewed as female, but the hormone treatments have eliminated the erections that embarrassed me.
>
> I continue to feel aroused at the thought of feminization. The frequency of my masturbation has greatly decreased since starting hormone therapy, but I still use feminization fantasies during autoerotic activity. To date I have not told anyone else about this aspect of my transgendered nature. I have told my therapist about some of my fantasies but not about the erections when dressed. This is from fear of not being accepted as a true transsexual and being categorized instead as a transvestite or cross-dresser. I have a strong desire for SRS

and do not want to jeopardize my chances by appearing in any way skewed from the "classic" transsexual profile. (001)

Most narratives were submitted by middle-aged males, but I received some from informants in their 20s. Here is an example:

I'm a 28-year-old male who has experienced arousal from autogynephilia since the age of 12. I always thought I was weird, because I've never been effeminate. When I hit puberty, around age 12, I remember being aroused seeing girls growing boobs and also seeing my stepmother's bras and panties in the laundry area. I remember being attracted to girls themselves but having extreme arousal over the thought of being a girl and growing boobies. I already fantasized about being a girl and having a vagina before the boob thing started. It's hard to pinpoint when I realized I was highly aroused by this, but I believe it was when I saw some girls in my class at a play wearing leotards and tights or pantyhose at a school play. I wanted so bad to have a vagina and be free of my penis while being able to express myself in a way not accepted in a man's world.

Since then, I have been through the same thing over and over, hoping that I would somehow grow out of it. I'm an attractive guy; I've had sex with at least 20 women, but I have never had an orgasm with one of them. I came close once, when a girlfriend sucked and played with my nipples. I rarely cross-dress anymore, because I get so unbelievably aroused that I shake and tremble and ejaculate much too fast. This is not because of the clothes as much as the more realistic feeling of being an actual woman with female genitalia. I know that I don't simply have a cross-dressing fetish, because my greatest sexual fantasy is going through puberty again as a girl and experiencing breast development, as well as being in pillow fights and bubble-gum blowing contests with other girls. I've only tried makeup on once but got sexually aroused by it. Other things that have aroused me are shaving my legs, sitting with my legs crossed in a feminine way, blowing bubble gum bubbles (something I've always associated as being feminine), and sitting with a bunch of women as the only male and listening to "girl talk."

I'm probably more aroused than ever at the thought of being a woman. I'm getting ready to go on hormone therapy, because I'm at my wits' end as a man. I can't enjoy sex with women as a man—I've lost almost all interest. What I do enjoy with women is snuggling and getting close. As a woman, I could be free to enjoy sex again and be free to cry at a sad part of a movie and free to be chatty and get close with a mate. I have to admit that the thought of growing boobies while on hormone treatment is so arousing that it makes me shake and tremble, literally. This thought just blows me away, and the thought of getting a vagina is just as arousing. (002)

Only a few narratives were submitted by informants in their teens; here is one of the best examples:

After reading about autogynephilia, I suddenly became a lot less apprehensive about my decision to begin to transition. I'm 18 years old and am about to tell my parents. I'm optimistic about their reactions; my mom's always wanted a daughter. I'm seeing a psychiatrist starting tomorrow. This is not a new thing; I had been in therapy most of my early life.

I was worried that the fact that I feel sexually aroused by the idea of being a woman was a reason to doubt my gender dysphoria. I've always identified with women more than men but was never extremely effeminate. I am heterosexual, but only because I can't imagine myself having sex with a man as a man. My first realization of my desire to be feminine was in summer camp, when I was 12 years old. I was making a short video starring myself and I imagined a completely unnecessary scene involving my wearing various beautiful dresses and wigs. I was surprised to be aroused by this and actually ejaculated for the first time after masturbation. After the fantasy had ended, the desire did not retreat and has plagued me ever since. I would guiltily sneak into my mother's closet when she was away and wear as many combinations of her clothes as possible. I was almost always turned on by it, but I mostly did not masturbate. Instead, I'd condemn my penis for getting in the way. My friends still can't understand why I hate my penis so much, even after I told them that I am very committed to the idea of becoming a woman.

I fantasize about having sex as a woman. I can vividly imagine myself being penetrated. I fantasize about having long, beautiful hair, having it braided, having it on my face, having it short and cute. I try to do these things to my short guy hair and practically cry at feeling so inadequate. Wearing women's clothing is always something that initially turns me on, but when that damn penis of mine eventually becomes flaccid, I feel very comfortable and natural. I imagine having breasts. I tried taping my chest [to create the appearance of cleavage], but I'm too thin to generate a satisfactory appearance. I had a brief period during which I would only be attracted to women I would want to be.

I feel that it is perfectly natural for transgender people to be turned on by sexual situations involving being who they believe they are. Having your biological self in a sexual fantasy can completely ruin it. (003)

Some informants stated that they had rejected the idea of undergoing sex reassignment, even though they intensely wanted it; usually they cited inability to pass as a woman or family obligations as the principal reasons.

I am an autogynephiliac. I want to be female, but I don't already feel female inside. Rather, I have a deep, hard-wired longing built into me that I can't shake or get rid of and that I can remember having since I was a child. I feel like I am looking through an unbreakable glass window at a place I want to be and a life I want to have yet am unable to reach. This desire feels hardwired: As much as I don't want to want it, it is still there, taunting and frustrating me. The thought of being female turns me on so much that it's my primary sexual attraction mechanism. But my body is such that I could never transition convincingly.

This feels way deeper than what I imagine a fetish to be. There are countless days where I experience little in the way of feeling "turned on," yet I still have this deep aching inside of me to somehow be transformed into the object of my desires. Some days it is just a fleeting feeling on the edge of my peripheral awareness. Other days I feel it so strongly that I want to scream in frustration. I do have a separate, unrelated fetish, and I can feel a significant difference between that fetish and my autogynephilia. With the fetish, I can be turned on very strongly, but I don't actually want it to be made manifest; it's just a fantasy. But with the desire to be female, there is nothing I want more, even though it usually doesn't turn me on quite as much as my fetish.

I don't feel that I am a woman in a man's body. As a child, riding my bike and playing with robots and guns and blowing up toy cars was more interesting to me than playing with dolls and dress-ups. Clothes and fashion never really interested me. I am attracted to women, not to men; I can remember always wanting a girlfriend. I am competitive and driven to win and achieve. I sometimes feel masculine aggression at thoughts like winning a fight or defending my family. I love logical, analytical activities and write software and web applications professionally.

My attraction to women has never involved a desire to have sex; at no point have I ever looked at a woman and had a sexual response to the thought of having sex with her. My desire for a girlfriend, I think, always related to the need for acceptance and companionship. When I am really in the midst of a fantasy, imagining myself as a female, my interest in women decreases, though not completely. My sexual desires and fantasies take on that of a heterosexual woman, including all of the normal acts that would occur in the bedroom. I can even start to fantasize about being pregnant, breast-feeding, getting married, and so forth. When I think of myself in a male body, though, none of that appeals to me, and it even repulses me. (004)

Most informants did not explicitly report their nationality, but I assumed that they were predominantly from the US. Among informants from outside the US, most resided in Australia, Canada, or the UK; here is an example from a Canadian informant:

> I am a 50-year-old Canadian male. My first memories of identifying with the opposite gender were in early childhood. By the time I was 12 or 13, I was secretly experimenting with makeup, wearing my mother's lingerie, and curling and styling my hair as a girl would. I honestly do not recall whether my cross-dressing was erotically motivated, but from my experiences later in life, I would say that my motivation was erotic.
>
> In my early teens, I became interested in girls for reasons other than wearing their clothes. In an attempt to purge myself of my longings, I plunged myself into the world of competitive athletics. I was very athletic and not feminine at all. I won seven provincial championships in two different sports. My success in sports did not, however, eradicate my feminine yearnings: They survived and would resurface over and over again.
>
> I recall my first erotic fantasies of becoming female in my late teens. In addition to cross-dressing when I could, I would also purchase Playboy and Penthouse magazines and imagined myself as the models in the pictures, with their breasts and genitals. These are my first memories of anatomic autogynephilia. I have never had or wanted a relationship with a male, although I have fantasized about having a male penetrate me as a woman.
>
> I met my wife in high school and we were married during my first year of college. I continued to dress en femme when the opportunity presented itself; the motivation was purely erotic. The thought of having breasts and a vagina aroused me. Seeing myself in a mirror appearing like a woman was erotic, but it also made me feel "better." In 30 years of my marriage, I have been through the cycles of the desire to be female and cross-dress, followed by shame, guilt, purging and the return of my desire to be female. Although I say that my desire returned after purging, I don't think it ever really went away.
>
> About 15 years ago, my desire to dress and be feminine became overwhelming. I would take every opportunity to fulfill my needs, including taking days off work. I often thought of telling my wife but couldn't bring myself to do it. Then one evening I decided it was time for us both to face the truth. To my surprise, she took it remarkably well. Since my wife found out about my gender dysphoria, I have made great strides in becoming the person I want to be. I have had approximately 125 hours of electrolysis and my facial hair is almost all gone. I started hormone therapy but stopped after my breasts had developed sufficiently to satisfy me.
>
> I am still aroused by the thought of having a female body, but the requirement to masturbate has all but disappeared. The dysphoria, however, has not subsided. Although I have small breasts, and virtually no body or facial hair, the longing to be a female in all physical aspects has persisted and grown stronger. I have reached the point where I want SRS and am taking steps towards that end. (005)

Fewer than a dozen narratives were submitted by informants who resided in non-English speaking countries in Europe; below is one unusually detailed account:

> I am a 28-year-old male from Greece and a PhD student in engineering. I think Blanchard's theory describes me 100%. I was not one of those boys who were feminine in childhood. Around the age of 6 or 7 years, I had my first crush on a girl. I loved her in the way a young boy feels love. I never felt attraction for a boy, only for girls.
>
> At the age of 4, I had my first autogynephilic experience. It was so intense that I still recall the smallest details. My mother kept some of her lipsticks in the bathroom. One day I went inside, climbed the tub, reached the lipsticks, and immediately tried one. My heart was pounding and my hands were trembling. I felt a strange mixture of anxiety, happiness, tranquility, and fulfillment. I admired myself in the mirror. I remember saying exactly these

words to myself: "I can be a great woman!" When I was 7 or 8 years old, I remember looking at my mother's panties and feeling a compulsion to try them on. The laundry basket became my magic box; I tried on all the panties I found inside. I hadn't discovered sexual pleasure yet; it just felt nice wearing female underwear.

I had seen my younger sister naked, and I felt the urge to change my genitals. I wanted to make my penis disappear and have a vagina; I wanted to be forced to sit to pee. I created a method of tucking my penis using sticky tape. Every time I was alone in the house, I transformed my genitals. I don't remember my first orgasm in detail, but it was certainly after genital transformation with the tape. During that period, I could never achieve an orgasm if I hadn't first transformed my genitals. After a time, I found that I could just fantasize that I was a girl; then I could achieve orgasm easily. All my fantasies had one common thing, my becoming a girl; I usually had to do some feminine thing, like sitting to pee, or having to wear a dress to go outside.

During the same period, I felt a great need to use sanitary napkins. The thought of menstruating turned me on, and the first time I used a pad I had a feeling as intense as the first time I tried the lipstick. I started using pads regularly. Every time I changed my body to become more feminine or did something that only girls do, I got that same feeling. I started wearing my mother's high heels at home and tried on her pantyhose. My usual ritual when left alone in the house was transforming my genitalia, wearing female underwear, a pad, clothes, shoes and jewelry. Every such session ended with masturbation and my fantasizing that I was a woman having sex with a man. The moment after I ejaculated, I got a very negative feeling, a mixture of remorse, sadness, disgust, disappointment, and humiliation.

At about age 12, I discovered the ultimate genital transformation: instant glue. I applied a large amount of glue to my genitals, in order to have a firm tuck and be able to go to the bathroom like a girl. The result was quite good: My genitals were hidden perfectly, giving me a smooth crotch. If I wanted to go to the bathroom, I had to go in the feminine way: No other way was possible. Even if I wanted to get free, it would be impossible to do it easily. This feeling of inevitability triggered an explosion of autogynephilic feelings, from the inevitability of being female. I admired my body in the mirror. The price for all this pleasure was two painful hours of sitting with a mirror between my legs, taking off millimeter-by-millimeter the glue that had covered the scrotal and perineal area. Many times the skin was damaged and there was bleeding, and I had to clinch my teeth to stand the pain. Every time I swore that I wouldn't do it again, but not only could I not keep my vow, at times I tried again after only a few hours. I also experienced the urge to have breasts and be obliged to wear a bra. I enjoyed wearing my mother's bras and I loved the marks they left in my skin after taking them off.

At the age of 17–18, I had my first relationship with a girl. It lasted for almost 6 months. The frequency with which I had transformation sessions decreased. I was functioning more like a normal guy, but there were times that autogynephilic feelings occurred, even with my girlfriend. When she was dressed in very feminine clothes, like a miniskirt and pantyhose, I envied her. Whenever I saw a beautiful woman, I couldn't tell whether I was attracted to her as a man or whether I envied her for being a woman. Any arousal that I might feel looking at her was only because I was imagining myself in her position. At the age of 19, I went to University. I plucked up the courage and bought my own female underwear, pantyhose, pads, etc., and built a small wardrobe. I spend whole days locked in my apartment, dressed like a woman.

I was surprised by the abrupt alternation of my feelings that occurred in fractions of seconds when an "en femme" session ended with an ejaculation (and most of the time I ended by masturbating). Before orgasm, I was ready to sacrifice everything to become a woman. And suddenly, after having an orgasm, the feeling was totally reversed! I was flooded with powerful remorseful feeling, which made me unhappy and miserable.

I knew that as soon as an orgasm was achieved, the desire to be female would disappear for a time. For that reason, I often tried to delay orgasm or avoided orgasm at all. Whole weeks sometimes passed before I masturbated. All this time, I went out wearing female underwear under my clothes and generally tried to do normal female activities, avoiding masturbation and orgasm. I also noticed a considerable reduction in the orgasmic aim I used to have; it did not matter too much if I hadn't had an orgasm. It was more important to experience the everyday aspects of a woman's life. I found enjoyment in reading women's magazines, shopping, and grooming my nails and eyebrows. Of course, the sexual urges never stopped, but the remorseful feelings were greatly reduced. Autogynephilic feelings may at first depend on sexual drive in order to be expressed; after a while, though, one associates them with general pleasure and a good feeling.

I occasionally met girls with whom I had sexual intercourse. Kissing and cuddling was nice, but when it came to intercourse, I could only have an orgasm by fantasizing that I was female. At age 24, I met my present girlfriend. She has a sweet face and looks tiny and fragile, which triggers my male protective instincts. I promised myself a new beginning and threw all my female clothes away; I wanted to live a normal life as a man. From the beginning, I had a big problem having sex with her. First I couldn't achieve an erection, and then when I achieved it, I couldn't have an orgasm unless I fantasized that I was a female. After 8 months, I could no longer resist and tried on her underwear. After that, I again started building a new female wardrobe.

Every day is a constant fight between the things that I have to do and the autogynephilia that creates disruptive thoughts. It is not easy to study when your mind pops up thoughts of being a girl. It is impossible to concentrate at your job when you envy the pantyhose that a stranger outside wore. It is hard to maintain a healthy relationship with your girlfriend when you envy her for being female. (006)

Only a few narratives were received from informants living in Asia; here is one of the best examples:

I am a 20-year-old Chinese Singaporean. I've always had thoughts of being female since I was 10 or 11. I would always dream of becoming a lady. But, due to social expectations, I've always shelved my desires. As I went through puberty, I started wearing lingerie, since I was 14. I felt extremely aroused when I wore a brassiere and imagined myself having breasts. These sessions always ended with me stimulating my anal cavity, imagining it was a vagina. I was also very fascinated with menstruation and wished I could have that also. I proceeded to try that; the first time I wore a sanitary pad was when I was 10. It was so arousing I had an erection. I always had more girlfriends than guy friends. I find it so fascinating just observing them. At times I just wished so much I could be one of them. I tried cross-dressing once when I was 15. It was such a wonderful experience and I felt so sexually charged when I used the ladies room for the first time. I get rid of the hair on my legs, and I've tried all sorts of stuff: wax, creams, etc. It just gave me such a feeling of sexual arousal when I lay there, waiting for the treatment to work, enduring the pain and smell. I used female deodorant and sweet-smelling shower gel. I would just get aroused anywhere when I fantasized about being feminine.

I'm now engaged in a romantic relationship with an 18-year-old girl, and I'm trying to tell myself that I am male and I should remain that way. I'm just so afraid to hurt the girl that has been my best friend for 16 months. But I still have the tendency to cross-dress, albeit not in public. And I still can't suppress my feminization thoughts. I have also questioned myself on whether I'm gay. But I just don't think so, as I have never really thought of having sex with a guy when I'm physically male. At the same time, I have also fantasized myself being a woman and being gang raped. I'm just so confused with all these feelings. I have never confided in anyone before and I feel embarrassed about expressing myself so explicitly, due to the social mindset that was inculcated in me since childhood. (007)

Major Themes in the Narratives

The examples above illustrate most of the major themes found in the narratives collectively. Some men who experience gender dysphoria, desire sex reassignment, or have begun or completed sex reassignment feel that the concept of autogynephilia accurately describes them. Furthermore, these autogynephilic transsexuals:

- Often express relief and gratitude at having found a description of their condition that seems accurate.
- Often state that their autogynephilic feelings caused them to doubt whether they were "really" transsexual.
- Often report that they hesitated or refused to disclose their autogynephilic feelings to helping professionals and significant others.
- Often report that their autogynephilic fantasies or behaviors began in childhood, usually well before puberty, and sometimes were associated with overt erotic arousal.
- Usually concede that they were not overtly effeminate during childhood but instead displayed many male-typical interests and behaviors.
- Often report that autogynephilic erotic arousal has continued throughout their lives, including after sex reassignment.
- Usually give a history of erotic arousal associated with the fantasy or act of wearing particular items of women's clothing.
- Almost always report a history of erotic arousal associated with the fantasy or reality of having female breasts or genitalia.
- Sometimes give a history of erotic arousal associated with fantasies of menstruating, breast-feeding, or being pregnant.
- Often report a history of erotic arousal associated with the fantasy or act of engaging in behaviors considered typical or characteristic of females.
- Often describe a history of erotic arousal associated with the fantasy or act of having sex with a man as a woman, even though they are not otherwise sexually attracted to men.
- Typically state that most or all of their sexual partners have been women or that they are primarily attracted to and tend to fall in love with women.
- Often experience autogynephilia and heterosexual attraction as competing with each other, in that autogynephilic feelings decline when a new heterosexual relationship begins and re-intensify when the novelty of a heterosexual relationship wanes.
- Sometimes describe autogynephilia as feeling like a variant, misdirected, or self-directed form of heterosexuality.
- Occasionally experience little or no sexual attraction toward other persons.
- Often report that autogynephilic fantasies or behaviors are obligatory to achieve orgasm during partnered sex and masturbation.
- Sometimes observe that their desire to be a woman temporarily disappears following orgasm and is replaced by feelings of disgust or remorse.

- Sometimes describe other co-occurring paraphilic sexual interests.
- Sometimes experience autogynephilic erotic arousal or associated penile erections as unwanted or unpleasant.
- Typically report that feminizing hormone therapy reduces, but rarely eliminates, autogynephilic arousal.
- Sometimes state that autogynephilic feelings were an important motivation for their seeking sex reassignment, in that sex reassignment enabled them to actualize or manage their autogynephilic feelings.
- Sometimes believe that autogynephilia is an effect, not a cause, of their cross-gender wishes and behaviors.

Chapter 4
Confronting Autogynephilia

Discovering the Concept of Autogynephilia

The theory that one form of MtF transsexualism is an outgrowth of autogynephilia—erotic arousal to the thought of being a female—was not widely known until recently. One of the topics informants most frequently discussed in their narratives was discovering the concept of autogynephilia for the first time. They often reported feeling amazement, relief, delight, and gratitude when they realized that the concept applied to them and could help them better understand themselves and their desires to be female. Many were reassured by the knowledge that other transsexuals shared similar feelings. Some said that the concept of autogynephilia helped them to feel more legitimately transsexual. In particular, it helped them to resolve the cognitive dissonance ("craziness") that arose from believing that they were genuinely transsexual but having been told repeatedly that "real" transsexuals did not experience sexual arousal with cross-dressing or cross-gender fantasy. Not all informants described self-recognition as an autogynephilic transsexual to be a positive emotional experience, however: Some reported that it was associated with feelings of distress, sadness, or shame.

Encountering the concept of autogynephilia prompted several informants to reflect on their encounters with psychologists or psychiatrists who had informed them that they could not really be transsexual because of their autogynephilic feelings. Others described misrepresenting or concealing their autogynephilic feelings in past or ongoing interactions with psychotherapists. Informants also reflected on the extent to which they believed that autogynephilia was a motivating factor in their desire to be women or to seek or undergo sex reassignment; they expressed a range of opinions, from "definitely" to "not at all."

A.A. Lawrence, *Men Trapped in Men's Bodies: Narratives of Autogynephilic Transsexualism*, Focus on Sexuality Research, DOI 10.1007/978-1-4614-5182-2_4,

Discovering an Accurate Description

Informants frequently stated that the concept of autogynephilia provided an authentic, true-to-life description of their feelings and experiences. Some were surprised to find their desires, fantasies, and behaviors portrayed with seemingly uncanny accuracy:

> When I came across your paper on autogynephilia, I felt for the first time that I was reading about myself. (008)
>
> After reading through the identifiers associated with autogynephilia, I realized that I related to each and every one. (009)
>
> Your article on autogynephilia describes exactly how I have felt since age 6 or 7. (010)
>
> When I read about autogynephilia, I saw myself so clearly that it hit me like a rock. (011)

Autogynephilia as a Revelation

For some informants, the concept of autogynephilia and the recognition of themselves as autogynephilic transsexuals had a revelatory quality: They felt that a profound personal mystery had been explained at last.

> Thank you for your writings on autogynephilia. I thought I knew almost everything about transvestism and transsexuality, but I am speechless, as it described my entire journey much more accurately than the "woman trapped in a man's body" explanation. For me, the idea of autogynephilia as a root or driving cause of transsexualism is a revelation. (012)
>
> Autogynephilia has just been flat out revelatory to me. Over the last 5 years, I've been increasingly thinking that I'm transsexual but was always dismayed at not being able to find myself in the transsexual literature. I read your article and sat there smiling, laughing, and rereading and rereading it. (013)

Several informants used the word "epiphany" to describe what the concept of autogynephilia meant to them:

> Discovering autogynephilia was an epiphany. The theory, the essays, and the personal accounts spoke directly to me. (014)
>
> It is only since discovering Blanchard's concept of autogynephilia that I've been able to finally make some sense of who and what I am. Since reading about autogynephilia, I've been able to accept the idea that my preoccupation with the female side of myself is rooted in sexual desire. It seems so obvious, but, as such personal epiphanies usually are, it was invisible until someone else pointed it out. (015)
>
> Thank you for your articles on autogynephilia: I feel like I have had an epiphany, a revelation, an "ah-hah moment" of self-recognition. (016)

For a few, discovering the concept of autogynephilia was not only a revelatory experience but an intensely emotional one as well:

> I have just finished reading about autogynephilia, and all I can say is, thank you from the bottom of my heart. I have tears in my eyes as I write this: At 54 years of age, I have found

> information that has liberated my thinking about myself. I had struggled for years to place myself in categories that did not seem right for me. Now I read about autogynephilia and all I can do is weep. It is like a homecoming. (017)

We will subsequently observe, however, that informants' emotional reactions to learning about autogynephilia were not always so positive.

Facilitating Understanding and Clarity

Many informants reported that discovering an accurate description of their feelings and experiences facilitated greater self-understanding. Here are some representative comments:

> The description of anatomic autogynephilia comes closer to my own personal experience than anything I have ever read on the subject of transsexuality and has helped me tremendously to understand my own transgendered feelings. (018)

> I identify strongly with the anatomic type of autogynephilia. Your article has provided the first sensible discussion of how transgenderism applies to me. I am now motivated to review my life in a new context. (019)

> I had not been able to explain the almost inexorable force that continues to drive me to want to have the body of a woman until I read about autogynephilia. Now I understand. (020)

In several narratives, the word "clarity" was used to describe individuals' improved insight into themselves and their desires:

> I had not heard of the word "autogynephilia" before. Everything rang utterly true for me. Never in all my research on this topic has any explanation nailed things down with such total obvious clarity for me. (021)

> Autogynephilia is an amazing concept. When I found out about it, it was as if I finally saw this aspect of myself with complete clarity for the first time in my life. This is me! (022)

> The information you published on autogynephilia has given me a sudden clarity into what I have experienced my whole life. I feel almost like a weight has been lifted off of me. (023)

One informant who had transitioned 3 years earlier observed that recognizing herself in the descriptions of autogynephilic transsexualism had helped her reach a more nuanced understanding of her status as a transsexual woman and come to terms with some personality traits that were not traditionally feminine:

> I began my transition at age 26 and completed sex reassignment surgery 3 years ago. Reading about autogynephilia has helped me shed many of my pretensions, which has helped me to become more grounded and not as easily hurt when my femininity is questioned. Indeed, I have come to accept the dual nature of myself as a thinking male with a female emotional life. (024)

This excerpt illustrates how the theory of autogynephilic transsexualism cannot only promote personal understanding in a dramatic and revelatory way, but also in more subtle ways, by encouraging MtF transsexuals to reflect on the origins and meanings of their cross-gender identities.

Opening Eroticism to Discussion

A few informants observed that the concept of autogynephilia provided a descriptive term and an explanatory schema that addressed feelings and desires that were rarely discussed openly: the erotic feelings that provided the impetus, at least in part, for wanting sex reassignment:

> As a transsexual who finds her own transsexualism to be the continuing culmination of many erotic fantasies, I want to thank you for eloquently expressing the importance for many of us of the "sexual" in transsexual. (025)

> I was delighted to read about autogynephilia. It is very much the idea and fantasy of having a woman's body and enjoying it that I find intensely arousing. It is a great relief to have this topic brought out into the open. (026)

> I have yet to read an explanation that more closely and accurately describes the motivation I feel than the concept of autogynephilia. This is the first time anybody has ever said it is ok to have sexual feelings and motives. (027)

The concept of autogynephilia not only puts the erotic dimension of transsexualism on the table for discussion but also implies that individuals can participate in such a discussion with less worry about whether they are "genuinely" transsexual.

Finding a Theory That Feels Applicable

Several informants reported that the theory of autogynephilic transsexualism provided a better explanatory framework for making sense of their feelings and experiences than other theories of MtF transsexualism they had encountered. Other theories, they felt, either didn't seem to apply to them or were missing some important element.

> You've published the concept I've been searching for, which finally explains my feelings. I've read all the traditional theories, yet I've always felt I was different. I've been trying to decide what to do, feeling I didn't match the standard descriptions, yet knowing I had to do something. With this cloud of confusion lifted, I can make clearer decisions. (028)

> I think the ideas of autogynephilia match my feelings and understanding of my desires. I never really felt that the "politically correct" motivations matched my situation. (029)

> Your articles on autogynephilia, especially concerning the physical aspect of feminizing one's body, hit home for me. I have always sought a reason for my gender dysphoria but have not been satisfied with most of the theories. Your articles describe me to a T. (030)

> I am convinced of the validity of the autogynephilic model of transsexualism. Unlike other theories I have read about, the autogynephilia model seems to exactly match up with my intuitive understanding of my own experience. (031)

Because MtF transsexuals are eager to make sense of their seemingly inexplicable feelings and desires, they are often intensely interested in scientific theories that attempt to explain the etiology or development of transsexualism. Finding a theory that is congruent with their personal experience is satisfying emotionally as well as intellectually.

Discovering Others Feel Similarly

Another major theme expressed by many informants was relief upon learning that they were not alone in experiencing autogynephilic arousal. The discovery that others shared similar feelings was frequently a source of comfort and hope:

> I have struggled to find information that fits my story. Your articles for the first time have described my feelings. It feels good to realize that my feelings are felt by others. (032)

> I definitely recognized myself in what I read about autogynephilia. Reading other people's stories and learning that I am not alone is really a relief. (033)

> Thanks for making me aware that I am not alone in my fantasies and feelings. I know there are plenty of transsexuals, but I really felt that many of my thoughts and fantasies were unique. (034)

> I guess that I had simply never thought that someone else might feel the same way. It isn't something that we talk about. Finding out that autogynephilia is not just something with me, uniquely, has made a difference in my status as a transsexual. (035)

Discovering that others shared the same feelings was not only emotionally gratifying but could also provide the impetus to seeking professional help:

> The fact that I am not the only person who feels like a "man trapped in a man's body" makes me hope that there is some way to mitigate my increasing distress. Thanks for writing the article. It made me feel less lonely and encouraged me to seek professional help. (036)

> Your article on autogynephilia resonated so directly with my own experience that I was able to finally reconcile myself to my nature and move forward with treatment. I have accepted myself as transsexual and have begun counseling for hormone therapy as a result. (037)

Feeling Legitimately Transsexual

Another significant theme in the informants' narratives was relief and gratitude that their histories of autogynephilic arousal did not disqualify them from being considered genuinely transsexual. The theory of autogynephilic transsexualism validated their experience of transsexualism as legitimate and helped to dispel their doubts and fears:

> I have often had doubts about my own transsexuality and have felt like I was not a real transsexual. Now I have a better understanding of what I truly am. (038)

> I feel like your essay on autogynephilia totally validates my desire to transition. I have been sexually aroused by fantasies of being a woman since puberty. I was seriously considering transition when I was 36 or 37, but I felt like I didn't meet the requirement of feeling like a woman trapped in a man's body. (039)

> The description of anatomic autogynephilia has hit the nail right on the head. I never knew that there was a term for what I have been experiencing all my life. I thought at first that I was transsexual; but I held off from transitioning because something just didn't seem right about the definition of a transsexual and what I experience. (040)

Several narratives referred to the commonly held belief that anyone who experienced sexual arousal in connection with the fantasy of being a female was merely a transvestite or heterosexual cross-dresser, not a "real" transsexual:

> I think that autogynephilia is why a lot of MtF transsexuals initially feel, as I did, that they are not really transsexual and must be transvestites. You shouldn't enjoy these thoughts, and if you do, then you're not really transsexual. It isn't until you discover more about the subject that you understand that you can have these feelings and be transsexual. (041)

> I have been involved with cross-dressing behavior since I was 5 or 6 years old and it has been sexually arousing for me. I had always been of the opinion that I was just a transvestite until recently. (042)

> I did worry that I was not truly a transsexual due to the erotic nature of my fantasies, which are usually associated with transvestism. (043)

> When I considered transition in the past, I quickly rejected the idea. I felt that my sexual gratification proved I wasn't a "real" transsexual, rather just a cross-dresser. Your essay finally makes it clear that these two categories are not mutually exclusive. (044)

The last informant realized that one of the implications of the concept of autogynephilia is that "transsexual" and "cross-dresser" are not distinct and mutually exclusive conditions, but are merely points on a spectrum of symptomatology (see Lawrence, 2009b). Over time, greater awareness of the concept of autogynephilia may lead to a more sophisticated understanding of the relationship between these two closely related clinical entities.

No Longer Feeling Crazy

Before reading about the theory of autogynephilic transsexualism, several informants had felt "crazy": They knew that, according to prevailing stereotypes about MtF transsexualism, experiencing erotic arousal in association with the idea of being female disqualified one from being genuinely transsexual. They knew that they had experienced such arousal, but they also knew that they were severely gender dysphoric. The inability to reconcile their feelings with the prevailing stereotypes was disconcerting and distressing.

> I thought I was crazy, looking at myself as possibly transsexual but not fitting the general stereotypes. But as I read about behavioral autogynephilia, my eyes widened and I felt a sense of understanding to a question that has driven me insane for 8 years. (045)

> Until I started reading the comments of others, I thought I was alone or crazy. I was having an incredible problem reconciling my desire to physically change my sex with most of the literature I had read on transsexualism. (018)

> I have been so confused about my gender dysphoria. I went to a therapist and he kept trying to get me to believe transsexualism is solely about gender identity. Then I came across your essay about autogynephilia and it helps me confirm what is actually going on in my head and that I'm not crazy. (046)

Disconcerting Self-Recognition

Recognizing oneself to be an autogynephilic transsexual was not always a joyful, liberating experience for informants. On the contrary, it was a disconcerting realization for some. Several informants reported that acknowledging that they were autogynephilic transsexuals carried overtones of doubt, sadness, or shame. I consider the narrative excerpts describing these reactions to be especially important. Here are some representative comments:

> I read most of your article on autogynephilia with my mouth open or my hand up to my face. It made me uncomfortable to read something that so closely described my cross-gender urges, which don't seem to fit the transsexual norm. (047)

> For most of my life, I have been sexually aroused both by wearing women's clothing and the fantasy of being a woman. I am desperately seeking a way to cross over to femininity, but admitting the sexual arousal part of my gender dysphoria is difficult. (048)

> The only time that I am at peace with myself and my desires is when I am progressing toward my goal of being a woman. My therapist is confident that I am on the right course, but I sometimes doubt myself because of my sexual fantasies. (049)

> I very often need feminization fantasies to achieve orgasm. My partner has told me not to be ashamed of it. But there's something about it that has made me feel so inauthentic. As if maybe, despite the incredible ease of my transition, I'm not for real after all—that I'm just a messed up guy. I'm still bothered by it, I have to be honest about that. (050)

One informant expressed distress and sadness that her self-focused pattern of autogynephilic erotic desire seemed to preclude genuine sexual intimacy with other persons:

> When I read one of your articles on autogynephilia, it blew my mind. You described Blanchard's thesis as an epiphany, and it was like that for me, too. However, it was also upsetting to realize that my sexual desire had always been centered on myself, rather than involving an intimate sharing with someone else. I felt really cheated out of something that seemingly was effortless for others. (051)

This informant's statement is reminiscent of the one made in Chap. 1 by Ms. Z, who described her obligatory reliance on autogynephilic imagery during partnered sex as "a profound, disabling defect in her ability to feel genuine sexual love for other people." One of the most distressing aspects of intense autogynephilic eroticism is that it often precludes real intimacy with one's sexual partners; several informant's descriptions of this phenomenon will be presented in Chap. 7. In my opinion, interference with interpersonal intimacy during sex constitutes one of the strongest bases for considering clinically significant autogynephilia to be a genuine mental disorder.

Several informants used the word "pervert" to describe themselves, based on their recognition that their sexual arousal pattern was paraphilic:

> Your article on autogynephilia explains the way I feel and what I have thought about myself all my life. I have always been honest about why I want to transition, but I feel like some kind of pervert when I tell any shrink. (052)

> You hit the nail right on the head with the theory of autogynephilia. This is truly about my sexual orientation. It is quite a kick in the butt to realize that you are a pervert

> or a deviant, but I'm also smart enough to know that I can't rationalize my sexual desires away. (034)

> Reading your essay on autogynephilia, I made sense of my transsexual feelings for the first time in my life. I cannot begin to express the misery of the self-loathing resulting from the fact that the object of my sexual desire is an abstract concept. For a very long time I regarded myself as a total pervert. (053)

Although I consider the word "pervert" to be unnecessarily pejorative, I admire the insight and honesty of these informants: Autogynephilia is indeed a paraphilia—a condition formerly known as a perversion. Therein lies one likely reason why Blanchard's theory of autogynephilic transsexualism has not gained much traction among MtF transsexuals: It requires unusual honesty and courage to embrace a theory that tells you that you have a paraphilia. Some psychotherapists may have been reluctant to accept Blanchard's ideas for a similar reason. It requires a high degree of professional integrity to embrace a theory that tells you that some of your clients—clients whom you genuinely want to help and support—suffer from a paraphilia.

I would argue that, from a psychotherapeutic perspective, validation of a client's experience of psychopathology (and addressing associated issues of shame and stigma) is ultimately a more powerful and effective intervention than attempting to "depathologize" a condition that is genuinely pathological. The following two narrative excerpts support the value of this approach:

> Your description of paraphilic autogynephilia in transsexuals is right on the mark, so far as my life has been concerned. I am glad and greatly relieved that the paraphilic condition of autogynephilia has been recognized. (054)

> I have always been sexually aroused at the thought of my feminization. Many transsexuals who are brave enough to look at themselves objectively will admit to some level of autogynephilia. The problem is that our society has put such shame on sexual perversion that many people feel they have to put on a big front and avoid the issue. (055)

I will discuss feelings of shame about autogynephilic transsexualism in detail in Chap. 12.

Anxieties About Consequences

In contrast to the more positive views expressed in many of the earlier narratives, two informants expressed concerns about possible negative consequences for themselves or for MtF transsexuals generally if it became widely recognized that one form of MtF transsexualism was the outgrowth of a paraphilia.

> My wife was initially accepting of my cross-dressing desires as a fetish, but became very opposed when it became clear to her that it wasn't just a sexual turn-on. She feels this will harm our children, so she is trying to limit me to supervised visitation only. I am a little concerned about the effect of me being viewed as having a paraphilia, as opposed to being purely "a woman in a man's body," on the court case. (056)

> I think we need to be very careful with study of this subject. If you are not transgender, this stuff will blow your mind, although if you are transgender, it makes sense. That's why the

> concept of autogynephilia is dangerous. I think we need to move toward an understanding of gender dysphoria on a deeper level than sexual gratification, which is where autogynephilia puts it. And it is not about that. Sure, it's part of it, but a small part. People are starting to see us transsexuals as something other than freaks, so please don't screw that up. (057)

The latter informant's belief that the concept of autogynephilia implies that gender dysphoria is exclusively about sexual gratification is not accurate, as I explained in Chap. 2. Unfortunately, misconceptions of this kind concerning autogynephilia are not uncommon among MtF transsexuals and the psychotherapists who provide care to them.

Invalidation by Psychotherapists

More than a few informants reported receiving invalidating statements from their psychologists and psychiatrists, who sometimes suggested that an informant's history of autogynephilic arousal meant that she was not genuinely transsexual:

> I have had autogynephilic sexual fantasies for as long as I have had sexual fantasies—of having a woman's body and responding the way a woman would. This part of my life has always been intensely sexual. For decades, professionals told me that I could not really be a transsexual, because I was oriented toward women. Reporting my fantasies got an equally negative response. (058)

> My thoughts of being female almost always were accompanied by erotic feelings. I was bitter for years because of the rejection I met in the psychiatric community when I acknowledged that many of my thoughts had a sexual element involved. "Well, you're just a transvestite, then," was the dismissive message I received. That's ridiculous and naive. (059)

> The evaluation at the John's Hopkins gender clinic was interesting. They asked questions about my fantasies, about arousal during cross-dressing, and lots that seemed to be related to latent homosexuality. Their conclusion was that I wasn't transsexual because I wasn't homosexual and was aroused by cross-dressing. (056)

> By the time I was 22, I was sure I was a good candidate for MtF sex reassignment surgery. Unfortunately, I had a psychologist at that time who did not see me as a "true transsexual" because of my autogynephilia. The autogynephilia really did have me thinking that I was merely a hopeless paraphiliac and not a realistic candidate for sex reassignment surgery. (060)

With respect to the last informant's comment: One of the implications of the theory of autogynephilic transsexualism is that paraphilic individuals can sometimes be very appropriate candidates for SRS.

Reluctance to Discuss Autogynephilia with Therapists

Reluctance to disclose autogynephilic feelings to psychotherapists was a common theme in the narratives, especially when dealing with therapists who were in a position to grant or deny approval for hormone therapy or SRS. Several informants concluded that being honest about their feelings was simply too risky:

> I haven't broached the subject with my therapist. I think that a lot of women are apprehensive about telling someone that they get excited in this fashion, because that is what is associated with transvestites, and it would potentially hurt their transition goals. (041)

> The definition of autogynephilia describes me perfectly. My life-long desire to have feminine urinary function and female genitalia was definitely a major reason for my sex reassignment surgery. However, I never explained this to my therapist, fearing he would not support my planned surgery. (061)

> When I first came across the concept of autogynephilia, I identified strongly with some of the personal accounts by autogynephilic transsexuals. I have never discussed or admitted my sexual feelings to the psychiatrists at Charing Cross for fear of being labeled a fetishist and losing access to treatment and sex reassignment surgery. (062)

> I am in my second year of transition. More often than not, I have had to indulge in forced feminization fantasy to enable me to orgasm. I feel that forced feminization fantasies are probably normal for most transsexuals, regardless of what they say. Let's face it, though: Tell that to a psychiatrist gatekeeper and see how far you get. I think most of us know what we want and just play the game to get there. (063)

> I am a 42-year-old male, currently living full-time as a woman and approved for SRS. While I do not believe that sexual fantasy is my primary motivating force towards seeking sex reassignment surgery, it is certainly one of the factors. But it is a factor I cannot even mention to my therapist, for fear of having sex reassignment surgery denied me. Although I want to trust my therapist, she is a gatekeeper and could easily put an end to my sex reassignment surgery with a phone call. Obviously, this attitude greatly skews any data collected on this subject. (064)

> I am seeing a psychiatrist about my gender dysphoria. To see some of my autogynephilic feelings described makes them less scary to me, but I'm still leery about sharing them with my psychiatrist. In my opinion, we all must keep some of these feelings private and keep the smokescreen of pure and simple gender dysphoria at the forefront. I think that most therapists would interpret some of these feelings as fetish-driven and try to protect us from ourselves by placing barriers in the way of gender reassignment. (057)

Other autogynephilic transsexuals similarly concluded that the safest approach to take with psychotherapists was to present themselves as "textbook cases" of MtF transsexualism, not only refusing to disclose their history of sexual arousal with cross-dressing or cross-gender fantasy but lying about this if necessary. Their attitude is consistent with data from Walworth's (1997) survey of 52 MtF transsexuals, who reported that sexual arousal with cross-dressing was the single most common topic about which they had lied to or misled their psychotherapists.

> One comment on why transsexuals may be so unwilling to talk to therapists on this issue: I didn't bring it up because I wanted sex reassignment surgery. I figured out early on that I had to present what they wanted to see, not what I really was. I had no belief at all that I could get approval without lying, so I lied. (065)

> Before I began transition, I read your writing about autogynephilia. I felt that the concept applied to me somewhat, although I did not want to tell anyone that, because I was determined to have a flawless, "by-the-book" case of transsexualism so that I could pursue sex reassignment surgery. (066)

> I'm considering finding a therapist so that I can begin moving toward transition. Sadly, it seems apparent that, if I'm honest with my therapist about my autogynephilic feelings, she will consider me inappropriate for sex reassignment surgery. So, I'm left with having to find a therapist and parrot the lines they want to hear in order to get my letter. (067)

Explanations like these might partly explain why many psychotherapists who specialize in gender issues report that they rarely encounter clients for whom autogynephilia is a significant issue.

Counternarratives: Acceptance by Psychotherapists

In contrast to the experiences described above, some informants disclosed their autogynephilic feelings to their psychotherapists and did not encounter invalidating reactions:

> I showed your article to my psychiatrist on my first visit and said that it was closer to my own feelings than anything else I had read. He had not heard of the term autogynephilia, although he probably has seen other cases. He is nonjudgmental and this action does not seem likely to have any adverse effect on my diagnosis. I certainly feel much better about this than creating a package of lies to meet my expectations of what I think "they" want to hear. (068)

> I received my surgery about 2 years ago. When I was in the throes of making my decision, some of the issues in your article about autogynephilia concerned me a great deal. I was lucky that I had a very understanding therapist and I was able to openly discuss those feelings. (069)

> I have just gotten my letter of approval for genital surgery from my therapist. I identified as autogynephilic from the get-go, and my therapist was willing to work with me anyhow. (070)

Perhaps such accepting reactions from psychotherapists will become more prevalent as the concept of autogynephilia becomes more widely known and its explanatory value becomes more generally appreciated.

Invalidating Reactions from Peers

Some informants reported that other MtF transsexuals had told them that a history of autogynephilic arousal disqualified them from being genuinely transsexual. Others feared that disclosing their autogynephilic feelings to other transsexuals might elicit such responses.

> I transitioned in my early 20s. The fact that I was sexually excited by being a woman made other transgender people label me a cross-dresser or a fetishist and not a true transsexual. (071)

> When I was still preoperative, I would sometimes tell some of my transsexual friends that I really wanted to have sex as a woman and that it was one of the primary motivating factors, not so much in my transition, but in the desire to have sex reassignment surgery. I quickly learned that an admission like that was not really a good idea: I usually got an earful about how I couldn't be transsexual. (072)

> I've never honestly discussed my feelings within the transsexual community, because I know that admitting to autogynephilia would lead to being ostracized. (062)

It is easy to find examples of such invalidating assessments on many of the Internet sites maintained by high-profile MtF transsexual activists. These individuals often state or imply that autogynephilic transsexuals are not genuinely or legitimately transsexual. Ironically, the transsexual activists who maintain these Internet sites often have demographic profiles that are strongly suggestive of autogynephilic transsexualism, although the activists usually deny or minimize any history of autogynephilic arousal. As I noted in Chap. 1, counterfactual denial of autogynephilic arousal by genuinely autogynephilic persons is a well-documented, well-understood phenomenon (Blanchard et al., 1986; Zucker et al., 2012).

Reluctance to Alienate or Upset Others

Some informants stated that they were reluctant to disclose their autogynephilic feelings to professional or nonprofessional persons, either out of shame or a wish to avoid controversy:

> I fit the autogynephile description. In my own mind, I don't feel the need to hide behind a gender-based excuse or explanation for my desire to have a woman's body. But I've felt the need to express it to others cloaked in the terms of "gender reassignment," simply because my paraphilia seemed indefensible. How could I admit to being intensely sexually interested in an altered version of my own body? I don't want to alienate others by admitting what society has asked me to be ashamed of: the fact that nothing turns me on more than the idea of inhabiting a woman's body. (073)

> I hope I can find a good way to explain why I am doing this without having to reveal just how perverted this is. How ironic: When I live as a woman, I will have to live a lie. (034)

> I don't talk about autogynephilia much with other transgender persons, since it upsets them. They feel that it invalidates them or something. (070)

> Your descriptions of autogynephilia are very consistent with my experiences. I have had the opportunity to discuss these topics with others in my local transgender support group. As you might imagine, it was not always a popular topic. (074)

If the concept of autogynephilia were to become more widely known and appreciated, autogynephilic transsexuals might eventually be able to discuss their feelings with fewer concerns about negative social consequences.

Considering Autogynephilia as a Motive

Several narratives contained reflections on the implicit theory of motivation that is associated with the concept of autogynephilia. Not surprisingly, informants expressed differing opinions about whether autogynephilia was a motive for their cross-gender expression or for seeking sex reassignment.

Autogynephilia as a Principal Motive

Several informants reported that the desire to actualize their autogynephilic feelings was the principal driving force or motivation for their cross-gender expression or for their decision to seek sex reassignment:

> I kept denying that there was a sexual component to my transgendered feelings until I read your paper concerning autogynephilia. I now realize that the driving force for my transgender behavior is the sexual feelings in becoming a woman. For the first time, I understand the motivating factors. (075)

> The autogynephilic hypothesis makes plenty of sense to me, as it is self-sexual desire that has driven my fantasies and my desire to change my body. (076)

> I have always had highly charged erotic feelings associated with the development of female sex characteristics. It seems to me it's been the root cause of a greater commitment to transsexuality and it's what drives me from one step to the next. (077)

> I transitioned in my early 20s. I started hormones at 21 and was full-time at 22. The idea of being a woman sexually excited me. I was literally driven to go for facial feminization surgery and to get SRS by this urge. (071)

> My sexuality and pleasure comes from the thought of myself as a woman. In my case, being a woman is all I ever wished for. My most intense feelings are bound up in this idea. It has been the driving force of my life. (078)

> I am a 55-year-old MtF, nearly 4 years post-op. The concept of autogynephilia helped provide an understanding of my behavior. Sex is a powerful force for some of us and certainly me. I just wanted to add to the ever increasing body of evidence that many of us are indeed motivated to undergo sex reassignment surgery by our autogynephilia. (079)

An informant who had not yet transitioned likewise felt that her autogynephilic eroticism would eventually lead her to sex reassignment:

> I have always found cross-dressing extremely erotic. I still find women's clothing and the thought of becoming a woman sexually exciting. I feel like the erotic feelings are eventually going to drive me to start hormone therapy, electrolysis, and eventually surgical reassignment. (080)

Another observed that the impetus to actualize her autogynephilic sexual desires was comparable to the impetus to actualize her other sexual desires, such as engaging in sexual activity with preferred partners or undergoing erotic piercing:

> My fantasies of feminization of my body are intertwined with piercing fantasies and practice, both genital and other (facial, nipples, navel), and with heterosexual desire and fantasies. As such, they are a very strong force in my pursuing SRS, like piercing fantasies are for pursuing being pierced and sexual desire is for pursuing heterosexual sex. (081)

Yet another informant observed that sexuality was such an important aspect of life that it seemed wrong to forego the opportunity to actualize her autogynephilic desires:

> Your views about autogynephilia made a lot of sense to me. To be a woman, to be taken, to have orgasms as a woman—I have a compulsion to experience those feelings. It seems wrong to live as a conventional man, imagining sexually being a woman, and just leave it at

that. You can minimize it all, say, oh, well, it is just sex, and sex is just one aspect of life among many. Yes, but sex is like the tip of the pyramid of life. (082)

In a lengthy meditation on her motive for wanting to transition, an informant proposed that, in her case, autogynephilia led to the creation of a powerful cross-gender identity ("will to be a woman") that she felt she had to express in order to live a truly vital life:

> No matter how much effort I put into the project of developing a female personality, the final product will not be equal to my male personality in terms of integration and authenticity. At best, it will have elements of phoniness, insecurity, and awkwardness. Why exchange something good for something poor? The answer is that a female personality will afford a superior link to my subconscious and therefore will be better in certain very important areas. I prefer to explain this in terms of autogynephilia. Just as a forest fire can develop into something that is categorically different—namely, a fire storm, which generates its own weather patterns—so can autogynephilia develop into something that is categorically different than a mere sex drive: It can give rise to a subconscious will to be a woman. Once this subconscious will to be a woman has been born, life can only truly be vital when one is consciously projecting oneself toward being a woman. How important are the relatively rare moments when life is truly vital? To me they are extremely important. I would trade a good deal in the area of the practical to be able to have states of conscious will that were "supercharged" with energy from the subconscious. (083)

Although I might quibble with the term "subconscious," I feel that this informant makes several excellent points. First, we autogynephilic transsexuals often observe that autogynephilia seems to exert its motive force indirectly, by giving rise to our strongly held, highly valued cross-gender identities. Second, our lives often do feel as though they lack vitality and purpose if we fail to express our cross-gender identities. Finally, we often pay a heavy price for expressing our cross-gender identities, because we are not naturally feminine and because the female personas we create sometimes appear unusual or inauthentic—to ourselves as well as to others. I will discuss these issues in more detail in Chap. 12.

Autogynephilia as a Possible or Partial Motive

Other informants acknowledged that autogynephilia was probably or definitely part of their motive for seeking sex reassignment. Many of them suggested, however, that other factors—especially female gender identity—played a significant part as well. Regrettably, the latter informants rarely addressed the question of whether their female gender identities might have been direct outgrowths of their autogynephilic feelings or whether their cross-gender identities had developed independently of autogynephilia.

> I think the increasing pervasiveness of those autogynephilic sexual fantasies have contributed to my decision to transition. I could, within the acceptable range of male behavior, wear feminine clothes, have sex with men, knit during school lessons, work in a kindergarten and so on. I have done all this, and it has given me some relief as to my struggles with my male gender identity. At a certain point, I realized that I had done everything possible to accept my male gender, and it still didn't work. I have thought a lot about the reason for this,

> and after having read your article it becomes more clear that the fact that I see myself as a woman in my sexual fantasies may have a say here. (084)

> I am a 39-year-old heterosexual anatomic autogynephilic transsexual. I am now seriously considering SRS. I have declined in the past, simply because I have known that my motives were sexual. My motives now are less connected with my sexual desire and more to do with an ever-deepening desire to be female generally. (053)

> While I do not believe that sexual fantasy is my primary motivating force towards seeking sex reassignment surgery, it is certainly one of the factors. (064)

> I am 49 years old and have been approved for hormone therapy by a gender therapist. We have talked about my belief that elements of autogynephilia are part of the reason that I want to pursue such a course. While the thought of being female has and continues to be somewhat arousing to me, there was no time in life that I didn't want to be the opposite sex. Based on my experience, I think one can be a blend of autogynephilic and so-called "legitimate" tendencies. (085)

> I guess in some ways sexual desire did play a part in my decision to transition, but certainly it was not the entire reason. I did it because I have felt this way for as long as I can recall. (086)

> I am a 41-year-old postoperative transsexual. I don't think it is as simple as saying that wanting a sex change is purely driven by sexual fantasies or not. I think that it is a factor that is woven into a complex set of emotions and feelings that drive one to undergo such a dramatic change in life. I admit that I have had many sexual fantasies about being female and having a female body, a life long dream for me. I am not ashamed that I am sexually turned on by being female now, nor do I think that it was a wrong motivation for transitioning. (069)

Other informants conceded that autogynephilia might constitute a principal or partial motive for seeking sex reassignment but were unable to say so definitely:

> I did not transition until age 36. I've never understood what might have been the spur for the gender dysphoria, but perhaps in my case the autogynephilia acted as positive reinforcement. After all, if I feel the best ever (and sexy) when fantasizing as a female, that would be a powerful incentive to promote and enlarge that fantasy. (087)

> I have been exploring transsexualism actively for maybe 6 months. Cross-dressing in the closet has been my outlet for 25 years. The thought of being a woman transports me. I don't seek only to be a woman in appearance, I want the full experience. Is it arousing? Sure. Is it the reason? I don't think so, but it is hard for me to differentiate. (088)

Desire to Engage in Sex as a Woman as a Principal Motive

The desire to engage in sex as a woman was emphasized as a principal motivation for seeking sex reassignment in a few narratives. This desire is plausibly a manifestation of behavioral autogynephilia, although some informants offered other explanations for it.

> I am a 35-year-old who has undergone therapy for gender dysphoria over the past 2 years. My erotic thoughts have always been fueled by my thinking of myself as female, and having sex as a woman was a great motivator in my pursuit of SRS. (066)

> I'm not sure whether my feelings are really completely autogynephilic. I believe I would have transitioned anyway, because there were a whole variety of nonsexual experiences that I wanted to have. But at the same time, the thought of having sex as a woman was

strong—very strong—and I'm not sure I would have gone through sex reassignment surgery without it. (072)

Sexual feelings have been very important in my decision to transition. For a long time, I've had sexual fantasies about men, but physically I couldn't have a relationship, because in my mind I've always had an image of myself as female, and having a male body kept me from being able to experience the type of sex I wanted. (089)

I read a statement about some autogynephilic transsexuals "becoming the women they love." I'm becoming what I'm attracted to, and at the same time, I'm hoping to attract a woman who is like me and likes that aspect of me. There is a sexual motivation for my pursuit of SRS, but it is not for personal gratification, it is to feel whole and complete, able to function with a woman the way I want to. (090)

Autogynephilia Not a Motive

Other informants who acknowledged a history of autogynephilic eroticism denied (or doubted) that autogynephilic feelings played any significant part in motivating them to seek or undergo sex reassignment:

I have experienced sexual arousal from all the things on your list and conform with all else I've read about autogynephilia. I always was attracted to women. These desires were NOT the reason for transitioning; the understanding of my really being transsexual was. (091)

My thoughts of being female almost always were accompanied by erotic feelings. But I don't believe it would be accurate to say that I transitioned because of erotic feelings, for I might well have done so anyway. (059)

One informant observed that her autogynephilic fantasies disappeared after she began hormone therapy; she concluded from this that autogynephilia had not been a significant motive for her transition.

I must admit that I have had sexual fantasies of forced feminization and having a feminine body. After I started hormone therapy, though, feeling sexual desire in this manner became nonexistent. Even before hormones, wearing women's clothing had lost any appeal to sexual desire for me. I don't think sexual desire played any large role in my decision to transition. (092)

Another informant believed that the process of sex reassignment was too arduous to undertake simply for the sake of living out her sexual fantasies. She conceded, however, that actualizing her fantasies would be an "unexpected benefit" of transition:

Regarding autogynephilic sexual fantasies, I experienced many of these things much more intensely when I was younger, but the feelings are still there to a certain degree. Now, being out and accepted as just one of the girls is more of a goal for me. I feel out of place in my male body and aware that the male walls I had constructed around myself were nothing other than protection from my true self. Sure there are sexual desires within me, but I can experience sexual pleasure without transitioning and can act out many of my fantasies without transitioning. So why would I want to put myself and everyone around me through the costs and hell of transition? To finally find peace with myself. Living out some of these fantasies in a female body would be an unexpected benefit of transitioning, not a motivating factor. (093)

Narratives such as this are not unusual and are worth considering carefully. Blanchard's theory proposes that the cross-gender identity of an autogynephilic transsexual is a manifestation of her autogynephilic sexual orientation: Her "desire to be a female" is an outgrowth of her autogynephilic sexual desire to be a female. From this perspective, an autogynephilic transsexual's wish to express her "true self" (feminine gender identity) in order to "finally find peace" can be understood as driven or motivated, at least initially, by autogynephilia. Therefore, to claim that autogynephilia is not a motivating factor in such a case is merely to say that autogynephilia exerts its motive force indirectly, through the intermediary of the transsexual's gradually developing cross-gender identity. After one's journey toward finding peace has gone on for years or decades, it is seemingly easy to forget the autogynephilic sexual desires that originally gave impetus to that journey.

Must Revelatory Knowledge Remain Private Knowledge?

In the narrative excerpts presented in this chapter, informants often reported that discovering the concept of autogynephilia was a revelatory experience. Many felt that the concept and the associated theory of autogynephilic transsexualism accurately described their feelings, facilitated greater self-understanding, and reassured them that they were genuinely transsexual. But this revelatory information did not always cause informants to rejoice: Sometimes it was an occasion for sadness or distress. None of the informants felt that autogynephilia was anything to be proud of, and some clearly considered it shameful.

Moreover, many informants felt that they could not safely disclose their autogynephilic feelings to anyone. Disclosure to psychotherapists was risky, because therapists might withhold access to treatment if they believed an autogynephilic client could not be genuinely transsexual. Disclosure to other transgender persons was risky, too, because autogynephilia was controversial and disclosure might elicit invalidating responses. For many informants, then, the concept of autogynephilia was revelatory knowledge, but it seemed prudent to treat their personal experience of autogynephilia as private knowledge.

Given these realities, it will probably be challenging for the concept of autogynephilic transsexualism to become widely known and generally accepted. Transsexuals who experience autogynephilia and could testify to its applicability and explanatory value are often reluctant to talk about their experiences, deterred by shame and the very real practical consequences of disclosure. Because such individual testimonials are rare, autogynephilic transsexualism can too easily be dismissed as "just a theory"—and one that describes only a tiny minority of MtF transsexuals. This, in turn, makes autogynephilic transsexualism feel even more unusual and shameful to those who experience it and makes the possible consequences of disclosure potentially more serious. The resulting vicious cycle of ignorance, secrecy, shame, and fear of disclosure will probably be difficult to break. In Chap. 12, I will offer some suggestions about how the process might begin.

Chapter 5
Developmental Histories

Theorizing Developmental History in Autogynephilic Transsexualism

If one accepts the theory that autogynephilic transsexuals are "men trapped in men's bodies"—men who are unremarkably masculine except for the paraphilic sexual orientation that makes them want to turn their bodies into facsimiles of women's bodies—one would predict that the developmental histories of these transsexuals should resemble those of other heterosexual men in most respects. Exceptions should be limited to traits or characteristics that are a result of their paraphilic sexual orientation. These predictions are consistent with observations by Whitam (1997), who offered this summary of the early developmental histories of transvestites and MtF transsexuals of the nonhomosexual type:

> Often their only cross-gender behavior [during childhood] is cross-dressing, which may not appear until just before, during, or after puberty and is often done in secret. Many transvestites and transsexuals of the heterosexual type have childhood experiences indistinguishable from those of boys who later become nontransvestic heterosexual men. (p. 192)

Whitam's observations are also largely consistent with the developmental histories provided by the study's transsexual informants, albeit with a few exceptions.

The first indications of men's eventual sexual orientations sometimes become evident in early childhood, as I will discuss in detail in Chap. 10. For example, some pre-heterosexual boys develop crushes on girls or special friendships with them, or fantasize about eventual marriage with them (Bell, 1902; Hatfield, Schmitz, Cornelius, & Rapson, 1988); some pre-homosexual boys have comparable feelings or experiences involving boys. These early indications of eventual sexual orientations appear well before puberty. Many of the study's transsexual informants similarly reported that the first indications of their eventual autogynephilic sexual orientations became evident in early childhood, taking the form of cross-gender wishes and fantasies or cross-dressing behavior. Unequivocal indications of men's eventual sexual orientations, manifesting as genital arousal in response to stimuli

A.A. Lawrence, *Men Trapped in Men's Bodies: Narratives of Autogynephilic Transsexualism*, Focus on Sexuality Research, DOI 10.1007/978-1-4614-5182-2_5,

involving preferred sexual objects, usually become evident at or during puberty. This is usually true of pre-heterosexual and pre-homosexual boys, and it was also true of the transsexual informants: In nearly all cases, they described having experienced unambiguous autogynephilic genital arousal in connection with cross-dressing or cross-gender fantasy during their early teenage years.

Most heterosexual men display typically masculine interests and behaviors during childhood and adolescence and choose male-typical occupations in adulthood (Lippa, 2002). Because autogynephilia is theorized to be a variant form of heterosexuality (Blanchard, 1992), one would predict that the same should be true of autogynephilic transsexuals: Their childhood interests and behaviors and adult occupational choices should theoretically be similar to those of other heterosexual men. With occasional exceptions, informants' narratives were consistent with these predictions.

The familiar trope that describes pretransition MtF transsexuals as "women trapped in men's bodies" is suggestive of a particular developmental history: It implies that MtF transsexuals will have developed psychological and behavioral characteristics that are typical of natal women, despite their incongruent male bodies. The theory of autogynephilic transsexualism implies a very different developmental history: It suggests that autogynephilic transsexuals usually will have developed psychological and behavioral characteristics that are typical of other heterosexual men; any exceptions will involve characteristics that derive from their autogynephilic sexual orientations (e.g., tendencies to cross-dress and engage in cross-gender fantasy). Consequently, one would predict that autogynephilic transsexuals would often reject the "woman trapped in a man's body" description or at least be skeptical of it; some autogynephilic transsexuals might even endorse the countertrope I proposed and agree that they resemble "men trapped in men's bodies" (Lawrence, 1998). For the most part, informants' narratives were consistent with these predictions as well.

Men's sexual orientations usually if not always remain stable throughout their lives, although strength of genital arousal and frequency of sexual behaviors often decline with advancing age. Because autogynephilia is conceptualized as a sexual orientation as well as a paraphilia, one would predict that autogynephilic transsexuals' sexual orientations—manifesting as feelings of arousal from, attraction to, and love for the idea or reality of resembling women—would continue throughout their lives, including after sex reassignment. Once again, informants' narratives were generally consistent with these predictions, although not in every case.

Age of Onset of Cross-Gender Fantasies, Behaviors, and Associated Arousal

Most informants who discussed the age of onset of their cross-gender fantasies and behaviors reported that these began in early childhood, usually between ages 4 and 6. This is somewhat earlier than most reports in the published literature.

The nonhomosexual gender dysphoric men studied by Blanchard et al. (1987) reported the onset of cross-gender wishes at a mean age of 9.8 years and the onset of cross-dressing at a mean age of 9.6 years. In a study of 232 MtF transsexuals who had completed SRS (Lawrence, 2003), I observed that the mean age at which participants first felt the desire to be the other sex or to change sex was 8 years. In the current study, it is possible that informants who experienced an especially early age of onset of cross-gender wishes or behaviors might simply have been more likely to mention this fact than those who experienced a later and seemingly less remarkable age of onset.

In contrast, the ages at which informants first experienced explicitly erotic feelings in association with their cross-gender fantasies and behaviors varied widely. Some informants reported that their cross-gender wishes and behaviors were explicitly erotic from earliest childhood or were "exciting" or "thrilling," implying possible erotic feelings. Others reported that associated erotic feelings developed only at puberty or, more rarely, well after puberty.

Early Childhood Onset of Cross-Dressing and Associated Arousal

More than a few boys cross-dress at least occasionally during early childhood. In a study of US children, Friedrich, Fisher, Broughton, Houston, and Shafran (1998) found that about 14% of 2-to-5-year-old boys and about 6% of 6-to-9-year-old boys had "dressed like the opposite sex" at least occasionally during the previous 6 months, according to reports by mothers or female caregivers. In an earlier study of US children, Friedrich, Grambsch, Broughton, Kuiper, and Beilke (1991) found similar but slightly lower figures: about 6% of 2-to-6-year-old boys and about 3% of 7-to-12-year-old boys were reported to have cross-dressed during the previous 6 months. Some boys who cross-dress during early childhood will become homosexual men, heterosexual transvestites, or MtF transsexuals in adulthood, but many or most probably will not.

Childhood cross-dressing by boys is sometimes, but certainly not always, associated with erotic arousal. The published literature contains two case reports of boys younger than age 3 who expressed the desire to wear girls' or women's clothing and who developed penile erections when allowed to do so (Stoller, 1985; Zucker & Blanchard, 1997); these reports suggest that autogynephilic sexual arousal can begin very early in life. In a study involving 36 transvestite participants, Doorn et al. (1994) found that 8 participants had begun cross-dressing before age 7, whereas only 5 or 6 (the article is unclear on this) denied that their cross-dressing was initially fetishistic, implying that at least 2 or 3 participants had experienced fetishistic arousal associated with cross-dressing earlier than age 7.

In the current study, several transsexual informants reported that they had experienced penile erections or definite erotic arousal or had engaged in masturbation in association with cross-dressing or cross-gender fantasies beginning in early childhood, typically between ages 4 and 6. Some informants distinctly remembered having had erections in association with cross-dressing:

> I have experienced sexual arousal from both imagining that I am a woman and looking at myself wearing feminine clothing since 4 years old. Long before my testes started to function at age 14, I could always get an erection by just putting on the panties, bras or petticoats of my sisters. (094)

> I can relate to the autogynephilic model to a great degree. I dressed often, up until about the start of elementary school, when my interactions with other children caused me to suppress this behavior. My mother never complained about my dressing up; in fact, she was quite encouraging. I remember at an early age getting erections while wearing my mother's silken nightgowns. I started dressing again in earnest about the time male puberty started, around age 12. (095)

Other informants reported that cross-gender fantasies alone were enough to induce penile erections in early childhood:

> I can remember vividly at the age of 6 getting a hard-on while wearing my mother's clothing. I did this whenever I got a chance, which was hardly ever. Because I hardly ever got a chance to dress up, I discovered that merely fantasizing about wearing my mother's clothing also gave me a hard-on. (096)

> From the age of 4, I had thoughts of wanting to know what it felt like to be a girl. I would make a wish, hoping that I would turn into a girl. I would develop an erection when I thought about becoming a girl; when I developed an erection, I thought some magical being was granting me my wish and I was going to become a girl. The erections were pleasurable, even after I knew that I wasn't going to become a girl. This lasted until I was 8 or 10. It went away until I was 11 or 12, then it all came back very strongly. (097)

Another informant reported penile erections in early childhood from daydreaming about being the maid of an attractive next-door neighbor and wearing her clothes:

> At about the age of 6 years, I became besotted by a lovely lady living next door. She must have been about 30, with a body to die for. In my dreams, both day and night, I was her maid and assistant, who was required to help her dress and provide assistance in her bathing and personal hygiene. I seem to remember getting a form of erection; however, my biggest wish was simply to grow up like her and be able to wear such lovely clothes. (098)

Yet another informant recalled masturbating in early childhood to the image of having female rather than male genitalia:

> When I was 6 or 7, I used to masturbate with a piece of clothing—it did not need to be gendered clothing, I just did not want to touch my penis—and fantasize about not having a penis, but having a vagina. I was not sure how that all would work, but I was sure that this was what I wanted and should have. (099)

Still another informant reported having experienced orgasms starting at age 6 and strongly implied that these occurred in association with cross-dressing or cross-gender fantasy:

> I have highly developed skill at using my mind to facilitate orgasm, and what stimulates me the most is to be a female. From my earliest recollections at age 3 or 4 years, I have been able to do this. I got great pleasure wearing my sister's skirts, and I was extremely paranoid about being discovered. I can remember orgasm from the age of 6. (100)

Some informants did not describe penile erections or masturbation but nevertheless reported definite erotic excitement or arousal associated with cross-dressing or cross-gender fantasies in early childhood:

> I have vivid memories starting from about age 6 or 7 of wanting to be a girl and of sexual desires which accompanied it. I also remember feeling ashamed of those feelings, though I do not remember any particular incident which instilled such feelings. Fantasies of intentionally becoming a girl began around age 10. (101)

> I have had the autogynephilic sex drive since I was a small boy; I have memories of it that go back to around age 6. (102)

> Your discussion of autogynephilia seems to fit me to a tee. I was dressed as a girl at age 4 or 5 and found it arousing then. Whenever I was presented with the chance to be alone and wear my mother's or sister's clothes, I did so. (103)

These narratives demonstrate that for some autogynephilic MtF transsexuals, cross-dressing and cross-gender fantasies in early childhood are erotically charged phenomena.

Early Childhood Onset of Cross-Dressing and Possible Erotic Feelings

Several informants reported that cross-dressing or cross-gender fantasies during early childhood were thrilling, exciting, or associated with sensations similar to the explicitly erotic sensations of adulthood. These feelings, too, are plausibly erotic.

> As a very young child, age 4, I already had the urge to have my ears pierced and alter my sex. My mother let me try her collection of clip-on earrings, which excited me beyond belief. The exploitation of these feelings for eroticism occurred much later, of course, but I don't think that proves that autogynephilia was not manifest in my early childhood. For example, I remember being thrilled by stories of boys allowed to wear dresses and long hair. (081)

> The concept of autogynephilia describes to a tee what I have been feeling all my life. Since age 4, I remember being excited by the thoughts of becoming and being a woman. After puberty, the only sexual fantasies that would bring me to orgasm involved me being a female. (104)

> I have always wanted to be a female. As long as I can recall, I have always had this desire. When I was around 5 years old, I remember sneaking into my mother's closet and wearing her hose and girdles. I found this so exciting. (105)

> I have always found crossdressing extremely erotic and very sexually satisfying. It all started at the age 15, when I discovered my mom's panties. That was when I had my first sexual experience. However, I remember feeling different from other boys in kindergarten. I would compare myself and my frail body to girls my age. This sent a shivering and tingling sensation throughout my entire body. These thoughts were with me at a very young age. (080)

> My first understanding that I desired to be a woman and its following excitement came when I was around 5 years old. This occurred watching a Doris Day movie and at first involved the wonderful clothes she wore. The idea of the clothing continued to both

> fascinate me and cause an excitement that I did not know what to do with at that age. My first cross-dressing incident was directly an attempt to emulate Ms. Day. By the age of 8, I cross-dressed "regularly"—meaning every chance I could find. I would find reasons to stay at home when my mom went visiting friends. By about age twelve, the early-on "excitement" began to be associated with the beginnings of sexual arousal the clothing seemed to cause. (106)

> I can distinctly remember being excited as young as 6 or 7 at the prospect of becoming a girl and living a girl's life. While too young to be really sexually stimulated by these thoughts, they certainly stirred an erotic side of me that has remained strong to this day. (107)

> I apologize for my limited knowledge of written English (I am Spanish). When I was 4 or 5 years old, I was playing with a girl friend of mine who was the same age. We were in her house, because our parents were friends. I don't remember the reason, but her mother put me in the clothes of that girl that evening. I experienced some kind of happiness that I still remember. It was a physiological pleasure, and though I was just a child and couldn't understand the nature of what I was feeling, it was something similar to the sexual pleasure I have experienced when I became an adult. It wasn't the clothes I was wearing, I think it was that I felt I was like that girl friend of mine. (108)

The final narrative excerpt is a particularly instructive one. The informant was not able to truly understand what he experienced at the age of 4 or 5, but the episode was obviously memorable. He remembered feeling a "physiological pleasure"—a *bodily* pleasure, at least by implication, and one similar to the bodily pleasures of adult sexuality. He also remembered that this physiological pleasure came from *feeling he was like a girl*—not from, say, some tactile or esthetic quality of the clothing itself. These two highlighted features comprise the irreducible core of the autogynephilic experience: pleasurable erotic arousal associated with the idea of being female.

Early Childhood Onset of Cross-Dressing, Pubertal Onset of Erotic Feelings

Other informants reported that they first cross-dressed or engaged in cross-gender fantasies in early childhood but did not develop explicitly erotic feelings associated with these activities until puberty. This is the classic pattern described in much of the published literature (e.g., Whitam, 1997).

> I first became aware of my feelings at age 4, my earliest recollection. At that age, I loved getting in my mother's closet and playing in her high heels. At age 5, I remember fantasizing I was a beautiful American Indian princess. At age 6, I remember secretly identifying with lead female characters in movies and cartoons. Ages 7–12 are filled with fantasies of me being a male hero: a cowboy, a patriot, a Roman soldier, and so on. By age 10 or so, stories of Christine Jorgensen were in the news. It fascinated me and I wished I could be her. I wished I was Natalie Wood; I wished I was Brenda Starr. At age 12, I picked up a copy of one of my dad's adult papers, containing pictures of cute, partially clothed girls. On the cover was a photo of French actress Noelle Noblecourt, age 19, wearing a frock that was split at the sides so you could see her thighs. I stole the paper and kept it; I started wishing I was her. One night, I was rubbing myself on my mattress, fantasizing being a girl on an all-girl island where everyone wears outfits like Noelle's. I imagined

> myself as Noelle, my first femme identity. As I rubbed myself, something happened: It was my first ejaculation. Soon I was ejaculating several times a night, wishing I was a girl. (109)

> My first cross-dressing experience was at age 5. When I was a child, prior to 11 years old, I had occasional interest in having things girls had—long hair at first. Later, as I became more aware of other differences between boys and girls, I wanted the additional things I knew girls had. At age 11, I began cross-dressing regularly—the experience of seeing and imagining myself as a girl and later as a woman was nearly always erotic for me. (110)

> At 6 years old, I wanted to be a girl. I loved to go through the Sears catalogue and wish I could wear all the pretty clothes the little girls were wearing. Every night when I went to bed, I'd dream about how the world stopped and I could go into stores and pick out all the pretty clothes and wear them. I wore my mother's clothes whenever I could without being caught. As a teenager, I would wear women's panties and masturbate into them. (111)

> I wanted to be a girl since age 5 or 6. I dressed in my sister's clothes and somehow got away with it. As I reached puberty, my frustration at not being able to do anything about the physical changes was overwhelming. Although my desires clearly did not begin as sexual, sex certainly became the focus. (112)

The first of the four narrative excerpts above is notable for its report of the development of male hero fantasies between ages 7 and 12 that temporarily pushed aside the informant's earlier cross-gender fantasies. This example illustrates that the existence of occasional or even frequent cross-gender fantasies during childhood does not necessarily imply the existence of a strong and persistent cross-gender identity during childhood.

Other Patterns of Onset of Cross-Gender Behavior and Erotic Feelings

One informant recalled the onset of cross-gender fantasies in later childhood, with associated erotic feelings developing just before or at puberty:

> The idea of "becoming a woman"—that is, being changed physically—was indeed a source of sexual stimulation for me. I remember this starting in my pre-teen years. Before that, I remember longing to be a girl, but without any distinctly sexual feelings; this I can recall to about age 9. (113)

Two others recalled the onset of cross-gender fantasies or cross-dressing in childhood, but no associated erotic feelings until well into adulthood:

> When I cross-dressed, as a child and growing up, not once did I feel sexual arousal—that is, until I married and began having intercourse with the woman who is now my ex-wife. When I dressed, a sense of "rightness" overtook me, a feeling of much more completeness than existed while dressed in my male role. (114)

> I am almost 100% sure that my desire to be a woman is more established than autogynephilia, which I also recognize in myself. The former has been rather stable since the age of 6, whereas I don't recall any remotely autogynephilic fantasies before the age of 20. (084)

In interpreting histories like these, it is useful to recall that inaccurate denial of autogynephilic sexual arousal by persons who are known or presumed to be autogynephilic is a well-documented phenomenon (Blanchard et al., 1986; Zucker et al., 2012).

The statement by the last informant that her desire to be a woman had been "rather stable since the age of 6" deserves comment. It seems quite possible that her desire to be a woman had continued *in some form*, perhaps continuously but more probably intermittently, until she submitted her narrative at age 32. Elsewhere in her narrative, she stated that she had then been living as a woman for 4 years, so she probably had a strong and persistent cross-gender (female) identity at that time. I would conjecture (but obviously cannot know) that she probably did not have a strong and persistent cross-gender identity at age 6; for example, I doubt that she had yet taken a female name. If my conjecture is correct, her claim that her desire to be a woman had been "stable" over the intervening 26 years would constitute a significant exaggeration.

One should not read too much into cross-gender wishes in early childhood. It is not uncommon for young boys to occasionally express the wish to be the opposite sex, but most boys who do so do not develop strong, persistent cross-gender identities in adulthood. Friedrich et al. (1991) observed that about 7% of 2-to-6-year-old boys and about 2% of 7-to-12-year-old boys had "talked about wanting to be the opposite sex" at least occasionally during the previous 6 months, according to their mothers or female caregivers. Friedrich et al. (1998) subsequently found that about 6% of 2-to-5-year-old boys and about 4% of 6-to-9-year-old boys had expressed the wish to be the opposite sex occasionally or more often during the previous 6 months. Goldman and Goldman (1982) observed that 8% of 5-year-old boys and 13% of 7-year-old boys from their North American sample would choose to be a girl rather than a boy. Studies of boys in the Netherlands and Belgium have revealed slightly higher figures: Friedrich, Sandfort, Oostveen and Cohen-Kettenis (2000) observed that, in two different groups of Dutch children, about 10% of 2-to-6-year-old boys and about 15% of 4-to-6-year-old boys had at least occasionally talked about wanting to be the opposite sex during the previous 6 months, according to reports by their mothers. In a study of Dutch and Belgian children, Sandfort and Cohen-Kettenis (2000) found that about 10% of 0-to-11-year-old boys (about three-quarters of whom were between 2 and 6 years old) had expressed the wish to be the opposite sex at least occasionally in the past 6 months. Many heterosexual cross-dressing men who have no desire to be women also retrospectively report cross-gender wishes during childhood: Buhrich and Beaumont (1981) found that 8% of American cross-dressers and 26% of Australian cross-dressers who reported no desire to be women had "often" wished to have been born a girl between ages 6 and 12 years.

Wishing at times to be a girl, however, is not the same as having a strong and persistent cross-gender (female) identity. Strong, persistent cross-gender identities usually develop many years or decades after the onset of erotic cross-dressing in nonhomosexual men and are preceded by episodes of complete cross-dressing, public self-presentation as a woman, and adopting a feminine name (Docter, 1988). The last of these is "the most explicit statement that a cross-gender identity has emerged"

(Docter, 1988, p. 209). Based on his studies of nonhomosexual MtF transsexuals and other nonhomosexual cross-dressing men, Docter observed that:

> Among our subjects, 79% did not appear in public cross dressed prior to age 20; at that time, most of the subjects had already had several years of experience with cross dressing. The average number of years of practice with cross dressing prior to owning a full feminine outfit was 15. The average number of years of practice with cross dressing prior to adoption of a feminine name was 21. Again, we have factual evidence indicative of the considerable time required for the development of the cross-gender identity. (p. 209)

Boys who are destined to be nonhomosexual or autogynephilic MtF transsexuals often experience episodic, unsustained cross-gender wishes and fantasies in early childhood but rarely, if ever, develop strong, persistent cross-gender identities that can act as the driving force for a decision to seek or undergo sex reassignment until they reach young adulthood. In contrast, boys who are destined to be homosexual MtF transsexuals usually experience sustained cross-gender wishes and fantasies in early childhood and often meet full diagnostic criteria for GID in childhood; their adult transsexualism is often merely a continuation of their childhood GID (Cohen-Kettenis & Pfäfflin, 2003). Childhood cross-gender wishes and fantasies in boys who are destined to be autogynephilic MtF transsexuals are important primarily because they constitute one of the earliest indications of an autogynephilic sexual orientation; I will discuss this concept in detail in Chap. 10.

Gender Expression in Childhood and Adulthood

Many boys without known gender identity issues sometimes play with traditional girl's toys during early childhood, and some express a preference for girls rather than boys as friends or playmates or occasionally take female roles in fantasy play. Friedrich et al. (1991) observed that about 63% of 2-to-6-year-old boys and about 31% of 7-to-12-year-old boys had played with girl's toys at least occasionally during the previous 6 months, according to their mothers or female caregivers. Friedrich et al. (1998) similarly found that about 57% of 2-to-5-year-old boys and about 55% of 6-to-9-year-old boys had played with girl's toys occasionally or more often during the previous 6 months. Sandfort and Cohen-Kettenis (2000) reported that about 60% of 0-to-11-year-old boys (most between ages 2 and 6 years) in the Netherlands and Belgium had played with girl's toys at least occasionally during the past 6 months. Goldman and Goldman (1982) observed that 23% of 5-year-old boys and 32% of 7-year-old boys from a North American sample would choose a girl rather than a boy as a friend. Several studies (Friedrich et al., 1991, 1998; Sandfort & Cohen-Kettenis, 2000) have demonstrated that between 17% and 20% of boys at least occasionally "pretend to be the opposite sex while playing" during early childhood.

There is disagreement in the scientific literature about whether the childhood behaviors and interests of autogynephilic transsexuals are usually male typical—which would include the possibility of at least occasional play with girl's toys or choice of female friends or female roles in fantasy play, as described above—or whether the behaviors and interests of autogynephilic transsexuals are sometimes or often female typical. Observations by some researchers (e.g., Blanchard, 1990; Whitam, 1987, 1997) support the former point of view, but observations by other investigators support the latter. For example, Buhrich and McConaghy (1977a) found that most members of a sample of 12 MtF transsexuals with a history of fetishistic cross-dressing reported that, during childhood, they avoided rough-and-tumble play, preferred girls' company and games, and had been called "sissy" at school.

Observations by Doorn et al. (1994) provide the strongest support for the idea that many late-onset MtF transsexuals (LOTs; most of whom are nonhomosexual and putatively autogynephilic) and even some transvestites (TVs) display female-typical preferences in childhood. Note that all of Doorn et al.'s data concerning childhood cross-gender behaviors involved informants' *preferences*, not actual behaviors (i.e., "preference for female toys," rather than "usually played with female toys"). Doorn et al. found that roughly one-quarter to one-third of LOTs reported that they preferred female-typical toys and games and female playmates during childhood and that roughly 15% of TVs reported that they preferred female playmates (p. 191); these figures were substantially higher than those reported by male control subjects. Additional percentages of LOTs and TVs reported combinations of female-typical and male-typical preferences in childhood. Doorn et al. argued that the higher than expected prevalence of self-reported female-typical preferences during childhood in these groups required a reevaluation of Docter's (1988) theory about the late-life development of cross-gender identities in LOTs and TVs:

> The major finding is that LOTs and, to a lesser degree, TVs show much more feminine behavior in their early years than expected. Doctor's [sic] theory is therefore only applicable to a small proportion of the LOTs and to most, but clearly not all TVs. Many of the LOTs and an important proportion of the TVs show signs of clearly developing feminine gender identity aspects in early childhood. (p. 196)

Once again, I would note that Doorn et al.'s informants reported more female-typical preferences than expected—not necessarily more female-typical behaviors.

A crucial issue in interpreting the Doorn et al. (1994) data is whether the retrospective reports by late-onset MtF transsexuals and transvestites concerning female-typical preferences in childhood are accurate or not. One should bear in mind that Walworth (1997) found that "preferring girls' games and toys as a child" (p. 359) was one of the most frequent areas in which MtF transsexuals reported having lied to or misled their psychotherapists. Moreover, Blanchard, Clemmensen, et al. (1985) observed a significant positive correlation between socially desirable response style and self-reports of female-typical interests and behaviors during childhood in a group of heterosexual male gender patients. Finally, as previously noted in Chap. 3, many experienced clinicians (e.g., Bancroft, 1972; Fisk, 1974; Lukianowicz, 1959; Sørensen & Hertoft, 1980) have observed that MtF transsexuals often distort their histories to make them conform more closely to accepted stereotypes about MtF transsexualism. Consequently, I believe that both the data and the conclusions reported by Doorn et al. should be interpreted with a high degree of skepticism. One possible explanation of the data is that many of the LOT and TV participants who reported female-typical preferences in childhood might have displayed behaviors that were far more male typical than their recalled preferences would imply.

In the current study, most informants who described their gender expression in childhood or adulthood denied effeminacy or female-typical interests or behaviors. There were some clear exceptions, however.

Male-Typical Interests and Behaviors in Childhood and Adulthood

Several informants reported that their childhood interests and behaviors had been male typical and that they had never been effeminate. Here are some representative accounts:

> As a child, riding my bike and playing with robots and guns and blowing up toy cars was more interesting to me than playing with dolls and dress-ups. Clothes and fashion never really interested me. (004)

> I was never effeminate. I wasn't into dolls or girl's play, and I enjoyed sport and was okay, if not good, at it. I liked music and drawing and collecting and gemstones and many non-gender-specific things, too. (115)

> I was never effeminate, although I often wished I was in order to "validate" my desire to be a woman. As a young male, I was an athlete, served in the military, and became a husband and father. (110)

Other informants reported that, although most of their interests and behaviors were male typical, they felt different from other boys in certain ways, especially in their lack of interest in or aptitude for team sports:

> Growing up, I never fit in well with other boys and was not into sports or many other boyish things. But at the same time, I also preferred male toys like cars, guns, trains, etc. I was not confused about my gender. (023)

> I was not successfully masculine. In a village culture that defined boyhood around baseball, I was hopeless at hitting, throwing, and catching. But I did try to be a boy, constructing my alternative masculinity around the outdoors in the woods surrounding the village, water-skiing, cross-country running, and becoming cadet lieutenant-colonel at the military high school I attended. (116)

It is surprising that a boy who became cadet lieutenant-colonel at his military high school and was an avid water-skier and cross-country runner would conclude he was "not successfully masculine" simply because he was not proficient at baseball. Green (2008) observed that MtF transsexuals sometimes hold stereotyped views of masculinity and femininity and are apt to conclude that, if they deviate from the masculine stereotype in any way, they cannot really be men. Green gave the example of a gender dysphoric patient who concluded he was transsexual in part because he was not interested in cars and football. Although Green makes an important point, another explanation might be that autogynephilic men who are unremarkably masculine but experience a strong and seemingly inexplicable desire to be female might be eager to find evidence, however insubstantial, of psychological femininity or unmasculinity that would help them make sense of their cross-gender wishes.

Other informants' narratives discussed only their adult interests and behaviors, which they usually described as male typical:

> I have an advanced degree in chemistry and have led a successful life as a male. I grew up as a normal male and I played a wide range of sports in both high school and college. I still enjoy outdoor activities and lead a rather active life. (075)

> I am a 49-year-old who has been on and off hormones many times. I am the classic male: Naval Academy, US Marine Corps, weightlifter, etc. (117)

> I am a 47-year-old male, athletic and muscularly built. I played college sports. I am an avid outdoorsman and love to hunt and fish. (105)

One informant observed that she, like other MtF transsexuals of her acquaintance, had made typically masculine occupational choices:

> I might have had thoughts of being a girl at a very young age, but that didn't keep me from being a very good athlete and later a Navy pilot. I personally know 3 fighter pilots other than myself who are postoperative transsexuals. My roommate is a 64-year-old postop who was once a semi-pro baseball player and has a doctorate in chemistry. (118)

Male- and Female-Typical Interests and Behaviors in Childhood

A few informants reported a combination of male- and female-typical interests and behaviors during childhood:

> I had friends of both sexes. I would have been a tomboy if I was a girl. My sister was my best friend, and we played with dolls and girlish fantasy games, but I also played cowboys and softball and ran around the badlands with my boy friends. (119)

> In my early childhood and when I first went to school, I preferred the company of girls and played "girly" games regularly with neighbors and my female cousins. I liked dolls and although I never had anything much more than a teddy myself, I used to play with them, especially in bed. After a couple of years of primary school, I was sent to an all-boys school. I learned to act the part eventually, never showing my feminine side at school or in the company of boys. It became difficult for me to play with girls in this environment and I concentrated my creative side on model railways and airplanes alone. I hated sports and did my best to avoid rough playground games. Instead I concentrated on softer activities such as swimming, chess, and painting. (120)

Although these histories do mention a few feminine interests and behaviors, they seem otherwise ordinary in most respects and similar to what many men without gender dysphoria might report.

Female-Typical Interests and Behaviors in Childhood

A few informants described primarily female-typical interests and behaviors in childhood, although their narratives did not state whether these persisted into adolescence or adulthood:

> I do not conform to the portrayal of standard characteristics of autogynephiles, as I was feminine as a child. (121)

> I didn't fit in with boys. I loathed sports and fighting or war-related role playing. I was quite drawn to trying on my mother's and sister's things, including clothes, makeup, perfume, and jewelry. My favorite toys were all my sisters'—the dolls and the easy bake oven. (122)

> Throughout my childhood, I always engaged in behaviors and activities which have been considered feminine. All of my friends were female up until about the age of ten, when pressure from peer groups caused me to branch out. (095)

> At a very young age, I would play pretend games and hide and go seek with neighborhood girls my age. I also had a couple of dolls as a young child. (080)

> I always preferred dolls and frilly things to the toys my parents wanted to buy me. When I was really small, 4–6 years old, I would love to go to my grandparents' house and I would play with the dolls she had. She also had a small sewing machine that I would try to use. (089)

Another informant described some female-typical interests and behaviors in passing, without saying whether or not they were representative of her ordinary day-to-day childhood experiences:

> I look back on my past, when I was five and wearing perfume, or making pretty necklaces out of colored beads, or arranging flowers, or when I was 7 and volunteering to play "Mother Goose" in the school play. (123)

In my clinical practice, I not uncommonly elicit histories like these from nonhomosexual gender dysphoric male patients. In many cases, the feminine behaviors in question turn out to be a few isolated and unrepresentative episodes (e.g., "For a time my closest playmate was a girl"—for 2 months one summer; "When I was 6, I used to play with dolls"—on three or four separate occasions). These isolated episodes of feminine behavior nevertheless feel quite meaningful to the men who experienced them. I almost never get the sense that these patients are trying to mislead me by portraying these childhood episodes as more representative than they genuinely are. Instead, I believe that these patients are desperately trying to make sense of their powerful cross-gender wishes and are grasping at straws in an effort to find evidence of childhood femininity that might help to explain their adult feelings.

Male-Typical Versus Female-Typical Occupational Choices in Adulthood

Nonhomosexual MtF transsexuals rarely choose occupations that are typically preferred by women; their career choices are usually unremarkably masculine. As Whitam (1987) observed, "Heterosexual transvestites and trans-sexuals [sic] tend to have traditionally masculine occupations such as engineer, mechanic, salesman, or produce manager" (p. 198). The limited data provided by the transsexual informants was generally consistent with this observation.

Only 24 (9.6%) of the 249 transsexual informants reported their occupation. Although these 24 informants cannot be assumed to constitute a representative sample, it is notable that most of them reported occupations preferred by men more than by women. The reported occupations, with the number of informants reporting each, were:

- 4 physicians (1 psychiatrist, 1 surgeon, 2 unspecified)
- 4 military service members (1 Marine, 1 Navy pilot, 1 unspecified Navy, 1 unspecified)
- 3 computer professionals (2 software developers, 1 programmer)
- 3 engineers (1 electrical, 1 mechanical, 1 unspecified)
- 2 business managers
- 2 firefighters
- 1 airline pilot
- 1 attorney
- 1 experimental psychologist
- 1 truck driver
- 1 factory worker
- 1 medical technologist

Lippa (2002) provided gender preference data for 50 different occupations, including 8 of the 12 listed above. Fourteen of the 24 informants reported occupations that men prefer significantly more than women according to Lippa's data (military service member, computer professional, engineer, business manager, airline pilot, and attorney). Four of the 24 reported an occupation that men and women prefer about equally (physician). Only 1 reported an occupation that women prefer significantly more than men (psychologist). The remaining 5 informants reported an occupation not listed by Lippa, but 3 of these—the 2 firefighters and 1 truck driver—chose occupations that Govier and Feldman (1999) described as male typical. Eight of the 24 informants—the engineers, military service members, and pilot—reported occupations that were among the five most strongly preferred by men over women, according to Lippa's data.

Why do so many autogynephilic transsexuals decide to pursue male-typical occupations? Brown (1988) proposed that some MtF transsexuals go through a "hypermasculine phase of transsexual development" (p. 527), during which they choose stereotypically masculine or hypermasculine occupations (e.g., military service) in a last-ditch attempt to suppress or eliminate their feminine personality traits. This could account, at least in part, for the male-typical occupations that many nonhomosexual MtF transsexuals choose. Some MtF transsexuals would probably be inclined to offer this socially acceptable explanation to their therapists—and some therapists would probably uncritically accept it. But a more parsimonious and more plausible explanation—albeit a less socially acceptable one—is that nonhomosexual MtF transsexuals choose male-typical occupations primarily because they genuinely prefer them. For example, I have heard too many MtF transsexuals describe with relish their enjoyment of firing automatic weapons, blowing things up during demolition training, practicing hand-to-hand combat skills, and flying jet fighters in real or simulated combat to believe that they chose military service primarily to suppress their intrinsic femininity. In my experience, the occupational choices of nonhomosexual MtF transsexuals are at least as male typical as those of nontranssexual men. The occupations of the last 10 nonhomosexual MtF clients I have seen in my practice included 3 information technology professionals, 2 aircraft assembly technicians, 1 physicist, 1 security guard, 1 shipyard worker, 1 loss-recovery specialist, and 1 manufacturer's representative in hardware sales.

Applicability of the "Woman Trapped in a Man's Body" Trope

As noted earlier, the description of pretransition MtF transsexuals as "women trapped in men's bodies" connotes a particular developmental history: It implies that MtF transsexuals will have developed the same psychological and behavioral characteristics that are typical of natal women. For rhetorical purposes, I have sometimes described autogynephilic transsexuals as "men trapped in men's bodies" (Lawrence, 1998), which connotes a different developmental history: It implies that autogynephilic transsexuals will have developed psychological and behavioral characteristics that are typical of other heterosexual men, except in those areas that reflect their autogynephilic sexual orientations. Many informants spontaneously commented on the applicability of either the original trope or my counter-trope.

Five informants invoked the original trope or something close to it. Three of them provided little or no explanation or qualification:

> I always felt like a girl trapped in a man's body. (124)

> I wanted to feel a vagina between my legs as I masturbated instead of a penis. I view this as a supremely normal thought for a girl trapped in the body of a male. (125)

> I have not always felt like a woman trapped in a man's body: It is only now starting to feel close to that. (126)

Two other informants who also invoked the original trope offered longer, more complicated explanations of their feelings. I will present excerpts from their narratives in Chap. 10.

Four informants thought that my revised version of the trope described them accurately; here are two of their comments:

> I now realize that I am a "man trapped inside a man's body." (014)

> For me, there's a strong sexual compulsion to look female. I am a man trapped in a man's body. (127)

Nine other informants rejected the original description without proposing an alternative. Here are a few representative examples of their comments:

> I have never felt like a woman trapped in a male body. (128)

> I have never regarded myself as a "woman trapped in a man's body." (129)

> I don't really feel like a woman trapped in a man's body. (108)

Two others who rejected the original trope distinguished between the belief that one *is* a woman and the *desire to be* a woman; the latter was what they experienced.

> I never felt like I was "a woman trapped in a man's body" but instead just wished I were a girl. (130)

> The best phrase to describe my belief about myself is that "I desire (or need) to be a woman with all my heart, in every way," as opposed to feeling "I have always been a woman." (042)

The distinction that the last two informants made is important but is one that autogynephilic transsexuals too often fail to make.

Yet another informant poignantly expressed her doubts about the accuracy of the original description in her answer to a rhetorical question:

> I really want to be a woman with breasts and a vagina. I guess I'll have to accept everything else that goes with it. Is this the same as feeling like I am a "woman trapped in a man's body"? Possibly not. (068)

Nine other informants provided their own variations on the original trope; some of the more instructive ones are presented below. Two informants described themselves as lesbians trapped in men's bodies:

> I feel like I am a lesbian trapped in a man's body, since I have intense sexual desires for women and also want to be a woman myself. (131)

> I knew I was a lesbian trapped in a male body by the time I was 13. (132)

Presumably the implication here was that the informants felt like typical women except that they were attracted to females. Other informants provided their own unique descriptive variations:

> Frankly, most of us are not far from being men trapped in men's bodies. I would tweak that a bit and suggest maybe tomboys trapped in men's bodies. (025)

> I do not feel as if I am a woman trapped in a man's body. Rather, I have always felt more of a hermaphrodite. I am neither solely male nor female, but both. (022)

Still other informants stated or implied that the "wrong body" metaphor was indeed applicable to them, even if the original trope was not:

> I have had the persistent feeling that I am trapped in the wrong body, that the gentleness of my mind and spirit and my creative nature could never be free in this male body. (095)

> I've very rarely felt like a "woman trapped in a man's body," but I do feel like I should be a woman, and there is an erotic component to that feeling. (067)

> I want to become what I have so deeply wished to be: a human in a female body. (081)

Two informants admitted that they considered it prudent to at least appear to personify the original trope, whether or not it was genuinely accurate:

> I am conducting myself like the standard vanilla "woman trapped in a man's body," and the prospect of my carrying out a successful transition, including changing gender in my present job, seems to be good. (047)

> My "girl next door" image is simply a ploy for minimizing the impact of my intended transition and for winning support by appearing to be a genuine case of a "girl in a man's body." (053)

I consider the informants' overall degree of skepticism about the original trope to be an encouraging sign. In my opinion, there is an off-putting hubris about autogynephilic transsexuals who describe themselves as women in men's bodies. We have not been raised as women, we have never experienced female physiology or embodiment, and we have benefitted from male privilege throughout our entire lives; to assert that we are, in effect, women like any other natal women seems to me to represent both lack of insight and remarkable insensitivity. Before undergoing sex reassignment, we autogynephilic transsexuals are not women: We are only men who want to become women. If we live as women and attempt to conduct ourselves recognizably as women, I believe we earn the right to call ourselves women, but we should nevertheless be quick to acknowledge that our womanhood is atypical. In short, it behooves us to display and feel a little humility. We autogynephilic transsexuals generally choose other women as partners (if we find partners at all) and often live our posttransition lives, by choice or necessity, primarily in the company of other women. If we claim to be other than what we truly are, we risk alienating the women upon whom we are likely to depend for friendship, support, love—and ongoing education in how to better emulate them.

Autogynephilia Over the Life Course and After SRS

Men's sexual orientations tend to be stable over the course of their lives. If autogynephilia is a sexual orientation, then one would predict that its manifestations—sexual arousal from, attraction to, and love for the idea or reality of resembling a female—would continue over the life course for most or all autogynephilic transsexuals, including after SRS.

Many transsexual and transgender persons who acknowledge a history of autogynephilic arousal report that their autogynephilic feelings have continued throughout their lives; others, however, state that their autogynephilic feelings have waned or disappeared. Nuttbrock, Bockting, Mason, et al. (2011) examined one form of autogynephilia, transvestic fetishism (TF), in a large group of MtF transgender participants. Among 58 nominally heterosexual participants who acknowledged a history of TF, 49 (84%) reported that their TF was "lifecourse persistent"; among 65 nominally bisexual participants who acknowledged TF, however, only 43 (66%) reported lifecourse persistent TF. Most participants in both groups appeared to have been in their 40s or 50s when surveyed. In a survey of 232 MtF transsexuals who had completed SRS and were mostly nonhomosexual, I observed that 84% of participants reported having experienced one or more episodes of autogynephilic arousal before SRS but only 44% reported having done so after SRS (Lawrence, 2005). In interpreting these figures, it is important to remember that autogynephilic arousal is probably greatly underreported, for the reasons explained in Chap. 1.

In the current study, many informants stated that they had continued to experience autogynephilic arousal throughout their lives, including after SRS. There were exceptions, but they were uncommon.

Continuation of Autogynephilic Arousal over the Life Course

Many informants unequivocally stated that their experience of autogynephilic arousal had been a lifelong phenomenon.

> I am in my 60s. I have suffered with autogynephilia since I first became aware of my feelings at age 4. Cross-dressing still arouses me. (109)

> I am a 52-year-old heterosexual male. From about age 12 or 13, the idea of being able to wear women's clothes and present and live as a woman was an amazing sexual turn-on, and it remains so to this day. (133)

> I've been experiencing autogynephilia since the first time that I tried on my mother's nightgowns and wigs. I'm now a pre-op transsexual taking hormones, and nothing has changed. As a man, I had to fantasize that I was a woman to get excited sexually. Now, as a female, I get aroused at times by the thought of just being female. (134)

> At age 50, the erotic aspects of my condition have subsided somewhat. I am still aroused by the thought of having a female body, but the requirement to masturbate has all but disappeared. (005)

> I am in my 60s. Imagining myself a woman has always been sensually pleasurable, whether accompanied by climax or not. I would like to say the arousal and pleasure are now gone or irrelevant, but I would be lying. There is still deep pleasure that is sexual and compelling. There is an imagination of myself as the object of my own desire. (135)

Continuation of Autogynephilic Arousal After Sex Reassignment

In my original solicitation, I specifically invited potential informants to comment on whether autogynephilic arousal had continued after SRS. Several informants addressed this issue, and most who did stated that autogynephilic erotic arousal had indeed continued following SRS:

> Wearing women's clothing and feminizing my body has always been sexually exciting for me, even after SRS. It was and still is sexually exciting for me to have female body functions. (061)

> I am 7 months postoperative. I was extremely autogynephilic. My fantasies were of my feminization, which still continue, despite not having testosterone. (136)

> I am 6 months postop now, and at 46 years old, still get sexually aroused when I think of the entire transformation that I just completed. (132)

> I am a 41-year-old postoperative transsexual. I received my surgery about 2 years ago. I admit that I have many sexual fantasies about being female and having a female body, a lifelong dream for me. I am not ashamed that I am sexually turned on by being female now. (069)

> I am a 31-year-old MtF post-op. After starting hormone therapy and living in female role for a while, the fantasies continued like they always had, only now there was more satisfaction from having them. (072)

> I am nearly 4 years post-op. The concept of autogynephilia helped provide an understanding of my behavior. Sex is a powerful force for some of us, and certainly me. Even now, I embrace my autogynephilic fantasies as part of my sexuality, which is alive and very well. (079)

Others, however, reported that feelings of autogynephilic erotic arousal had become less frequent or intense after SRS, although they still occurred periodically.

> Several years after SRS, I still have erotic feelings about being female, although they are not nearly so compelling as in the old days. But sometimes I'll look in the mirror as I head out to work and feel a flush of excitement over who I have become. (059)

> I underwent SRS 22 years ago. Preoperatively, I had some sexual arousal when wearing women's clothes; postoperatively, I have felt arousal in the vulva when wearing lingerie. Preoperatively, when I was fantasizing myself to be a woman with a vagina, I was strongly sexually aroused and got an orgasm. Most of the preoperative feelings of arousal stopped gradually after SRS. The urges diminished in intensity but are still present. (137)

> There have been times when I was totally turned on by the whole experience of becoming a woman, but mainly it has been more a sense of happiness and peace, as I can now relax and be myself. But I have had moments where I have had a total orgasmic rush because of the transformation in myself and my body. In self-pleasuring, I do think about what I have done at times and that does sexually excite me, I must admit. (086)

> I first fantasized about being a girl at an early age. In my teens, I behaved like a typical transvestite, cross-dressing and masturbating in private. I also had the usual forced feminization fantasies, so typical of transvestites, and now I realize, transsexuals, too. Now, a year postop at age 41, I feel great about it all. Yet, I am far from a typical woman. Sexually, I still get aroused by forced feminization fantasies and being the woman among men. (115)

I will say more about forced feminization fantasies, which were mentioned by the last informant, in Chap. 9.

Some informants reported that arousal to the thought or image of being female continued to occur in the context of masturbation later in life and that autogynephilic fantasies were sometimes necessary for orgasm after SRS:

> During puberty, I began to fantasize about physically being a girl, and the thought of this aroused me. I went full-time at age 41 and had SRS at age 43. Even though I only rarely masturbate now, I typically do so while looking at myself in the mirror. I get off on my appearance. (096)

> I'm 3 years postoperative. Many of my sexual fantasies as a kid were feminization fantasies. I'm still wired the same way. I very often need those fantasies to achieve orgasm. (050)

One informant observed that during and after sex reassignment, engaging in and observing the results of self-feminization resulted in a feeling of "warmth" that was hard to distinguish from the feeling of sexual arousal:

> I am 46 years old, 23 years postoperative. The occasion of my first estrogen injection was a real high. I was jubilant and warm all over. I don't think that it was entirely hormonal. The first week after surgery was almost manic in its happiness. Standing naked in front of a mirror was all that was necessary to renew the warmth that I felt. I have been sexually aroused since surgery and would readily admit that the sensation is indistinguishable from the above mentioned warmth. (138)

The observation that autogynephilic arousal sometimes, perhaps often, persists after SRS is of theoretical interest for at least two reasons. First, this observation supports—or is at least consistent with—the theory that autogynephilia is (or resembles) a sexual orientation. Second, this observation calls into question an alternative explanation of autogynephilia that has been proposed by some critics of Blanchard's theory. This explanation asserts that autogynephilia is merely an epiphenomenon that emerges when males who have female gender identities and incongruent male bodies fantasize about having female bodies in order to have satisfying sexual experiences. Serano (2010) summarized this explanation:

> It makes sense that pretransition transsexuals (whose gender identity is discordant with their physical sex) might imagine themselves inhabiting the "right" body in their sexual fantasies and during their sexual experiences with other people. Indeed, critics of autogynephilia theory have argued that such sex embodiment fantasies appear to be an obvious coping mechanism for pretransition transsexuals. (p. 184)

This alternative explanation implies, however, that autogynephilic arousal should disappear after hormone therapy and SRS have largely corrected the incongruence between embodiment and gender identity that MtF transsexuals experience. The observation that autogynephilic arousal sometimes, perhaps often, persists after SRS suggests that Serano's explanation has limited, if any, ability to account for autogynephilic transsexualism.

Cessation of Autogynephilic Arousal After SRS

One informant reported that, after completion of SRS, she no longer experienced autogynephilic arousal. She submitted her narrative only 1 month after SRS, however.

> I am 47 years old, post-operative by 1 month, and clearly identify with the feelings you describe. I was aware that something like autogynephilia could be driving me and I made sure that I could function in a female body before committing to my surgery. I never have these kind of thoughts now. (139)

To put her report in perspective, consider this narrative from an informant who described revisiting her earlier autogynephilic fantasies after undergoing SRS one year earlier:

> About a year after SRS, I realized that I'd lost touch with my sexuality and I wanted to reclaim it. I revisited old thoughts and fantasies and ultimately found that some of those fires still burned. To make it happen, I had to "turn up the heat," so to speak, and add intensity and violence to them. I still like to play with some of the old fantasies, but they are much more gentle and loving now. (059)

In my professional practice, I have sometimes been consulted by autogynephilic transsexuals who have been unsuccessful in achieving orgasm after SRS. Among other things, I often advise these clients to experiment with using the same autogynephilic fantasies they found exciting prior to SRS. In many cases, resurrecting their earlier autogynephilic fantasies facilitates high levels of erotic arousal and eventually enables clients to achieve orgasm. In my first review article on autogynephilia (Lawrence, 1998), I recounted the case of a MtF transsexual friend of mine—now a prominent transsexual activist and opponent of the theory of autogynephilia—who had for a time been unable to achieve orgasm following SRS but eventually had succeeded with the help of fantasies of forced feminization.

Concluding Comments on Developmental History

The narrative excerpts presented in this chapter demonstrate that, among autogynephilic transsexuals, autogynephilic erotic arousal not uncommonly begins in early childhood, usually is evident by the time of adolescence, and often continues throughout life, including after SRS. The excerpts also demonstrate that significant numbers of autogynephilic transsexuals report that they were not effeminate in childhood or adulthood but were instead unremarkably masculine in their interests and behaviors, even though they intensely desired to make their bodies resemble women's bodies and live and be recognized as women.

Are (or were) nearly all autogynephilic transsexuals unremarkably masculine men whose gender dysphoria was simply an outgrowth of their paraphilic desire to turn their bodies into facsimiles of women's bodies? I believe that the narratives presented in this chapter support that interpretation, but they obviously cannot settle the issue. The value of these narratives does not lie in their ability to prove or disprove any theoretical proposition, but in their capacity to inform the decisions that severely gender dysphoric autogynephilic men face.

The narratives in this chapter are important because they demonstrate that some autogynephilic transsexuals truly are, by their own account, "men trapped in men's bodies": unremarkably masculine men who experience the paraphilic wish to have women's bodies—and who sometimes overcome the skepticism of the psychiatric establishment and many of their peers to successfully complete sex reassignment and lead happier lives thereafter (Lawrence, 2003). This information is likely to be of significant value to severely gender dysphoric autogynephilic men who are considering sex reassignment but feel deterred by the realization that they lack intrinsic femininity. These men may or may not eventually decide that sex reassignment is the best option available to them, but they will be in a better position to seriously consider this option if they realize that they are neither unique nor unusual—except, perhaps, in being unusually honest.

Chapter 6
Manifestations of Autogynephilia

Four Main Types of Autogynephilia

Blanchard (1991) described four distinct types or categories of autogynephilic fantasies and behaviors: *transvestic* (involving wearing women's apparel), *anatomic* (involving possessing female anatomic features), *physiologic* (involving having female physiologic functions), and *behavioral* (involving engaging in stereotypically feminine behavior). Yet another type is *partial* autogynephilia (Blanchard, 1993a, 1993b)—more precisely, *partial anatomic* autogynephilia—in which individuals desire to have only partial, not complete, female anatomy. The most prevalent type of partial autogynephilia involves the desire to have women's breasts but no desire to have female genitals. It is debatable whether individuals who experience this type of partial autogynephilia should be considered transsexual; for purposes of this study, I have chosen to categorize them as nontranssexual. Chapter 11 includes several narrative excerpts by informants who experienced partial autogynephilia.

The four types of autogynephilia that Blanchard described are conceptually useful but are not mutually exclusive. Some autogynephilic fantasies and behaviors could easily be classified under more than one category; for example, wearing a menstrual pad could be considered a manifestation of transvestic, behavioral, or physiologic autogynephilia, depending on its meaning to the person wearing it. The various types of autogynephilia also tend to co-occur; in particular, most individuals who experience anatomic autogynephilia also experience transvestic and behavioral autogynephilia. There are some notable exceptions to this pattern, however: A few informants who reported anatomic autogynephilia denied any desire to engage in female-typical behaviors or to live in a female-typical gender role.

One particular type of behavioral autogynephilia, the act or fantasy of engaging in sexual activity with a man as a woman (a manifestation of *autogynephilic interpersonal fantasy;* Blanchard, 1989b) is both highly prevalent and of particular theoretical and clinical significance; it will be considered separately in Chap. 8.

A.A. Lawrence, *Men Trapped in Men's Bodies: Narratives of Autogynephilic Transsexualism*, Focus on Sexuality Research, DOI 10.1007/978-1-4614-5182-2_6,

Transvestic Autogynephilia

Transvestic autogynephilia is the most prevalent type of autogynephilia; almost all autogynephilic males probably experience it. Most informants acknowledged or alluded to transvestic autogynephilia in their narratives. The narrative excerpts in this section illustrate important general principles about transvestic autogynephilia, are noteworthy or unusual, or emphasize fetishistic elements not generally associated with MtF transsexualism.

Several informants reported that they favored the kinds of apparel—lingerie, short skirts, high heels, etc.—that men generally find sexually alluring when worn by women and that are stereotypically associated with transvestic fetishism. Here are three representative accounts:

> I am a transgender woman currently undergoing estrogen treatment. The fact that my body is feminizing is both a source of arousal and joy. My earlier "closet" phase involved the ritual of dressing as a normal woman: lingerie, nylons, dresses, shoes, etc., and applying full makeup and perfume and becoming so turned-on by my femme image in the mirror that the ritual often terminated in masturbation. (140)

> I am 58 years old and a preoperative MtF transsexual. I began crossdressing when I was about age 7. I was especially sexually aroused wearing girdles and nylon stockings. By my mid-20s, I had very strong desires to dress as a female on a full-time basis and to attract attention as a sexy, feminine woman. I have worn sexy feminine fashions, especially bras, lingerie, pantyhose, short dresses, lace fashions, mini-skirts, high heels, etc., at home since my mid-20s. Wearing sexy lingerie, a bra, a girdle with nylon stockings or sensuous sheer pantyhose, and high heels, imagining myself as a female, still often sexually arouses me, leading to an erection, masturbation, and orgasm. (141)

> I am a 44-year-old male. My counselor classifies me as a transsexual and has offered to refer me for hormone therapy. In high school, I cross-dressed in my mom's clothes and can't deny the arousal. In college and law school, under the guise of being a hippie, I wore long hair, women's jeans, and women's T-shirts. I married, and my cross-dressing became the secretive wearing of my wife's clothes, always in front of a mirror. It was arousing. Presently I cross-dress on a limited basis, and it's still arousing. When I am aroused by a woman, it feels good. But cross-dressing adds so much more: In front of a mirror, it gives the visual image of a woman in my presence, the touch of silk fabrics and feminine underclothes, the touch of smooth skin, the smell of cosmetics, etc. It just feels so good to be dressed and acting as a woman that nothing else compares. (142)

Note that the last two informants mentioned not only the appeal of the clothing itself but also the way in which wearing the clothing allowed them to see or imagine themselves as being female. This illustrates why it is useful to think of transvestism as "transvestic autogynephilia": cross-dressing that facilitates the thought or image of oneself as a female. Blanchard (1991) explained:

> The rationale for subsuming transvestism under the heading of autogynephilia is that the transvestite's excitement results from making himself, in some sense, more like a woman .... In fact, most transvestites do fantasize themselves as females when they are cross-dressing and may also act this out in their behavior. (pp. 237–238)

One informant described this type of anatomic visualization as the rationale for her transvestism:

> In the case of cross-dressing, it was using the prop of the clothing to imagine a female body underneath that turned me on, not the clothing itself. (087)

Another informant made the same point more explicitly, explaining that the greatest excitement associated with wearing women's attire arose from the imagined anatomic features that certain items of women's clothing implied (note: this informant had not undergone SRS):

> My interest is not in underwear and outerwear that are deemed by some to be sexually provocative (six inch heels, nylons and garter belts, low-cut blouses, etc.). No, it is the "form follows function" aspect of women's clothes that excites me most. Thus "having" to wear a bra for supporting my breasts, or "having" to wear panties that have a closed crotch, in recognition of the fact that my penis has been removed and that I now have the external genitalia of a female. (143)

Clinicians other than Blanchard have also observed that the associated mental image of oneself as a female is an essential aspect of transvestism. Levine (1993) commented that

> I cannot ever recall speaking to or hearing about an adult cross-dresser who did not have a fantasy of himself as a female. I now assume that the cross-dressing and the autogynephilic fantasy are the external and internal manifestations of the same phenomenon. (p. 135)

Money (1988) similarly explained that "Wearing women's garments is, however, in all likelihood only a partial manifestation of a more extensive gender crosscoding from male to female that includes also the body image." (p. 94).

One informant who was especially aroused by wearing women's panties early in her cross-dressing career reported that the scope of her erotic cross-dressing subsequently broadened to include other items of women's attire:

> I have always found crossdressing extremely erotic and very sexually satisfying. It all started at age 15, when I discovered my mom's panties. That was when I had my first sexual experience. I never developed any type of normal sexual relationships with girls in my teens. I was more interested in what style of panties they were wearing or what I was going to wear when I got home from school. Panties were my obsession. By age 20, I probably had collected over 200 pairs of women's panties. In my twenties, I began to acquire bras, nightgowns, nylons, and other types of lingerie. Next was women's clothes, wigs, makeup, and heels. Every dress-up session always ended in a very intense masturbation session. It was like clockwork. I now have a huge collection of women's clothing, makeup, lingerie, and jewelry. I am usually completely dressed in women's clothes while I am at home. (080)

Wearing specific kinds of women's footwear was a prominent element of transvestic autogynephilia for some informants. Two individuals favored high-heeled shoes:

> Your article on autogynephilia very accurately characterized the core experience of my life. As a 16-year-old, I tried on a tight shirtdress of my mother's. The sexual excitement that resulted permanently altered my sexuality. My earliest fantasies simply involved being a cute little female with large breasts. This evolved over time into enormously detailed fantasies,

> which included taking showers as a woman (but wearing high heels) and different sorts of sexual intercourse. In my fantasies, I imagine the sensation of a man's hands on my hips, pulling me down to make penetration deeper. I find it hard to imagine sex any other way, with one exception—standing up, my skirt around my waist—and in both cases, with heels on. For quite some time, sex with women has required me to pretend that I'm the female being penetrated to achieve orgasm. I press my legs together and arch my feet as if I've got heels on. Frankly, I wish I were in her shoes—literally. (144)

> I feel so sexy in my high-heeled boots and skirt with my long red hair. I loved putting on makeup, doing my hair, and getting dressed. I just love heels. I am 6 feet tall, like all the runway models, with a size 9-1/2 women's pump, and open toe strappy sandals are my favorite. Even though my age should call for a cooled-down version of attire, I much prefer the hotter, younger styles. I have been playing ice hockey for years, and my behind and long legs are really something to see. (145)

The latter informant's preference for "younger, hotter styles" rather than more age-appropriate attire is not unusual. Autogynephilic transsexuals are theorized to want to become facsimiles of the kinds of women to whom they are sexually attracted, so it is not surprising that most would prefer to resemble young, sexually desirable women and would be drawn to the attire that young women who wish to project a sexy image stereotypically favor.

One informant had a special fondness for another particular type of women's footwear, Keds tennis shoes:

> I remember finding my mother's stockings and garters sometime around age 8 or 9, and that is when I started trying women's clothes on. I found it to be exciting and sexually arousing. My wife understands that I wish that I was female and lets me buy and wear women's clothing; for the most part I do it when I am alone. Sometimes it is a sexual thing and other times it is just because it feels good. I wear things like women's sandals, Keds tennis shoes (I have found Keds very sexy since I was in third grade), panties, tops, pants, shorts, and bathing suits. (146)

Other informants emphasized that wearing women's clothing was not so much arousing for its own sake, or even for the female anatomy it implied, as for its ability to facilitate or necessitate female-typical behavior. Their reports could be interpreted as describing transvestic autogynephilia that occurred "in the service of" behavioral autogynephilia. The following narratives are illustrative:

> I began cross-dressing shortly after puberty in my older sister's clothes. Later, I would occasionally borrow one of my wife's dresses when she was out of town. I would always fantasize about women and assuming the role myself when dressed. And it was always an erotic experience. I have come to realize that for me, being a cross-dresser has not merely been the activity of a transvestite, but of a transsexual. The clothes themselves are but an adornment that allow me to take on the intended role. Just as "clothes make the man," I feel they make the woman as well. A skirt or dress, because of its very construction, makes a woman vulnerable, which is a female attribute. (020)

> The restrictions imposed on me by wearing female clothes are also tremendously exciting—having to sit with my legs together when wearing a skirt. Trying to keep hold of the hem of a skirt or dress on a windy day. Trying to avoid a neighbor's excitable little terrier causing a run in my pantyhose when he runs to greet me. (143)

Here again, the point that comes through clearly is that transvestism represents transvestic autogynephilia: cross-dressing that contributes to or facilitates the thought or image of oneself as a woman.

Transvestism as a Relaxing or Comfortable Activity

Heterosexual transvestites, who resemble autogynephilic transsexuals in many respects, often report that cross-dressing makes them feel relaxed or comfortable. In a survey of 33 heterosexual cross-dressers, Buhrich (1978) found that the most prevalent feelings his subjects described during cross-dressing were "comfortable, relaxed, at ease" (p. 147). Buhrich's subjects reported that during adolescence, these feelings had been slightly more prevalent than sexual arousal; in later adulthood they were much more prevalent than sexual arousal. In the current study, several transsexual informants similarly reported that cross-dressing was not only sexually arousing but also made them feel comfortable or relaxed. Here are some representative narrative excerpts:

> When I reached adolescence, I started cross-dressing discretely and would get aroused and masturbate. After the sexual part of the experience, I would remain dressed as long as was safe and would feel comfortable and cozy. (056)

> I had a persistent desire to cross-dress and did so from as early as I can remember. It was interesting that, although I was excited to get dressed in female clothing, once dressed, I was always very relaxed and any emotional excitement subsided. (147)

> Since I told my wife that I cross-dress, it has stopped being sexually exciting. I still dress, but it is more a stress reliever now than a form of sexual arousal. To me it feels nice, relaxing, maybe thrilling, but not sexually so. (148)

How should one interpret such reports of relaxation and comfort associated with cross-dressing? Blanchard was quoted (in Bloom, 2002) as expressing skepticism that nonhomosexual cross-dressing is genuinely relaxing:

> "Of course it's not relaxing," Blanchard says, with some heat. "Heels and makeup and a wig and a corset? It's preposterous. Even women don't find that relaxing. Relaxing is a pair of sweatpants, clothing that doesn't even feel like clothing. Crossdressers want to normalize this, to have it seen as relaxation." (pp. 66–67)

Docter (1988) was also skeptical of reports by heterosexual cross-dressers that habitual cross-dressing (e.g., underneath male clothing) is eventually experienced as relaxing or calming rather than sexually arousing:

> The experience most often reported by those who wear women's clothing beneath their male clothes for extended periods of time is that of a calming effect. It may be that the experience of relaxation or calmness is a major reinforcer which reduces sexual tensions, thereby becoming reinforcing. The mediating events for such a response pattern are not understood if, in fact, this is what takes place. Another hypothesis would be that the mild sexual arousal that may accompany concealed fetishistic cross dressing is subjectively interpreted as calming despite what may be mild physiological arousal. (p. 117)

Docter's hypothesis is consistent with the observation by Blanchard et al. (1986) that nonhomosexual cross-dressing men who deny experiencing sexual arousal in association with cross-dressing nevertheless display physiological genital arousal when they listen to audio recordings describing cross-dressing scenarios.

Yet another explanation of cross-dressing being experienced as comfortable or relaxing is suggested by Blanchard's (1991) observation that "many men, after years of marriage, are less excited by their wives than they were initially but continue to be deeply attached to them" (p. 248). One can imagine such men saying—to recast the ideas expressed by the informants above—"Early in my marriage, I was very turned-on by my wife; nowadays I just feel relaxed and comfortable around her." Longstanding romantic relationships with other people can be sources of relaxation and comfort after associated erotic excitement has diminished or disappeared; perhaps longstanding "relationships" with activities like cross-dressing or with one's own feminized body can also be sources of relaxation and comfort after associated erotic excitement has declined or become less important.

Anatomic Autogynephilia

Blanchard (1993a, 1993c) observed that anatomic autogynephilia, especially sexual arousal to the thought or image of having female genitals, was the type of autogynephilia most closely associated with gender dysphoria and the desire for SRS. Several informants described feeling aroused by the fantasy or reality of having a feminized body or specific elements thereof:

> Autogynephilia describes my sexual life. My sexual arousal and fantasies have always been about being transformed into a female. When I see a beautiful woman, I wish I had such a body. As I've grown older, the feeling has only gotten stronger. (149)

> It is self-sexual desire that has driven my fantasies and my desire to change my body. As my body has become more curvy, with breast development, redistribution of fat on my ass, and a noticeable feminization of my facial features, I have become more aroused daily. (076)

> Visualizing my body as having a female form is a primary source of sexual excitation. Viewing my flat pubic area and bra is a regular part of sexual foreplay. For years I have applied various forms of pressure and wraps on the penis that limited erections and have contributed to a tiny flaccid shaft. It is now usually inverted into my body and held in place with moderate pressure from support-style panties. (150)

Some informants emphasized that cross-dressing per se was less important than having female anatomic features:

> My first experiences at age 13 involved masturbation. I was slightly fat at the time and would imagine myself to have larger breasts and push my penis up into my body cavity. Much later in my teens, I would masturbate while wearing women's clothing, makeup, and other aids, while looking into the mirror and fantasizing about having a female body. In the case of cross-dressing, it was using the prop of the clothing to imagine a female body underneath that turned me on, not the clothing itself. Overall in my transition, the idea of changing has been incredibly exciting. The first 6 months when my breasts were developing were great. I'd look in the mirror and it wouldn't matter how small the change was, it'd cheer me up. And while I still could, I'd jerk off to my own naked reflection. A standard masturbation technique was to squat in front of the dresser mirror so that my penis was not visible in the reflection. Then I'd concentrate on that while I touched myself. It worked, and I liked the idea of finding my own body to be sexy. (087)

> I am a 35-year-old biological male who has undergone therapy for gender dysphoria over the past 2 years. My fantasies are almost purely based on the physical elements of being female: having breasts, a curvy body, a big butt, a vagina, a pretty face, long hair, etc., and not so much based on clothing or activities. Once puberty hit and I was aroused by females, I always wanted to be like them. The thought of being like them was always very arousing. I remember when I began masturbating, using porn magazines or videos, I would find myself thinking things about the women, like "I wish I were you. I wish my body was like yours." And the more vividly I imagined that and the more I imagined myself as a woman, the more excited I became. That behavior has never left. (066)

> I'm 44 and scheduled for sex reassignment surgery in 3 months. I never really got into cross-dressing. I did, however, from an early age fantasize about having breasts and a vagina and being accepted among women as a woman. I will admit that my initial transition did have a component of sexual desire, but it has faded, along with everything else sexual. My basic goal is to be able to fit right into tight clothing and swimwear. And, I admit, urinating in the female manner is a major goal of my upcoming sex reassignment surgery. (151)

> I am anatomically autogynephilic. Since the age of 5 or 6, I have had dreams and fantasies of being turned into a girl. Occasionally, I would get off by putting on my mom's, and later my ex-wife's, nylons; but I never had any other thoughts of cross-dressing. I am considering surgery and have begun talking to my therapist and psychiatrist about it. (152)

It was not unusual for informants to report that their most intense source of sexual arousal was imagining themselves having female genitals:

> I feel more asexual than anything, but I still must admit my greatest arousal comes from fantasizing or imitating having female genitalia. Even dressed to the hilt, if I cannot see or feel myself as a woman, with a woman's anatomy, I feel more sad than aroused. (124)

> I have always felt vulva envy. To me, being a woman is to be [sic] a vulva between the thighs—nothing more, nothing less. The beauty of being a woman comes from the vulva and is in the vulva and only there. To wear the most beautiful clothes, to have a pretty face, to have breasts, round hips, can mean nothing to me in the absence of the vulva. When I have my vulva, I will feel beautiful enough to me, and to wear feminine clothes in public will be just a consequence of that. (153)

Some informants reported that they experienced sexual arousal to the fantasy or reality of undergoing orchiectomy, penectomy, or complete SRS. In other words, the process of physical feminization was sexually arousing, not just the outcome of that process:

> I've always been turned on sexually by the idea of having a woman's body. Finally my compulsion drove me to have an orchiectomy, which was perhaps the greatest thrill of my life. A girlfriend who is a medical student came with me to the procedure. I can't tell you how thrilled and amazed I was when my testicles were removed and the process was described by my friend. It was sort of the ultimate forced feminization. (154)

> I remember reading, many years ago, about the case of the twin who lost his penis during circumcision and being tremendously envious and sexually excited. (155)

> I have always had highly charged erotic feelings associated with the development of female sex characteristics. I will have my sex reassignment surgery in about 6 months. At the moment I even have erotic fantasies derived from finally having my penis removed. (077)

> I have several fantasies I use to achieve orgasm. All are autogynephilic in one way or another. In one, I re-live my orchiectomy, albeit somewhat embellished by a more dominant group of women being the ones castrating me. My actual surgeon obliged that fantasy

> somewhat by acquiescing to my request that his female surgical assistant cut my spermatic cords. (156)

> The sexual stimulation of thinking of myself as a woman—that is me in a nutshell. Some of the sex games with the spouse involved pretend castration and forced feminization. The real desire, to have a vulva, is overpowering. Even the idea of the surgery process can arouse me. (157)

> When I was 14, I imagined lying down on the operating room table for my sex reassignment surgery. I also imagined, with horror, that I would become sexually aroused. How would I explain this? How could I even understand it myself? I didn't know why, when I thought those thoughts, I became excited. (123)

Two of the above informants mentioned forced feminization fantasies, which are extremely common in autogynephilic transsexuals. I will discuss these fantasies in Chap. 9.

Other informants described the intense excitement they felt at seeing their bodies being feminized by hormone therapy:

> I've had all of the feelings associated with autogynephilia, from early childhood to today. I feel that I'm addicted to feminizing myself with hormones. I can't seem to stop, because of the feelings I get from seeing myself change to a more female-looking body. I wish that I could stop at times, but the high I get from seeing the change is never ending. (158)

> I've been on hormones for 4 years now and have the usual physical developments, which I dearly love. My endocrinologist gives me my prescriptions and I love her performing physicals on my developing breasts and atrophying testicles and male organ. She always measures me, and I love to hear of the developments since my last visit with her. I am so mentally aroused as my breasts are measured. (159)

As I observed in Chap. 1, cross-gender identity and gender dysphoria seem to operate as two sides of the same coin in many or most autogynephilic transsexuals. The autogynephilic erotic wish to have female-appearing genitals (a manifestation of cross-gender identity) is not uncommonly accompanied by dislike or disgust for one's male genitals (a manifestation of gender dysphoria). Some informants reported that they had tried to damage or anesthetize their genitals or had attempted to castrate themselves because they disliked their male anatomy; sometimes these attempts were explicitly linked to an erotic desire to have female genitals:

> Changing into a woman was the dominant fantasy that I had even at early childhood. When I started to hear about sex change operations, I wanted one. I'd heard about horses being castrated by slowly tightening a strap of leather around their testicles. I tried to duplicate the effect. I gathered together rubber bands and wrapped them tightly around my testicles and penis. I even tried to hang myself by my genitals. (122)

> I remember wearing my older sister's panties and being very disappointed that they didn't seem to fit me properly because of my genitals. I hate my male genitals. A couple of years ago, I tried to modify my genitals, but I had to stop and take myself to the hospital because of the bleeding. If I didn't fear bleeding to death, I think that I would have removed my genitals before now. (160)

> I have always felt aroused by the fantasy of having a female body, with or without a partner. I find clothes are of little help in the arousal if I cannot disassociate myself from the penis. Experimentation in desperation has made me find ways to numb and damage my penis over the years. I confess that sex reassignment surgery to me is as much a sexual high as it is a completion of reality for my own identity physically. (161)

Note that the last informant made an explicit connection between anatomic autogynephilic arousal and her attempts to damage her penis.

Anatomic Autogynephilia Without the Desire to Live in Cross-Gender Role

As I discussed in Chap. 3, some informants reported a desire to have female genitals—and usually other female anatomic features as well—but no strong inclination to live in a female-typical gender role. Conceptually, this could represent anatomic autogynephilia unaccompanied by significant transvestic or behavioral autogynephilia. Blanchard (1991) described this pattern in the case history of Philip, a patient who experienced anatomic autogynephilia but had never cross-dressed as an adult. Alternatively, persons who give such histories might actually experience significant transvestic and behavioral autogynephilia and prefer to live as women in an ideal world but conclude that cross-living would be unfeasible in their particular circumstances. Consequently, they might decide not only to forego cross-living but to disavow any desire for it. Instead, they might seek SRS (and sometimes additional physical feminization) but continue to live as men as a compromise solution.

Based on the reports of several informants, the phenomenon of anatomic autogynephilia unaccompanied by the desire to live in a cross-gender role may be more prevalent than is generally assumed. Here are some representative narratives:

> I am a 30-year-old man, currently in therapy regarding my desires to become a female and on a hormonal regimen. My problem is that I want to go through the process, up to and including SRS, but afterwards continue living my life as a male, in a male role. I feel that I would be more comfortable living in that role. I am trying to explain this to my counselor, but I fear that she would reject me for the SRS part of transition if she really knew my goal. I don't want any surgical enhancements to my body other than SRS. I would not want to transition fully, as I have no desire to live as a female. (162)

> I am 20 years old and in college. As long as I have been sexually aware, I have been aroused exclusively by the thought of myself having a female body—specifically, a vulva and large breasts. My thoughts have been consumed by the possibility of having SRS and breast augmentation but continuing to live as a heterosexual male. It seems like the only way I could satisfy the only sexual feelings I have ever known. Since middle school, I have thought I might be a candidate for a sex change operation, but the thought of becoming a girl seemed both socially impossible and not necessarily desired. Unlike a number of autogynephiles, I have no history of cross-dressing. My arousal seems to be focused on having female anatomy. (014)

> I am 47 years old. For many years, I have wanted to have a female body, particularly breasts and a vulva. But I don't want a female face, I don't want to wear female clothes, and I don't want to have a female lifestyle. Moreover, although I want a vulva with a clitoris and outer and inner labia, I don't want a vaginal canal or to have sexual intercourse like a woman. (163)

> I want genital modifications but don't want to become a woman. After the modifications, I want to continue to live socially as a man. I do not like to use my penis to urinate, because I do not like to touch it and see it. I like to look at a woman urinating, with the secret hope

to be able to urinate like that one day myself. During masturbation, I take pleasure from imagining that I no longer have a penis but a pretty vulva. For me, my penis is useless and I want to remove it and the testicles and to replace them with a vulva. But I do not want to become a woman or live like a woman. (164)

I have wanted to be female all the way back to the age of 6 or 7. I am 6′4″ and 265 lbs., a little large to pass as a female. I love my job and could not transition without giving it up. I am also in a wonderful relationship with a woman, so I will probably do nothing more than cross-dress and continue the hormones I have been on for 12 years. But if she should pass before me, I do intend to seek SRS. The inflexibility of the Standards of Care on this issue is unreasonable. They cannot see that, at least in my case, being a female living as a male makes sense. It would hurt no one, and yet it would complete me. As a result, if that day ever comes, I will be forced to go underground and find a surgeon overseas and probably not one who will do the best job of SRS. (165)

I feel arousal at the thought of having female genitalia. Since I was a child, I have had dreams about becoming female from the waist down. I try to will those thoughts away, but they keep resurfacing. I don't want to live in the female role, and I am not attracted to men. I actually fantasize about lesbian sex with my wife. If it were possible, I would probably have genital surgery, but nothing else. Most men would feel sick at the thought of losing their penis and testicles, but I would actually feel a sense of relief. I hope the Standards of Care will change to allow for genital surgery based on a diagnosis of autogynephilia. (166)

The last two informants were referring to the *Standards of Care for Gender Identity Disorders* (Meyer et al., 2001)—recently renamed the *Standards of Care for the Health of Transsexual, Transgender, and Gender Nonconforming People* (World Professional Association for Transgender Health [WPATH], 2011)—which are widely viewed as authoritative. The Standards of Care specify that having "lived continuously for at least 12 months in the gender role that is congruent with [one's] gender identity" (WPATH, 2011, p. 21; the language in Meyer et al., 2001, p. 25, is almost identical)—the so-called "real-life experience"—is a prerequisite for SRS. For persons who want to obtain female-appearing genitals through SRS, the gender role that is congruent with one's gender identity is usually assumed to be something resembling a female-typical gender role, although the Standards of Care are not explicit on this point.

A few informants reported, however, that they had managed to obtain SRS with little or no real-life experience in a female-typical gender role:

I am a 28-year-old postoperative MtF transsexual. However, unlike the vast majority of postoperative transsexuals, I do not live in a full-time female role. I first remember wanting to be female at a very early age, and the desire to become female continued as an obsession throughout my life. By my 20s, I was living a successful life as a male, with a profession and a well-paid career. My strong desire to become a woman continued, but the practical consequences of taking the conventional route for obtaining gender reassignment surgery would have been huge. I would have lost my job and would have found it hard to reestablish myself in my profession. Furthermore, there were some aspects of my male life (certain social interests, networks, etc.) that I preferred to retain. My overriding goal was not so much to live full-time as a female, but rather to acquire the physical characteristics of a female. Looking at the practical consequences, I felt that I should try to achieve my desire of undergoing physical feminization through a female hormone regimen and sex reassignment surgery. I achieved this goal without substantial difficulty. (167)

> I underwent SRS in Thailand 4 months ago. I had a referral letter from my therapist for SRS, but there was something of an unspoken agreement that I had performed a full 1-year real-life experience, when in reality I did nothing more than dress in an androgynous manner for 3 or 4 months prior to SRS. My sexual fantasies and desires have always centered around having a vulva; I don't recall any instances of female clothing ever arousing me. I never actively lived my life as a female. I remain "male" even now. I have a gender-neutral name. I am not taking testosterone or estrogen, and I live day-to-day as a male, although I am postoperative. I've been in contact with some other people who live as I do, but we are admittedly rare. I've found a small network of six post-op "male-to-female" persons who remain living as men postoperatively. (168)

I will have more to say in Chap. 12 about men who experience severe gender dysphoria as a result of anatomic autogynephilia but do not want to live as women or do not feel that doing so would be feasible.

Physiologic Autogynephilia

Sexual arousal to the thought or image of having female physiologic functions (i.e., menstruation, pregnancy, or lactation) was first mentioned by Hirschfeld (1918), who described a case of "pregnancy transvestism" ("Schwangerschaftstransvestismus"; p. 168). Money (1988) also described transvestites for whom being a pregnant woman was a feminine ideal and who cross-dressed accordingly:

> She [sic] may have dozens, if not hundreds of photographs of herself in many different poses and outfits, to suit each occasion, including pregnancy, that is construed as womanly in her idealized conception of womanhood. (p. 95)

Buhrich and McConaghy (1977b) described the prevalence of fantasies (albeit not necessarily erotic ones) involving pregnancy and menstruation in small samples of MtF transsexuals and heterosexual cross-dressers. Most of the transsexual patients were probably homosexual, so their data are of less interest; but 3 of 35 transvestites fantasized about pregnancy and 1 fantasized about menstruation.

Physiologic autogynephilia is probably the least prevalent type of autogynephilia, but several transsexual informants in the current study reported sexual fantasies involving all of these female physiologic functions:

> I'm 31 years old. When I was age 12 or 13, I was sexually aroused by wearing my sister's clothes and later by my mother's. As I became older, I wanted to be a woman full-time. Now, with one year to go before sex reassignment surgery, I want more than that. I have fantasies of breast feeding and getting pregnant or menstruating. (169)

> Wearing women's clothing was about the least of my fantasies; being female and being made love to, made pregnant, and having children played prominent roles in my fantasies. (170)

> I've been on hormones now for almost 7 years. I've experienced arousal from the fantasy of having a woman's body. I've also fantasized about having periods and cycles. I've imagined being pregnant and carrying my child, created with my special other's seed deeply implanted inside my womb. Breast-feeding from my breast would be so heavenly. (171)

Other informants emphasized particular aspects of female physiologic function; one informant was especially aroused by simulating menstruation:

> Wearing women's clothing and feminizing my body has always been sexually exciting for me. Also, it was and still is sexually exciting for me to have female body functions. Before my sex reassignment surgery, I would pretend to menstruate by urinating in sanitary pads. I particularly enjoyed wearing the old-fashioned belted pads with long tabs. (061)

Several informants were particularly aroused by the fantasy of being pregnant, with or without arousal to the fantasy of lactation or breastfeeding:

> I am a 38-year-old male. I have felt that I should be a woman since I was about 12. I find the thought of having female genitalia very erotic. I have also fantasized about becoming pregnant. I used to do this by stuffing a pillow under a dress or pair of jeans when I was a teenager. (172)

> I am transitioning at 46 and have been approved for sex reassignment surgery. I fantasized as a youth about being a teenage girl. I have been interested in breastfeeding and becoming pregnant and have been known to wear maternity clothing. I was never aroused by the idea of breastfeeding, just by the idea of becoming pregnant. (173)

> I underwent sex reassignment surgery 22 years ago. Preoperatively, when I was fantasizing myself to be a woman with a vagina, I was strongly sexually aroused and got an orgasm. Sometimes I imagined being pregnant, also with sexual arousal. (137)

> I consider myself a transsexual. Of my thousands of sexual experiences, both with women and masturbatory, probably 98% or more centered around autogynephilic themes. In one favorite fantasy, I am married to a feminist career woman. When she gets pregnant, we agree that we should split child care completely fairly. We also want the baby to be breast-fed. We decide that I should start taking the appropriate hormones so I will be able to lactate. Because of the pressure of her work, I eventually take over all the nursing. We find out that a procedure has been perfected whereby men can be made able to receive the couple's fertilized egg, becoming pregnant. This is perfect for her career, and I willingly bear our second child. (174)

> Since puberty, I have been filled with powerful sexual feelings by the thought of dressing as a woman, having a woman's body, being pregnant and nursing my baby, and being made love to as a woman. When my longing to be a woman becomes more than I can bear, I resort to masturbation, accompanied by fantasies of being a nursing mother. (175)

Behavioral Autogynephilia

Behavioral autogynephilia—sexual arousal to the act or fantasy of engaging in stereotypically feminine behavior—was reported by many informants. The most prevalent behavioral autogynephilic fantasy of autogynephilic men is having sexual intercourse with a male partner as a woman (Blanchard, 1991); I will address this topic separately in Chap. 8. The following narrative examples involve other kinds of behavioral autogynephilia.

Some informants reported that they found a wide range of stereotypically feminine behaviors arousing or appealing:

> I'm 53 and am confessing to what I have told so many fellow transsexuals: I am obsessed with the desire to be female. I have been sexually aroused by imagining using a feminine

> voice, a feminine name, a feminine walk, tossing my hair, and opening my legs. My greatest moments of joy would be being told I am a true born woman, being told I am indeed one of the girls, or shopping for earrings or makeup in a shop where salesladies treated me as a normal woman. I love the idea of being accepted in women's locker rooms, wearing a towel like a dress, wearing tampons, and urinating sitting down always. I dream of feeling and getting wet under panties or sometimes having hot waves or itching in this area. (176)

> Although I have not yet transitioned, the thought that I will someday do so is extremely exciting to me. My mind is constantly filled with sexually exciting thoughts of living a regular daily life as a woman: getting up in the morning and putting on women's underwear and clothing; going to work at a traditional woman's job; and having everyone who interacts with me believe I am a woman. (104)

> I am 58 years old and a preoperative MtF transsexual. By my mid-20s, I had very strong desires to dress as a female on a full-time basis. I use a variety of feminine hygiene products; these include panty-liners, maxi-pads, vaginal creams, tampons, etc. I have often wished I could have been a saleslady, selling feminine fashions at a Victoria's Secret store, dressed as a woman and appearing to be a female at my job and in public. As a male, I have always been reluctant to make sexual advances; but, imagining myself as a female, I have wanted to be seductive, wear sexy, feminine fashions, and initiate physical intimacy, especially with other women. (141)

Other informants reported that they found certain specific feminine behaviors particularly arousing. Being obliged to sit to urinate or experiencing the inconvenience associated with seated urination was sometimes experienced as sexually arousing:

> I always wanted to have to sit on a toilet just like a woman. For years I would wear arrangements (so as not to touch or direct my penis) to simulate female urination. For example, I would wear the old-fashioned sanitary belt and pad, with the inner pad removed from the outer covering. The mesh covering would hold my penis in a downward position and produce a feminine stream. Also, I would void through pantyhose, or glue or tape my penis in a downward direction. For me, the greatest joy of my sex reassignment surgery is the constant reminder, every time I use the bathroom, that my maleness is gone. I am still sexually excited knowing that my urination process is just like a woman's. (061)

> I find the thought of becoming a woman and "having" to urinate as women do incredibly arousing. I thought that I was completely alone in finding this so arousing. (143)

> I empathize with the other writers who expressed excitement at going to the bathroom as a female. It's intensely exciting to think of having no choice but to squat to urinate, and I'm very envious of those transsexuals who have attained the ability to experience female urination. In fact, I go out of my way to make sure I always use a stall to pee, even when it's very inconvenient to do so. I consider this good practice for what I will have no choice but to do once I am female. (104)

Some informants described even seemingly trivial female-typical activities and behaviors as having been sexually exciting:

> The idea of owning a girl's bike has aroused me. (174)

> I definitely have that erotic turn-on from thoughts of myself as a female, sometimes doing ordinary things: When I'm alone or driving, I sometimes fancy myself a middle-aged, attractive woman with a husband. (177)

> I had my first experience at 15 with a 16-year-old girlfriend. Later with the same girlfriend I did some amateur feminization, including makeup and nails and the most amazing part: I got to take the non-hormone reminder pills from her birth control pills a few times. (178)

Others were sexually excited by the idea of being with other women in a gym or locker room and feeling as though they genuinely belonged or deserved to be there. Here are two representative examples:

> I started hormones about 6 months ago and am awaiting approval for sex reassignment surgery. The most sexually exciting thing about being a woman is fitting in as a woman and finally feeling I have a place to belong. I often fantasize being postoperative and being able to go to the gym and finally being able to shower with other women after having a nice workout. I am really turned on by the idea of going into the women's shower and being surrounded by femaleness and of just being able to legally belong in the women's restroom. What I'm saying is that to truly fit in as another woman in these places means a great deal sexually to me. (089)

> After reading about autogynephilia, I think that I have come a long way in understanding myself and my motivations and desires. Most of my early masturbatory fantasies involved being transformed into a woman and living as a woman. I don't really care about the clothes. It is about being able to see myself as a woman or at least with feminine qualities. My most enjoyable moments are imagining experiencing the more tame parts of life as a woman (e.g., playing golf, going to the women's room or locker room, being able to shop for feminine clothes and shoes, and being seen as a woman.) The few times I have been in a women's locker room have been overwhelming. The smell is so inspiring and alluring and the idea of being able to go there and be accepted as a woman—I certainly can understand why people go completely through the surgery. (107)

It is important to emphasize that the narratives that mentioned wanting to be with other women in a gym or locker room never carried overtly voyeuristic overtones. What was arousing to the informants was being accepted as a woman by other women, not the opportunity to view nude or scantily clothed female bodies. In fact, one informant explained that experiencing the *absence* of male-typical feelings was what made the locker room scenario arousing:

> I am deeply aroused by the idea of being in a locker room with other women and having no male sexual feelings. (179)

Another informant reported that shopping for women's clothing was arousing primarily because it is something that only women normally do:

> I've often become aroused by wearing women's clothing or thinking about having a woman's body. The desire to become a woman or more like a woman has encouraged me to just walk right into a department store and into the women's department and go right up to the lingerie counter and ask for what I want. Often when I've done this I've had a mixture of guilt, shame, and embarrassment and at the same time felt excited, proud, relieved, and happy. There are also times when it feels exhilarating, because I'm doing something that normally only a woman would do and start to feel like a woman shopping for her personal needs. (180)

Yet another informant was especially sexually aroused by the fantasy of receiving a manicure in a beauty salon. She apparently found the actual event arousing, too—she implied that having undergone castration was all that prevented her from exhibiting an erection:

> When I first read about autogynephilia, I knew instantly that it described me to a T. I was surprised that hormones and orchiectomy did not eliminate my sex drive. My erotic fantasies have evolved considerably over time. I have several fantasies I use to achieve orgasm.

> All are autogynephilic in one way or another. In one, I enjoy an afternoon being totally pampered at a beauty salon. The centerpiece is always a manicure. It's kind of the sine qua non of feminine indulgence and is the one female affectation forbidden to men. Two months ago I felt confident enough to finally indulge my manicure fetish. I felt I had earned a set of acrylics. Had I not been castrated it could have been a very awkward moment. But instead it was anticlimactically but perfectly normal. My manicurist gave no indication that she suspected I was anything but a woman. (156).

The fantasy of being in a lesbian relationship with a woman was particularly appealing to another informant. She emphasized that what was exciting about this fantasy was not the opportunity to have sex with a woman but the opportunity to enact the role of a lesbian.

> I'm a 50-year-old MtF transsexual, in transition about 10 years. I fit into the behavioral autogynephilic pattern. I am currently and always have been attracted to females. My conscious memory of gender dysphoria really began at age 13 with dressing up, which was always connected with sexual arousal and orgasm. This early fantasy was of being a girl and being with a girl. I had a real interest in reading lesbian love story paperbacks, which aroused me. I started to go out with girls at age 15 or 16. From 16 on up, I never really had any great desire to have intercourse, but I was really interested in a lesbian relationship, usually with a clothes fantasy. My sex life with my girlfriend from ages 16 to 18 was what I fantasized as a lesbian relationship. We never had intercourse: She was trying to be moral and I had no real interest in intercourse. (181)

Another informant admitted to feeling aroused by having a female name and gender designation on her identity documents, because this carried implications of now being "forced" to live permanently in the female gender role, a theme that is a staple of transvestite and transsexual erotic fiction:

> I will confess that officially changing my name and changing my driver's license and ID over to "female" did sexually excite me, as I felt I had pushed myself to a point of no return. The notion of now being trapped in my new gender reminded me of all of the little pink storybooks of "forced transitions" I had bought and been stimulated by earlier. (182)

The anonymity provided by the Internet allowed some informants to enact their behavioral autogynephilic fantasies by posing as women and engaging in female-typical behavior in cyberspace:

> I have lived as a woman in the cyber world for the last few years, taking on a woman's name and identity. I spend a lot of my time on the net every night, living out my fantasy of being a woman. (183)

> I really do wish I could be an attractive woman. But that is impossible, so I become one in cyberspace. When I first created a female identity on the Internet, I would become the attractive, 5′1″, 100 lbs., black-haired beauty who wears red lipstick and pearls. (109)

Perhaps the most unusual instance of behavioral autogynephilia involved a 61-year-old informant who aspired to be the "trophy wife" of a wealthy businessman or successful male professional:

> I am a 61-year-old preoperative transsexual. I have had liposuction and will have an almost total facial package done within the next several months. My thing is not to have a female body, though I am definitely an anatomic autogynephiliac. My thing is to have a super-sexy female face and body. I want to be the woman that men look at and know that, unless they're the CEO or extremely successful professionally, they can't afford me. I feel like I'm

> an ideal candidate to be the wife of an extremely successful person. I've seen the male side of things and I'm going to have extraordinary empathy for his side. Even though I'll be a sex-bomb, I won't be an airhead. I'll be the best combination of two worlds. (184)

Wealthy male CEOs and other professionals rarely choose 61-year-old natal women as trophy wives, even if the women in question are or were extremely beautiful, love men, and have decades of experience in pleasing and catering to their male partners. The idea that a wealthy male CEO or other professional might choose to marry a 61-year-old autogynephilic MtF transsexual strains credulity. This narrative illustrates the naiveté with which many autogynephilic MtF transsexuals approach the prospect of romantic or sexual relationships with male partners. I will examine this topic in greater detail in Chap. 8.

Concluding Comments on the Diverse Manifestations of Autogynephilia

As these narrative excerpts demonstrate, the manifestations of autogynephilia are highly diverse. The key to understanding this diversity is the realization that autogynephilic transsexuals can envy and eroticize any aspect of femaleness or femininity, from the most fundamental and essential to the most trivial and mundane. Autogynephilic transsexuals can and do eroticize fundamental biological aspects of femaleness, such as having female anatomy and physiological functions. They almost invariably eroticize wearing women's clothing—the most prevalent manifestation of autogynephilia. They can eroticize any aspect of female-typical behavior, from the cross-culturally universal to the most culturally specific. They can even eroticize aspects of women's experience that most women dislike, such as societal expectations to conform to standards of dress or behavior that are restrictive, inconvenient, or uncomfortable. One of my clients even described being turned-on by the fantasy of experiencing sexism: having her opinions ignored or dismissed because she is a woman, or being treated as incompetent in technical subjects in which she had been expert while living as a man. Any aspect of women's experience is seemingly fair game for an autogynephilic fantasy.

The unusual or quirky manifestations of autogynephilia are undeniably fascinating, in part for what they reveal about current cultural ideas concerning femaleness and femininity. It is important to remember, however, that autogynephilic transsexuals—whatever the nature of their erotic fantasies—experience real gender dysphoria, develop real cross-gender identities, and often transition to live as social women in a world where being somewhat recognizable as a woman makes one's life easier, safer, and more rewarding. The aspects of female-typical appearance and behavior that autogynephilic transsexuals eroticize are, for the most part, the same aspects that they envy, admire, love, and want to emulate. Autogynephilic transsexuals who undergo sex reassignment and want to thrive in the real world are well advised to try, at least to some extent, to look like and act like natal women. If they find the prospect of doing this somewhat erotic, so much the better.

Chapter 7
Autogynephilia and Heterosexuality

Autogynephilia Resembles and Complicates Heterosexuality

Blanchard (1991, 1992) theorized that autogynephilia is a variant or misdirected form of heterosexuality that usually coexists with ordinary heterosexual attraction to women but also competes with that attraction. Consistent with Blanchard's theory, several informants reported that their autogynephilic feelings seemed to resemble or be closely connected to their feelings of heterosexual attraction. The sexual desire they felt toward specific women was often accompanied by the desire to look like or become those same women, such that the two desires were at times difficult to separate or distinguish from one another. Some informants observed that intense sexual attraction to a woman could temporarily lessen their autogynephilic feelings, but that autogynephilia would inevitably return in force when the intensity of heterosexual attraction waned. Many informants reported that they usually or invariably engaged in cross-gender fantasies when they had sex with female partners; some stated that heterosexual performance was possible only when they utilized such fantasies. Several informants observed, however, that obligatory reliance on autogynephilic fantasies seemed to diminish or preclude genuine intimacy. In some instances, autogynephilic arousal overshadowed or displaced heterosexual attraction and behavior almost completely: Informants were aroused by the fantasy or reality of themselves as female, but they reported little or no attraction to potential female sexual partners. A few informants reported what they considered a late loss of virginity and theorized that this might be a consequence of their autogynephilic feelings.

A.A. Lawrence, *Men Trapped in Men's Bodies: Narratives of Autogynephilic Transsexualism*, Focus on Sexuality Research, DOI 10.1007/978-1-4614-5182-2_7,

Autogynephilia Feels Closely Related to Heterosexual Attraction

As noted in Chap. 2, a few transsexual autobiographers have observed an apparent connection between their desire to be women and their attraction to women. Hunt (1978), for example, said about girls, "I seethed with envy while at the same time becoming sexually aroused—I wanted to possess them even as I wanted to become them" (p. 60), and Zander (2003) reported having experienced "a slightly schizophrenic feeling whenever I met an attractive girl…I used to call this my 'Have her and be her' fantasy" (p. 104). Some clients in my practice have recounted similar feelings; one described masturbating while looking at a photograph of an attractive woman and rapidly alternating between the fantasy of having sex with her and the fantasy of being her, with the result that the two fantasies seemed to merge.

In the current study, several informants also observed that their autogynephilic feelings seemed to be closely related or connected to their feelings of attraction toward women. Indeed, their desires for women and their desires to be women were sometimes hard to separate from each other:

> I have understood for a long time that my desire to be a woman and my attraction to women were somehow linked. (185)

> For me, gender, sex, and desire might be easy concepts to separate in theory, but in practice they are so interwoven that they are very difficult to separate. When I was in my teens, my desire to be a woman was so strong I was unable to separate "I wish I was her" from "I wish to have sex with her." (186)

> Seeing a woman's body, with all its aesthetic and erotic qualities, can feed both gynephilic and autogynephilic emotions. The sight of a beautiful girl sensually dancing and expressing her femininity can drive me wild, although it's impossible to separate my envy from the normal mechanisms of the masculine psyche. (081)

> I am in my 50s. My earliest sexual fantasies were about being female. If I saw a naked woman, to some degree I would want to have sex with her, but the more prominent thought was that I would want to be her. This was pretty confusing. (187)

The last informant mentioned the confusion that arose from feeling attracted to women and also feeling aroused by the thought of being a woman. I believe that such confusion is not uncommon in autogynephilic men, especially during their teenage years.

Some informants observed that when they saw a woman they considered attractive, they usually fantasized about becoming her, rather than about engaging in sex with her:

> At the very moment young males are first becoming aroused by the opposite sex, there apparently is a group of us that are becoming aroused at being the opposite sex. I remember with a great deal of clarity—I became aroused by those blossoming young girls in their short skirts and wishing I was them. (018)

> I realized that when I admired a female, I was not wishing to have sex with her but wanting in some way to be her. (051)

> I felt detached from the male world because I didn't like the normal sex talk about wanting to have women. I wanted to be a woman I was attracted to, not have a woman I was attracted to. (056)

> I have always been exclusively attracted to girls, but in order to be aroused by them, I must go through the extra mental step of internalizing their voluptuous features as existing on my own body. In other words, I am romantically attracted to girls, but the actual physical lust has needed to come from the idea of having their bodies. (014)

Other informants reported having had similar reactions to photographs of models or nude women: They fantasized about being these women, rather than having sex with them.

> Lingerie ads, nude photographs of women, stimulate me in the sense that I identify with the person, not to have intercourse with them, but to be like them. (157)

> I will never have the body of a model, but seeing pictures on covers of magazines, I do not desire the model but rather desire to look like her. (128)

Another informant described how two of her female partners had concluded on their own that she might be more interested in becoming them than in making love to them:

> I always felt a compulsion to disclose my femme side to my girlfriends but only did it with a handful. Two "read" me with no prompting on my part. One of them observed bemusedly that I wanted to be her making love to myself. The other asked me if I wanted to be her or fuck her. (156)

A few informants reported that they had sexual fantasies about looking like or wearing the clothes or hairstyles of specific girls or women to whom they felt especially attracted:

> When I reached adolescence, I started cross-dressing discretely and would get aroused and masturbate, fantasizing about myself in the clothes but also with a female appearance: for example, the hair and face of an actress I admired or a girl in school I thought was attractive. In adolescence, I had a strong attraction to certain actresses (e.g., Dianna Rigg from *The Avengers* and Mary Tyler Moore). I would get aroused by fantasies involving having my appearance changed to match that of these actresses. I fantasized about being forced to dress as a woman. When I was attracted to some girls in school, I would fantasize about being forced to wear their clothes and have hair like theirs. (056)

> My fantasies have generally involved me as a very attractive woman – often taking the form of whatever girl I had a crush on at school – in a lesbian relationship with another very attractive woman. (014)

Other informants described how their initial attraction to women had turned into or been supplanted by the desire to become women themselves. In other words, their original heterosexual desire had evolved into or been replaced by autogynephilic desire:

> When I look at an attractive woman on the street, I no longer think the male thought, "Mmm, I'd like to sleep with her." Instead, I think, "Mmm, I wonder what it's like to be her." And I am jealous. (188)

> My experience with transsexualism started with a love for the female body, followed by the wish to "embody" that femininity inside me. I remember feelings of attraction to women when I was a child, perhaps when I was only 6 or 7, and fantasizing about a beautiful teenage girl who lived next door. I remember having the urge to sneak into her home and "possess" her body. I was too young to appreciate what sex means; all I understood was that I wanted to see and hold her naked body. At that point, "possess" meant to me to enjoy it as

an outsider. But subsequently, my desire changed to wanting to "possess" it as an insider: I began to wear my mother's underwear and fantasize about my being a girl. (189)

There is one culturally sanctioned way to "possess" a female body, heterosexual sex. I tried and tried for 30 years to sexually possess a female body. Finally at 40 I had the awareness that what I really wanted was to be a female (body), versus to have a female body. The sexy body I was always looking for in a woman turned out to be my own after transition and surgery. The person I was looking for in a woman turned out to really be me. I never found that person except in myself. (190)

I am still exclusively attracted to women romantically, albeit no longer obsessively. My attraction to them has been redirected inward. When I regard my now very feminine self in the mirror, I am get a slight rush from the sense of fulfillment I never had as a male, even when I enjoyed the love and affection of very beautiful women. (156)

Autogynephilia Competes with Heterosexual Attraction

Blanchard (1992) observed that autogynephilia and conventional heterosexual attraction often exist in a state of competition. Nonhomosexual MtF transsexuals often report that their autogynephilic fantasies and behaviors or their associated feelings of gender dysphoria become less compelling or disappear altogether when they fall in love with women. There are several published case reports documenting this phenomenon (e.g., Marks et al., 2000; Shore, 1984; Steiner, 1985). Conversely, nonhomosexual MtF transsexuals sometimes report that their autogynephilic fantasies or their feelings of gender dysphoria become stronger after an existing heterosexual relationship ends or loses its novelty (e.g., Marks et al.). As noted in Chap. 2, Blanchard (1992) referred to this phenomenon as *dynamic competition* (p. 275). Dynamic competition between autogynephilia and heterosexual attraction was an especially frequent theme in the informants' narratives; here are some representative examples:

Whenever I had a girlfriend or was in love, my autogynephilia would recede so deeply that I would actually forget that I ever had it. I cannot overstate this. Even when I would think of my autogynephilia during these periods, it would seem like it was just nothing. But it would keep coming back. And each time it came back it would be a little bit stronger. I am now age 53, and my autogynephilia is the only sex drive I have. (102)

I have been in many short-term, turbulent relationships with women. At the beginning of a relationship, my gender dysphoria is almost nonexistent, but after a period of three months to a year, I start having erotic fantasies about being a woman. Eventually, I need to fantasize about being a woman to perform sexually. (018)

My transsexual feelings diminished significantly, but not entirely, when I started having sex with the woman who became my wife. I still remember that odd look she gave me when I once used the words "my pussy" in sex talk. Like a pendulum, however, my transsexual desires increased as the novelty of the sexual relationship diminished. It is now stronger than ever. (191)

I began taking contraceptive pills on a daily basis and seriously considered how and where I could transition. As a start, I booked a long holiday, which I intended to spend partly as a woman. At this critical juncture, I met on holiday a lovely girl with whom I immediately bonded. I had to rebuff her first sexual advances, as I was by then incapable of an erection. After a week, she had to go home. A few days later, after much agonizing, I decided I was really serious about her and stopped taking the pills and disposed of all the female items I had begun to accumulate. By the time we met again, two months later, I was able to sustain an erection. However, my sexual drive remained quite low, and I used transsexual and feminization fantasies to help my arousal. (129)

I got a prescription for Premarin from a doctor and continued taking it off and on for a year. Finally I went to see a therapist, who said I was clearly transsexual. I separated from my wife, and I dressed as a female essentially full-time. However, I still considered myself heterosexual, interested in women. I met a wonderful woman, and we married and had a child. I've never breathed a word about cross-dressing to her. However, after suppressing the desires for about 2 years, they have come back. I have obtained hormones from a reputable source and have started taking them again. (192)

I began fantasizing myself as a woman, and I discovered that it was just as sexually arousing as having intercourse, if not more so. My fantasy evolved into my desiring to change my body. In my late 40s, my marriage ended and I soon found myself overwhelmingly attracted to a lovely, warm, and very sexual woman. I purged myself of my past and dove into my new relationship. But, several years into my second marriage, the feelings crept slowly back into my life. I eventually reconstituted my collection of underwear and I resumed my erotic feminization fantasies and self-pleasuring. No matter how good the marital sex, I would fall asleep dreaming about becoming feminized. (193)

Dynamic competition also appears to occur between autogynephilia and attraction to other MtF transsexuals. This might plausibly represent a somewhat different phenomenon than the dynamic competition between autogynephilia and attraction to natal women, but it is conveniently addressed here. Nonhomosexual MtF transsexuals not uncommonly find themselves sexually attracted to other MtF transsexuals. In some cases, this appears to reflect a preferential, paraphilic attraction to the MtF transsexual somatotype; this paraphilia is called *gynemimetophilia* (Money, 1986). Several narratives by transsexual and nontranssexual informants with gynemimetophilia will be presented in Chaps. 9 and 11. MtF transsexuals with this paraphilic interest typically have a history of repeated infatuations or involvements with other MtF transsexuals, but they do not necessarily or ordinarily put aside their plans for sex reassignment when they fall in love with MtF transsexuals.

In other cases, however, nonhomosexual MtF transsexuals without any apparent history of paraphilic attraction to the transsexual somatotype fall in love with other MtF transsexuals, find that their autogynephilia and associated gender dysphoria temporarily go into remission, and put aside their transition plans to pursue romantic relationships as men with their MtF transsexual partners. This phenomenon has been described in a few case reports (e.g., Marks et al., 2000; Person, 1995; see also Ovesey & Person, 1976), as has a closely related phenomenon involving transvestites who temporarily give up cross-dressing after becoming romantically involved with MtF transsexuals (Guze, 1969).

In the current study, two informants reported that they stopped taking hormones or lost their desire for sex reassignment after falling in love with another MtF transsexual:

I was on hormones for 6 months until about a month ago, when I fell head over heels for another girl in transition. Hormones had killed my libido, but after stopping hormones, it's

> not coming back very quickly. While I dearly love the girl I fell for, I find that spontaneous erections are not as good as when I fantasize about forced feminization and/or becoming a woman. (130)

> For many years I cross-dressed and would become sexually aroused at the sight of myself in the mirror. This would lead to furious masturbation. One night I went to a club for cross-dressers and transsexuals. I met a sultry transsexual who was in transition. I was very aroused. She suggested that I go home with her, and it was the most surprising and transforming experience of my life. I stopped being tormented with a desire to transition or cross-dress. Instead, I became obsessed with transsexual women. (194)

Do the experiences described by these informants reflect a type of dynamic competition between autogynephilia and attraction to individuals who closely resemble natal women? Or do they perhaps simply represent the unmasking of previously unrecognized gynemimetophilia? The final sentence of the second narrative above is suggestive of the latter possibility.

Falling in love with another MtF transsexual allows autogynephilic gender dysphoric persons the opportunity to experience the actualization of their own cross-gender wishes by proxy; this probably represents part of its appeal. Person (1995) observed that:

> Fantasy may be gratified through bonding with someone who has already actualized one's own fantasy. This mechanism is particularly apparent among people with cross-gender disorders… .What is particularly prominent in love is that the identification process allows us to enjoy our fantasies vicariously, that is, at one remove, without suffering guilt or anxiety. (p. 131)

One might speculate that this same dynamic is probably also operative, at least to some extent, in dynamic competition between autogynephilia and heterosexual attraction to natal women.

Autogynephilia Complicates Heterosexual Expression

Informants frequently stated that autogynephilia had complicated their relationships with their female sexual and romantic partners. Many reported that they habitually needed to resort to autogynephilic fantasies to become sufficiently sexually aroused to engage in sexual intercourse with female partners or achieve orgasm during intercourse. Here are a few representative comments:

> When I married and sex became a part of our relationship, it was awkward from the beginning, and the only way—and I emphasize the ONLY way—I would achieve sexual arousal would be by taking the role of the female via fantasy and actually believing I was the one being made love to. (114)

> I have always imagined swapping places with my female partner and feeling what she is feeling and possessing her body and genitalia. Actually, that is basically the only way I can achieve an orgasm. (095)

> I am married to a lovely lady who has been my wife for 23 years. I love her, but the only way I can have sex is to dream I am a woman with breasts and a vagina. (195)

> I am attracted to women. I can only orgasm during sexual intercourse if I see myself as female and believe that I'm being penetrated. (196)

> I have always found the idea of being a woman sexually arousing. Indeed, I can only climax with my wife by thinking that I am female. (197)

> I can't understand why I can only make love to a woman by fantasizing that I'm her in every way. (198)

> I was married for years, and the only way I could get aroused was to think about how great it would have been to be my wife. (199)

One informant stated that he found it difficult to function sexually as a man with a female partner, even with the help of autogynephilic fantasies:

> I am currently in a long term relationship of nearly 7 years and I have a lot of difficulty getting aroused by the thought of having sex with a woman. Often I have fantasies like: I wish she had the penis so that she could make love to me. I often imagine myself as a woman to achieve ejaculation. I don't really get a proper orgasm very often. (200)

Others reported experiencing performance difficulties during acts of heterosexual intercourse in which they attempted to take the traditional male role or were unable to engage in autogynephilic fantasies:

> The central themes of my erotic fantasies were my becoming female and having sex with women as a woman. The fantasies allowed me to have a sexual relationship with my wife, but when she wanted me to act like a man, my sexual feelings disappeared, except for my private ones about being a woman. (132)

> I can never have sex with a female without thinking about myself as a female. It is always about me and never my partner. The more attractive they are, the easier it is for me, but that's just because I'm wishing or thinking about being them. When I was 19, I met the woman who would become my wife. She hated it if I closed my eyes during sex, but the only way I can become aroused is to think of myself in feminine ways. So for years, we would have sex only sporadically, because I had to be real horny to have sex with her and keep my eyes open. (034)

Another informant similarly reported that he never looked at his female partner while he engaged in intercourse but instead imagined what she was feeling:

> I previously had a heterosexual relationship in which I had intercourse. I enjoyed the physical sensations, but when I think about what I was doing at those times, I realize that I don't recall ever actually looking at her while we were having intercourse. I do remember sometimes imagining what the sex felt like for her. (043)

Obligatory reliance on autogynephilic fantasies for arousal during sex with female partners felt wrong or embarrassing to some informants:

> Making love as a man to a woman was always very confusing, it just didn't have that knockout punch, unless I fantasized I was a woman, but that seemed wrong when you were making love to your wife. (201)

> In my marriage, the vast majority of the time with my wife in bed was spent in fantasy. What I was doing to her, in my mind, was really being done to me by someone else. It was me that was the beautiful woman. The reality of the situation, that I was a man in bed with a woman, was by far wholly insufficient to arouse me much. I never wanted to admit to myself or anyone what a turn on just thinking about all this was to me. (021)

Other informants reported that their autogynephilic feelings had led them to limit or eventually stop engaging in sex with their female partners or even to give up entirely on the prospect of having satisfactory sexual relationships with women:

> My fantasies about being female have not been good for my relationship with my wife of the past 15 years. I enjoy having a more feminine body. That, of course, is the root of my sexuality. My wife and I are on a "friends" basis now, because I cannot fulfill her desire for a man and my sexual desire involves myself as a woman. (066)

> I have told my wife of these fantasies, some have been acted out, some rejected, some not understood. My feelings have diminished our sex life substantially. I often have to fantasize I am a woman to achieve orgasm; she wants a man in her bed more than a woman. (093)

> I suffer from autogynephilia. The mental image of myself becoming female is definitely erotic. As a matter of fact, the only sexual feelings that I have relate to this. My spouse and I once had a pretty close physical relationship, and that is now nonexistent. (202)

> About sex: I usually do it myself, with pictures of women in dresses. I imagine that I am one of the women, stuck in the role. I had a girlfriend for a while, but this mode of excitation was not something that she could deal with. (035)

> I got married hoping that it would cure me; it hasn't. I have sex with my wife out of obligation about once a year. When I do, I am the woman with a vagina and she has the penis. (177)

> The idea of becoming a woman—that is, being changed physically—was indeed a source of sexual stimulation for me. I have had some relationships with women, but dismissed them as futile in my early 20s. I could not cope with the autogynephilic feelings and be in a relationship. (113)

One informant observed that her obligatory reliance on autogynephilic imagery for sexual arousal precluded genuine intimacy during partnered sex and sometimes made her feel awful:

> I can't remember a time when I was able to have an orgasm without fantasizing myself as a woman. Whether I was making love to a woman or pleasing myself, nothing could happen for me without an accompanying fantasy that I was a woman. My own pleasure is all but guaranteed, as long as I can conjure up the right fantasy. But there's also a dark side: There is almost no way for me to have intimate and loving sex. The simple act of giving to my partner is turned topsy-turvy by my need to imagine myself as her. At rare times it works out, and both of us are happy. More often I end up feeling really awful. And sometimes my need for this fantasy leaves me feeling like some kind of bizarre emotional vampire. Then sex becomes a chore, even a threat, to me; it's no fun any more, and it stops happening. (203)

Why would consistently resorting to autogynephilic fantasies during sexual intercourse make one feel like an "emotional vampire"? Perhaps because vampires take something they require from their victims without giving anything back (or at least anything good). Nearly everyone needs and wants emotional intimacy during sex, but habitually resorting to autogynephilic fantasies can make autogynephilic men feel that they are receiving such intimacy without giving any back to their partners. Money (1988) graphically described this absence of reciprocated intimacy:

> One paraphilic patient equated intercourse with his wife with masturbating in her vagina. In his paraphilic fantasy, she was a stage property, not a participant actor. (p. 143)

It is easy to imagine why partnered sex might feel really awful and eventually stop happening if one's partner is merely a prop.

Integration of Autogynephilic Elements into Heterosexual Lovemaking

A few informants reported that they had sometimes managed to integrate their autogynephilic desires into lovemaking with their female partners. Here are two representative accounts:

> My wife is really supportive. She has bought me clothes, makeup, shoes, a wig, and other things. When I wear them, I get aroused and we have the best sex I have ever had with her. My wife and I bought a realistic looking penis/dildo. She uses it on me and I fantasize about my anus being my vagina and I have great orgasms. (046)

> Even though my wife is a natural female, I can block her out and make believe she is penetrating me; or, when I am lucky, she will play along and tell me what a pretty girl I am. (124)

One informant reported that she was intensely sexually aroused by being unable to penetrate female partners and needing to use a strap-on dildo to pleasure them:

> As I began to lose my ability to have sustainable erections, my fantasies began to shift. I tried to have sex with women at times—especially gay or dominant women—and I soon realized I got a tremendous thrill from the fact that I could no longer perform sex as a man. One of the most intense sexual experiences occurred when I was with a woman who asked me to put on a strap-on to satisfy her. The strap-on was the most powerful sexual symbol of my new status. (077)

Some informants stated that they preferred to engage in sexual intercourse with their female partners on top, presumably because this placed the informants in the traditional female position and thereby enhanced their autogynephilic fantasies:

> My wife and I have intercourse regularly. I have persuaded her that I perform best if she mounts me, rather than the other way around. I am not sure whether I could now have intercourse if I were on top. I can only achieve orgasm through fantasizing about forced feminization. (143)

> For years I have imagined myself as a beautiful woman and have had fantasies about receiving pleasure sexually as a woman. I ask my wife to be on top frequently, and she obviously can tell how this arouses me. (103)

Heterosexual lovemaking was commonly accompanied by the fantasy of being in a lesbian relationship:

> My wife has been very supportive of my efforts of growth and inner discovery. We proceeded to adapt our lovemaking to reflect my long hidden desires to be submissive and "soft." We have had the warmest, most loving experience of our lives these past few weeks, as I openly enjoy real sex while being treated as a woman. Is it fair to say we are acting almost as though we are lesbians? She certainly is not, but we are doing a lot more caressing, oral sex, and conversation. (204)

> I am currently married to a very supportive woman who treats me at home like a female lover. My wife and I decidedly relate to each other on a lesbian level, with sexual practices being almost exclusively manual and oral. Regular copulation, when used, is with her usually being the dominant top partner and both of us fantasizing that we are using a double-ended dildo (i.e., my penis). God, I can't believe I wrote that, but it is the truth. (038)

> I had always been attracted to women and lesbian sex was highly erotic. When I entered my first sexual relationship, I began to fantasize that we were lesbian lovers. I actually convinced her to assist in the fantasies occasionally. I don't think she ever really understood what it meant to me. (101)

It is not unusual for wives or female partners to remain in relationships with MtF transsexuals who initiate or complete sex reassignment. In a follow-up study of MtF transsexuals who had completed SRS (Lawrence, 2005), among 153 participants who had been married before SRS, 17 (11%) still lived with their spouse or ex-spouse following SRS.

Autogynephilia Is Sometimes Associated with Marital Discord or Divorce

In contrast to the previous reports of successful integration of autogynephilic behaviors into heterosexual relationships, several informants stated that their partners were annoyed or turned-off by their autogynephilic fantasies and behaviors or eventually found them intolerable.

> My ex-wife used to become extremely jealous and angry because I would masturbate while dressed. I cannot get off sexually with a woman or through masturbation without fantasizing about being a woman. (048)

> During marriage, I was only turned on by my wife telling me stories of men making love to me. I don't know why, but this is what turns me on. I guess sex for her was not that great. She said she was tired of feeling like she was having a lesbian relationship. (205)

> With one girlfriend and now with my wife, I have managed to incorporate some cross-dressing activities into our sex life, but only very minor. I can rapidly lose my connection with my partner and become absorbed with my own fantasies, which is a big turn-off for them. Mostly I keep my fantasies and certainly the extent of them to myself. (107)

> Early in my former marriage, I used to fantasize with my wife about switching sexes with her or even switching bodies. She participated in these fantasies and seemed to enjoy them early on, but later, as I started to cross-dress more and more, she got upset and turned off by them. (206)

> My current wife of 11 years was initially accepting of my cross-dressing desires as a fetish, but became very opposed when it became clear to her that it wasn't just a sexual turn-on. For example, she hates that I wear my hair in a somewhat feminine style and shave my legs. (056)

One informant reported that his wife seemed to regard him as an alien being who had somehow taken possession of her husband's body:

> The feeling of my growing breasts and softening skin is more sexy to me than anything or anyone outside myself. My wife sees me as a totally selfish person, one who has killed and inhabited her husband's body and is ruining what is left of him. (073)

In my practice, I have more than once heard reports of spouses invoking images of alien or demonic possession to describe the powerful forces that seem to have taken control of their husbands' bodies and lives.

A few informants stated or implied that autogynephilia had been a contributing factor in their divorces, although narratives explicitly attributing divorce to cross-dressing or other cross-gender behaviors were surprisingly infrequent. Here are a few examples:

> I cross-dressed a few times in secret while I was married and was caught on one occasion. My wife's reaction was disapproving. She was prepared to forget the matter, provided I assured her it wouldn't happen again, but ultimately my revelation that I did it for sexual pleasure sealed the fate of the marriage, and we are now going through divorce. (053)

> I started electrolysis and hormones and gave myself one year to start living full-time as the woman I'd always wanted to be. My wife demanded a divorce, and I moved out of the house. I was very sad to lose her, but overjoyed by my new freedom. (182)

> After seven years, she called it quits and asked for a divorce. She found some of my things, which included breast forms, wigs, lingerie and other items. She could not accept this part of me and said she wanted a real man. Plus, I was a complete failure in bed. I was not sexually attracted to her and spent all my time fantasizing about dressing or becoming a woman. These feminine thoughts blocked out any feelings for her. (080)

One informant expressed the hope that severely gender dysphoric autogynephilic men would learn about the meaning and significance of autogynephilia before deciding to marry and have children; her unstated but clear implication was that it might be better for these men to avoid marriage:

> I only hope that other men like me will find this information and learn to understand themselves earlier in life, when they have more time to consider their options and before they marry and have kids. (044)

I feel that this informant's advice is wise: Severely gender dysphoric autogynephilic men should consider their feelings carefully and think twice before entering into marriage.

Autogynephilia Sometimes Overshadows and Replaces Heterosexual Attraction

As previously noted, autogynephilia and heterosexual attraction usually coexist to some extent, but the balance between their relatives strengths can shift over time; this shifting balance is called *dynamic competition*. Blanchard (1992) also described another type of competition between autogynephilia and heterosexual attraction, *developmental competition* (p. 275); it is so called because it putatively occurs early in psychosexual development. Blanchard theorized that developmental competition establishes a kind of "baseline" balance between the relative strengths of autogynephilia and heterosexual attraction; this baseline balance can subsequently be shifted through the operation of dynamic competition.

Blanchard (1992) further theorized that, in a few cases, developmental competition establishes a baseline balance of relative strengths in which autogynephilia is so much stronger than heterosexual attraction that the former overshadows and effectively crowds out the latter. This formulation accounts for the existence of autogynephilic transsexuals whose sexual interest is directed almost exclusively toward themselves and who experience little or no sexual attraction to other persons. These transsexuals are referred to as *analloerotic* (not sexually attracted to other people; Blanchard, 1989a). In a survey of 232 MtF transsexuals who had completed SRS, I observed that about 12% of participants reported little or no sexual attraction to other persons and were plausibly analloerotic (Lawrence, 2005).

In the current survey, several informants reported that their autogynephilic feelings were not accompanied by any significant heterosexual attraction or that they had no desire to engage in sexual activity with female partners. Here are some of their observations:

> In the street, I look at a girl, and think, "god, I want to be in that body." I have never had any kind of attraction to men, nor to a girl, except for being envious of that body and lifestyle. (207)

> My self-conception as a female and the subsequent self-feminization was enough to offer me a sexual delight so high and so intense as I never felt again till after my transition. The sole thing interesting to me then was not to be with someone else but to become female. (208)

> I have never had any thoughts of wanting to have sex with a female. I am attracted to females, but not so much by physical lust, but by personality displayed in interaction and through facial features. My fantasies involving relationships have focused on the emotional and companionship aspects, not the physical ones. I have recently longed to be able to relate to females as other females do. (209)

> I am sexually aroused by the thought of being female and the thought of making love as a woman to a man. I have had a desire since early childhood to be female, but I'm attracted to neither sex, except in my sexual fantasies. (210)

> My transsexuality does have erotic elements. I get so turned on to myself that my heart pounds with horniness and wantonness but also joy and exhilaration. I honestly am not attracted to anyone else. I guess you could call me anallophilic. Maybe I could be attracted to someone else, but I'm not and haven't been for most of my life. I am my own pleasure. Yes, indeed: love of oneself as a woman. (211)

> I lost my virginity at age 26 by frequenting a sex worker. It became apparent that there was little difference between intercourse and masturbation for me. While others were out chasing each other, I had no attraction to anyone, but masturbated furiously by myself. I had passes but didn't know what to do. I had no experience in responding to any of this. (087)

> I have always found cross-dressing extremely erotic. I never developed any type of normal sexual relationships with girls in my teens. I never looked at Playboy magazine or naked women. They never really did anything for me sexually. I did not have a girlfriend until I was 19. I never found her sexually attractive, but I absolutely loved her panties. We were together for two years and were like two sisters or best friends. We never had sex during that time. My only sexual interest in her was fantasizing and imagining it was me who was wearing those panties. (080)

> I have always felt a deep, unshakeable longing to be female. I have an attraction to women and not to men; I can remember always having wanted a girlfriend. My attraction to women, however, has never involved a desire to have sex. At no point have I ever looked at a woman and had a sexual response to the thought of having sex with her. I've tried fantasizing about having sex, but it really does nothing for me at all. My desire for a girlfriend, I think, always related to the need for acceptance and companionship. (004)

The last informant alluded to one of the most significant issues that analloerotic autogynephilic transsexuals face: How to satisfy their longing for intimate, affectionate interpersonal relationships and the comfort provided by human touch in the absence of genuine sexual desire for other persons. Ms. Z described this situation in Chap. 1: Tired of the emptiness and futility of partnered sex, "eventually she resigned herself to celibacy, although she missed the comfort of another woman's body pressed against her own." On the basis of my clinical and nonclinical experience, I believe that many autogynephilic transsexuals feel lonely, isolated, and touch starved; but perhaps none so much as analloerotic autogynephilic transsexuals.

Late Loss of Virginity in Autogynephilic Transsexuals

Several informants reported that they had lost their virginity unusually late in life or had never lost it. Usually these informants implied or stated explicitly that they felt their delayed experience (or absence of experience) of sexual intercourse was somehow related to their autogynephilic sexuality. Here are some representative comments:

> I have often masturbated while wearing sexy feminine fashions and looking at pictures of women wearing sexy, feminine clothes. I have often wished I were these women and had their female bodies. I was a virgin until I was about 39. (141)

> At age 29, without any sexual experience and feeling guilty over being a virgin, I thought it was time to settle down with someone and try to live a normal life. I met someone whom I thought I could learn to love physically. I finally lost my virginity, but it was only through fantasizing about being dressed as or becoming a woman. (080)

> It took me until my later 20s to lose my virginity, and I had trouble getting fully aroused with my first girlfriend, the only proper girlfriend I've had. I have not sought out sex with women as avidly as my friends, because my desires are always autogynephilic, which can detract from that kind of motivation. (023)

> I have experienced autogynephilia since childhood, in a fairly classic pattern. At 32, I am still effectively a virgin, never having had the right kind of drive or "know-how" to pursue women, even though I am definitely attracted to them. (212)

> I relate very strongly to the descriptions of autogynephilia. Since I was 5, I have had a strong desire to be a girl, and since puberty, I have been filled with powerful sexual feelings by the thought of dressing as a woman and having a woman's body. I am 48 years old and a virgin; women have always attracted me, but I have been too much in awe of them to take the initiative and have never been attracted to the idea of playing a man's role. (175)

The last informant's explanation of being "too much in awe of [women] to take the initiative" brings to mind Freud's classic essay *On the Universal Tendency to Debasement in the Sphere of Love* (1912/1957). Freud observed that heterosexual men's respect for women is fundamentally antierotic:

> The man almost always feels his respect for the woman acting as a restriction on his sexual activity, and only develops full potency when he is with a debased sexual object. … It sounds not only disagreeable but also paradoxical, yet it must nevertheless be said that anyone who is to be really free and happy in love must have surmounted his respect

> for women.... Anyone who subjects himself to a serious self-examination on the subject of this requirement will be sure to find that he regards the sexual act as basically something degrading. (pp. 185–186)

If Freud was correct that men's respect for women is antierotic, perhaps the almost worshipful idealization that some autogynephilic men feel toward women can act as an impediment to their engaging in sexual intercourse with female partners.

In a review article on autogynephilia (Lawrence, 2007), I observed that nonhomosexual MtF transsexuals commonly reported that their attraction to women "was not expressed with typical masculine confidence" (p. 514). One can imagine several possible reasons for this, in addition to feelings of extraordinary admiration and respect for women: for example, uncertainty about gender identity or sexual orientation, or simply a paucity of other-directed sexual interest in the case of analloerotic or near-analloerotic autogynephilic transsexuals.

Autogynephilia Versus Heterosexuality

The narrative excerpts in this chapter are consistent with Blanchard's ideas about the relationship between autogynephilia and heterosexual attraction, and they vividly illustrate the ways these ideas play out in real life. Blanchard (1991, 1992) theorized that autogynephilia was a variant form of heterosexual attraction, and that is precisely what informants described: Their autogynephilic desires felt similar to heterosexual desire and arose in similar circumstances, and the two feelings were sometimes hard to distinguish. Blanchard (1992) theorized that autogynephilia and heterosexual desire would often exist in dynamic competition, and informants reported that this was indeed the case: Their autogynephilic feelings often diminished temporarily when they began a new heterosexual relationship, but autogynephilia returned in force when the relationship lost its novelty. Blanchard also theorized that developmental competition between autogynephilia and heterosexual attraction would sometimes favor autogynephilic desire so powerfully that heterosexual attraction would be almost negligible by comparison; this situation, called analloeroticism, was also described by a few informants.

Perhaps the most surprising aspect of so many of the narratives was the relative lack of intensity of the informants' erotic desire for women. Even when heterosexual interest was strong enough to draw an informant into a sexual relationship with a woman, it was rarely strong enough to guarantee the informant's orgasm during heterosexual intercourse. Over a dozen informants reported that cross-gender fantasies were always necessary to achieve orgasm during sex with female partners; only one or two informants stated or implied that such fantasies were optional or rarely necessary. I suspect (but cannot say for certain) that many less severely gender dysphoric autogynephilic men—many heterosexual cross-dressers, for example—do not experience this kind of obligatory reliance on cross-gender fantasies for orgasmic release during intercourse: At least occasionally, they plausibly find the bodies of their female partners sufficiently arousing to facilitate climax. It seems possible that the invariable necessity of engaging in autogynephilic fantasies to achieve orgasm during sex with female partners may be indicative of an especially strong autogynephilic sexual orientation, unusually intense gender dysphoria, or both.

Although some informants found female partners who would cooperate with their autogynephilic fantasies during partnered sex, many others described their female partners as having been unaccepting. Some informants had given up on heterosexual relationships entirely because they could not find cooperative partners or were unwilling to subject themselves or their partners to obligatory paraphilic enactments that felt dishonest or empty of real intimacy. It may be that long-term heterosexual relationships are inherently problematic for autogynephilic transsexuals. Both men and women, but women especially, want to feel desired by their partners (Brotto, Heiman, & Tolman, 2009). Autogynephilic transsexuals, however, experience a self-directed erotic desire that is "greater than the desire for any person" (Bloom, 2002, p. 94) and is likely to be inimical to interpersonal intimacy and satisfying sexual expression, whether it is concealed from female partners or disclosed to them. It seems to me that severely gender dysphoric autogynephilic men should feel great hesitancy about entering into marriage or long-term committed relationships with women; although such relationships may not inevitably be doomed, many if not most will probably either fail or prove to be highly unsatisfactory. In my opinion, most severely gender dysphoric autogynephilic men would be well advised to forego marriage altogether.

Another theme running throughout the narrative excerpts in this chapter, albeit sometimes only implicitly, was the profound confusion informants felt about their simultaneous experience of heterosexual attraction and autogynephilic desire. Many appeared to have been so confused that they entered adulthood without a firm commitment to either heterosexual relationships or cross-gender expression; others went on to make unfortunate relationship choices that plausibly reflected this same confusion. Making sense of autogynephilic desire and its relationship to heterosexual attraction is inherently challenging, but the almost total absence of self-help resources and role models for young autogynephiles greatly compounds this problem. Teenage boys and young men who experience same-sex attraction often feel confusion, too; but at least they have educational resources to help them make sense of their feelings and "out" gay men to serve as role models. Autogynephilic teenagers and young adults—who may be almost as numerous as their gay counterparts, according to some estimates (see Lawrence, 2009a)—are not so fortunate. Perhaps someday young autogynephiles will have self-help educational resources that summarize the facts about autogynephilia, along with "out" autogynephilic transsexual role models who can put a human face on the phenomenon they experience. Such aids to self-understanding are desperately needed and long overdue. I will say more about this topic in Chap. 12.

Chapter 8
Sex with Men

Autogynephilic Fantasies of Sex with Men Are Prevalent

Behavioral autogynephilia can be defined as the propensity to be sexually aroused by the act or fantasy of engaging in stereotypically feminine behaviors, those that "symbolize femininity to the affected male" (Blanchard, 1991, p. 236). Blanchard observed that "the most common behavioral fantasies of adult autogynephilic men involve the thought of themselves, as women, engaging in sexual intercourse or other erotic activities" (p. 237), especially engaging in penile–vaginal intercourse with a man. Consistent with Blanchard's observation, many transsexual informants submitted narratives describing fantasies involving sex with men.

The allure of this autogynephilic fantasy is predictable: It is difficult to think of a female-typical behavior that is more basic, culturally universal, or archetypal than being the recipient of vaginal penetration by a man; only breastfeeding and child care would seem to come close. The female reproductive role is the quintessential female role, and the fantasy of enacting the most dramatic aspect of that role is understandably powerful for most autogynephilic transsexuals.

Blanchard argued that autogynephilic transsexuals who report that they are sexually attracted to men are not genuinely aroused by male bodies: He believed that their underlying sexual orientation is toward females, and their supposed attraction to men simply reflects their wish to have their femininity validated by interaction with a male partner. Consequently, these nominally "bisexual" transsexuals can more accurately be thought of as *pseudobisexual* (Blanchard, 1989b, p. 622). He explained:

> The effective erotic stimulus in these interactions, however, is not the male physique of the partner, as it is in true homosexual attraction, but rather the thought of being a woman, which is symbolized in the fantasy of being penetrated by a man. For these persons, the male sexual partner serves the same function as women's apparel or make-up, namely, to aid and intensify the fantasy of being a woman. (p. 617)

A.A. Lawrence, *Men Trapped in Men's Bodies: Narratives of Autogynephilic Transsexualism*, Focus on Sexuality Research, DOI 10.1007/978-1-4614-5182-2_8,

Blanchard further observed that bisexual autogynephilic transsexuals, in comparison to their heterosexual or analloerotic counterparts, were especially likely to report that they were sexually aroused by "the sexual fantasy of being admired, in the female persona, by another person" (p. 619). Nearly all of the narratives that discussed sexual fantasies or behaviors involving male partners were consistent with Blanchard's formulations.

Although Blanchard distinguished between genuine androphilia (sexual attraction to men) and the autogynephilic fantasy of assuming the female role in relation to a male partner, he suggested that this distinction was probably lost on almost all autogynephilic transsexuals:

> Even the most scrupulously honest heterosexual male gender patients do not (and probably can not) intentionally distinguish, in their self-reports, between the nature of their interest in sexual intercourse with males, which is related to fetishism in that it derives from the symbolic meaning of a male partner, and true homosexual attraction, which is based upon erotic arousal by the male physique per se, in particular, by the sight or feel of the external genitalia. (Blanchard, 1985a, p. 253)

In fact, Blanchard may have overstated the case somewhat: Although many informants seemingly were unable to make this crucial distinction, a few did so clearly and eloquently.

It is important to note that the allure of enacting the female reproductive role and the appeal of having one's femininity affirmed by the admiration of others are probably not the only reasons that some autogynephilic transsexuals express an interest in having men as sexual partners. Yet another reason might be that having a male partner signifies that an autogynephilic transsexual is, in at least some respects, *normal*. To be an autogynephilic transsexual is to be deviant. To be able to think of oneself as a "heterosexual woman"—a woman attracted to men—allows one to feel and appear more normal. Steiner (1985) described this phenomenon in an explanation that referenced Laud Humphreys' (1976) concept of *the breastplate of righteousness*—a Biblical phrase that Humphreys used to denote a public facade of social conformity that conceals secret deviance:

> Many writers have noted the extremely traditional and rigid stereotyped sexual and bonding roles that most transsexuals, male or female, adopt. Within the context of public sex in male washrooms or "tearooms," Humphreys (1976) has noted that participants often expound "exaggerated conservative" attitudes concerning acceptable social and sexual behavior, and he has termed this *the breastplate of righteousness*. He has suggested that this exaggerated righteousness is an example of extreme public conformity as a method of compensating for this "deviant" behavior. Feinbloom *et al.* [1976] suggest that the male-to-female transsexual may be expressing a similar conservatism, as exemplified by the usually complete acceptance of the rather limited, rigid, and stereotyped male and female roles that are more common to Victorian standards than to present-day standards. These authors further suggest that this breastplate-of-righteousness attitude accounts for the fact that the male[-to-female] transsexual, at least publicly, rejects lesbianism as a sexual option. (pp. 359–360)

Although MtF transsexuals no longer invariably reject lesbianism, some of them go to great lengths to maintain a facade of "heterosexual normality." One can observe this phenomenon on a few Internet web sites belonging to MtF transsexuals who fit the autogynephilic demographic (formerly married to women, male-typical occupational history, etc.) and have found men willing to marry them. On their web sites, these transsexuals clearly convey their pride in their status as married women; sometimes they even display their wedding photographs, which are often redolent of the kind of Victorian traditionalism that Steiner described.

Attraction to Men Often Reflects Desire for Validation of One's Femininity

Several informants who described their sexual attraction to, sexual fantasies about, or sexual interactions with men perceptively observed that their interest in men primarily reflected their erotic desire to have their femininity validated:

> I am clearly much more physically attracted to women than men. Yet my primary fantasies are about being a woman with a man. As I think about this, I would concede that this may have much more to do with feminine validation than attraction. The very idea of being desired by a heterosexual man is erotic for me. (018)

> Before the transition process started, I often fantasized I was a woman having sex with a man. A little while into transition, my sexual submission with men seemed to validate my feminine feelings. To have intercourse with men seems to be as womanly as anyone can get. (213)

> I had sex with a real man. He made me feel like literally a whole new person. It is as if I have finally discovered sex; like having sex with a man who affirmed my womanhood was some kind of ultimate fantasy. (035)

> I have had sexual encounters with eight men. These have been generally less than ideal, since they have all had trouble maintaining erections. None the less, I found I enjoyed the physical aspects of this type of sex and felt I was confirming my womanhood by being a passive partner. (068)

> I fantasized about being penetrated by a man and wanted a boyfriend to confirm my femininity. (200)

> I am a postoperative transsexual. I have found that I get the most sexually excited now when I fantasize about being sexy and beautiful and when someone else sees me that way. In fact, adoration from someone else plays into it. (069)

> It occurred to me that I should consider sex with men—what better way to confirm my new status as a woman? The idea of sex with men used to disgust me, but little by little that changed, and I became tremendously turned on by the superior physical strength men have and my growing ability to turn them on just by flaunting my stuff. Getting men aroused gives me an incredible sexual thrill and confirms my desirability as a woman. (077)

> I met a man who fell in love with me. When I was with him, I was happy to be submissive, I was excited to be looked after and to feel pretty and sexy. (214)

> I sometimes have the sense that what really thrills me is not my sexual partner (i.e., the supposed object of desire) but rather what he makes me feel like. I would feel thrilled to be a sexy woman capable of arousing a man—a real, straight, masculine man. (189)

> When I am a woman, I want to be with a man, acting like a woman, being treated like a woman and being loved like a woman. I know that this would be the ultimate for me. While

> I was living full-time, I had a boyfriend that I communicated with by e-mail. I even had a date with him when he was in my town. I enjoyed very much being treated like a lady. (215)

> I am powerfully sexually excited by the idea of being desired by men and by the notion of being thought of as beautiful. The turn on is not me, but to attract others. (216)

In all of the preceding narrative excerpts, the informants emphasized the validation they experienced from real or fantasized interactions with men. They described how the real or imagined men they interacted with made them feel about themselves: womanly, desirable, submissive, sexy, beautiful, attractive. They notably did not emphasize how they felt about specific men or about men in general (e.g., they did not describe falling in love with specific men or feeling aroused by specific men's bodies—or by men's bodies generally).

One informant reported that she experienced similar feelings of validation of her womanhood after being anally penetrated by another preoperative MtF transsexual:

> I was with an Asian pre-op. She was totally functional, and I bottomed (anal) for her for about a half hour. It didn't hurt at all, and I felt so feminine. I loved that I could cause a penis to orgasm the same way a natal female can. It was so great to be totally submissive. I loved being an object of pleasure for someone. (034)

As this informant suggested, the ability to take a woman's sexual role (or something like it) in relation to another person's penis is sometimes all that is necessary to experience validation of one's femininity. The gender of the person who possesses the penis may be of secondary importance.

Imagined Male Partners Are Often Vague or Anonymous Figures

Blanchard (1991) believed that, in the case of autogynephilic transsexuals who are aroused by fantasies of having sex with men as women, "the male partner represented in these fantasies is usually a vague, anonymous figure rather than a real person and probably has little excitatory function beyond that of completing the fantasy of vaginal intercourse in the female role" (p. 237). Blanchard was not the first to call attention to this phenomenon: Person and Ovesey (1974a) described so-called primary MtF transsexuals—those whom Blanchard (1989b) would later call analloerotic—as typically masturbating "either with no fantasy at all, or with a vague heterosexual fantasy in which the patient saw himself as a woman. The fantasies were impersonal, and the partner was usually a stylized man rather than a real person" (p. 16).

In the current study, many transsexual informants reported that the male figures in their fantasies closely conformed to these descriptions. Here are several representative examples:

> My most common sexual fantasy now is that I am a woman having sex with a man. No man in particular, just a male. Often he doesn't even really have a face; he's just there inside me as I imagine how that would feel. (148)

> I dreamed and fantasized about having sex as a woman with a man penetrating my vagina, yet it was always a faceless, generic man. (217)
>
> I did fantasize about having sex with men as a woman, but it was indeed with faceless male stereotypes instead of real individual men. (122)
>
> I fit in the mold of those who see men as faceless objects, necessary only to fulfill the fantasy. (184)
>
> My current fantasies involve becoming a woman. I imagine that I need to have a man penetrate my new vagina as a sort of rite of passage into womanhood; the man is faceless, and I don't enjoy the sex. (056)
>
> It was bewildering to identify with images of women when sexually aroused and imagine I was them. Who was penetrating me? I don't know, I left it blank. (082)
>
> I was now imagining that I was a woman and a man was making love to me. This man was faceless: He had a head, but no facial characteristics. (006)
>
> My sexual submission with men seemed to validate my feminine feelings. It was just like one of the articles described: a fantasy in which he was a prop. (213)
>
> The thought of sex with a man is erotic, provided I am a woman. In line with your assertions, the man in question is symbolic and featureless. The sexual contact is restricted to penetration only and does not extend to kissing the man, which I find distasteful. (053)
>
> My fantasies of being made love to have occasionally involved a faceless, symbolic man, but I am not attracted to men. (175)

The last two excerpts shed light on a question that might seem to have an obvious explanation but is actually rather subtle: Why are the male figures in so many of these autogynephilic fantasies faceless? It would be easy enough to conjure up the mental image of a specific man—a movie star or celebrity, for example—if one chose to. The obvious explanation assumes that a kind of mental parsimony operates in the creation of fantasies: Because the male figures in these fantasies are purely symbolic, there is simply no need to give them faces or turn them into specific, identifiable men. I suspect that the more accurate and more subtle explanation is that fantasies involving specific, identifiable men could often be experienced as antierotic: Faceless, abstract men can be useful as symbolic fantasy elements, but real men are not only unattractive but also potentially distasteful and even disgusting. Abstract men can enhance fantasies, whereas real men can potentially spoil those fantasies. This conjecture provides a convenient segue to the next topic.

Male Partners Are Often Arousing in Fantasy but Unattractive in Reality

Many informants stated that, although they were aroused by fantasies of having sex with men, they did not actually find men sexually attractive:

> When I masturbate now, it is either to the fantasy of being "humped" by a man or imagining myself as my wife being penetrated by a man. I don't get erotic feelings just from thinking of myself as a woman, but I do when I think of being a woman having sex with men, although I'm not especially attracted to men. (218)

> Even though I would love to be with a man as a woman and even have normal sex, I am not attracted physically to a man. (215)

> I flirted with the idea of having sex with a man; I was very curious, but I never did anything about it. I still didn't see men as being at all attractive, even though I wanted to have sex with them. I just wasn't attracted to men. (217)

In an alternative formulation, some informants reported that they experienced no sexual attraction toward men when they were in the male role but found men attractive when they were in the female role. This suggests that the male partner himself was not intrinsically attractive but that the opportunity to assume the female role in relation to a man was the essential precondition for the experience of sexual "attraction":

> I have an increasing sexual desire oriented toward men. I always fantasized myself to be a woman during the sexual act, both with women and with men. I never feel drawn to a man when I come to him as a man, but thinking of myself as a woman makes me regard a man as the most attractive sexual partner. (219)

> As a man, I am never attracted to other men. But, when I think of myself as a woman, I do fantasize about being penetrated and giving oral copulation. I would never want a relationship with a man full-time, though. (127)

Some informants went still further and observed that, although they were aroused by the fantasy of having sex with a man as a woman, they actually found men or men's bodies to be disagreeable or disgusting:

> By the time I was 13, I would occasionally fantasize about what it would be like to have a man between my legs with his penis inside me. It was during this erotic fantasy that I had my first orgasm. Later in life I did experiment with men, but I didn't find it satisfying and actually found it a bit disgusting. (220)

> I live alone and often entertain men for sexual pleasure while I am dressed as a woman. I met a man who took me to dinner as a woman. I slept with him and was very much aroused by the experience. I enjoyed sucking his penis but I thought the balls were disgusting. (214)

> I transitioned a little over 2 years ago. I have had strong erotic fantasies in which I was a woman who was sexually submissive to a man. The thought of actualizing this fantasy does not interest me in the least. I can enjoy thinking about it to the point of orgasm, but I'd hate to do it. (186)

> I created a female identity on the Internet and had cybersex with many males as a woman. It felt wonderful to get them to come. This really made me feel like a woman. While cybersex is fine, I find males unattractive and think it would be disgusting to really be with one sexually. (109)

In the late 1990s, I became friends with an autogynephilic transsexual who had completed SRS; I will call her Ms. Y. She provided me with a memorable description of her sexual interaction with a male partner, and her account graphically illustrates some of the ideas discussed by the informants above. Note that some details of Ms. Y's history have been changed to conceal her identity. Ms. Y was in her mid-40s and held a doctoral degree in a clinical behavioral science. She had been married twice to women and had been heterosexually active while living as a man. She had engaged in only incidental sexual interactions with men before transition.

She was familiar with and accepted Blanchard's theories about autogynephilia, but she nevertheless claimed that after her transition, her sexual interest had become directed primarily toward men. She had found a male partner with whom she was regularly sexually active. I asked her to describe what she and her partner did together sexually. She explained that her preferred sexual activity with her partner was to kneel before him, blindfolded and with her hands tied behind her back, and perform fellatio on him. It seemed to me that Ms. Y had found the perfect behavioral expression of the fantasy that many of the above informants described: She was able to have oral sex with a "faceless" man—at least a man whose face she could not see—and was required to have contact only with his penis, the only part of his anatomy necessary for her to feel that she was enacting the female sexual role.

Attraction to Men Rarely Extends to Feelings of Romantic Love

Sexual orientation is usually assessed by asking subjects whether they are sexually attracted to men or women. An alternative approach, possibly a superior one, is to ask subjects whether the first person they fell in love with was male or female or whether they habitually fall in love with men or women (e.g., Fisher et al., 2010) or with boys or girls (e.g., de Vries, Steensma, Doreleijers, & Cohen-Kettenis, 2011).

Although many informants described sexual attraction to men, almost none raised the issue of romantic love for men, either by reporting such love or by denying it. Only one informant claimed that she sometimes fell in love with men; her unusual account is presented in detail toward the end of this chapter. A few informants specifically denied that they fell in love with men. One reported that she was aroused by the fantasy of having sex with men but fell in love only with women:

> I started having crushes, but only on girls. This was very confusing. I dreamed and fantasized about having sex as a woman with a man penetrating my vagina, yet I still didn't see men as being at all attractive, even though I wanted to have sex with them. I just don't get it. Why all the cruising of personal ads for men who like girls like me, when the people I fall in love with and like to look at are women? (217)

Another informant stated that she only wanted to have long-term romantic relationships with women:

> I have commonly loved women in long-term relationships and men in short-term relationships. At some point in transition, I began to be more attracted to women. Sex had more and more of an emotional component, and my connections with women keyed into that in a way I had never experienced before. (099)

My clinical experience leads me to believe that autogynephilic transsexuals routinely fall in love with women and rarely or never fall in love with men. This is a neglected area of clinical research, however, and I am not aware of any formal investigations of this issue.

Attraction to Men Sometimes Reflects Men's Propensity to Mistreat Women

One reason some autogynephilic transsexuals find men attractive is that men more than women have a propensity to mistreat women and some autogynephilic transsexuals are sexually aroused by the idea of being a woman mistreated or raped by a man. MtF transsexuals are hardly unique in having sexual fantasies about being mistreated or raped or in being sexually aroused by fantasies that they would never want to experience in reality; many natal women have similar fantasies and feelings (Bivona & Critelli, 2009; Critelli & Bivona, 2008). The point is simply that arousal to the fantasy of being mistreated or raped by a man seems to mediate some cases of autogynephilic transsexuals' attraction to men: It is simply one more way to be a woman in relation to a man.

One informant was aroused by the idea of being forced by a man to have sex against her will and being verbally degraded by men:

> The men in my fantasies are usually much larger than myself and extremely well-endowed. A feeling of "Oh my God, I don't know if I can take this, but I have to continue submitting to this pseudo-rape (it's scary, and the urge to beg him to stop is so strong) now that I've let him start" is the key to mind-blowing orgasms. My fantasies usually begin with the whole feminization process and proceed to my going out and prowling bars in a seedy neighborhood looking for my first sexual encounter with a straight man. I often end up getting it from several men on a pool table after hours, reveling in the degrading way they talk to and about me. (060)

Other informants fantasized about experiencing rape:

> I have several fantasies I use to achieve orgasm. One fantasy is being taken sexually by a man. I am always very feminine and totally submissive. My partner is so passionate he would simply overpower any resistance on my part. Sometimes I imagine resisting and he date rapes me. (156)

> I have never thought of having sex with a guy when I'm physically male. At the same time, I have fantasized myself being a woman and being gang raped. (007)

Some of these fantasies contain features (e.g., being described in a degrading way) suggestive of sexual masochism, a paraphilia that commonly co-occurs with autogynephilia. I will discuss sexual masochism in autogynephilic transsexuals in more detail in Chap. 9.

Reports of Increased Attraction to Men During Transition Are Frequent

Several studies and case reports have documented that MtF transsexuals with a history of sexual attraction to women sometimes report that their self-described sexual preference has shifted toward greater (and occasionally exclusive) sexual attraction to men during the gender transition process and especially following cross-sex hormone therapy or SRS (Daskalos, 1998; De Cuypere et al., 2005; Lawrence, 2005; Muirhead-Allwood, Royle, & Young, 1999). Whether this phenomenon represents a genuine change in sexual orientation or merely greater expression of the autogynephilic wish to have one's femininity validated by a male partner is open to dispute, although I consider the latter explanation far more plausible. Sexual orientation in males is probably essentially immutable in adulthood (Swaab, 2007). Whitam (1997) was willing to declare categorically that "it is well known that sex reassignment surgery does not change sexual orientation" (p. 202); I agree with his statement, at least as it applies to MtF transsexuals.

Accordingly, I hypothesize that all or almost all reports of changes in sexual orientation by autogynephilic transsexuals simply reflect greater autogynephilic interest in validation of one's femininity by a male partner, not a genuine change in somatotypic preference. The issue has received little formal study, however: I know of only one investigation in which a nonhomosexual MtF transsexual who described a change in sexual orientation toward men following SRS underwent physiologic measurement of her sexual arousal pattern in a laboratory setting (Lawrence, Latty, Chivers, & Bailey, 2005). In this case, consistent with my hypothesis, measurement of neovaginal blood flow did not confirm the subject's reported change in sexual orientation.

However one interprets self-reported change in sexual orientation in autogynephilic transsexuals, several informants stated that they had experienced such a change. They often described the change in a casual, unelaborated way, as though it were the most natural thing in the world:

> I have never been attracted to men, but lately, I have begun to look at men in a different light. I look forward to pursuing this when I make the complete transition. (188)

> I'm also at the point in my evolving sexuality where, through no effort on my part, men are starting to look good. (144)

> I have an increasing sexual desire oriented toward men. I still have sex with women, but a sexual act with a man seems more satisfying day by day. (219)

> I began experimenting with sexuality with men (I never had before) and found it arousing and this has essentially replaced the female imagery as my arousal mechanism. (139)

Indeed, some informants suggested that such a reversal of sexual orientation was entirely normal:

> Now I find I am aroused far more by the opposite sex. My fantasies have evolved from my origins as male with a female before transition to me being female with a male. I look at men entirely differently now as well. I never had a desire to be with a man ever before transition and I assume that this reversal is somewhat normal for my accepting and being a woman mentally and socially. (221)

> I had always considered myself heterosexual. My sexual preference after starting transition actually flipped over to liking men for the first time in my life. It felt completely normal, and I now simply considered myself a heterosexual female. (182)

One informant, however, concluded that the dramatic change in her sexual orientation after transition represented the actualization of her long-standing fantasies of being treated as a woman by a man and taking a woman's sexual role in relation to a man:

> As a man, I was simply not attracted to men. But now, as a woman, I have found great happiness and fulfillment being in a relationship with a wonderful man for the last 10 months. Am I still attracted to women at all? Not with him around I'm not! Reality at this point is finally much closer to what I have always wanted and seen in my mind. Now I am the woman having her cheeks kissed by a loving man. Now I am the woman having her breasts fondled by a man who only sees her as a beautiful woman. Now I am the woman taking her lover's penis into her mouth. I never wanted to admit to myself or anyone what a turn on just thinking about all this was to me. (021)

This informant's description is consistent with Blanchard's explanation that purported changes in sexual orientation in autogynephilic transsexuals reflect actualization of behavioral autogynephilic fantasies.

Two informants explained that they believed it was possible to learn to be sexually oriented toward men, perhaps through a kind of conditioning process:

> If a MtF fits your description of an autogynephiliac, finds sexual relations to be the ultimate validation of femininity, and is an unapologetic heterosexual, then a migration in orientation is both necessary and logical. I will even go out on a limb here to further suggest that these MtFs can actually learn to be aroused directly by men through some sort of conditioning process. If an autogynephiliac believes that the ultimate validation of a female body is to have sexual relations with a man, she then learns how to be aroused by men. (018)

> Even though I would love to be with a man as a woman and even have normal sex, I am not attracted physically to a man. But I might learn to like it or even love it for the man that is with me. I would love him for accepting me and that would provide the motivation to become sexually attracted to him. After all, women are not attracted to all men, only certain ones; and if the man shows them that they are loved, they are attracted even more. (215)

In fact, there is a great deal of data—most of it from gay men who desperately wanted to become heterosexual—demonstrating that it is essentially impossible for men to change their sexual orientation in adulthood, through conditioning or any other means. Summarizing these data, Swaab (2007) concluded that "there can be little doubt that sexual orientation has become fixed in adulthood and is beyond influencing later" (p. 434).

Repression of Genuine Attraction to Men Due to Homophobia

A few informants with a history of sexual attraction to women believed they had really been attracted to men all along (or had been destined to be so attracted) and had merely repressed their attraction to men because they had internalized the homophobic values of society:

> I am a pretty classic autogynephilic transsexual. Yet, I think I could have equally easily been a classic homosexual transsexual if circumstances had been slightly different. When I was younger, I was fearful of being known as a cross-dresser, but I was even more fearful of being gay. Though I had thoughts and feelings that I was attracted to men and not women,

> I kept them more suppressed than even my wish to be female. In hindsight, I was homophobic, probably because of the environment I was raised in. Did the environmentally induced homophobia inhibit my homosexual transsexuality? I almost had an experience with a guy in 10th grade. Had I had that experience, it's possible that I would have realized I was not attracted to women and I might have sought relationships with men. I wonder how many of the transsexuals who eventually are attracted to men actually suppress their true orientation in order to fit into society. (222)

> I was very repressed. I was almost homophobic. If I was repressed and I was trained to prefer girls as acceptable behavior and trained not to prefer men, then I would outwardly and inwardly lie and prefer women. So, I would suggest that as I begin to acknowledge my transsexual nature and my true feelings, I find myself more attracted to men and less to women. (074)

> I also eventually discovered that I really was attracted to men underneath my homophobia, and found that attraction very enjoyable and natural. (119)

> I admit that I enjoy being desired and made to feel attractive by straight men as a validation of my femininity. My heterosexual past was entirely due to internalized homophobia. (115)

Note that this "repression of attraction to men due to internalized homophobia" explanation cannot account for the fact that the great majority of homosexual MtF transsexuals and other homosexual males, who are also exposed to ubiquitous homophobic messages from society, somehow manage to become aware of their genuine sexual attraction to men during adolescence or early adulthood, even if they do not immediately act on their feelings. Consequently, I don't find explanations like these to be very persuasive. These explanations are, however, psychologically revealing.

Why might it be important for some autogynephilic transsexuals to be able to tell themselves that they were "really" attracted to men all along or should have been? Some other informants, whose accounts appeared earlier, were perfectly content to assert that their previous attraction to women had been genuine but that their sexual orientation had simply shifted toward men as a result of social transition or cross-sex hormone therapy. I think the answer lies in the fact that any deviation from the "classic" transsexual pattern ("has felt and acted feminine from earliest childhood, has never been sexually aroused by women's apparel, and is romantically inclined toward males"; Blanchard, Clemmensen, et al., 1985, p. 508) can potentially feel discrediting to one's status as a legitimate transsexual. Some of these deviations probably feel more consequential than others to particular individuals. Perhaps the informants who strongly believed that they were really attracted to men all along (or should have been) simply considered a history of sexual attraction to women to be a particularly discrediting feature. Interestingly, all of them acknowledged and most made no attempt to explain away their history of autogynephilic arousal, which many people would probably consider far more discrediting than a history of sexual attraction to women. There is still much to be learned about the elaborate explanations that autogynephilic transsexuals sometimes create to try to make sense of their feelings and histories. I will address some of these explanations in greater detail in Chap. 10.

An Autogynephilic Transsexual "Exclusively Attracted to Men" (with Limitations)

One unusual narrative was submitted by a self-described autogynephilic transsexual who also described herself as "exclusively sexually attracted to men." She had been evaluated at the former Clarke Institute of Psychiatry in Toronto ("the Clarke"), where Blanchard conducted his pioneering studies of autogynephilia in the 1980s and 1990s. She was familiar with Blanchard's theory and accepted much but not all of it. She stated that she fell in love with and was attracted to men—at least some men—because she was attracted to their spirits, albeit not to their bodies. This informant also stated that she loved another MtF transsexual because she admired her confidence and found her beautiful, despite not being attracted to her body. This informant further conjectured that her love for and attraction to some individuals might be mediated by their gender-atypical traits. Her account is lengthy but fascinating:

> There's a boy where I go to school who I think is absolutely smashing. I was talking to another student, Heather, who is married with two children, saying how amazing I thought it was that she was able to balance all these things. The boy turned to us and said, "She's a better woman than I am." We all just about died laughing! But what I saw in him was such incredible support for his friend and such confidence in himself without being fearful for his gender. I just thought he was the most magnificent and wonderful man I had ever met (although I have to admit that it doesn't hurt either that he holds doors open for me and wishes me a nice day all the time). The point is that, although there always seems to be a gender-bending connection, I am directly attracted to him. I think he's amazing! But I do concede that my attraction stems from an attraction to his spirit, not his body. Likewise, there is a transsexual woman of my acquaintance who I think is without a doubt the most beautiful woman I've ever met. She projects such femininity and self-confidence. I think she's incredible. When I was a patient at the Clarke, they placed so much emphasis on "are you attracted to men, or are you an autogynephile?" My response was that I was exclusively sexually attracted to men, but I am an autogynephile. They said, "But these men you think about—they're faceless, aren't they?" What I'm saying is, that isn't the case. I fall in love with and am attracted to real live men. (I'm not saying I think my transsexual friend is a man; I am saying I love her but I'm not sexually attracted to her body). Perhaps, though, my autogynephilia is somehow connected with a love and appreciation of people who don't follow the gender scripts they're handed. (123)

Although this informant claimed that she was "exclusively sexually attracted to [some] men," she seemed to be attracted to their personality traits (e.g., their supportiveness, self-confidence, and androgyny), not their physical traits. This is such an unusual and idiosyncratic use of the term "sexual attraction" that it renders the informant's description of her sexual orientation almost meaningless. But the phrase "exclusively sexually attracted to men" has been widely used in the professional literature about MtF transsexualism, and it has historically functioned almost as a "seal of approval" in certain gender programs. It was—and in a few programs still is—how one needed to describe oneself in order to be taken seriously as a MtF transsexual. It is understandable, then, why some autogynephilic transsexuals would want to claim this specific description, whether or not it is genuinely applicable to them according to conventional definitions.

It is also interesting to notice that this informant, generalizing from her attraction to an androgynous man and her love for another MtF transsexual, pointed to a "gender-bending connection" as the common thread. This is plausible, of course, and it sounds progressive and avant-garde. But another common thread—if one were willing to be politically incorrect—might be "some masculine traits in evidence"; this might arguably be what one would expect from someone supposedly exclusively sexually attracted to men, and its absence is telling. As one who accepts Blanchard's theories, I tend to notice another common thread, "some feminine traits in evidence." I believe that autogynephilic transsexuals tend to fall in love with women; consequently, the men they are likely to find most appealing should be those who most closely resemble women, especially in their physical characteristics.

An Autogynephilic Transsexual with Substantial Sexual Experience with Men

Because autogynephilia is theorized to be a misdirected form of attraction to women, it would be logical—and correct, I believe—to conclude that the primary sexual orientation of autogynephilic transsexuals who declare themselves attracted to men is toward women and that their supposed attraction to men is wholly a secondary phenomenon, mediated entirely by autogynephilia. One might consequently assume that autogynephilic transsexuals who engage in sex with men are likely to have only a few male partners and that their sexual activity with men is likely to be rare and of little real importance.

As a statistical generalization, this is not entirely incorrect. For example, in a study of 232 MtF transsexuals who had completed SRS (Lawrence, 2005), I observed that, among 92 MtF transsexuals who were behaviorally bisexual before SRS (i.e., who reported at least 1 male and 1 female partner), the median number of female partners before SRS was 7, whereas the median number of male partners before SRS was only 3, with one-third of the participants reporting only 1 male partner. There were some notable exceptions to this pattern, however: 8 (9%) of the bisexual participants reported 11–20 male partners and 2 (2%) reported 21 or more male partners. These latter respondents reported considerable experience with men by almost any measure.

Some autogynephilic transsexuals not only report substantial sexual experience with men but may have had many more male than female partners and may even have identified as homosexual men in the past. The following narrative excerpt was submitted by an informant with such a history:

> I am 38 years old and 8 months postoperative. I had begun cross-dressing as a child and had fantasized about being female. From puberty onwards, I was sexually aroused by the idea of being a woman, wearing women's clothes, and being made love to as a woman by a man. I identified early (age 12 or 13) as gay or bisexual. I did not date as a teen and was very friendly with girls. I was not particularly effeminate and physically fitted in well with men.

> At college, I came out and had numerous affairs with men and, surprisingly, women (much less, more awkward). In college, I met a woman, fell in love, and married. We had two children, and I stopped cross-dressing for 7 or 8 years. With the birth of my first child, a girl, I began to dress again. This continued through the birth of our second child, a girl also. Throughout this time, I was most turned on by the idea of being made love to as a woman by a man. However, I still conceived of these fantasies in terms of homosexual relationships (penises played a big role—mutual penetration and oral sex). At around 30, I began to attend transgender support groups. At this time, in my sexual fantasies, I first conceived of myself as a female being made love to by a man. After my marriage broke up, I dated men. The turn-on was the idea of being accepted by them as female. At that time, I met my current partner. He stayed with me through surgery and we are happily living together. Today, I am powerfully sexually excited by the idea of being desired by men and by the notion of being thought of as beautiful. Thus, I suppose I am still sexually motivated. Yet the turn on is not me but to attract others—in particular men, but I also enjoy being able to attract lesbians. (216)

This MtF transsexual stated that she identified as gay or bisexual at puberty, engaged in numerous affairs with men in college, entered into an unsuccessful marriage with a woman, subsequently resumed dating men, and successfully partnered with a man after SRS. A clinician who did not elicit this informant's history of sexual arousal with cross-dressing and cross-gender fantasy, lack of childhood effeminacy, numerous affairs with women, and falling in love with a woman might mistakenly conclude that the informant was a typical androphilic MtF transsexual. A clinician who elicited these historical details but was not attuned to the fact that the real turn-on for the informant was not her male partners' bodies but the idea that they accepted and treated her as a woman (i.e., that she was not genuinely androphilic) might mistakenly conclude that the informant was both autogynephilic and androphilic. Consequently, it is important for clinicians to bear in mind that some autogynephilic transsexuals have considerable sexual experience with men. When evaluating behaviorally bisexual MtF transsexuals, it is important to ask about a history of autogynephilic arousal, who they habitually fall in love with, and what element of sex with men—their partners' bodies or the validation of one's womanhood that male partners provide—is experienced as primarily arousing.

Making Sense of Autogynephilic Attraction to Men

A few years ago, I was consulted by a gender dysphoric male client with a history similar to those given by many of the informants in this chapter. He was married to a woman, and he had engaged in several romantic relationships with women before marriage. He had never been attracted to a man while presenting himself as a man. He had not been effeminate as a child, he had served in the military in an elite combat unit, and he held two advanced degrees in the physical sciences. By his own description, he experienced transvestic, anatomic, and behavioral autogynephilia, but the last of these predominated. His most intense erotic arousal came from engaging in sex with men while presenting himself as a woman. His intelligence was in the very superior range, and he had read most of what I had written and much of what

Blanchard had written about autogynephilia. His presenting concern was deciding whether or not he was "really" androphilic—sexually oriented toward men.

It seemed evident to me that this client was not genuinely androphilic: He was clearly an autogynephilic man whose most intense source of erotic arousal involved the most common type of behavioral autogynephilia, autogynephilic interpersonal fantasy involving a male partner. But what was evident to me was not at all evident to this client, even though he was probably more intelligent than 99.9% of the population and had read more about autogynephilia than most psychologists and psychiatrists who specialize in the treatment of gender dysphoria. The most intense and rewarding sexual experiences of this man's life had involved sex with male partners. How could he not wonder whether his real sexual attraction was toward men? His uncertainty about an issue that seemed so straightforward to me was a reminder of how profoundly confusing this type of behavioral autogynephilia can be, even to highly intelligent, well-informed people. Eventually, this client recognized that he was not genuinely androphilic, but this realization occurred only gradually.

Unfortunately, I suspect the kind of confusion this client experienced is likely to remain widespread among autogynephilic gender dysphoric men for the foreseeable future, for several reasons. First, many professionals who specialize in the treatment of gender dysphoria dismiss Blanchard's ideas about autogynephilia for reasons that are primarily political rather than scientific: that is, because his ideas "directly contradict basic tenets of the worldwide transgender movement" (Nuttbrock, Bockting, Mason, et al., 2011, p. 249). Consequently, these professionals are not attuned to the concept of behavioral autogynephilia manifesting as a desire for sex with men; they are unlikely to ask about it or recognize it and are unlikely to be willing or able to educate their clients about it.

Second, there exists a naive but prevalent belief that sexual orientation in nonhomosexual MtF transsexuals can sometimes genuinely change, especially after cross-sex hormone therapy, in contrast to the more skeptical view that this treatment merely sets the stage for more confident misinterpretation and misreporting of an underlying sexual orientation that not only remains unchanged but is, in fact, unchangeable. Consider this passage by Meyer-Bahlburg (2010), who is one of the smartest and best informed gender specialists in the world:

> One feature of animal models of the sexual differentiation of brain and behavior that has not yet found sufficient consideration in human research on gender development is the observation in rats that males have the neural circuitry of all aspects of female sexual behavior. That circuitry is usually blocked by perinatal sex-hormonal defeminization, but can be activated by the induction of an atypical sex-hormone milieu in adulthood (de Vries & Södersten, 2009). Perhaps related mechanisms…contribute to the sexual orientation change observed in many trans[sexual] persons after onset of cross-gender hormone treatment. (p. 466)

Does female sexual behavior in rats (i.e., lordosis) really provide a useful model for something as complex as androphilic sexual orientation in humans? What about the fact that the female sexual behavior that de Vries and Södersten (2009) referred to had been elicited by a very specific combination of estrogen and progesterone that is quite unlike the type of cross-sex hormone therapy that most MtF transsexuals receive? Meyer-Bahlburg's statement demonstrates that even knowledgeable experts will sometimes clutch at straws to avoid the unpleasant conclusion that most or all nonhomosexual MtF transsexuals who report a change in sexual orientation after hormone therapy are simply engaging in unintentional self-deception. The willingness of some serious scholars to suggest that sexual orientation in nonhomosexual MtF transsexuals is potentially malleable lends an air of validity to the idea that a formerly heterosexual man could actually become genuinely androphilic.

Third and finally, the belief that some nonhomosexual MtF transsexuals experience a change in their sexual orientation can serve as a basis for rejecting all sexual orientation-based typologies of MtF transsexualism (see Cohen-Kettenis & Pfäfflin, 2010), including Blanchard's. Such a blanket rejection lends credence to the idea that Blanchard's concept of autogynephilia and his MtF transsexual typology are simply inapplicable to many nonhomosexual MtF transsexuals. It thereby gives some clinicians a further excuse not to take the concept of autogynephilia seriously and not to learn about it, ask about it, or educate their clients about it.

Can anything change this state of affairs? Perhaps the accumulation of more narratives like the ones in this chapter can eventually effect a change. These narratives demonstrate that the "attraction to men" that some autogynephilic transsexuals experience looks nothing like genuine androphilia. Unlike genuine androphilia, autogynephilic attraction to men is validation seeking rather than object seeking; it values faceless abstractions over real male bodies, which are experienced as unappealing or disgusting; and it rarely, if ever, extends to romantic love. These characteristics are indeed manifestations of a sexual orientation, but that sexual orientation is autogynephilia, not androphilia.

Chapter 9
Other Aspects of Autogynephilic Sexuality

The narratives submitted by the transsexual informants addressed several other aspects of autogynephilic sexuality in addition to those discussed in the previous chapters. Many informants observed that autogynephilic fantasies were always or almost always necessary to achieve orgasm in all sexual situations, including during masturbation. Some described autogynephilic arousal as being, at least at times, unpleasant, psychologically distressing, or unwanted. Informants reported a variety of unpleasant feelings immediately following orgasms that had been achieved with the help of autogynephilic fantasies. Several narratives discussed the effects of feminizing hormone therapy on autogynephilic arousal. Others described additional paraphilic sexual interests that co-occurred with autogynephilia.

Autogynephilic Fantasies Required for Orgasm

As noted in Chap. 7, several informants reported that autogynephilic fantasies were always necessary to achieve orgasm during sexual intercourse with female partners. Still others observed that achieving orgasm was contingent on autogynephilic fantasies in all sexual situations, including during masturbation. Here are some representative excerpts:

> As an adolescent and young adult, I would often masturbate, but I couldn't get aroused without picturing myself as a woman. It is still impossible for me to have an orgasm without some form of autogynephilic fantasy. (056)

> From a sexual standpoint, I can not have an orgasm unless I am thinking about being a woman. (223)

> I have never been able to orgasm without thinking of being a woman. (049)

> For me, sex always involved visualizing myself being a woman in some variation: clothes, sexual situations, genitalia, breasts, the whole gamut. I still cannot orgasm without visualizing something about being a woman. (224)

A.A. Lawrence, *Men Trapped in Men's Bodies: Narratives of Autogynephilic Transsexualism*, Focus on Sexuality Research, DOI 10.1007/978-1-4614-5182-2_9,

One individual conceded that she had managed to climax a few times without resort to an autogynephilic fantasy but that such occurrences had been rare:

> Just about every time I masturbated, I'd be fantasizing about being a woman, being transformed into a woman, or having sex with a woman while being one, too. I can count on one hand the times I successfully masturbated to the thought of having sex with a woman being a man, and those times it was through speed alone (having a limp dick) that I was able to climax. (225)

Altogether, about two dozen transsexual informants—roughly 10%—spontaneously volunteered that autogynephilic fantasies were always or almost always necessary to achieve orgasm during masturbation or partnered sex, even though the issue of obligatory reliance on autogynephilic fantasies for orgasm was never asked about or alluded to in any of the survey solicitations.

Discomfort with Autogynephilic Arousal

Gender dysphoric men and other men who cross-dress sometimes report that sexual arousal associated with cross-dressing is unwanted or bothersome (Blanchard & Clemmensen, 1988; Buhrich, 1978). In the current study, several informants similarly reported that they disliked or were made uncomfortable by autogynephilic arousal. Some stated that their autogynephilic feelings made them feel driven, were intrusive, or interfered with their concentration:

> I was extremely autogynephilic. My fantasies were of my feminization, which still continue, despite not having testosterone. My sexual urges have virtually disappeared since surgery. I hope I get horny again, but I am very happy not to be as driven as I once was. (136)

> Every day is a constant fight between the things that I have to do and the autogynephilia that creates disruptive thoughts. It is not easy to study when your mind pops up thoughts of being a girl. It is impossible to concentrate at your job when you envy the pantyhose that a stranger outside wore. It is hard to maintain a healthy relationship with your girlfriend when you envy her for being female. (006)

The latter narrative implied that both autogynephilic erotic arousal and the intrusive feelings of envy and longing it caused were experienced as disruptive factors.

Other informants observed that autogynephilic arousal acted as an unpleasant reminder of their unwanted maleness:

> I am 23 years post-op. I would like to distinguish between the sense of well-being resulting from being a girl and the sexual arousal of a male body. The former was always welcome; the latter wasn't. If fantasy or crossdressing was leading to arousal, I'd generally either try to avoid it or speed it up to get it out of the way. (138)

> I began crossdressing when I was 10. I was having a shower and my sister's bathing suit was hanging there. I put it on and had an erection; it felt nice to wear it, but I hated my penis. I wanted the erection to go away. For the next 9 years, my cross-dressing increased, the erections persisted, and I continued to hate my penis. (214)

> Like many others, I, too, have always had these feelings of arousal at the mere thoughts associated with being female. And it always pissed me off! I hated that putting on a dress or wearing other feminine attire or even just fantasizing about being a normal woman would elicit such an "un-female" response both physically and mentally. I wanted so badly for the things I was doing to simply be and feel normal. I didn't want to be aroused by them! Because of my attitude, I never felt right feeding these reactions to cross-dressing by masturbating during them. I was therefore never fetishistic with any clothing or with anything, a fact I took comfort and pride in. (021)

These narratives suggested that the informants found autogynephilic arousal to be both physically distressing and invalidating to their cross-gender identities.

Practical considerations, especially the difficulties of wearing women's clothing in the presence of an erection, were also emphasized in some narratives:

> Two years ago, I started wearing my mother's clothes, particularly her underwear. Every time I used her clothes, I had erections. I do not like having erections during my cross-dressing sessions; sometimes I let my mother's underwear somehow get wet. I try not to have these erections doing my cross-dressing sessions; a big penis makes it hard to put on skirts and look feminine. It is not something I like and I definitely prefer not having them. (207)

> I would guiltily sneak into my mother's closet when she was away and wear as many combinations of her clothes as possible. I was almost always turned on by it, but I mostly did not masturbate. Instead, I'd condemn my penis for getting in the way. My friends still can't understand why I hate my penis so damn much, even after I told them that I am very committed to the idea of becoming a woman. Wearing women's clothing is always something that initially turns me on, but when that damn penis of mine eventually becomes flaccid, I feel very comfortable and natural. (003)

> In the early days, I would become aroused whenever anyone—a sales clerk, a casual stranger—would address me as "Ma'am" or perform some courtesy, such as holding a door for me. This arousal led to a heightened fear of discovery, i.e., that my erection would give me away. (001)

> When I reached adolescence, I started cross-dressing discretely and would get aroused and masturbate. After the sexual part of the experience, I would remain dressed as long as was safe, glad that I didn't have an erection to ruin the lines of the dress or skirt. (056)

Taken together, these accounts make it clear that autogynephilic transsexuals do not always enjoy autogynephilic arousal but sometimes experience it as invalidating, distressing, inconvenient, or otherwise undesirable.

Postorgasmic Reactions: Disgust, Remorse, and Remission of Gender Dysphoria

Several informants described their feelings immediately following orgasms that were associated with cross-dressing or cross-gender fantasies. Many reported temporary remission of their gender dysphoria, feelings of disgust or remorse about their cross-dressing or cross-gender fantasies, or a combination of these.

Consequently, they not infrequently tried to avoid having orgasms or postponed them for as long as possible. Some narratives emphasized negative feelings immediately following orgasm:

> I went for extended periods with no sex or masturbation, because I believed that being aroused by sex-change fantasies was a mental illness. Also, I found that orgasms immediately made me feel masculine and ruined the feminine fantasy. (119)

> Though I liked the pleasure associated with orgasm, I did not like the feeling afterward. I felt dirty, and for a short time after it lowered the intensity of my cross-gender feelings. Because of these feelings, I masturbated infrequently, mostly to get rid of sexual energy that had no other outlet. (222)

> Eventually I was completely taken over with my feminization fantasies. There were times the urge to be transformed into a female was overwhelming. After I shaved my legs or took a Premarin pill, I would climax and suddenly feel dirty and disgusted with myself. I kept having these fantasies, and I couldn't help it. (097)

> Many years ago, before hormone therapy, I did obtain a certain sexual satisfaction from cross-dressing. I masturbated to orgasm with thoughts of being a woman and having a woman's body. But immediately afterwards, I always felt a crushing loss that the fantasy was not a reality. I loathed the sight of my male-shaped body and face so much I couldn't bear to look in a mirror. (062)

> When I was younger, after orgasm I felt rather ashamed about my thoughts. I began to cross-dress so I could better imagine myself as female, and after orgasm I would rush to remove all traces of womanliness from my body. I was embarrassed and didn't want to be caught doing something wrong. (066)

Other informants emphasized the dramatic and almost instantaneous, albeit only temporary, remission of their gender dysphoria or desire to be female:

> I was surprised by the abrupt alternation of my feelings that occurred in fractions of seconds when an "en femme" session ended with an ejaculation (and most of the time I ended masturbating). Before orgasm, I was ready to sacrifice everything to become a woman. And suddenly, after having an orgasm, the feeling was totally reversed! I was flooded with powerful remorseful feeling, which made me unhappy and miserable. (006)

> I wanted to be a girl since age 5 or 6. Although my desires did not begin as sexual, sex certainly became the focus. I found that, after orgasm, my entire thoughts on the subject reversed. I couldn't believe I could think that I wanted to be a girl! Within minutes, however, my "normal" state of mind returned. (112)

> Every time I have an orgasm, including to this day, the strong sexual urge to imagine myself as a woman goes away completely. It is like flipping off a light switch in my brain. Then, anywhere from a couple of hours to many days later, it always reappears. I have noticed that during periods of great stress, the length of time it takes for these feelings of autogynephilia to return is shortened. (127)

> When the woman sexual feeling is aroused in me, I can't make myself not act on it. When ejaculation happens, I always lose my woman sexual feeling, and I really hate this. I feel guilty and don't know what to do. My mind becomes that of a man again for a while, and this is so confusing. (226)

A few informants, aware that their desire to be female would quickly if only temporarily dissipate once orgasm occurred, tried to prolong their feelings of sexual arousal and their resulting desire to be female for as long as possible by postponing or avoiding orgasm.

I knew that as soon as an orgasm was achieved, the desire to be female would disappear for a time. For that reason, I often tried to delay orgasm or avoided orgasm at all. Whole weeks sometimes passed before I masturbated. All this time, I went out wearing female underwear under my clothes and generally tried to do normal female activities, avoiding masturbation and orgasm. (006)

Autogynephilic gender dysphoric clients I have seen in my practice have also described postponing or avoiding orgasm in order to prolong their feelings of sexual arousal and their resulting desire to be female. We ordinarily tend to think about erotic desire and sexual arousal as emotional/motivational states that prepare individuals for action—specifically, in the case of men, for sexual behavior leading to ejaculation and orgasm (Janssen, 2011). Consequently, it might seem counterintuitive that a person would try to prolong these feeling states, rather than trying to promptly discharge or resolve them through orgasmic release.

I can think of at least two plausible reasons, however, why autogynephilic gender dysphoric men might enjoy the feeling of autogynephilic arousal and the resulting desire to be female and want to prolong it, apart from simple avoidance of any dysphoric feelings associated with orgasm itself. First, experiencing autogynephilic arousal or the autogynephilic desire to be female can potentially reduce stress by concentrating the individual's attention and directing it away from unpleasant feelings or cognitions. As Docter (1988) noted, "by having something specific to concentrate upon, the unpleasant or anxiety-laden thoughts, which are derived from our daily experience, are somehow pushed into the distant background" (p. 118). Docter went on to observe that "both transvestism and transsexualism are, in part, mood altering behavioral strategies. They generate pleasurable excitement and a sense of well-being" (p. 118). It is hardly surprising that individuals would seek to prolong such feelings of pleasurable excitement and well-being. Second, to the extent that autogynephilic arousal and the autogynephilic desire to be female are "action tendencies," they can plausibly motivate other desired behaviors, not merely their discharge through orgasm. For example, a few of my patients have told me that they are more likely to adhere to their weight loss and exercise regimens and save money for feminizing surgical procedures when they can maintain or prolong their feelings of autogynephilic arousal and their associated autogynephilic desire to be female.

Postorgasmic Remission of Gender Dysphoria Implies that Transsexualism Is Paraphilic

A few informants independently concluded that the rapid disappearance of their gender dysphoria following orgasm confirmed that their cross-gender wishes were a direct outgrowth of their autogynephilic sexual desires and, by implication, that their transsexualism was a paraphilic phenomenon:

Something that I have not seen anybody write about with regard to autogynephilia is the phenomenon of the urge to be a woman disappearing for a time just after sexual climax. I find that before and during masturbation, the feelings of autogynephilia are very strong,

> and I find myself wishing that this feeling would continue after climax. Yet in almost every instance, I can feel it ebb away, much to my chagrin. This lessening of the feeling of autogynephilia right after orgasm may seem a trivial and frivolous matter, but it is of importance to me because it relates to my opinion of how "serious" I am about wanting to be a woman. It makes me think that somehow it is more of a sexual perversion than a true wish, even though the autogynephilic feelings usually return fairly quickly (but sometimes recede for days at a time). (212)

> When my longing to be a woman becomes more than I can bear, I resort to masturbation. The result of my masturbation is a decrease in my desperate desire to live as a woman. That yearning never goes away, but it is controllable with sexual release. I consummate my feelings with fantasy and masturbation, the sense of urgency decreases, and I carry on with my unsatisfactory life. This makes me more aware of the vicious circle I am in. My sexual roller-coaster has undermined my belief in my essentially transsexual nature. Clearly, my transsexual feelings are intimately intertwined with my sexual desires. (175)

The assumption implicit in both of these narratives is that transsexual desires that are "true" or genuine should not be evanescent; they should not suddenly recede, even temporarily, after a sexual climax. The disappearance or significant diminution of one's desire to be a woman immediately after orgasm, even if it is temporary, feels like incontrovertible evidence that this desire is an erotic phenomenon: One's desire to be a woman seemingly requires a certain level of sexual drive or tension to exist, because when sexual tension falls to zero immediately after an orgasm, the desire to be a woman falls to zero or greatly diminishes, too.

I admire the keen insight and fearless honesty of these informants. They accurately observed that in their own cases, as in autogynephilic transsexualism generally, the desire to be a woman is a paraphilic phenomenon, deeply entwined with autogynephilic erotic desire. I differ with these informants, however, concerning their assumption that one's desire to be a woman is somehow less true or genuine if it derives from a paraphilia (i.e., autogynephilia). Many or most cases of MtF transsexualism in Western countries occur in nonhomosexual individuals, most of whom are putatively autogynephilic. In my clinical experience, autogynephilic transsexuals unquestionably suffer from real gender dysphoria, exhibit strongly held cross-gender identities, and experience their autogynephilic sexual orientations as essential aspects of their personalities.

Although autogynephilic arousal and gender dysphoria are sometimes present from an early age, it apparently takes time and experience for autogynephilic men to develop strong, persistent cross-gender identities—ones that will not disappear, even temporarily, following orgasm. Docter's (1988) studies of autogynephilic cross-dressers and transsexuals, discussed in Chap. 5, revealed that autogynephilic men typically develop strong, persistent cross-gender identities only after years or decades of experience with cross-dressing. Once this has occurred, however, these cross-gender identities feel like and operate as powerful forces in the lives of the autogynephilic transsexuals who experience them. In particular, these cross-gender identities become strong enough to withstand the temporary reduction in autogynephilic arousal that follows orgasm.

Effects of Hormone Therapy

Feminizing hormone therapy, which usually consists of estrogen with or without an antiandrogen, exerts its effects not only through the feminizing effects of estrogen but also through the demasculinizing effects of decreased testosterone production. Both estrogen and antiandrogens act to decrease testosterone levels. The diminution of male sex drive that occurs with hormone therapy is a direct result of decreased testosterone levels.

Several informants described the effects of feminizing hormone therapy on their sex drives, autogynephilic feelings, gender identities, and cross-gender behaviors. Some reported a gratifying loss of sex drive and autogynephilic arousal with hormone therapy:

> I used to find the idea of being a girl erotically arousing. In the UK, we are usually prescribed Androcur, an antiandrogen. Within quite a short time of commencing the Androcur, my male sex drive began to lessen and soon went away completely. I was quite happy about this, and it was part of my intention. In consequence, I was no longer aroused by my own body or the prospects of becoming female. I realize that there is a possibility I may no longer be able to achieve orgasm when postoperative. This has never deterred me, since I believe I'm motivated by the need, the desire, to be female, rather than by the possibilities of sexual gratification. (227)

> I've experienced autogynephilia strongly while wearing women's clothes. I went to my doctor and asked if she could give me anything to stop my strong sexual feelings. She warned me that my sex drive would go and my desire to dress might also go. My compulsion to dress did not alter, just my sex drive, which I hated anyway. I went on to live full-time as a woman, and I'm due for SRS at the end of the year. (201)

> I am using hormones simultaneously to suppress my libido, which drives me to distraction, while achieving as much feminization as possible. I am totally infatuated with what development I have achieved. (193)

All of these informants stated that one of their reasons for wanting feminizing hormone therapy was to reduce or eliminate their unwanted sex drive, in addition to the physical feminization hormone therapy provided. Their statements are consistent with several previous narratives that described autogynephilic sexual feelings as sometimes distressing or invalidating. Two of the informants stated or implied that their desire to live as women had continued unchanged, despite the reduction in their sexual feelings: Evidently their cross-gender identities were strong and persistent enough to survive the reduction or elimination of autogynephilic sexual desire.

Other informants painted a more complicated picture: They not only lost their sex drive but also their cross-gender identification or their desire to continue hormone therapy:

> I used to take hormones, birth control pills. The first time was about 2 years ago. It started with a very intense woman-pressure. I went to the drug store and told the seller what I needed. I got home and began to take it daily, one by one. When the pills were almost gone, my woman sex emotion was suddenly gone, too. I hated this feeling and didn't know what to do next. (226)

> After 4 months on hormones my old male urge to "jerk off" ceased. I was very pleased over this at the time. My breasts were just starting to develop and I felt fit and sexy. But—nothing seemed to work. My nipples were just too sensitive at the time, and I seemed to lose all my sexual fantasies as well. It was hard to masturbate at all in the old way, and if I did get an erection, it was labored and felt afterwards like someone had placed an iron band around it. In this case there was little incentive to continue. (087)

In the latter case, the informant's loss of the ability to enjoy a satisfying sexual response felt like a sufficient reason to discontinue hormone therapy, despite her satisfaction with the physical feminization and reduction in sex drive that hormone therapy produced.

Another informant lost both her sex drive and her desire to transition after 3 months of hormone therapy. She concluded that her desire to live as a woman was an outgrowth of her autogynephilic sex drive:

> Last year, things progressed to the point where I left my wife and began living full time, taking hormones and antiandrogens. After I had been taking the hormones and antiandrogens for 3 months, I totally lost my sex drive. That's when I got lonely and missed my wife, and she was more than willing to have me come back. That was 8 months ago, and now that my sex drive is back to normal, I am again struggling. I think about going back to living full-time as a woman, an experience that more than exceeded my wildest dreams. This desire does not go away, but the hormones caused me to lose my desire temporarily. I would only be satisfied with a level of hormones and antiandrogens that would maximize my transformation. I don't want the male sex drive. I don't like my male body and the body hair. But even though it is such a pleasant, wonderful feeling when I am fully transformed into a woman, that feeling unfortunately is generated from my male sex drive. I would end up the same way again if I tried to transition. (215)

This informant described one of the key dilemmas that many autogynephilic gender dysphoric men confront: They are troubled by their sex drive, but their desire to be a woman (and to continue to use hormones) disappears when their sex drive disappears.

A physician informant similarly described how her desire to cross-dress waxed and waned with her changing testosterone levels. In her case, this was caused by the addition or withdrawal of transdermal testosterone following her orchiectomy, rather than by stopping or starting feminizing hormones:

> I am a licensed, board certified surgeon who is transgendered. I want to describe my recent discovery of the overwhelming (and seemingly contradictory) role of testosterone in this process. During my entire life, I have had the strong desire to be female and make a sex transition. I had a persistent desire to cross-dress and did so from as early as I can remember. Although I was excited to get dressed in female clothing, once dressed, I was always very relaxed and any emotional excitement subsided. I found hormone therapy very comfortable. Although I have taken hormone therapy for several months at a time, I have never been on hormones for more than 3 months continuously. During those times, however, I never experienced a decrease in the desire to dress in female clothing. I became comfortable with a plan for a slow transition and felt I was ready.
>
> Approximately 18 months ago, I had a bilateral orchiectomy, as I felt it would make the transition easier and would allow me to use lower doses of estrogen. Even without any hormone therapy, the physical changes became progressive and dramatic. My body hair almost totally disappeared, my skin became smoother, and I began to lose muscle mass and strength. Around this time, I found it necessary to briefly postpone the final transition.

> Interestingly, I totally lost the drive to cross-dress. I was still comfortable dressed as a female, I just lacked the urge to do so. When I developed rather troubling symptoms of hot flashes and sweats and I began using the new topical testosterone, the drive and urge to crossdress again became prominent. I was fascinated with this finding; I tried again, stopping and starting testosterone (without taking any estrogen) and the phenomenon repeated. I know that this is a one-person experiment and that I am not an unbiased observer. However, I am expert in conducting controlled clinical trials. The point is that the result was totally unexpected, and although I believe I have read just about every article on transsexualism, transgender, and transvestism, I have never seen it mentioned. (147)

One could hardly ask for a more convincing demonstration that the desire to cross-dress that autogynephilic men experience is a sexual phenomenon—one that increases in strength with the administration of testosterone.

Yet another informant described how a high dose of estrogen and antiandrogen eliminated both her libido and her desire to present as a woman, whereas a low dose of estrogen—insufficient to completely suppress testosterone—preserved her desire to present as a woman:

> From the earliest time I can recall, I felt like I wanted to be female. I wore my sister's clothes in secret and sometimes under my normal clothes. Cross-dressing usually involved a pattern of dressing up, masturbating, and intense feelings of guilt and shame. An on-line gender therapist suggested I take Diane-35 [an estrogen/progesterone combination] to help alleviate the tensions I felt. I started taking it and, to my surprise, these worked just like they were described. My libido went down, my erections were nil, and I even lost the compulsion to present as a woman. Because of the risks of Diane-35, I later switched to 1 mg estradiol per day, an intentionally low dose. Estradiol has had a calming effect and I am a much happier person when I am on it. While I was on Diane-35, I was happy and had no sex drive at all and little or no desire to present as a woman. Now on estradiol, I feel good, but I still want to present as a female. Testosterone drives my libido. When I get horny, I want to look as much like a female as I can. This would explain the compelling desire to present as a woman. (228)

I have observed this same phenomenon in a few autogynephilic transsexual clients in my practice, who began feminizing hormone therapy and initially found the experience very gratifying. If they stayed on a low dose of estrogen, they continued to find the mild feminizing effects satisfying, and their desire to transition remained strong. But if they began taking fully feminizing doses of estrogen and antiandrogen, which reduced their testosterone levels to the normal female range, their desire to transition suddenly disappeared. After they discontinued feminizing hormones and their testosterone levels returned to normal a few months later, their desire to transition reappeared. Sometimes this cycle occurred more than once in the same client.

Although some autogynephilic clients lose their desire to transition after taking fully feminizing doses of hormones, others do not: Their desire to transition remains strong, even after the complete loss of their sex drive and associated autogynephilic arousal. I hypothesize that individuals are more likely to want to continue hormone therapy and gender transition, despite a complete loss of sex drive and autogynephilic arousal, if their gender dysphoria is more intense, of longer duration (and therefore associated with stronger and more persistent cross-gender identification), and more intensely focused on anatomical features (i.e., driven primarily by anatomic autogynephilia). I am not aware of any formal research on this issue, however.

Co-occurring Paraphilias

Paraphilias tend to cluster or co-occur: Men with one paraphilia have an increased likelihood of having one or more other paraphilias as well (Abel & Osborn, 1992; Wilson & Gosselin, 1980). Because autogynephilia is conceptualized as a paraphilic phenomenon, it is not surprising that many informants described other paraphilias as well. These included sexual masochism and forced feminization, gynemimetophilia and gynandromorphophilia (attraction to feminized men), pedophilia, autonepiophilia (infantilism or adult baby syndrome), abasiophilia and autoabasiophilia (leg brace paraphilia), and unspecified paraphilias.

Sexual Masochism

Sexual masochism is a paraphilic sexual interest in which affected individuals are intensely sexually aroused by fantasies or behaviors involving "being humiliated, beaten, bound, or otherwise made to suffer" (APA, 2000, p. 573). A few reports have suggested that sexual masochism not uncommonly occurs in association with MtF transsexualism (e.g., Bolin, 1988; Walworth, 1997), although these reports have not distinguished between homosexual and autogynephilic subtypes.

In the current study, some informants described masochistic fantasies or believed that there were connections between their autogynephilic feelings and sexual masochism.

> One thing I can affirm about autogynephilia, based on my personal experience with it: It has a masochistic dimension to it. Being feminized is perceived as humiliation, and this sense of humiliation is a basic ingredient of the sexual turn-on. (102)

> My school age fantasies always started off something like, "Will she tie me up and then when can I dress up like her?" Since junior high school, I have been involved in relationships that involved cross-dressing and being submissive. I had my first experience at 15 with a 16-year-old girlfriend; she was dominant. The understanding of the sexual desire to be a woman is so clear when I am doing sadomasochism. I somehow feel a punishment for not being a woman and yet can get as close to a woman as possible. (178)

One informant described masochistic fantasies during adolescence involving dismemberment and dehumanization—fantasizing herself as a female farm animal being butchered. These fantasies later evolved to emphasize having female genitals:

> I grew up on a farm. I was masturbating by around age 13 or 14. My first fantasy was that I was a cow and my penis was the teat of a female cow. Then I imagined I was a mother sheep and I ended up getting slaughtered, because animals on farms get that done to them. I saw myself as all these pieces of meat. I thought this probably was not a very good thing to fantasize about. I developed the fantasy about having a vagina, which still remains. (229)

The evolution of this informant's fantasies provides an example of an interesting phenomenon in which very distressing or ego-dystonic paraphilic fantasies sometimes become superseded by less distressing, more acceptable ones. The paraphilic fantasy of having female genitalia undoubtedly felt more acceptable to the informant than the paraphilic fantasy of being butchered. I will present other examples of this kind of "paraphilic substitution," in which unacceptable paraphilic fantasies are replaced by more acceptable ones, later in this chapter and in Chap. 11.

Forced Feminization

A particular genre of masochistic fantasies and behaviors involves forced or coerced feminization; the masochistic aspect of feminization derives from "its humiliating associations" (APA, 2000, p. 572). Forced feminization fantasies are a staple of transgender erotica (Beigel & Feldman, 1963), although there is disagreement about how prevalent and popular they truly are (Buhrich & McConaghy, 1976). In earlier chapters, several informants mentioned such fantasies in passing, with little elaboration. Other informants described their forced feminization fantasies in greater detail:

> My main fantasies revolved around being forced by a woman into becoming one myself. I started buying the little pink trans novels at the bookstores and became obsessed with their visions of my wife burning all my male clothing, injecting me with giant syringes of hormones, and hauling me off to the beauty parlor against my will. (182)

> About sex: I usually do it myself, with pictures of women in dresses. I imagine that I am one of the women, stuck in the role; often forced into it by a man. I imagine myself with breasts and with no choice but to live as a female. (035)

> My sexual fantasies usually involve being made into a woman in some way, usually against my will. Specifically, I experience erotic fantasies of being coerced or duped into being a woman, against my will initially but then gradually being won over until I can't go back. (212)

> I fantasized about being forced to dress as a woman as a punishment for various offenses, such as not acting masculine enough. I would also combine the cross-dressing fantasy with being dominated by a woman. Sometimes this woman would make me look like her. When I was attracted to some girls in school, I would fantasize about being forced to wear their clothes and have hair like theirs. Sometimes I would add to this fantasy being bound and forced to watch them have sex with their boyfriends. My current fantasies involve becoming a woman. I imagine myself forced to become a woman in dress, manner, and physique (through hormones and surgery). (056)

Another informant reported that she was attracted to the idea of observing a man who was "trapped" in the body of a woman; she imagined this to be a real-life instance of forced feminization.

> I became obsessed with transsexual women. To observe a young man being transformed into a woman was now my fantasy. I haunted clubs where they would gather. I was particularly attracted to transsexuals who were "women" in every way except one. I dated transsexuals who could pass in public but who had not yet had final surgery. Although I dated post-operative transsexuals, I was only satisfied with pre-operative transsexuals. I still date genetic females, but I catch myself longing for signs—a slightly deeper voice or some other evidence that she is a transsexual—that will arouse my ardor. I am particularly attracted to transsexual women who are autogynephilic. The idea of a man "trapped" in the body of a

> transsexual, experiencing the daily humiliation and degradation of being a woman, forced to wear women's clothes and lipstick, is extremely attractive to me. (194)

I have not been able to find a satisfactory explanation in the literature as to why forced feminization fantasies are so powerful and exciting for so many of us autogynephilic transsexuals. The conventional explanation is that being forced to become feminine absolves us of responsibility and thereby relieves us of guilt. One informant proposed this exact explanation:

> I believe that the forced feminization scenario is particularly stimulating to a lot of transsexual women because it relieves us of the guilt of wanting to be feminine. Someone else is forcing us, and we have no choice in the matter. No guilt, all fun, and you are experiencing life in the body you desire to be in. (041)

Personally, I don't find such explanations very convincing. Relief from guilt might make fantasies more pleasant, but it would not necessarily make them more exciting; in fact, I suspect the opposite would be true. Some psychoanalytically inclined writers have attempted to explain forced feminization fantasies as reenactments of childhood experiences in which a boy's masculinity was devalued by powerful female caregivers (e.g., Stoller, 1975) or as attempts to deal with unresolved oedipal wishes and conflicts (Beigel & Feldman, 1963); interested readers are referred to these accounts for details.

One might ask why forced feminization fantasies should succeed at all as masochistic fantasies for autogynephilic transsexuals. Why should we identify with male protagonists who feel shame and humiliation at being turned into girls or women—isn't becoming a girl or a woman precisely what we want? Wouldn't we experience pride and gratitude instead of shame and humiliation if someone turned us into women? The whole premise of forced feminization fantasies should mystify us: Why should we identify with male protagonists who need to be forced into becoming girls or women—aren't these precisely the outcomes we seek voluntarily? Surely no one would need to force us to become women, so it makes no sense that we should identify with protagonists who need to be forced.

Reality is, of course, considerably messier. We do, in fact, consider becoming feminized—becoming women—to be shameful and humiliating. We grew up receiving an unending stream of explicit and implicit messages—from the boys and men we knew and from society at large—about women's inferiority. We believed these messages and internalized them. Even though we now genuinely desire to be women, we find the idea of becoming women profoundly humiliating. Probably we will always feel that way to some extent. That is plausibly why forced feminization fantasies continue to work as masochistic erotic fantasies for many of us, even years or decades after we have completed sex reassignment: We never entirely get over our shame.

Interestingly, forced feminization fantasies are also symbolic representations of our actual life experiences. Because we find the prospect of becoming women so shameful and humiliating, we really do have to be forced into it. We are forced by our unremitting gender dysphoria, by our powerful erotic desires, by our love and admiration for women's bodies and our wishes to turn our bodies into facsimiles of them, and by our need to honor our strongly held cross-gender identities in order to give meaning and vitality to our lives. If we are prudent, we autogynephilic transsexuals undergo sex reassignment only if we feel we have no other viable alternative: We transition because we feel forced to do so. Forced feminization is, in a very real sense, the story of our lives.

Gynemimetophilia and Gynandromorphophilia

Money and Lamacz (1984) coined the term *gynemimetophilia* to describe paraphilic sexual attraction to surgically or hormonally feminized men who had not undergone SRS (often called *she-males*; Blanchard, 1993b). Money (1986, p. 262) later broadened the definition of gynemimetophilia to include paraphilic attraction to feminized men who *had* undergone SRS (i.e., postoperative MtF transsexuals). A few years later, Blanchard and Collins (1993) coined the closely related term *gynandromorphophilia*, which they used to describe paraphilic sexual attraction to feminized men who had not undergone SRS—a group that included transvestites as well as she-males, but did not include postoperative MtF transsexuals. Thus, those of us who study and describe paraphilias are presented with the confusing situation of having two very similar terms with overlapping but not identical applicability. To summarize: Men with a paraphilic interest in transvestites are properly called gynandromorphophiles. Men with a paraphilic interest in postoperative MtF transsexuals are properly called gynemimetophiles (Money, 1986). Men with a paraphilic interest in she-males are properly called by either term.

A narrative by an informant who was sexually attracted to MtF transsexuals was presented previously in connection with the discussion of forced feminization. Several other informants also described their experience of particular sexual attraction to transvestites, she-males, or postoperative MtF transsexuals. In some cases, their gynemimetophilia or gynandromorphophilia dated from a time prior to their identifying as transsexual or beginning the sex reassignment process.

> Early in my transsexual days, I had crushes on more advanced transsexuals. I decided to start dating again, and I find myself dating heterosexual crossdressers. I find myself appreciating the feminine in my lovers. (230)

> When I was 29 years old, I met a beautiful pre-op transsexual who was also a street prostitute and a glamorous showgirl. I fell in love and my first experience with a transsexual was wonderful, although I was unable to orgasm. She was not fond of my cross-dressing and although she fell in love with me, couldn't be physically involved because I was a cross-dresser, which was looked down upon in the homosexual drag community. (214)

> I have been involved with cross-dressing behavior since I was 5 or 6 years old and it has been sexually arousing for me. I met a drag queen almost 6 years ago at a gay bar, and within minutes we were heavily petting on a pool table. I had never been this aroused by anyone so quickly. We have been together ever since. As our relationship continued, she was the "female" and I was the "male" of the relationship, literally. I was allowed to dress on Halloween but at no other times. I became increasingly unhappy about my role and inability to be who I wanted to be. I would sit in extreme jealousy when she would get dressed to go out and I began to realize that I wanted to be who she was. She is very attractive and I found

> myself dreaming constantly of changing my appearance to be feminine. She will not accept my transition in any way and I can not bring myself to leave her. For the longest time, I felt confusion as to whether my sexual orientation would change with time and exposure to hormones. When I read about MtF-to-MtF attraction, I realized that my sexual orientation was and still is towards other transsexual women. (042)

Some informants emphasized how much they identified with and envied the MtF transsexuals to whom they were attracted.

> I am astounded that doctors perform so many sex changes. There must be hundreds of thousands of transsexuals, and when I see pictures of them, I am aroused as well. I look at photos of lovely young boys transitioning and am jealous of them, or want to be with them, or wish I were one of them. (133)

> I am obsessed with the desire to be female. My first experience picking up a transsexual was at age 18. I was very excited to hold a large manicured hand and see a hotel full of "girls." I ended up submitting to anal intercourse, which hurt, but I did not object. My greatest moments of joy would be spending hours with transsexual prostitutes, watching them dress and prepare and joining them. My favorite photos are of groups of transsexuals together at parties, dancing, taking baths, etc., with me as one of them. I can function sexually with women or transsexuals, but I don't feel much thrill with women. (176)

It is important to note that some cases in which autogynephilic transsexuals become sexually involved with other MtF transsexuals do not necessarily represent instances of gynemimetophilia. Some informants who described sexual involvement with other MtF transsexuals did not explicitly describe any special or specific attraction to the MtF transsexual phenotype:

> I began picking up and having sex with transsexual prostitutes, first acting as "the man," but as my guard lessened, wanting to simply be around them, observe and learn from them, and also act feminine. (179)

> I have noticed that there are two types of transsexuals. In fact, I am dating someone of the other type now. My transsexual girlfriend is of the "primary" type. She was able to transition early and has always maintained her interest in men, before and after transition. (074)

In my experience, MtF transsexuals often partner with each other, before and after SRS, for reasons that have more to do with mutual acceptance and an absence of other viable alternatives than with specific sexual attraction to one another. Indeed, many of these partnerships appear to be affectionate but largely asexual.

Pedophilia

One informant stated that she was aroused by the fantasy of having sex with female children, although she claimed that she had never acted on her fantasies:

> I have been diagnosed as transsexual by four separate therapists, and I am taking hormones. I live full time as a woman and have for almost five years. I have fantasized about sex with a man a time or two, but mainly I have been aroused by the idea of penetration with female children. I don't have these fantasies anymore, as I am chemically castrated and have gotten

> relief from them by being on hormones. I have never done any of these things I have fantasized about; I would not be free very long if I did. (231)

Co-occurrence of transsexualism and pedophilia has been reported (Abel & Osborn, 1992), but it appears to be rare.

Autonepiophilia (Paraphilic Infantilism or Adult Baby Syndrome)

Autonepiophilia is a paraphilic sexual interest involving sexual arousal to the thought or image of being an infant, often an infant wearing diapers specifically (Money, 1986). It is sometimes referred to as paraphilic infantilism (Money, 1986) or adult baby syndrome (Kise & Nguyen, 2011). One transsexual informant reported this co-occurring paraphilia:

> When I was younger, maybe 8 years old, I had always wanted to wear diapers and pee in them. Around this same age and later, I would often put my penis and testes down and cross my legs, so as to hide them and see how I'd look with female genitalia. I remember that I wanted the feeling of it getting wet "down there," near my butt, like I imagined it was for a girl. In exploring erotic imagery on the Internet, I came across pictures of females peeing in their pants. This provided some validation that others got arousal from it, too. I also found pictures of people in diapers and subsequently found out about infantilists. I had a friend help me buy training pants, basically diapers, in the store. He assumed I wanted the boy ones. I said, "No! I want the girl ones." In exploring with these, I found that fantasizing about being a girl who didn't have full control over her bladder was immensely satisfying. I would imagine I was age 5 or so to pre-teen, something in there. I have been aroused by imagery of females in swimsuits, since they show the crotch area in all its smoothness. I have had this arousal for many years. Recently, I had the idea that I wanted to actually be this. I have never found breasts to be arousing. I'm more obsessed with the child female form. (209)

The co-occurrence of MtF transsexualism and autonepiophilia or infantilism has been reported previously (Kise & Nguyen, 2011), and I have seen one case of diaper fetishism in an autogynephilic transsexual in my practice.

Abasiophilia and Autoabasiophilia (Leg Brace Paraphilia)

The term *abasiophilia* refers to a paraphilic interest in "having a partner who is lamed, crippled, and unable to walk" (Money, 1990, p. 165). Money called the reciprocal paraphilia—sexual arousal to the thought or image of oneself being lamed, crippled, and unable to walk—*autoabasiophilia* (p. 166). The use of leg braces offers visible evidence of this kind of disability, and wearing or using leg braces is often the focus of abasiophilic and autoabasiophilic sexual interest. One informant reported experiencing both abasiophilia and autoabasiophilia:

> I am a 60-year-old retired psychiatrist who is currently in the hormonal and hair removal phase of my gender transition. Since my childhood, I have dressed as a crippled female, with this usually ending in masturbation. I have known my female gender identity since age

> 4, but negative messages about cross-gender behavior led me to repress the expression of it, except as a crippled female. I have also dated several brace-wearing females and was engaged to one. (232)

The occurrence of autoabasiophilia in an autogynephilic transsexual with abasiophilia is not unexpected. As I noted in Chap. 2, autogynephilia is theorized to reflect an erotic target location error (Freund & Blanchard, 1993): the tendency to be sexually aroused by the idea of becoming a facsimile of the kind of person to whom one is attracted. Men who are autogynephilic are attracted to women and are aroused by the idea of becoming women. Men who are autogynephilic and are also specifically attracted to women who wear leg braces would predictably be especially sexually aroused by the idea of becoming women who wear leg braces. This kind of specificity of autogynephilic arousal is apparently not uncommon; it will be discussed in greater detail in Chap. 11.

A second informant also reported autoabasiophilia, but did not describe abasiophilic attraction to other persons:

> I remember in about first grade being fascinated by posters of child polio victims wearing leg braces, particularly those showing little girls. My older sister wore a leg brace due to an injury when I was between the ages of 1 and 4. As an infant, I must have seen my sister getting love, sympathy, and attention because of her disability. Somehow I must have gotten the subconscious message that I must wear leg braces and be female to have that, too. Throughout my teen years, I remember reading all about polio and looking at pictures of children and women in leg braces. I had no idea why I would be fascinated by this and was embarrassed by it. As a teen, my most powerful masturbatory fantasies were of me being attended to as a disabled teenage girl. Occasionally in private I would pretend with clumsy props to be wearing leg braces. When I graduated from college, married, and finished grad school, I suppressed all of this, but sexual fantasies of my being female and sometimes female in leg braces continued to interfere with my sexual relations with my wife. My fantasy images kept interfering with what was right in front of my eyes. Eventually, when making love with my wife, the "in leg braces" part became less important and the being female part became overpowering, such that that was the only way I could stay aroused.
>
> I had never seriously cross-dressed until about 5 years ago, when I happened upon some leg braces that were about to be thrown out in the physical therapy section of a hospital. By happenstance, they were almost exactly my size. This was too much to ignore. I set about with intense, amazing energy to ready myself for a public experience as a woman wearing leg braces. In a short time, I read everything I could find about successful cross-dressing. Several months later, when I was ready for this foray in public, as I was completing my feminine look in private and without the leg braces on, I was absolutely overwhelmed about how natural and at home I felt as a woman. While the braces were the catalyst that set this going again so powerfully, now they were superfluous. I did go out a few times with the braces on, but it seemed silly and deceptive. And all the energy was around being female, not being disabled.
>
> At first, I thought I must be what writers referred to as a fetishistic transvestite. Gradually, I have come to realize that it is not the dressing, but the being female with a female body, that is such a powerful urge in me. My female identity and potential body seems to be my spiritual soul, my heart. It is certainly sexual, but much more. Somehow it seems my whole life before this has had a certain void at the center. At this point, I am on the verge of going full time and doing all the things necessary to be very passable, including SRS. (233)

This narrative offers another example of the phenomenon of "paraphilic substitution," which was discussed earlier in this chapter. Paraphilic substitution is the term I used to describe the process by which disturbing or unacceptable paraphilic fantasies are sometimes replaced by less distressing, more acceptable ones. Autoabasiophilic fantasies are not necessarily highly disturbing, but they were apparently more embarrassing to this informant—and surely more inconvenient to actualize—than her autogynephilic fantasies. The outcome was that the more embarrassing and inconvenient paraphilia, autoabasiophilia, receded and the more acceptable paraphilia, autogynephilia, assumed greater prominence.

I have observed a similar case of paraphilic substitution in my own practice: An autogynephilic transsexual client whose most intense paraphilic interest was autoabasiophilia eventually gave up her desire to live full time as a woman with a highly visible disability and decided instead to be content by simply undergoing sex reassignment. Her autoabasiophilic paraphilia did not exactly recede—the fantasy of being a woman wearing leg braces remained her most reliable source of erotic arousal—but she made a deliberate choice to deemphasize it. She stated that she reached this decision because "the leg brace thing just felt too crazy."

Unspecified Paraphilias

Two informants stated that they experienced other co-occurring paraphilias (or fetishes) but did not describe the content or focus of these paraphilias.

> The thought of being female turns me on, so much so that it's my primary sexual attraction mechanism. I do have a separate, unrelated fetish, and I can feel a significant difference between the fetish and my autogynephilia. With the fetish, I can be turned on very strongly, but I don't actually want it to be made manifest; it's just a fantasy. But with the desire to be female, there is nothing I want more, even though it usually doesn't turn me on quite as much as my fetish. (004)

> My autogynephilic fantasies probably kicked in with puberty. In the early days, I think they were more clothes/forced feminization-based. Later on they were more based on the idea of a change of genitals. Interestingly, autogynephilia is not, and never was, my primary paraphilia. I really can't trace autogynephilia back too much beyond adolescence. My primary paraphilia is rooted back to my earliest memory, and I can remember distinct interests at about 5 years of age. It began to manifest around age 10. It is now my only source of orgasm. (065)

Note that the second informant described her primary paraphilic interest as having been present from about age 5, roughly the same age at which many autogynephilic transsexuals first became aware of their autogynephilic interests.

Concluding Comments on Other Aspects of Autogynephilic Sexuality

This diverse collection of narratives concerning other aspects of autogynephilic sexuality illustrates three important themes that are fundamental to understanding autogynephilic transsexualism. First, autogynephilia resembles and operates as a paraphilic sexual orientation in autogynephilic transsexuals: Autogynephilic themes are central to the sexuality of most autogynephilic transsexuals and are often obligatory for achieving orgasm. Moreover, autogynephilia is accompanied by other paraphilic sexual interests in a significant number of autogynephilic transsexuals, which is consistent with the theory that autogynephilia is itself a paraphilia. Second, gender dysphoria and cross-gender identity in autogynephilic transsexuals are direct outgrowths of this autogynephilic sexual orientation: Autogynephilic transsexuals not uncommonly report that their desire to be a woman temporarily disappears immediately after orgasm, suggesting that this desire is driven by or dependent on some minimal level of sexual desire or tension, at least initially. Moreover, testosterone reduction associated with feminizing hormone therapy sometimes leads to the disappearance of autogynephilic arousal, gender dysphoria, and cross-gender wishes in autogynephilic transsexuals, suggesting that all of these phenomena are erotic and testosterone-driven, at least initially. Finally, although autogynephilic arousal is the defining and animating element of autogynephilic transsexualism, it is not always regarded as pleasant or desirable by those who experience it: On the contrary, some autogynephilic transsexuals describe autogynephilic arousal as distressing, invalidating, or inconvenient.

Chapter 10
Debating the Meaning of Autogynephilia

What Is the Meaning and Explanatory Significance of Autogynephilia?

All of the transsexual informants who provided narratives had experienced autogynephilic arousal, but they expressed widely varying opinions concerning its meaning and significance. Many seemed to accept Blanchard's formulation: They believed that autogynephilia was a paraphilic sexual interest that had been an important force in their lives, had given rise to their gender dysphoria and cross-gender identification, and had been an undeniable cause—albeit not necessarily the proximate or the only cause—of their wish to undergo sex reassignment.

This point of view, however, was not universal. To attribute real meaning and explanatory significance to autogynephilia is to disagree with the beliefs and attitudes held by most other MtF transsexuals and more than a few clinicians and researchers. Many autogynephilic transsexuals would understandably prefer to interpret their autogynephilic feelings in a way that would not "directly contradict basic tenets of the worldwide transgender movement" (Nuttbrock, Bockting, Mason, et al., 2011, p. 249). Several informants accomplished this by taking a compromise approach: They acknowledged that they had experienced autogynephilic arousal but rejected Blanchard's explanation of its meaning and significance. This served to minimize or deemphasize any disagreement between their life histories and generally accepted ideas about transsexualism.

Informants who did not attribute great meaning or explanatory significance to their autogynephilic feelings proposed various alternatives to Blanchard's formulation. Some suggested that autogynephilia might be only a symptom or an effect of their transsexualism or gender dysphoria, not a cause of these conditions. These informants often supported their opinions by noting that their cross-gender fantasies had begun well before puberty or had usually preceded overt autogynephilic arousal by many years. Other informants argued that autogynephilia was merely an

A.A. Lawrence, *Men Trapped in Men's Bodies: Narratives of Autogynephilic Transsexualism*, Focus on Sexuality Research, DOI 10.1007/978-1-4614-5182-2_10,

epiphenomenon—an incidental effect of their female gender identities interacting with their unwanted male bodies or some particular aspect of their male upbringings. Still others asserted that autogynephilia was not a paraphilic condition at all but rather a normal manifestation of female sexuality that could be easily observed in natal women. A few informants expressed more than one of these points of view.

In a related vein, a few informants proposed that MtF transsexualism had a specific biologic etiology; they usually believed that an abnormal hormonal milieu during prenatal development was wholly or partly responsible. Their unstated implication was that there was no need to consider the meaning or the significance of autogynephilia, because their transsexualism could be explained in terms of hormonal abnormalities during the prenatal period.

Autogynephilia Might Be a Symptom of Transsexualism

The idea that autogynephilia might be merely an effect or symptom of one's gender dysphoria or transsexualism rather than a cause of these conditions is an appealing one, because it denies the explanatory significance of autogynephilic arousal without denying the fact of it. Back in the days when I was trying to reconcile my belief in Blanchard's theory with the transsexual community's vehement rejection of it, I even proposed this idea myself (Lawrence, 2000), although I now regard it as specious.

Some informants similarly suggested, usually without much elaboration, that autogynephilia might simply be a symptom or an effect of their transsexualism or gender dysphoria. Here are some representative comments:

> I have numerous concerns with Blanchard's analysis, but I'll focus on just one: the assumption that autogynephilia is the cause or primary motivation for an individual's transsexuality. I have never been adequately convinced that this is the case, and it seems just as likely to me that transsexuality causes autogynephilia, or that transsexuality and autogynephilia are the shared result of some common root cause. (121)

> This erotic impulse created by the desire to be and live as a woman has probably been an important factor in my transition, although I believe, as I need to, that it is simply a manifestation of a deeper underlying condition. (110)

> I strongly believe that it is misguided to view autogynephilia as the ultimate cause of gender dysphoria or the wish to undergo SRS. I feel it is something I developed or crafted as a way of dealing with my gender dysphoria. (081)

> Reading about autogynephilia, I did have some strong pangs of truth, but I feel it is possibly one of the symptoms of gender dysphoria. I feel the fantasies are an escape outlet for my closed and shutdown reality and my cultural maleness. (234)

There is a certain superficial plausibility about the accounts offered in the last two narratives: If one wanted to become a woman but were unable to do so, one might understandably fantasize about becoming a woman. These accounts do not explain, however, why fantasies of becoming a woman would be so powerfully erotic.

Desires to Be Female Begin Before Puberty and Precede Autogynephilic Arousal

Children usually, if not invariably, display erotic and sexual interests and behaviors beginning in early childhood—long before puberty (Friedrich et al., 2000; Martinson, 1976, 1994; Yates, 2004). Erotic and sexual behaviors in young children are so ubiquitous and so easily observed that they have been taken for granted in most cultures throughout human history. In recent years, however, there has developed a countervailing cultural belief, especially in the United States, that eroticism and sexuality begin only at puberty.

In their interviews with nine MtF transsexuals, Schrock and Reid (2006) encountered several instances in which informants invoked the idea that sexuality begins only at puberty to justify their belief that their cross-dressing could not be an erotic phenomenon:

> Interviewees used cultural discourse on sexuality that paints preadolescents as asexual … as a resource to distance themselves from erotic transvestites. In telling their sexual stories, the six who had used women's garments during masturbation drew on the notion that sexual life begins only after puberty as a resource for identity work. Erin's account was typical: "I had been dressing for seven years before I had my first orgasm, so my reaching puberty and beginning to masturbate and becoming sexual was just coincidental with my cross-dressing." The implication was that because they crossdressed *before* puberty, that they were not, underneath it all, just transvestites. (p. 79)

In the current study, six informants reported that they had distinct memories of wanting to be female or cross-dressing before they went through puberty, at which time they first became conscious of autogynephilic sexual arousal. They argued, explicitly or implicitly, that this temporal sequence precluded the possibility that autogynephilic arousal was the cause of their gender dysphoria or cross-gender identity.

> I have had these feelings for as long as I can remember, and that is before puberty and issues of sexual arousal ever crossed my mind. Here is an example: My parents were the co-owners of a hotel when I was younger. During the summers, I would answer the phone and take down reservations. The callers, not expecting a 9- or 10-year-old to be answering calls, would identify me as a female receptionist. Until puberty, I played this role flawlessly, cherishing every moment. At this age, sexual arousal was the last thing on my mind, but I still loved to play the female, because I already at this age understood I wasn't meant to be a male. Though sexual arousal may play a certain role in my desire to be female, the actual concept of arousal from dressing up came many years after I figured out I wasn't like the other boys. (235)

> I had fantasies of acquiring a feminine body, and, yes, they were erotic. There is, however, something that seems inconsistent with this being my motivating factor to have SRS. I wished for SRS for several years prior to any sexual realization of myself. I have distinct memories of having wanted to be a girl beginning at age 4 or 5 years old. The sexual fantasies did not start for a good 6 years after that and were few and far between until about age 28, when I was married. I do not know if autogynephilia was more a reaction to my already strong desire to be the opposite sex (it was a product of my transsexuality) or the cause. I suspect it was a product rather than a cause, simply because it came later in life than the desire to change sex. (236)

> My earliest memories of dealing with this gender issue go back to age 3 or 4. Isn't this well before any sexual issues could be a source for these feelings? When I was about 9 or 10, I saw some Life magazine images of women who'd transitioned and I thought this is what I'd like to do. At the age of 11 or 12, I started cross-dressing in some of my mother's clothing. For the first time I experienced erotic feelings with my desire to be a woman. The point of all of this is to provide the history of my feelings and document that they preceded any sort of sex drive. So if I'm autogynephilic, which it appears that I am, how is it that my first thoughts about wishing I was a girl had nothing to do with sex drive? (130)

> I have had strong erotic fantasies around the subject of feminization. The fantasies very definitely came later than the desire to be female. As far back as I can remember, I have wanted to be a girl, but didn't start fantasizing about it in an erotic sense until after puberty. The things I used to fantasize about before puberty were more on the order of getting rid of a particular girl at school and somehow taking over her life. (186)

> My own feelings of dysphoria began at around 5 or 6 years of age, long before I experienced any sexual arousal or feelings at all. I remember thinking distinctly that I was both in the wrong body and the wrong role. Before puberty, it was almost entirely about the gender role, and the physical aspect was about form alone and was not sexualized at all. Around puberty, though, as my body became overrun with strong male hormones, I found myself constantly aroused at everything. My desire to be female quite suddenly expanded to include a new sexual aspect. So, my transsexualism predated a time when I was aroused by the idea of being female. (125)

> I don't think that autogynephilic sexuality is the reason I am transsexual. Rather, I think it is a symptom of my transsexualism. I had my first feelings of wanting to be female around the age of 3-1/2. All through childhood, I prayed that I could become a girl. I started cross-dressing around the age of 7. I was told I was a boy and would always be a boy no matter what, so I tried as best I could to get on with life as a male. Nowhere in those early years was autogynephilia present and yet my gender dysphoria was as intense, if not more intense, than it is now. It was only after puberty that autogynephilia began to display itself. (237)

In interpreting these narratives, it is useful to consider two questions: How confident can one be that the informants' implicit or explicit denials of erotic arousal in association with prepubertal cross-dressing or cross-gender fantasies are accurate? And how confident can one be that the informants' descriptions of their prepubertal desires to be female are accurate and not exaggerated? In both instances, I believe one should be skeptical about the accuracy of these accounts.

As several informants reported in Chap. 5, autogynephilic arousal associated with cross-dressing or cross-gender fantasy during early childhood is not unusual. Moreover, as I noted in Chaps. 1, 4, and 5, gender dysphoric men who display physiologic evidence of autogynephilic arousal in a laboratory setting often deny having experienced it (Blanchard et al., 1986), and adolescents who are clinically referred for transvestic fetishism often deny autogynephilic arousal as well (Zucker et al., 2012). Moreover, denial of autogynephilic arousal is associated with a socially desirable response style (Blanchard, Clemmensen, et al., 1985). All three of these studies involved denial of autogynephilic arousal that had occurred (or putatively had occurred) fairly recently. It would not be surprising, then, if inaccurate denial of autogynephilic arousal that putatively had occurred decades earlier, or simple failure to recall such arousal, might be a common phenomenon. Please note that I am not claiming that the six transsexual informants above who denied prepubertal autogynephilic arousal are *lying* (cf. Serano, 2010, p. 181); I am simply claiming that there is good reason to believe that they might not be reporting accurately—probably unintentionally—and, therefore, good reason to be skeptical of their denials.

How confident can one be that the informants' descriptions of their prepubertal desires to be female are accurate and not exaggerated? I have addressed the issue of childhood cross-gender wishes preceding autogynephilia in Chap. 5, and I will do so again later in this chapter. Occasional cross-gender wishes during early childhood are not unusual, even in boys without known gender issues (Friedrich et al., 1991, 1998, 2000; Sandfort & Cohen-Kettenis, 2000). Boys who will subsequently become autogynephilic transsexuals probably experience recurrent and perhaps frequent cross-gender wishes during early childhood and may also experience some episodes of gender dysphoria. But these symptoms do not necessarily indicate the existence of severe, ongoing gender dysphoria or strong, persistent cross-gender identification in early childhood. It is not uncommon for individuals who experience transsexualism in adulthood to inaccurately report significant cross-gender wishes occurring much earlier in life (Bancroft, 1972; Fisk, 1974; Lukianowicz, 1959). Consequently, I believe that one ought to be skeptical of the reports by transsexual informants in the current study who suggested or implied that they had experienced intense, persistent cross-gender wishes during early childhood.

I am not aware of any reliable third-person accounts—as opposed to retrospective first-person accounts—or clinical case reports documenting severe gender dysphoria or strong, persistent cross-gender identification during early childhood in adult autogynephilic or nonhomosexual MtF transsexuals. A report by Wallien and Cohen-Kettenis (2008), however, included one male patient who had been diagnosed with GID in childhood, exhibited persistent GID in adolescence, and reported heterosexual attraction in adolescence. A subsequent report by de Vries et al. (2011) included three male patients with childhood and adolescent GID, two of whom reported bisexual orientation and one of whom reported heterosexual orientation in adolescence (perhaps the same patient reported by Wallien & Cohen-Kettenis, 2008). It seems possible, then, that cases of males who met the diagnostic criteria for GID in early childhood and adolescence and later went on to developed nonhomosexual or autogynephilic transsexualism might exist; but such cases are probably very rare. In contrast, there are many reported cases of male patients diagnosed with GID in childhood who experienced persistent GID in adolescence or adulthood and developed a homosexual orientation (e.g., de Vries et al., 2011; Steensma, Biemond, de Boer, & Cohen-Kettenis, 2011; Wallien & Cohen-Kettenis, 2008). Until reliable third-person documentation exists, ideally in the form of actual case reports, I consider retrospective first-person accounts by autogynephilic transsexuals of severe gender dysphoria or strong, persistent cross-gender identification during early childhood to be suspect and possibly exaggerated—not out of willful deception, but out of the understandable need to find or create a coherent life story.

As I discussed in Chap. 5 and will discuss later in this chapter, an alternative possibility—and a more likely one, I believe—is that cross-gender wishes during early childhood in boys who grow up to be autogynephilic transsexuals are simply early indications of their autogynephilic sexual orientation.

Cross-Gender Fantasies Might Become Sexualized After Puberty

Some informants who reported that they had first experienced cross-gender fantasies or wishes in early childhood believed that their fantasies had originally been nonsexual but had become "secondarily" sexualized around the time of puberty, through the operation of some biological mechanism or psychosocial influence. Informants differed in the specific mechanisms to which they attributed the sexualization of their purportedly originally nonsexual feelings.

One informant believed that shame and fear of discovery had resulted in her cross-gender feelings and urges becoming sexualized:

> Before the age of 5, I felt as if I were female and began correcting anyone who claimed otherwise. However, the idea of me being female wasn't a sexual catalyst yet, because I wasn't the least bit afraid or ashamed of being a girl. In fact, I thought I was a girl. But then I began to feel ashamed, afraid to let anyone know my true feelings. Soon I became extremely sexually excited at the thought of all things female—not females in particular, but female articles of clothing on my body, etc. I became sexually excited by polishing my toenails, which hitherto had not happened. Surely you get the picture. Basically, fear was my sexuality back then. I didn't fear being a girl until I was taught to fear this, or at least taught to fear getting caught being a girl. (238)

Another speculated that her cross-dressing might have become sexualized because it was taboo:

> I'm a transsexual who has recently accepted what I am. I have been aroused by cross-dressing. I am attracted to women. What I've questioned is: Was and am I sexually aroused for the reasons you discussed, or because I knew that it was "taboo"? Taboo subjects can be highly erotic. (196)

Yet another believed that her cross-gender behavior had become sexualized because it was forbidden:

> I believe that, at least in my case, autogynephilia was a result of gender dysphoria, not a cause of it. I have realized that I had been denying my identity all along. My speculation is that the erotic response was the result of the identity conflict. It was my mind's attempt to deal with the contradictions. When I was trying to prove what I was, through the roles I lived, the forbidden feminine side was exciting and erotic. Now my mind is no longer in a state of confusion, and the erotic nature of doing something "forbidden" has given way to the new battlefront. I feel I have crossed over from a "marginal" or controversial transsexual classification to a more recognized definition. My anatomic autogynephilia is a result of the combination of a classic "woman in a man's body" definition of transsexuality, combined with years of self-delusion attempting to deny it. (204)

These explanations are problematic in part because they lack specificity. A wide range of behaviors in which children and adults engage or about which they fantasize—many antisocial behaviors, for example—are forbidden, taboo, prohibited, or shameful. These behaviors, however, presumably did not automatically become intensely sexualized for the informants in the way that their cross-gender behaviors did. The explanations these informants provided cannot account for the fact that cross-dressing or cross-gender fantasies *in particular* became sexualized, whereas other forbidden, taboo, prohibited, or shameful behaviors or fantasies presumably did not.

In contrast to the previous informants, who theorized that their cross-gender fantasies had become sexualized because they were shameful or prohibited, another informant proposed that her cross-gender fantasies had become sexualized because they enhanced her self-esteem:

> Starting with the premise of being a woman in a man's body, sexual desire is not as simple as becoming aroused while cross-dressed, fantasizing, or role-playing. Living within a body that feels alien, and sometimes even revolting, does not necessarily promote feelings of self-esteem, attractiveness, or sexual desire. An escape from perceived unattractiveness, however, may promote feelings of sexual desire. I propose that anyone, regardless of their motivation or gender, who feels more attractive and/or desirable will also experience increased sexual arousal. This is where, I believe, the line between fetishism and transsexuality has become blurred. For some people, cross-dressing is certainly the source of their sexual desire and gratification. It is nothing more. For myself, cross-dressing was a way of creating a positive self-image, which, in turn, often promoted feelings of attractiveness and sexual desire. Today, after transition and surgery, I still feel sexual energy from dressing up and looking my best for a night on the town. I suppose this could be confused for autogynephilia, when it is actually an issue of self-esteem. (239)

Again, this explanation lacks specificity. Many things large and small can enhance a person's self-esteem: a good haircut, a high grade on an examination, a compliment from a friend. This informant did not explain why cross-dressing *in particular*, and not other self-esteem-enhancing experiences, became sexualized for her.

Another informant opined that the male sex drive could potentially sexualize nearly anything, including cross-gender fantasies:

> I think that the male sex drive has the potential to be stimulated by almost anything—from the scent of a woman, through pornographic images, to the feel of latex. Almost anything one can think of has potentially erotic content and can generate arousal. It seems not at all surprising that a transsexual with a male sex drive should be aroused by the thought of having a female body and by seeing the results of, and experiencing, the feminization process. In fact, it would be surprising if this wasn't so. (227)

This explanation similarly lacks specificity: There is no attempt to explain why cross-gender fantasies *in particular* should become eroticized by the male sex drive, whereas many other fantasies, objects, and experiences presumably would not.

One informant provided an elaborate explanation of how her cross-gender fantasies had become sexualized during puberty through a process of conditioning that included exposure to her father's pornographic magazines:

> My own feelings of dysphoria began at around 5 or 6 years of age, long before I experienced any sexual arousal or feelings at all. Around puberty, though, as my body became overrun with strong male hormones, I found myself constantly aroused at everything. My desire to be female quite suddenly expanded to include a new sexual aspect. Soon after puberty began, I found a stack of Penthouse magazines in my father's garage cabinets. In the pictures, the women appeared to be in the throes of orgasm. It seemed from the photos that the mere physical fact of having a vagina and breasts was enough to send the owner

> into the throes of ecstasy. I began to sexualize the idea of being a woman, meaning that I began to correlate my desire to be a woman with having an erection. Since every masturbatory session I had was naturally associated with a fantasy that I was masturbating as a female, it was only natural that an erectile reaction to the thought of being female would soon occur. Due to the nature of the material I was exposed to, I honestly believed stroking a breast, or just standing with your legs slightly apart and looking down at your closed vulva, was sexually exciting for a woman. Simply put, the women in the pictures seemed to be turned on by their own bodies, and that affected my idea of what it would be like to be female. I feel strongly that my own autogynephilia was nothing more than a side-effect of the deeper problem of gender dysphoria, set in the context of raging male hormones, the "research materials" I had available at the time (porn), and the response of my penis due to episodes of masturbation when I (naturally) imagined I was a female doing the same thing. (125)

This informant's account is somewhat confusing, but it is helpful to highlight her recollection that "every masturbatory session I had was naturally associated with a fantasy that I was … a female." Thus, her explanation of her autogynephilic feelings appears to be circular: It starts and ends with the fact that her experiences of sexual arousal and orgasm were invariably associated with the fantasy of being female. This, of course, is the defining feature of autogynephilia.

Another informant proposed that her desire to be female was attributable to prenatal hormonal abnormalities and that she had developed transvestic fetishism because masturbation during cross-dressing allowed her to express her repressed cross-gender feelings through an "acceptable male activity":

> I believe that I became transsexual due to some birth defect (hormonal influx during weeks 12 to 16). As I began to live my life and become more self-aware, I began to notice something was wrong. How did it express itself? In the only way that it could have: I had been trained as a male, so I expressed my repressed feelings in the only acceptable way, a transvestic fetish. I concocted this really tough, impenetrable exterior and locked all the confusing feelings deep within myself, only to be let out during ritualistic masturbation practices, which are again an acceptable male activity. (074)

One might wonder whether most men or women would agree that masturbating while wearing women's clothing is an "acceptable male activity"—or that wearing women's clothing and masturbating is more acceptable than wearing women's clothing and *not* masturbating.

Other informants also theorized that their originally nonsexual, identity-related cross-gender fantasies had become secondarily sexualized during or after puberty but were more vague about the mechanism involved. They characterized the sexualization of their cross-gender fantasies as subconscious, a coping strategy, or a response to having concealed their fantasies:

> Why does the thought of wearing women's clothing and being a woman turn me on? My theory is that all transgenders, whether they are transvestites or transsexuals, are born with varying degrees of female gender identity. Because we are raised as boys, this basic need we have—the need to be the sex that we subconsciously view ourselves as being—is not satisfied. As time goes on, and this basic need is repeatedly not satisfied, day after day and year after year, we subconsciously eroticize this basic, fundamental need that has been denied us. In other words, we become autogynephilic. This would explain why

> autogynephilia always gets more intense as we age: because our basic, fundamental need has not been satisfied for that much longer. (096)

> I've read a few of the stories on autogynephilia and can relate to many of the experiences described. However, I believe that was because I was obsessed with wearing girls' clothes. At the time, the only thing I understood was that I wanted to wear girls' clothing all the time. So, as I went through puberty, I sexualized what I was obsessed with, wearing girls' clothes. As a youngster, I didn't have the information or vocabulary to say I was a transsexual. Instead, I engaged in the closest action that would represent being a transsexual, and that was wearing girls' clothes. What I'm trying to say is that, to cope with being a transsexual, I sexualized the wearing of the clothing. (240)

> At about age 4 or 5, I started to want to be a female. I have a twin sister and at that time, I dressed in her clothes to be a girl. As I started to develop sexually, I admit that I was getting aroused by wearing women's clothing. When I was about 19, I started to fantasize about having a female body to attain an orgasm. I felt very guilty about my female feelings as I was growing up and locked them inside. So, what I am saying is that I didn't start out with autogynephilic or any other sexual feelings. I just felt like I should have been born a girl. Because I locked in my feelings, they then later on in life developed into a sexual fantasy as a means of experiencing my female feelings. (241)

These explanations are so elaborate and convoluted that one might wonder whether it wouldn't be easier to simply say, "I've always been turned on by the thought of being a girl, but I have no idea why," and leave it at that. But some informants clearly believed it was important to attempt to explain their autogynephilic feelings as secondary, accidental, meaningless, or irrelevant phenomena. I believe that these explanations represent the informants' attempts to make their autogynephilic desires seem more conventional or acceptable and thereby make their histories seem to conform more closely to generally accepted ideas about MtF transsexualism.

Comment: Signs of Eventual Sexual Orientation Are Often Evident in Childhood

As noted earlier, several informants argued that their desire to be women could not possibly be a sexual phenomenon because they first experienced that desire during early childhood, well before puberty. Their argument is superficially plausible, but it ignores the crucial fact that children usually display erotic and sexual interests and behaviors beginning in early childhood, long before puberty.

More specifically, many children display genital and nongenital manifestations of their eventual sexual orientations well before puberty. This appears to be true for both normophilic and paraphilic sexual orientations, including autogynephilia. In some cases, the prepubertal signs of these eventual sexual orientations involve genital arousal or masturbation in connection with sexual play with other children or adults (Martinson, 1976, 1994); usually this play involves children or adults of the opposite sex, given that most children grow up to be heterosexual. In other cases, the prepubertal signs of eventual sexual orientation involve feelings and behaviors that are not explicitly genital but are associated with sexual attraction or love. Because most adults are unable to remember childhood events that occurred before the ages of 4 or 5 years (Multhaup, Johnson, & Tetirick, 2005), recalled experiences of childhood genital arousal, sexual attraction, or love that are indicative of eventual sexual orientation usually date from these or older ages.

Martinson (1976) described several cases of children between the ages of 6 and 8 who recalled genital arousal in association with sex play with other children or with romantic feelings directed toward other children or adults. He concluded that

> the capacity to relate to another person in an erotically intimate way and to experience sexual feelings and satisfactions (either homosexually or heterosexually) is clearly present before puberty. And we are being conservative, for most of the capacity and many of the experiences are present by five years of age ... and this in a society that is repressive of infant and child sexual behavior. (p. 255)

Children who grow up to be heterosexual often display affectionate or romantic behaviors toward specific opposite-sex peers between the ages of 4 and 8 years. In a classic article, Bell (1902) summarized 800 personal observations and accounts by 360 other observers (most of whom were teachers) involving 1,700 additional cases of "love between children" of the opposite sex. He concluded that:

> The emotion of sex-love may appear in the life of the child as early as the middle of the third year.... The presence of the emotion in children between three and eight years of age is shown by such action as the following: hugging, kissing, lifting each other, scuffling, sitting close to each other; confessions to each other and to others, talking about each other when apart; seeking each other and excluding others, grief at being separated; giving of gifts, extending courtesies to each other that are withheld from others, making sacrifices such as giving up desired things or foregoing pleasures; jealousies, etc. The unprejudiced mind in observing these manifestations in hundreds of couples of children cannot escape referring them to sex origin. (p. 330)

Decades later, Hatfield et al. (1988) used the Juvenile Love Scale (JLS)—a modified version of the Passionate Love Scale used with adults—to assess feelings of affection, preoccupation, desire for physical contact, desire for future marriage, etc. directed toward a specific boyfriend or girlfriend in children between the ages of 4 and 18 years. They observed that "even the youngest children reported having experienced passionate love. In fact, young children and adolescents received surprisingly similar JLS scores" (p. 35). Hatfield et al. added that "there is no evidence to support the contention that passionate love is fueled by the hormonal changes of puberty .... It is the youngest children and the oldest children who secure the highest scores" (p. 45).

Many boys who grow up to be homosexual similarly report that they first experienced sexual or romantic feelings directed toward same-sex peers between the ages of 4 and 8 years. Savin-Williams and Diamond (2000) surveyed 86 young same-sex attracted men and found that their recalled mean age of first same-sex attraction was 7.7 years. Isay (2009) presented several case reports describing the early onset of feelings of homosexual attraction in gay male patients and concluded that "it has become clear to me from working with these and other gay men that homoerotic fantasies are often present from 5 or 6 years" (p. 29). Spada (1979) presented excerpts from narratives by eight gay men who reported that their first attraction to males occurred between the ages of 4 and 7 years. Kulick (1998) reported a similar phenomenon in Brazilian *travesti* (male sex workers who wear women's clothes but identify as homosexual men), in whom "childhood [is] recalled as a period of erotic play with other boys and attraction to other males" (p. 46). Kulick described three *travesti* who stated that their sexual attraction to males had begun at age 7 or earlier.

Many adult males who have paraphilic sexual orientations also report that their paraphilic interests became manifest in early childhood. Gosselin (1979) found that, in a group of 100 rubber fetishists—men with an intense erotic interest in rubber items—42% reported that their interest in rubber items had begun at age 8 or earlier; the modal age of onset of their interest in rubber was 4 years. Men with transvestic fetishism—all of whom are putatively autogynephilic but many of whom are not gender dysphoric and some of whom do not have cross-gender identities of even mild intensity—often report an early onset of interest in cross-dressing. Doorn et al. (1994) found that, among 36 nontranssexual cross-dressing men, 8 (22%) reported that their cross-dressing began before age 7, and another 4 (11%) reported that it began between ages 7 and 10.

Thus, the earliest manifestations of sexual orientation often occur well before puberty, sometimes as genital arousal and sometimes as feelings of sexual attraction or love. In males, this has been observed for persons of heterosexual, homosexual, fetishistic, and transvestic-autogynephilic sexual orientations.

Early Cross-Gender Wishes, Guarded Conclusions

Some informants reported that their cross-gender wishes or fantasies had preceded overt autogynephilic arousal but were more guarded in their interpretations of this temporal sequence. One seemed unwilling to conclude that her early cross-gender feelings were nonsexual, given her awareness that children have sexual feelings before puberty:

> Does the sexual pleasure we get when we imagine ourselves becoming women lead to the urge to be a woman, or is the urge to be a woman there already, with the sexual pleasure simply an expression and result of it? I thought I should have been born a girl and wondered how to be one long before I experienced sexual pleasure and reinforcement of my fantasies. Of course, there is the question of prepubescent sexuality and sexual pleasure. (242)

Another felt that autogynephilia was more than just an erotic phenomenon and also encompassed feelings of love and envy. Based on this broader definition, she concluded that her early childhood desires to be a girl were indeed autogynephilic:

> I have interpreted autogynephilia to mean "loving" the woman inside oneself, as opposed to simply having a sexual attraction to her. If looked at that way, it seems to encompass feeling envious toward girls and wanting to be a girl long before knowing anything consciously about sex. That certainly was true for me. (243)

A similar view was expressed by a third informant: she felt that the early childhood manifestations of her cross-gender identity were indeed sexual, even if they were not yet associated with any physical evidence of sexual arousal:

> I have no doubt, as I look back on my past, that when I was five and wearing perfume, or making pretty necklaces out of colored beads, or arranging flowers, or when I was 7 and volunteering to play Mother Goose in the school play, that sexual motivation was a part of what I was experiencing. But I didn't understand that until I was 18. I didn't even notice the physical manifestations of sexual excitement accompanying those thoughts until I was 10, and even then, I didn't have a clue what it meant. (123)

Yet another individual distinguished between her early autogynephilic fantasies of being a girl (and her associated feelings of gender dysphoria) and her subsequent identification as a woman. She reported that her autogynephilic fantasies came first and therefore were not an effect of any preexisting cross-gender identity:

> My autogynephilic fantasies long pre-dated any notion of actually identifying as being a woman. On the surface, this seems to indicate to me that autogynephilia is a cause rather than an effect. Many respondents experienced their first episodes of dysphoria at the onset of puberty. This was true with me as well. At the very moment young males are first becoming aroused by the opposite sex, there apparently is a group of us that are becoming aroused at being the opposite sex. (018)

This informant's distinction between autogynephilic fantasies on the one hand and cross-gender identity on the other is significant. Autogynephilic persons often report the onset of cross-dressing, cross-gender fantasies, and episodic gender dysphoria in childhood or adolescence. But, as discussed in Chap. 5 and earlier in this chapter, autogynephiles do not typically develop strong, persistent cross-gender identities until adulthood—usually only after decades of cross-dressing (Docter, 1988). In short, the existence of cross-gender fantasies does not necessarily imply the existence of strong, persistent cross-gender identity in autogynephilic transsexualism.

An Alternative View: Autogynephilia Precedes Cross-Gender Identity

Some informants accepted an explanation similar to the one proposed by Blanchard: they believed that their autogynephilic erotic feelings had preceded and had given rise to their cross-gender identities. One stated:

> By the age of eight, I cross-dressed "regularly"—meaning every chance I could find. I would find reasons to stay at home when my mom went visiting friends. By about age twelve, the early-on "excitement" began to be associated with the beginnings of sexual arousal the clothing seemed to cause. By the age of fifteen, the sexual arousal was not a sufficient reason to dress in clothing designed for girls. Instead, I dearly wanted to *be* a girl. The thoughts or fantasies I had, and continue to have, centered on the desire to experience life as a female. This desire became much, if not most, of my fantasy life, whether sexual in nature, or in night and day dreams. I would say that these powerful sexually oriented night/day dreams largely shaped who I thought I was internally. (106)

Another informant offered a similar explanation: She proposed that, after years of experiencing autogynephilia, autogynephiles might end up believing they are female.

> I would like to share my thoughts on the mechanism that causes my condition. The underlying cause is definitely sexual. I believe that, pre-puberty, gender issues result in an unusual sexuality, autogynephilia. Autogynephilia then becomes a powerful driving force; if catered to, the sexual desires then switch to the personality level and the desire to become female becomes pathological. I think you could say that autogynephilia can eventually lead to a sexuality that mimics a heterosexual female. It transfers to the personality level, so you may end up believing you are female. (244)

These informants both touched on an important point that is too often ignored: We discover who we are and define our identities by observing our erotic desires. In both paraphilic and nonparaphilic sexual orientations, "erotic intentions shape identity" (Levine, Risen, & Althof, 1990, p. 95; see also Person, 1980).

Correct Embodiment Feels Important; Eroticism Feels Incidental

A few informants argued that their autogynephilic feelings were incidental or unimportant phenomena. They felt that their experience of wrong embodiment and their resulting desire to imagine themselves in bodies that were congruent with their identities were the genuinely important things, whereas autogynephilia per se was unimportant by comparison.

> Although I have been married for 25 years, I always fantasize that I am the woman and I need that to climax. I should have found a way earlier, but I am still a transsexual and I still want a vagina. It is not the sex, it is the thought of being just exactly what I always wanted to be. And of course with a vagina I could wear any dresses I wanted, even hot pants! I would love breasts, too. I do know that it is not a sexual thing, though, it is all about being in the right body. (120)

> I am certainly aroused sexually by imagining that I am, even for a second, a female in body as well as mind. As the pleasure of orgasm approaches, I imagine myself as a woman being penetrated by a man and in that brief instant, due to the extraordinary power of the human imagination, I really am female in body and soul. That is the core of autogynephilia: pleasure heightened to the level of sexual orgasm, coupled with and associated with becoming for just a second who you really are. Is it an aberration? Some would say yes, but I think rather that it is the expression of an extreme desire to exchange this male body for my real body. (245)

These two informants disagreed on several things, notably whether their autogynephilic fantasies were sexual phenomena, but they both agreed that their sense of wrong embodiment and their desire to have bodies that felt right were at the crux of their problem. Embodiment was important; autogynephilic arousal evidently was not. Of course, it is hard to argue with the statement, "That's simply not important." It is interesting, however, that these informants seemed to attach so little significance to the fact that autogynephilic fantasies were either necessary to achieve orgasm or were consistently associated with arousal and orgasm.

Autogynephilic Arousal Is Infrequent, Loss of Libido Is Acceptable

One informant believed that her desire to be a woman was unrelated to sexual arousal, because her cross-dressing led to sexual arousal only infrequently. While she conceded that her gender dysphoria might have begun as a paraphilia, her willingness to lose her sexual libido—presumably as a consequence of hormone therapy or SRS—led her to conclude that her current feelings were not paraphilic:

> I feel a strong desire to have a woman's body to match my inner self, which I feel is deeply feminine. I do not feel that my desire is directly related to sexual arousal, as 99% of the time that I am feeling the need to dress in women's clothes or wear makeup, etc., I'm not sexually aroused. My gender dysphoria has evolved slowly over the course of my life, and I feel that it may indeed have begun as a sexual paraphilia. Even today, I can still become quite sexually aroused when cross-dressing or wearing a tampon, but the majority of my waking hours are spent in a non-aroused state, wishing I was a genetic female. I have decided that I would rather lose all my sexual libido than continue to live in a male body. Since this is the case, I find it hard to consider my current condition a paraphilia. (246)

Blanchard (1991) addressed the observation that overt sexual arousal does not always accompany cross-dressing and cross-gender fantasy in autogynephilic transsexualism:

> The relationship between the cross-gender stimulus and sexual excitement is probabilistic rather than inevitable. An autogynephile does not necessarily become sexually aroused every time he pictures himself as a female or engages in feminine behavior, any more than a heterosexual man automatically gets an erection whenever he sees an attractive woman. Thus, the concept of autogynephilia—like that of heterosexuality, homosexuality, or pedophilia—refers to a *potential* for sexual excitation. (p. 238)

Does an individual's willingness to sacrifice her sexual drive in order to feminize her body imply that her gender dysphoria is not, or is no longer, a paraphilic phenomenon? Although many paraphilic men would undoubtedly prefer not to lose their capacity for sexual arousal, the definition of the term *paraphilia* does not include any requirement that paraphilic arousal be valued or desired or that individuals would necessarily resist its diminution (e.g., APA, 2000, p. 535). Money (1988) described the relentless compulsivity that often characterizes paraphilic arousal and emphasized the "personal and subjective discontent with having one's life dictated by the commands of a paraphilic lovemap" (p. 142). He observed that men with paraphilias sometimes appreciate the reduction of libido that antiandrogenic medications such as medroxyprogesterone can offer. Consequently, persons who wish to diminish or eliminate their feelings of sexual arousal to unusual sexual stimuli cannot ipso facto be assumed not to be experiencing paraphilic arousal.

Autogynephilia Might Occur in Natal Women

Several informants theorized that autogynephilic arousal was a common experience among natal women and therefore that their own autogynephilic arousal was simply a manifestation of their intrinsic femininity, rather than evidence of a paraphilia.

> I'm really searching for a way by which I can justify my autogynephilic tendencies as being characteristically female and thereby indicative of a bona fide link to universal femininity. Is a genetic woman's sexual arousal more dependent on physical self-image than a man's? If they were honest with themselves, how autogynephilic are genetic, heterosexual, so-called "normal" women? Are genetic women aroused by the thought or image of themselves as female? I'm not suggesting that they are attracted to themselves, but rather that their female self-image may contribute to their ability to be aroused or play an important role in their sexual arousal. If this were the case, it would be quite understandable that they would not publicly acknowledge this, and they might not even admit it to themselves. And this is no different than with transsexual women. (047)

> Most of the time when I go all out to look as good as possible, I get aroused. I believe the sexual gratification, in my case as with many genetic females, is associated with just trying to look as beautiful as possible. (235)

> I would say that the symptoms you describe are equally common among genetic women. Having fantasies about oneself, in a scenario involving a foggy partner, the presence of whom only serves to confirm one's female identity, may seem perverted for a person who still largely sees herself as a man. But it is perfectly normal for a genetic woman. Her psychologist may not use the term "autogynephilia", but may instead speak about "narcissism", which is a less clinical term, thus implying that the fantasies are completely normal. (084)

> For myself, fantasies about sex as a woman are important. So, strictly speaking, I am autogynephilic; but my nontranssexual women friends feel the same and were actually amazed that I had to ask them if they had such feelings, as they consider them completely normal. For me, fantasies like this are just a normal thing for me as a woman. (247)

> I wonder if a correlation could be made between the erotic feelings of having a female body in pre- and post-SRS transsexual women and the erotic feelings of having a female body in natal women. That could go a long way toward legitimizing the erotic component of having a female body and enjoying it. (020)

> There is a sexual motivation for my pursuit of SRS. I like being attractive. I like the comments, I like the attention. At the same time, there are women who will put on makeup and dress nicely, even if they will not see another human that day. I'm one of them as well. So, if it's a normal woman trait, why try to rip apart when we talk about transsexual women? If a woman looks nice for herself that's normal; if a transwoman admits to looking nice for herself, she's autogynephilic. (090)

> Having a male body and living a male life are not compatible with having a sex life for me; I can only experience sexual interest or pleasure as a female. How different is that from a lot of natal women? This leads me to wonder if I'm just experiencing a normal female reaction such as a natal woman would feel. (062)

One informant disagreed with these assessments, however:

> I can gain sexual gratification through thinking of myself as a woman, both dressed and looking beautiful and naked with a vagina. I think the thought of being a woman is not in itself arousing to a genetic woman. (248)

The informants who proposed that natal women also experience autogynephilia are not alone in so theorizing. Veale et al. (2008) reported the responses of 127 natal women to a modified version of Blanchard's Core Autogynephilia Scale (CAS; Blanchard, 1989b); they found that many natal women endorsed several items from their modified scale. In another study, Moser (2009) surveyed 29 natal women using a scale containing modified items from Blanchard's CAS and other scales created by Blanchard (for an analysis, see Lawrence, 2010d); he also found that many natal women endorsed one or more items on his modified scale, although he conceded that "it is possible that autogynephilia among MTFs and natal women are different phenomena and the present inventories lack the sophistication to distinguish these differences" (p. 544).

Unfortunately, both the Veale et al. (2008) and Moser (2009) studies had serious, arguably fatal, methodological limitations. The modified scales they utilized did not adequately differentiate between being aroused by wearing sexually provocative clothing or by imagining that potential romantic partners might find one attractive (which some natal women apparently do experience) and being sexually aroused simply by the idea that one is a woman or has a woman's body (which natal women arguably rarely or never experience). In my opinion, it remains to be demonstrated that natal women are genuinely sexually aroused simply by the fact that they are women. Moreover, with the exception of sexual masochism, paraphilic arousal of any kind is extremely rare in natal women (APA, 2000, p. 568).

Transsexualism Might Reflect a Feminized Brain in a Male Body

A few informants proposed that their transsexualism or gender dysphoria might wholly or partly reflect a mismatch between their male bodies and their putatively feminized brains. They usually believed that their brains had become (or had remained) feminized as a result of some hormonal abnormality—perhaps inadequate exposure to testosterone—in utero:

> I've felt for some time that the cause of transsexual needs in males was a mix of nature and nurture. I'm sure that the "feminized brain" theory is right and that stress in utero denies a budding male fetus of its due testosterone during brain formation. Studies in rats have indicated as much, with testosterone-deprived male rats taking up the female mating position when with males. Anecdotally, I feel this myself, as I naturally wrap my legs around a male partner's buttocks during lovemaking. (115)

> I am convinced that everything about gender dysphoria happens before birth, when the last surge of testosterone leaves us "half-way," with a male body but a female brain. In that female brain is the self-image of a woman, which we will try to bring out in many ways throughout our whole life: cross-dressing, sex reassignment, etc. I think that autogynephilia reflects the women we have been inside, since we were in our mothers' wombs. That means that we have been females always. (249)

These proposed explanations bear some resemblance to past or current biological theories of transsexualism that have been proposed in the scientific literature.

Regarding the theory of a "feminized brain in a male body," Swaab (2007) suggested that

> as sexual differentiation of the genitals takes place in the first 2 months of pregnancy, and sexual differentiation of the brain starts during the second half of pregnancy, these two processes may be influenced independently of each other, resulting in transsexuality (p. 431).

Unfortunately, the intriguing data that underlie Swaab's proposal and the limitations and possible interpretations of these data are too complicated to discuss in detail here. Interested readers are invited to consult a recent summary and critique (Lawrence & Zucker, 2012, pp. 616–617) as an introduction to the topic and a source of references for further exploration. Fortunately, it is not necessary to understand all the nuances of the "feminized brain in a male body" theory to appreciate why some informants might want to invoke this theory in a discussion of the meaning of autogynephilia. The theory provides a plausible biological explanation of transsexualism that neither involves nor requires autogynephilia as a causal or motivational factor. Invoking this theory allows an autogynephilic transsexual to say, in effect: "I don't know what my autogynephilia means or whether it means anything at all; I only know that biological factors account for my transsexualism and no further explanations are necessary."

It is worth noting that some informants were more skeptical about the "feminized brain in a male body" theory. One implied that she had previously believed in this theory but was no longer able to do so, after realizing that the concept of autogynephilia applied to her:

> I can say with certainty that the theory of autogynephilia applies in a way to me. This realization has added to my depression. It would be so much easier to believe that I was a hapless victim of a brain defect (i.e., having a woman's brain). (218)

Another had tried to convince herself that she displayed genuine feminine tendencies but had been forced to confront the realization that she was in most ways typically masculine:

> Over the years, I had started to believe that I had feminine tendencies. I had begun to form a "female identity" or a "girl within," as autogynephiles are said to do as an attempt to rationalize their feelings. But since I discovered the concept of autogynephilia, thoughts of being an actual girl have vanished. I now realize that I am a "man trapped inside a man's body." My closest friends have always been male, my role models have always been male, and I am not particularly feminine. (014)

This last informant recognized one of the most significant problems with the "feminized brain in a male body" theory as it applies to autogynephilic transsexuals: If our brains are indeed feminized, that feminization somehow doesn't seem to be very strongly reflected in our attitudes, interests, or sexual orientations. In fact, virtually the only thing feminine about autogynephilic transsexuals is our desire to be feminine. Of course, there are some MtF transsexuals who are genuinely quite feminine in their attitudes, interests, and sexual orientations, but these are homosexual MtF transsexuals, who represent an entirely different transsexual type.

The Case for Autogynephilia Having Explanatory Meaning

A chapter addressing transsexuals' opinions about the meaning and significance of autogynephilia would be incomplete without a brief statement of the case for autogynephilia operating as a meaningful explanatory factor in the lives of autogynephilic transsexuals, whether or not it is acknowledged as such. This is easily accomplished: With the exception of cross-dressing, we autogynephilic transsexuals rarely display female-typical behaviors, attitudes, or interests during childhood or adulthood (e.g., Blanchard, 1990; Whitam, 1987, 1997). Consequently, our gender dysphoria cannot plausibly be attributed to gender-atypical behaviors, attitudes, or interests. What can the gender dysphoria of autogynephilic transsexuals be attributed to? From what source does it derive? Autogynephilia provides the only obvious answer: Our gender dysphoria and our resulting cross-gender identities are direct outgrowths of our paraphilic desire to turn our bodies into facsimiles of women's bodies.

If autogynephilia is not considered a meaningful explanatory factor, then attempts to account for the gender dysphoria and cross-gender identities that we autogynephilic transsexuals experience quickly become circular, self-referential, and slightly ridiculous:

Q: Why do you want to become a woman?
A: Because I experience gender dysphoria.
Q: What does that mean?
A: That I experience persistent discomfort with my male sex and gender role.
Q: Why are you so uncomfortable with your male sex and gender role?
A: Because I want to become a woman.

Q: Why do you want to become a woman?
A: Because I have a strong and persistent cross-gender identity.
Q: What does that mean?
A: That I desire to be the other sex and live and be treated as a member of the other sex.
Q: In other words?
A: I want to become a woman.

I would argue that an account that treats autogynephilia as a meaningful explanatory factor offers at least a modest improvement:

Q: Why do you want to become a woman?
A: Because I experience a paraphilic erotic desire to have a woman's body.
Q: Is there anything else?
A: After having that desire for 20 years, I've started to think of myself as a woman, too.
Q: Anything else?
A: I love women and I have a desire to become more like the women I love.
Q: I'm beginning to understand—but it makes me think your sexuality is very odd.
A: You're right; but I can only play the hand I was dealt.

Perhaps someday we autogynephilic transsexuals will be able to forthrightly acknowledge the paraphilic hand we were dealt and play that hand without equivocation or apology. I will discuss this possibility in greater detail in Chap. 12.

Chapter 11
Narratives by Nontranssexual Autogynephiles

Transsexual and Nontranssexual Autogynephiles Resemble Each Other

As noted in Chap. 3, some individuals who submitted narratives about autogynephilia were either nontranssexual or not demonstrably transsexual. I had originally intended to collect narratives only from informants who were recognizably transsexual; I felt it was important to document that autogynephilia was experienced not only by the fetishistic transvestites with whom it had traditionally been associated but also by recognizably transsexual persons. I knew, however, that attempting to draw a definitive line between autogynephilic transsexuals and nontranssexual autogynephiles was a difficult if not an impossible exercise, even though I believed there were legitimate reasons for trying to do so. Consequently, I was not surprised to find that the narratives by transsexual and nontranssexual (or not demonstrably transsexual) informants resembled each other in many respects: Transsexual and nontranssexual informants provided similar descriptions of their reactions to learning about autogynephilia, developmental histories, sexual attractions to women and men, and other sexual attitudes and behaviors.

The principal differences between the two sets of narratives were that those by nontranssexual informants were less likely to describe severe gender dysphoria, anatomic autogynephilia, or the desire to live full-time as a woman. Interestingly, attempts to downplay the meaning and significance of autogynephilic arousal were also conspicuously absent in the narratives by nontranssexuals: Unlike their transsexual counterparts, the nontranssexual informants did not make any noticeable effort to describe autogynephilia as an effect rather than a cause of their cross-gender expression, as a nonsexual phenomenon that had become secondarily sexualized, as an epiphenomenon, or as a normal element of female sexuality. I speculate that nontranssexual informants may have been more willing to interpret their autogynephilic feelings as unambiguously erotic because, unlike their transsexual counterparts, they did not have well developed, highly valued identities as women that

A.A. Lawrence, *Men Trapped in Men's Bodies: Narratives of Autogynephilic Transsexualism*, Focus on Sexuality Research, DOI 10.1007/978-1-4614-5182-2_11,

could potentially be discredited or compromised if they acknowledged that their desire to be female was associated with paraphilic erotic arousal.

Given the similarities between the narratives submitted by the transsexual and nontranssexual informants, one might wonder why it would be useful to consider the latter narratives at all. There are at least three reasons. First, documenting the similarities between the two sets of narratives provides a further demonstration that autogynephilic transsexualism and less severe autogynephilic conditions are closely related clinical entities that exist on a continuum of symptomatology. Second, some of the narratives by nontranssexual informants contain informative descriptions of conditions that are closely related to autogynephilic transsexualism, such as partial autogynephilia. Third, some nontranssexual informants submitted unusually insightful or eloquent narratives that offer a more nuanced understanding of autogynephilia as it occurs in both transsexual and nontranssexual autogynephiles.

Representative Narrative by a Nontranssexual Autogynephile

The following account by a nontranssexual informant illustrates many of the similarities and key differences between the typical narratives submitted by transsexual and nontranssexual autogynephiles. Like many of the transsexual informants, this individual reported the onset of cross-gender wishes at an early age, feelings of envy and lust toward women, and overt erotic arousal with cross-dressing—arousal that diminished with time but never completely disappeared. In this and subsequent narratives by nontranssexual autogynephiles, I will identify informants by the parenthesized letters "NTS" (for nontranssexual) and a two-digit number.

> I am 65 years old, happily married, and father of two children. My life, however, has been complicated since about age 5 by a strong desire to be female. My earliest memories are of going past the girls' department in a store and wanting to wear the dresses and to be accepted as a girl. I also have early memories of being envious of the girls next door and wishing I could have long hair, polish my nails and wear pretty clothes. In middle school, when the girls were starting to become women, I began to feel cheated that they were becoming women and I was not. I envied the fact that they wore bras and nylons, dresses and heels. I wanted to be invited to their sleepovers. I, too, wanted to become a young woman, not to attract boys, but because I thought it would just feel really good to be a girl.
>
> This desire became so strong that I started trying on my mother's clothes. I would often dress fully and imagine what it would be like to be a woman. I do not believe that there was a conscious sexual component to my activities. I would also frequently dream that my mother or older female cousins would allow me to dress as a woman and permit me to be one of the girls. By high school, however, my dressing had taken on a strong erotic component and would usually end with an orgasm and a profound feeling of shame and self-loathing. By that time, I knew that there was such a thing as a transvestite, a type of pervert, and that I was one of them. At the same time, I actively dated and outwardly appeared to be a typical high school boy.
>
> In college, I had the freedom to pursue my interest in being feminine. Within a month, I bought my first pair of panties, which I would wear to bed and often under my male clothing. By my sophomore year, I was involved in a serious, physically and emotionally

intimate relationship. This gave me the courage to buy lingerie for my lover and sometimes myself. After a time, she would often permit me to wear her intimate items in the bedroom and on some level to be treated by her as a woman. Within a short time, I had accumulated a full feminine outfit, was exploring makeup, and was experimenting with trying to present as a woman.

After I finished professional school and moved to a large city to begin my professional career, my interest in dressing as a woman continued. Often, in the evening or on weekends I would fully dress with makeup and try to imagine myself as a woman. Within a year, I was beginning to go out to gay clubs dressed as a woman. It gave me a sense of well-being; I felt relaxed, as though on some level that was how I was meant to live.

After I married, my wife had no knowledge of my desires. I would keep my outfits hidden in storage and would from time to time take off for the evening, rent a hotel room, and explore going out as a woman. I began to work with a professional makeup artist on makeup application. I began to thin my brows, and I also started working with a woman who gave instructions in how to present as a woman: how to walk, how to move, and how to use the ladies' room. The better my feminine presentation became, the better I felt. By this time, I was going out to local clubs that catered to cross-dressers. I met other cross-dressers, which encouraged me even more.

By the mid-1990s, I was becoming reasonably comfortable going out for the day as a woman. During that period, I married for the second time, to a woman who was a clinical psychologist. Shortly after our marriage, she learned of my proclivity and was willing to accommodate my feminine pursuits. She would shop with me as a girlfriend and would assist me in purchasing clothing and makeup. I was free to accumulate a feminine wardrobe.

Over the past 10 years, I have become more comfortable spending time as a woman. It has become who I am. I regularly spend the day as a woman. I sometimes traveled as a woman, leaving home en femme and returning days later. I have found, however, that after three or four days, I need to get out of my feminine outfit and go back to my life as a man. For this reason, and in spite of my thoughts about living full-time, I don't think that it is reasonable for me.

Thinking honestly about my desire to be feminine, I admit that there is an erotic part to it. I get turned on by what I see in the mirror, and I do get aroused, but this is only a minor part of what is going on. The major part is my desire to be acknowledged as female and to "be one of the girls." I am probably most happy being out with other women, being treated as one of the girls. It relaxes me and somehow makes me feel that I am not pretending to be anything other than what I am. (NTS 01)

Unlike many transsexual informants, this individual did not report that he disliked his male secondary sex characteristics or was unhappy about being male. He did not describe any attempts to feminize his body, except for thinning his eyebrows. Although he enjoyed living part-time in a feminine gender role, he had no desire to do so for longer than a few days. He also did not report any fantasies of having sex with men, a manifestation of behavioral autogynephilia that is significantly more prevalent in nonhomosexual MtF transsexuals than in nontranssexual cross-dressers (Docter & Fleming, 2001; Doorn et al., 1994).

At first glance, this informant would seem to provide a textbook example of the ICD-10 diagnosis of *dual-role transvestism* (WHO, 1992), which is defined as:

The wearing of clothes of the opposite sex for part of the individual's existence in order to enjoy the temporary experience of membership of the opposite sex, but without any desire for a more permanent sex change or associated surgical reassignment, and *without sexual excitement accompanying the cross-dressing* [emphasis added]. (p. 365)

A clinician who was treating a client with a history like that of the above informant and who did not elicit any admission of erotic arousal accompanying the client's desire to present himself as a woman might mistakenly conclude that the ICD-10 diagnosis of dual-role transvestism was applicable. In fact, I believe this diagnosis is rarely, if ever, applicable to nonhomosexual transgender men.

Nontranssexuals' Identification with the Concept of Autogynephilia

Many nontranssexual informants, like their transsexual counterparts, regarded the concept of autogynephilia as a revelation and believed that it accurately described their feelings and experiences. Here are two representative examples:

> I'm a normal male, married with three children. I have a career as an engineer, a decidedly male-typical job. My sexual orientation is completely heterosexual. And yet, since I reached puberty, I have had almost exclusively sexual fantasies about looking like, dressing like, or being transformed into a woman. The description of autogynephilia was the first time I've read something that seemed to fit what I was experiencing. (NTS 02)

> I was completely overwhelmed by the information on autogynephilia. I have been searching for so long, not so much for a label, but for an answer to many questions that have plagued my life for almost 40 years. Transsexual, transvestic, transgendered, androgynous? The premises of autogynephilia are so in-tune with me that it almost makes me want to shout in joyful wonderment at this discovery. (NTS 03)

Nontranssexual informants suggested that the value of the concept of autogynephilia did not so much lie in providing a name for their condition as in offering an explanatory framework within which to make sense of their otherwise inexplicable feelings and behaviors.

Early Childhood Onset of Cross-dressing and Associated Arousal

Like their transsexual counterparts, several nontranssexual informants reported that they had experienced penile erections or definite erotic arousal in association with cross-dressing or cross-gender fantasies in early childhood:

> In one of your essays, you wrote of two cases of boys younger than age 3 who expressed a desire to cross-dress and became aroused when they did so. I found it odd that there were only two reported cases. I was around the same age when I cross-dressed for the first time. I was highly attracted to my mother's nylon stockings and I felt uncontrollably compelled to wear them. I have a very distinct memory of stealing a pair of stockings from my Mom's dresser and retreating to my room to try them on. I could not have been more than 3 or

> 4 years old, at the very most. It was a wonderful feeling to wear her hose, and I distinctly remember experiencing an erection. Wearing her stockings made me feel like a girl, and I thoroughly enjoyed it. (NTS 04)

> I used to watch my mother comb and braid my female cousin's long beautiful hair when she was staying with us. I was age 5 then and remember having strong erotic and sexual urges. I use to secretly want to wake up and be a girl; I so wanted my hair long. (NTS 05)

Other nontranssexual informants also described the onset of cross-dressing in early childhood but did not recall this activity as being definitely erotic until puberty. Here is a representative account:

> I am a 55-year-old cross-dresser. Another cross-dresser told me about autogynephilia, and it seems to fit me like a glove. I have distinct memories of dressing in my sister's clothes at probably about age 4; I cannot recall if it was sexually charged. There was no further activity until I was about age 12, and this time it was definitely erotic. From ages 12 to 17, I actively dressed in my sister's and mother's clothes. I have had rare moments when I felt like I would like to just remain a woman. I have always admired pretty women and feel like life in general might be easier as a girl. Probably 95% of the time, though, it's about the erotic aspect for me. (NTS 06)

Note that this informant reported a very early onset of cross-dressing, even though the subsequent manifestations of his autogynephilic orientation were almost entirely erotic. This illustrates that the onset of cross-dressing in early childhood is not necessarily predictive of a developmental course in which cross-dressing in adulthood has little or no erotic motivation.

Fantasizing Being Female During Cross-dressing

As discussed in Chap. 6, autogynephilic persons, transsexual and nontranssexual, typically cross-dress in order to create or facilitate the thought or image of themselves as female. This rationale was explicitly described by one nontranssexual informant:

> At age 40, I began to see myself as a heterosexual cross-dresser. I did not find that the sexual arousal associated with cross-dressing gradually went away with time, as Virginia Prince and others claimed. The gender aspects of cross-dressing and going out cross-dressed are an important part of my life, but so is the sexual aspect. And it is not clothing itself that is the primary source of my sexual arousal, but the perception of my body as being female. Even though I am fully male anatomically, in my mind I see myself having all the female parts. What the female garments, makeup, wig, jewelry, fragrance, etc. do for me is to enhance this feeling of myself as physically female. If I had been born later and found the social support I needed, I might eventually have sought SRS. Should I still call myself a heterosexual cross-dresser? Or am I a non-operative transsexual? (NTS 07)

This narrative also illustrates that the dividing line between heterosexual cross-dressing and autogynephilic transsexualism is often indistinct: This informant believed that he might have sought sex reassignment if his circumstances had been slightly different.

Comfort and Prolonged Erotic Arousal with Cross-dressing

The nontranssexual informant whose narrative appeared first in this chapter reported that he felt relaxed when he cross-dressed, just as some of the transsexual informants whose narratives appeared in Chap. 6 had reported. Other nontranssexual informants expressed similar feelings. One reported that he valued the comfort that cross-dressing provided more than any associated erotic arousal:

> I am not on the transsexual side of the transgender scale; I identify as a cross-dressing male, and becoming a woman was never a goal of mine. I do not believe that transitioning is something I need to pursue. I am simply a man who enjoys dressing in what is culturally considered to be feminine attire. Yes, there is an erotic component to this at times, but the reality is that, more often, sexual excitement is not the desired goal or even the end result. I simply find that I am comfortable dressed as a woman. This goes deeper than simply a sexual release or outlet. (NTS 08)

As discussed in Chap. 6, the relaxation and comfort that autogynephiles sometimes experience in association with cross-dressing might be analogous to the feelings of comfort and emotional security that men sometimes experience in long-term romantic relationships. Alternatively, these feelings might represent low intensity sexual arousal that is not always recognized or interpreted as such (Docter, 1988). Consistent with the latter interpretation, two other nontranssexual informants reported that they experienced and enjoyed the low intensity, long duration sexual arousal that resulted from extended periods of cross-dressing without orgasmic release:

> I wear very tight panties, 24/7; this controls penile erection and extends the time limits of sexual arousal. This never actually results in a full orgasm, allowing the dressing to go on a long time. Just to dress and masturbate is somewhat self-defeating. (NTS 09)

> I don't identify as transsexual, as I do not feel a need to transition fully. But I certainly recognize the strong presence within me of autogynephilic motivations. As a child, I experienced vaguely erotic feelings with the thought of wearing girl's clothes; with adolescence, these became very clearly erotic. In my 30s, it became more important to me to experience not an episodic and orgasmic eroticism, but a low level, long lasting "erotic buzz" from wearing something feminine secretly all day long. With increasing years (I'm now in my 40s), this changed into a desire to express myself as being feminine for others to see, with no (or very little) evident eroticism at all—but I still enjoy erotic fantasies of the old type at night. (NTS 10)

The low level, long lasting "erotic buzz" described by the latter informant may be a good example of what Docter (1988) was referring to when he observed that "transvestism and transsexualism are, in part, mood altering behavioral strategies. They generate pleasurable excitement and a sense of well-being" (p. 118).

Autogynephilic Fantasies Are Necessary for Orgasm

Several nontranssexual informants, like many of their transsexual counterparts whose narratives appeared in previous chapters, reported that autogynephilic fantasies were often or always necessary to achieve arousal or orgasm during masturbation or partnered sexual activity. Here are a few examples:

> I'm a 29-year-old male who's had autogynephilia since about 12 years old. I have always been strongly attracted to women and have absolutely no attraction to males. I have wanted so badly to live a normal guy's life, but I cannot enjoy sex with a woman unless I fantasize about being one. (NTS 11)

> Briefly, I am an autogynephilic man and always was. I can feel sexually excited only by imagining that I am a woman and doing something feminine. But I don't feel like a classically understood transsexual. I would like to be a woman only in sexual things. In all the rest of nonsexual human activity, I am a man and there is nothing feminine about me. (NTS 12)

> I am a university student in Denmark. Reading about autogynephilia concretized and made plain a number of things of which I had been aware but which I had been unable to express in so clear and lucid a manner. While having sex with my partner, I found it often necessary to fantasize about being a woman having lesbian sex with her in order to achieve orgasm. (NTS 13)

These narratives provide further support for the idea that autogynephilia operates as a sexual orientation in some autogynephilic nontranssexual men as well as in autogynephilic transsexuals.

Competition with Heterosexual Attraction

A few nontranssexual informants discussed competition between their autogynephilic feelings and their attraction to women. One observed that, whereas making love with women was exciting, imagining being a woman oneself was even more exciting:

> I loved dating and making love with girls, and I was highly aroused by their lovely bodies. But I especially loved that closeness with girls helped me to learn more about them and made my own feminine feelings more authentic. One night, making out with a girlfriend and undressing her, I noticed a large damp spot in her panties. I had a feeling of overwhelming excitement to put her panties on, to feel from the dampness the exact location of a girl's vagina on my body. Instead of making love with her at that point, I picked up her panties and faked a sudden need for the bathroom, so I could put them on and imagine I had a vagina and feel the dampness between my legs. This was one of the most exciting sexual experiences I had ever had. I didn't masturbate, but I made love to the girl fantasizing that I was her. After I married, I secretly collected a stash of women's clothes, lingerie, breast forms, shoes, and a wig. When I had the opportunity, I would dress up for the ultimate sexual experience. Feeling like a woman was far more exciting erotically than making love with one, and to this day I feel the same way. (NTS 14)

This informant's description of his eagerness to interrupt the progress of heterosexual intercourse in order to put on his partner's panties and imagine himself having her anatomic features suggests something of the power of autogynephilic eroticism relative to ordinary heterosexual attraction. Women's bodies are exciting, but imagining having a woman's body oneself is even more exciting.

Sex with Men

As discussed in Chap. 8, autogynephilic transsexuals sometimes engage in sex with men and often fantasize about doing so, even though they are not genuinely attracted to men's bodies. Some nontranssexual autogynephiles reported similar experiences; here is one representative example:

> I'm a 49-year-old male. I've lacked a good way of describing myself, but the concept of autogynephilia really describes me well. I am attracted to females as a male, but I fantasize intensely about engaging in sex with men with me being a woman or at least a highly feminized version of myself. Male-to-male contact as such is something I find especially unsexy. I've been with more than a dozen females and three males sexually; with the men, I made a point of appearing and feeling feminized or it would have been a total turn-off for me. I masturbate to fantasies about being way more feminized than now, and being with a man who is paying me for sex and is enthusiastically having sex with me from behind. (NTS 15)

As previously noted in Chap. 1, Blanchard (1989b) suggested that "bisexual gender dysphorics' interest in male sexual partners is mediated by a particularly strong desire to have their physical attractiveness as women validated by others" (p. 622). In the informant's fantasy, this validation of physical attractiveness is suggested by the imagined male partner's willingness to pay for sex and by his enthusiastic performance.

Specificity of Autogynephilic Arousal

Some autogynephilic persons fantasize about being women with certain specific features or characteristics, rather than simply fantasizing about being generic women. These specific characteristics are typically the same ones they find most appealing in the women to whom they are sexually attracted. Chap. 9 contained a good example of this kind of specificity of autogynephilic arousal: a narrative by an MtF transsexual who was specifically attracted to women who wore leg braces and who wanted to be a woman who wore leg braces. A few informants in Chap. 7 similarly reported that, when they were especially attracted to a particular girl or woman, they had sexual fantasies about looking exactly like her or wearing her hairstyle or clothing.

One nontranssexual informant described his specific attraction to women of a different ethnicity than his own and his erotic fantasies about being a woman of that same ethnicity:

> I have self-diagnosed autogynephilia. I fit all the autogynephilic criteria (transvestic fetishism, etc.), but it is not the only way for me to get aroused. I can remember fantasies of becoming a girl or wearing women's clothing before the age of 10. I have not seriously considered undergoing sex reassignment surgery, although I can appreciate the strong, albeit sexual, motivation to undergo such an operation. My experience of autogynephilia may further validate the theory that this paraphilia is a projection of one's object of desire onto oneself. I am an Asian male, but I do not fantasize about being an Asian woman, but rather a Caucasian woman, because I prefer and am most sexually attracted to Caucasian women. Thus, autogynephilia may not simply be the fantasy of being a woman, but the fantasy of being one's desired sexual object. (NTS 16)

In my clinical practice, I have sometimes had autogynephilic transsexual clients who stated that their most intense heterosexual attraction was directed toward women with a specific physical appearance or somatic type. Not surprisingly, the cross-gender identifications that these clients displayed were often specific in exactly the same way. One of my autogynephilic transsexual clients, for example, was particularly attracted to female bodybuilders and fantasized about becoming a female bodybuilder herself.

Autogynephilia and Female Beauty

One nontranssexual informant stated that he considered autogynephilia to be an emotional experience as well as an erotic one; he seemed to connect the emotional aspect of autogynephilia with his appreciation of female beauty and his interest in representing it through art. He also reported that, whereas he felt some sexual attraction to both women and men, he was only romantically attracted to women.

> Your explication and elaboration of the concept of autogynephilia resonated deeply with me and helped me to identify and admit the feelings I was having. I cross-dressed for the first time at age 13. I found it very arousing. For me, autogynephilia is a sexual experience, but it is also an emotional experience. I am fascinated by female beauty. I am an artist, and I have been drawing and painting beautiful women since puberty. I've never felt strongly motivated to draw the nude male body. At age 19, I discovered that I was bisexual. Yet, the percentage of males I have any interest in is very small, and I don't think I could ever have a romantic relationship with a male. My homosexual fantasies mostly just revolve around a penis penetrating me, rather than being about a complete man. When I am fantasizing about women, however, even imaginary ones, I will be thinking about the female form in its totality. (NTS 17)

In explicitly raising the issue of the appeal of female beauty, this informant touched on an important but infrequently discussed aspect of the cross-gender wishes we autogynephilic persons experience: our desire to turn our bodies into facsimiles of what we find beautiful—indeed, what we find more beautiful than anything else on earth. As John Updike (1991) perceptively observed, "A naked woman is, for most men, the most beautiful thing they will ever see; on this planet, the female body is the prime aesthetic object" (p. 5). We autogynephiles desire to become facsimiles of the most beautiful things on this planet.

Desire to Eliminate or Control Autogynephilic Feelings

Some nontranssexual informants believed that they would never be able to actualize their autogynephilic desires, because doing so would mean abandoning their obligations to their families. Consequently, they wanted to eliminate or control their autogynephilic desires, in order to feel less tormented by them.

> The article on autogynephilia hit the nail on the head with me. I am a 37-year-old male with a wife and two children. I have been having thoughts about being a girl that sexually excited me since I was 4 years old. I remember in nursery school that there was a ballerina's outfit I used to put on. I look at beautiful women and do get aroused; however, I cannot climax unless I think about becoming a woman. When I have sex with my wife, I have to think about becoming a woman in order to climax. Is SRS the cure? I hope there can be another cure. I couldn't go through transition and SRS in my situation; it would destroy my whole family. I wish there were something I could do that could cure this inner demon. (NTS 18)

> I'm in my early 40s and am quite masculine in appearance and manner. I have had physical and behavioral autogynephilic fantasies since puberty. Autogynephilic thoughts and images now dominate my mind much, if not all, of the time. The obsessive fantasy of being physically feminized using hormones, surgery, shaving, electrolysis, permanent cosmetics, etc., pretty much describes my sexual landscape. If I'm not thinking about it, I'm looking for porn about it or writing porn about it myself.
>
> Despite the urges, which are very intense at times, I've avoided acting on anything physically or behaviorally autogynephilic so far, for several reasons. First, I would never come even close to passing as a woman, and I'd be letting my sexuality lead me into an ostracized lifestyle and throwing away a lucrative, hard-won career. I don't see that as a path to greater happiness. Also, acting on my autogynephilic urges would not be faithful to the family responsibilities I've taken on.
>
> At this point, I'm seeking counseling and want to get on a course of antiandrogens to turn down the testosterone-induced heat on the autogynephilic fires. But it's also true that the thought of the feminization that will accompany the hormones is a source of excitement in and of itself. I suppose that, technically, some would then view me as a pre-op or non-op MtF transsexual, but I just consider myself a person with autogynephilia who is working to balance his sexual and nonsexual urges while trying to live a good life. (NTS 19)

These narratives are in some ways reminiscent of a few in Chap. 6 that were submitted by nominally transsexual informants who wanted to undergo SRS but live as men afterwards or who had successfully carried out such a plan. In both sets of narratives, the informants had decided that living full time as women was impossible or impractical, but they differed in the solution that they desired (or achieved): either attempting to suppress their cross-gender wishes or attempting to express those wishes to the extent that seemed feasible by undergoing SRS but not undertaking a gender role transition.

Wide-Ranging Autogynephilic Interests

A few nontranssexual informants provided narratives that described a wide range of autogynephilic fantasies and behaviors in great detail. One such informant reported that he experienced all four major types of autogynephilia (transvestic, behavioral, physiologic, and anatomic):

> I have all four varieties of autogynephilia. My desire to crossdress is intense and continual. I have all these beautiful angora dresses, sweaters, hats, muffs, bonnets, scarves, gloves, purses, slippers, etc. When I am dressed up, the erotic intensity is beyond words. I have an intense desire to wear certain female clothing items, ballet dresses (tutus) being the most significant. I have spontaneously ejaculated with no masturbation over many of these items.

> I love being with big groups of women and doing women's things, like my knitting. I have done this in the past wearing women's clothes and it was a great high. I have major fantasies about breast feeding, dressing as a lady pushing a baby carriage, and having periods. I have worn a Kotex belt and pad under my skirts and dresses. Fourthly, I fantasize about having a woman's body. I love wearing fuzzy dresses with silicone breast forms and a muff (made out of a wig) and hiking my skirt up and running my hands over my breasts and down over my muff, imagining myself as a woman. (NTS 20)

Another informant's narrative provided a detailed description of autogynephilic fantasies involving an imagined girlhood:

> I think of myself as a heterosexual male. However, I fantasize about being a woman. In this fantasy, I am bisexual and very sexually active. I also like to imagine performing other female activities: buying clothes, grooming myself, dating men and women, keeping house, having a period, having a baby, and getting married. Some of my favorite sexual fantasies include: being the submissive partner to a masculine lesbian, being swept off my feet by a gentleman, being a glamour model, being a housewife, and being a whore. I also find the idea of being raped as a woman very exciting. When I am sexually aroused, I get turned on by female things, not just sex as a woman. I think about what I would have been like as a little girl: my bedroom, school uniform, toys, being called "daddy's best girl," and having my first period. Even as I write this, I have an erection, thinking about getting dolls for Christmas, buying my first bra, having a boyfriend and letting him touch me inside my knickers. I could even get turned on by thoughts of having a Pap smear test or taking the pill. The idea of being a girl, of being treated like a girl, and of doing girls things is what I crave. (NTS 21)

This informant's final fantasy images, which eroticize Pap smears and oral contraceptive use, offer yet another illustration that virtually any aspect of women's experience can act as the basis of an autogynephilic fantasy.

Partial Anatomic Autogynephilia

Blanchard (1993b) used the term *partial autogynephilia* to describe "autogynephiles whose erotic self-images include a mixture of male and female anatomic features, most often women's breasts and men's genitals" (p. 71). As noted in Chap. 3, I decided for the sake of consistency to categorize as nontranssexual those informants with partial autogynephilia who reported the desire to have women's breasts but did not report any desire for SRS. Some informants who wanted women's breasts never expressed an opinion about SRS; those who did usually seemed to regard SRS as unnecessary rather than undesirable. In contrast to the cases of partial autogynephilia described by Blanchard (1993b), none of the informants with partial autogynephilia who wanted women's breasts emphasized that possession of male genitalia was an essential element of their desired sexual self-image. Here are several representative narratives by informants with partial autogynephilia who desired to have women's breasts:

> I can relate to most autogynephilic feelings, but I'm especially into breasts. I was jealous on seeing a woman with a large chest or a young girl who was beginning to develop. I bought breast forms to wear at home. A few years later I began to take hormones. They grew to the

point of having enough weight and volume to become bouncy; then I realized what I had always needed was having to wear a bra! Having to wear a bra and letting the world see them was such a great feeling. Since then I have had breast augmentation; I'm now a full 38C or baby D. I don't know if I will ever have SRS; that's not really a main goal of mine right now. I now live my fantasy: I now am one of those women I used to see with a large chest. (NTS 22)

I get aroused and excited when wearing women's clothing. I always have loved women with large breasts. However, I have discovered that my feeling for women involving their breasts is the wish that I had them. I have size 38DD breast forms; I wear them all the time now. To feel the way they move, how they get in the way of your movements, and the constant reminder that they are there due to their size, drives me crazy with the desire to have a set of my own. Any inconvenience of having large breasts would be a very small price to pay for the pleasure and feeling they would have for me. If it were possible to take a drug or something and wake up the next morning and be transformed into a woman with large breasts, I would do it in a second. (NTS 23)

The idea of developing breasts has been a strong driving force for me. I've always been jealous of women and their bodies since I was very young. As I got older, I began to cross-dress frequently, first in my mother's clothes, then venturing out to buy my own. My biggest thrill was buying a set of breast forms. This satisfied my urges and desires, at least for a while. The more I wore them, the more I wanted to wear them. My therapist finally directed me to a doctor who prescribed a low dosage of hormones for me. After about 6 months, I began to see some development. I am thrilled to death regarding these changes. It's hard to hide my breasts now, as they have grown to a B cup. I am trying to decide between going forward and living as a woman or just being a man with breasts. (NTS 24)

I am a 36-year-old male. I have cross-dressed ever since I can remember. In my late twenties, I began to focus on breasts: not just physical attraction to a woman's breasts, but to the idea of possessing them myself. I now want to develop breasts through hormone therapy or undergo surgery to augment my breasts. My whole arousal emanates from having breasts. My goal is to find a doctor who will prescribe hormones for me to develop breasts or a plastic surgeon to perform breast augmentation on me. Whatever the other effects on my body, it would relieve the frustration I feel now. (NTS 25)

I am a male in my mid-60s. I have had a fascination with breasts as long as I can remember. As a teen, I wore my mother's bra when no one was home and masturbated, fantasizing that the breasts were my own. This is the only physical change I want. If I had breasts, nothing would change towards the outer world. It would be my secret and fulfilled desire. My sexuality wouldn't change, except that feeling them grow and being able to play with them would bring me close to an orgasm. (NTS 26)

I am a heterosexual male in my late 20s. I first started fantasizing about what it would be like having very large breasts after I was intrigued by big-breasted pornographic models. I purchased very large breast forms and have worn them at least 5 hours a day when by myself. Typically I masturbate at least three times a day wearing them. The feel of having the weight on my chest is very erotic to me. I fantasize about getting breast augmentation, but I know I couldn't get them as large as I would like them. (NTS 27)

I am an autogynephilic person. I have a very strong desire to grow and augment my breasts. The desire is so strong that I have been taking hormones to enhance my bust, and I am also using breast pumps to get larger feminine nipples. I have no desire to do full SRS, as I only want large breasts and to appear feminine for sexual gratification. (NTS 28)

I am a 45-year-old straight male. I have a strong, unstoppable desire to develop female breasts. I have invested unbelievable amounts of time and energy over the last 17 years to develop them. But I have no desire to be anything other than a heterosexual male (with breasts).

> I have very little interest in cross-dressing and none whatsoever in presenting myself as a woman in public. I believe the existence of anatomic autogynephilia in heterosexual males should be recognized. I think it is possible that the inability of men like me to fulfill our unrelenting desire to have breasts may push many of us toward full SRS. I don't want to go that far. I like who I am, the way I am. I just want to hide a pair of breasts under my shirt and go about my life as usual. (NTS 29)

In my opinion, the concern expressed by the last informant—that the desire to have women's breasts might push some partial autogynephiles toward seeking SRS when they don't actually want it—is probably overstated. Nevertheless, he is correct in observing that there has been little recognition of the phenomenon of partial anatomic autogynephilia and little attention directed toward helping persons who experience the paraphilic desire to feminize their bodies but would be content with (or would prefer) something short of complete gender role transition and SRS. I discuss this issue in greater detail in Chap. 12.

Co-occurring Paraphilias

As discussed in Chap. 9, paraphilias tend to co-occur, and autogynephilic persons often report one or more other paraphilias in addition to autogynephilia. Several nontranssexual informants reported other concurrent paraphilias, including sexual masochism, amputation-related paraphilias, gynemimetophilia and gynandromorphophilia, and unspecified paraphilias.

Sexual Masochism

The following narratives expand on the masochistic themes described by the transsexual informants in Chap. 9. One nontranssexual autogynephile described masochistic fantasies and behaviors involving self-inflicted humiliation achieved by identifying himself as a feminized man or transvestite to strangers or casual acquaintances in public places:

> I have major fantasies of being dominated, feminized, dressed by women and laughed at and being humiliated by them. I love to dress outrageously and go out in public for the shock value and laughter it creates. I can go to a shopping mall for hours with a fake story for every clerk in every store that usually gets laughter or humiliation. I will tell women I need clothes for a sex change operation, or ask in front of a bunch of ladies if I can shop dressed as a lady, or ask if transvestites are welcome to shop here. I will say I am getting maternity clothes so I can host a baby shower, or buying purses or hats for a ladies' garden party, or buying dresses so my mother and I can doll up together. I will relate how my mother and friends caught me in my mother's clothes, or how my Auntie first dolled me up, or my career as a female impersonator, or my career as a dancing girl, or how much I love to dress as a ballerina and dance. I love going to beauty parlors and having the women make me up as a girl and laugh when I come out in some silly outfit. I love going to have my nails done, dressed as a lady. I see it as a paraphilia and feel that looking for laughter, humiliation, etc. is a form of masochism. (NTS 20)

Another nontranssexual informant reported masochistic fantasies involving both feminization and other traditional or stereotypic elements of sexual masochism, including bondage or loss of freedom, objectification, and sexual victimization:

> I believe I am an autogynephiliac, not a classical transsexual. I come from a fairly macho, Latin culture, and I'm aroused by the thought of being a submissive female having sex with an aggressive, macho man. There is always an element in my fantasies of being treated as an object, of being used in different ways. My fantasies often involve humiliation.
>
> I sometimes fantasize being a sexual slave. This generally involves kidnapping and bondage. The fantasies sometimes involve gradual feminization; in such cases, the first step is always getting my legs shaved and being forced to dress as a female. The scenarios sometimes involve prostitution. A recurring image is that I awake, not knowing where I am, and I'm gagged, blindfolded and bound to a bed, facing down, my hips raised by a couple of pillows. As I try to move, I realize I've been dressed as a female; my outfit always includes a bra, panties and skirt. A man climbs onto the bed, and, as he fondles my legs, I realize they've been shaven. As he positions himself for penetration, I feel his legs against mine; his are muscular and, importantly, hairy. Always, he lifts up my skirt and pulls down my panties before vigorously penetrating me. If he speaks, it is always to humiliate me.
>
> I also fantasize myself as an ultra-traditional wife. In these fantasies, it's like waking up in a parallel universe where I have always been female. My life revolves around sexually pleasing my husband, pregnancy, and breastfeeding. I only fantasize about the relationship with my husband in strictly sexual terms. The wedding itself isn't part of the fantasy, except for losing my virginity on my wedding night. The fantasy usually starts with fantasizing about experiencing female puberty. These fantasies are generally not taking place in my culture but in even more traditional ones, with arranged marriages. (NTS 30)

Yet another informant's most exciting masochistic fantasies originally involved being tortured and killed, albeit not specifically as a female. These fantasies gradually morphed into the fantasy of being a young female rape victim:

> I seem to fall pretty squarely into the group Blanchard calls autogynephilic. I have been married once, and all my sexual partners have been female. Starting when I was about three years old, I became conscious of an extremely pleasurable sensation from fantasies of sadomasochism. I found delight in the thought of being brutalized, humiliated, tied up, slashed, dismembered, and killed. At first, my imagined persona might be man, woman, child, or animal. After about age seven or eight, however, I usually liked to be a pretty young woman being tortured to death by a psycho. My fantasy would almost always end in being stabbed to death with a knife in the belly, which I found exquisitely satisfying and powerfully compelling. Shortly after I turned 14, one of these fantasies produced penile contractions and I soon discovered the concept of sex. I abandoned my longstanding childhood fantasy of being a pretty young woman being tortured to death and replaced it with the fantasy of being a pretty young woman being forcibly raped. Since that time, variations on the rape fantasy have always been my most compelling source of sexual excitement. These fantasies presume that I am a biological woman. Less commonly, but with increasing frequency in recent years, I have also enjoyed fantasies of being turned into a woman. These fantasies are less exciting than the rape fantasies. (NTS 31)

This narrative provides another example of the phenomenon of "paraphilic substitution." This is the term I introduced in Chap. 9 to describe the process by which very disturbing or unacceptable paraphilic fantasies sometimes become replaced by less distressing, more acceptable ones. Autogynephilic fantasies, even those involving rape, are probably less distressing than many other paraphilic fantasies (e.g., those involving being tortured to death). Consequently, it is not surprising that autogynephilic fantasies might take a prominent role in paraphilic substitution in individuals who experienced some autogynephilic erotic interest.

Acrotomophilia and Apotemnophilia (Amputation Paraphilia)

A paraphilic erotic interest in amputees as sexual or romantic partners is called *acrotomophilia* (Money, 1986). A paraphilic erotic interest in being an amputee oneself is called *apotemnophilia* (Money et al., 1977). In a review article (Lawrence, 2006), I proposed that apotemnophilia probably reflects an erotic target location error in men who are sexually attracted to amputees (i.e., who are acrotomophilic), just as autogynephilia represents an erotic target location error in men who are sexually attracted to women.

One nontranssexual autogynephile described experiencing both acrotomophilia and apotemnophilia. The colloquial terms *devotee* and *wannabe*, used by this informant in the narrative below, are commonly employed by acrotomophilic and apotemnophilic persons in reference to themselves (Bruno, 1997).

> I remember from my early development being turned-on at the idea of being a woman, but it was never all-consuming. What had been an overriding force was acrotomophilia and apotemnophilia, a blend of devotee and wannabe tendencies. As I understood it, the traditional notion of "woman trapped in a man's body" was generally something people were aware of from an early age. While there were signs I can see now, I missed them until a few months ago. With the apotemnophilic and acrotomophilic side of things, that's not the case. I was aware of odd feelings about amputees from a very young age, possibly as early as 4 or 5 years old.
>
> My earliest memory of anything to do with amputees was first noticing a couple of amputees while traveling with my parents; even at the time, it prompted an odd feeling. An occasional interest that triggered inexplicable feelings at that young age somehow became more important with the onset of puberty (i.e., I became turned-on). Seeing images of amputees, thinking about them, and sitting in certain positions that reminded me of them seemed to trigger the same sort of feelings as thinking about girls or seeing images of scantily clad women. I remember the first time I ever actually came was while sitting with both legs folded underneath me, as if I were a double above-the-knee amputee. That has to be an important moment for any teenage boy. I liked girls and the idea of amputees, so I guess it follows that amputee girls would be like a holy grail for me. That was true, but there was also something about the process of such extreme, generally involuntary, body modification that was fascinating.
>
> At college there were plenty of girls, so the amputee side of things took a back seat for a while. It was still there, though, and I started to collect a few images from the Internet. More importantly, I realized that I wasn't the only one who felt like this. In the past, I'd considered the idea of engineering a situation where I lost one or both legs, but I realized that the practicality was probably vastly different from the fantasy. While the permanence was part of the turn-on, I knew enough about myself to realize it was probably a bad idea. So, I stuck with pretending.
>
> A few months back, I started experimenting with cross-dressing. Somehow, I went from amputee pretending and some experimentation with a set of breast forms I'd bought earlier to trying on a dress to go with them. Soon I had some boots and a couple of wigs. I took several photos and I saw myself like I never had before. I actually liked the image; I couldn't stop

looking at the pictures. Realizing that I'd had autogynephilic tendencies in the past, I figured that I might have been suppressing this side of me the whole time. Of my two erotic targets, girls and amputees, at least one of them was looking viable. I realized that this was something significant and was reeling at the possibilities. Was I a transvestite or did I actually want SRS too? With time and reflection, I realized that I didn't want a full sex change but did want to go at least part of the way. I'd have breast augmentation tomorrow, given half a chance.

My apotemnophilia is still there, but it's not the overriding drive that it was before. I feel like the destructive force of wanting to become an amputee has been quelled to a large extent and replaced with a more positive notion of becoming something I love: me. I don't think I can expect the apotemnophilic feelings to just disappear, but now they are not the driving force. (NTS 32)

This narrative offers yet another example of the phenomenon of paraphilic substitution. The informant's intense but unacceptable paraphilia, apotemnophilia, was eventually superseded by a paraphilia that the informant considered more acceptable or benign, autogynephilia.

Gynemimetophilia and Gynandromorphophilia

As noted in Chap. 9, gynemimetophilia and gynandromorphophilia are closely related, partially overlapping terms that describe the paraphilic interest some persons have in transvestites, she-males, or MtF transsexuals as sexual or romantic partners. Two nontranssexual autogynephiles reported a specific sexual attraction to persons in these categories; the first of the informants offered this account:

I'm 31 years old. I was married for ten years and have two children. I'm now in a very loving relationship with a transsexual woman. I have fantasies of dressing and acting as a woman, but I've never had the desire to act on those fantasies; I'm primarily aroused by the *idea* of presenting myself as a woman. I'm also extremely attracted to cross-dressing males, whether they be drag queens or transsexuals. I have discussed this with my girlfriend, the MtF transsexual, and it's clear that we are very different. I'm not a transsexual like she is. But I'm extremely aroused by the thought of dressing like a woman and doing womanly things.

I definitely want to have sex with attractive drag queens or transsexuals when I see them. When I met my current girlfriend, I had no idea she was a man, and I found her extremely attractive. I emailed her right away and asked for a date. It was after that that one of my friends told me she was a transsexual, and I was even more attracted to her then. This was before her gender reassignment, and we enjoyed a few very good sexual experiences before her surgery. I still find her just as attractive and just as exciting after her surgery, but we haven't been sexually active yet. (NTS 33)

Although this informant had experienced extremely arousing erotic fantasies about dressing like or being a woman, he had never actualized these fantasies; instead, he dated and had sex with an MtF transsexual who had actualized her own desire to be a woman. This informant's narrative would seem to provide an excellent example of Person's (1995) observation, previously quoted in Chap. 7, that "fantasy may be gratified through bonding with someone who has already actualized one's own fantasy .... The identification process allows us to enjoy our fantasies vicariously, that is, at one remove, without suffering guilt or anxiety." (p. 131).

The second informant, a nontranssexual autogynephile who explicitly identified as gynandromorphophilic, provided this statement:

> Thanks for your 1997 paper on sexual attraction between autogynephilic transsexual women. You were way ahead of your time on this topic, based on the misinformation I hear from so many transsexual women. Based upon my own experiences and those of other gynandromorphophilic males, it seems painfully clear that we prefer as partners transsexual women with strong autogynephilic tendencies. To be more precise, we prefer men who are trapped in the bodies of fully transitioned pre-op transsexual women. I hope you can appreciate the distinction I have drawn from your own title "men trapped in the bodies of men." (NTS 34)

This individual was referring to one of my earliest conference presentations (Lawrence, 1997), in which I offered the following hypothesis:

> Could it be that some of us find other transsexuals especially desirable as partners because they exemplify the autogynephilia at the core of our desire? Because they mirror our own minds, are our own fantasies made flesh? Attending to our internal autogynephilic imagery, many of us metaphorically "make love to ourselves," whether we are by ourselves or with another. And when this feels too lonely, what partner could be better—and less distracting—than one who is essentially a clone of ourselves? (para. 22)

There is evidence that many gynandromorphophiles are themselves cross-dressers (i.e., transvestites or she-males) and are putatively autogynephilic. Blanchard and Collins (1993) studied personal advertisements placed by 88 gynandromorphophilic men who sought transvestites, she-males, or other cross-dressing men as sexual or romantic partners; of these, 37 (42%) described themselves as cross-dressers in their advertisements. The phenomenon of gynandromorphophilic men who are also autogynephilic is widely recognized within the MtF transsexual community: One of my MtF transsexual clients said of the gynandromorphophiles she had encountered, "They can't decide whether they want to have sex with us or be us."

Other Paraphilias

Another informant reported experiencing autogynephilia, sadomasochism, and several other unspecified paraphilias. He described his hope that putting greater emphasis on his sadomasochistic paraphilic interests might result in less pressure to act out his autogynephilic fantasies:

> I've never seen a more accurate description of my own inner struggle than the information you've published explaining physiologic autogynephilia. About 3 years ago, I figured out that I had a cluster of paraphilias—legal ones only, thank God. I noticed a distinctive pattern in the "forced-feminization" stories that I'm drawn to reading and writing. I just turned 40 and have reached a stage at which my interest in paraphilias has nearly crowded out interests in "vanilla" sexuality entirely. I find myself uninterested in relations with my wife and only novelty inspires an interest in nonparaphilic sexuality. I don't know where I'll go with all this; I'm in a politically sensitive field, public speaking is a large part of my job, and I'm not a great candidate for passing as female. Since about half of my paraphilias are sadomasochism-related and still spark interest, I'm considering moving back into that community, in the hope that satisfying the nonautogynephilic paraphilias will render the autogynephilic urges less urgent. (NTS 35)

This narrative once again describes the phenomenon of paraphilic substitution, here in the form of a deliberate strategy. After concluding that acting out his autogynephilic desires might lead to the loss of his job, and realizing that he would not make a very passable woman, this informant was considering putting greater emphasis on expressing his sadomasochistic paraphilic interests, in the belief that the pressure to express his autogynephilic fantasies might diminish accordingly.

Concluding Thoughts about Narratives by Nontranssexual Autogynephiles

Not surprisingly, the narratives submitted by the nontranssexual (or not demonstrably transsexual) informants were similar in content to those submitted by their transsexual counterparts. This is consistent with the idea that autogynephilic transsexualism and less severe manifestations of autogynephilia are part of a spectrum or continuum of symptomatology. Nevertheless, there were a few intriguing differences between the two sets of narratives.

The most interesting difference, in my opinion, was that the nontranssexual informants made no discernable effort to conceptualize autogynephilia as anything other than a paraphilic erotic phenomenon. They did not theorize that it was an effect rather than a cause of their fantasies of being female or suggest that it was originally a nonsexual phenomenon that had somehow accidentally become eroticized. They did not characterize it as unimportant, as an epiphenomenon, or as a manifestation of normal female sexuality. One could argue, of course, that autogynephilia in transsexuals and in nontranssexuals are actually two qualitatively different phenomena that only superficially resemble each other and that this accounts for the differences in the ways the two sets of informants thought about their feelings and experiences. Alternatively, one could argue that autogynephilia is the same phenomenon in both groups but that the transsexual informants had simply been motivated to reflect more deeply on their feelings and had arrived at a level of understanding that had escaped their nontranssexual counterparts. I'm confident that the opponents of Blanchard's theory will propose one or both of these explanations after this book is published.

I believe that the more likely explanation, however, is that the nontranssexual informants simply felt less incentive to make excuses for their autogynephilic feelings. Unlike their transsexual counterparts, they were not in the position of trying to justify their desires to undergo sex reassignment (or their past decisions to do so) in the face of the still widely accepted message that anyone who has been erotically aroused by the idea of being a female cannot be a "real" MtF transsexual. This message was ubiquitous in the older psychiatric literature and is still touted on some Internet websites run by MtF transsexuals who deny that they are autogynephilic. More recently, this same message has been circulating in an updated, amended form: A person who has been erotically aroused by the idea of being a female can be a "real" MtF transsexual, as long as that erotic arousal *doesn't really mean anything*: if it is accidental or is an effect rather than a cause of one's gender dysphoria or is just something that normal women experience. Thus, it is easy to understand why some of the transsexual informants in the current study were eager to insist that their autogynephilic arousal did not really mean anything.

The nontranssexual informants seemingly could afford to be more clear-eyed and candid: They were able to recognize autogynephilic arousal for the paraphilic phenomenon it genuinely is and acknowledge this without equivocation. Could more transsexuals who experience autogynephilia eventually achieve this same level of clear-eyed self-recognition and candor? I will address this possibility in Chap. 12.

Chapter 12
Autogynephilic Transsexualism in Perspective

Making Sense of Autogynephilic Transsexualism

In this final chapter, I offer a broader perspective concerning the nature and implications of autogynephilic transsexualism. My analysis is based on the narratives submitted by the 249 autogynephilic transsexual informants and the 52 non-transsexual autogynephiles, the clinical and research literature, and my experience with transsexual clients. I summarize some of the most important observations and reflections contained in the narratives and suggest how this information might help clinicians in case conceptualization and treatment planning for autogynephilic clients. I address the shame that many of us autogynephilic transsexuals feel about our condition and consider whether anything can be done to reduce it. I examine some of the options available to severely gender dysphoric autogynephilic men and their potential benefits and drawbacks. I describe a possible future treatment for autogynephilic transsexualism and discuss whether and how this treatment might eventually become available. Finally, I propose that, notwithstanding its many limitations, sex reassignment as currently practiced can offer autogynephilic transsexuals a pathway to a life of greater satisfaction, passion, and spiritual fulfillment.

Autogynephilic Transsexualism: Maybe Not So Rare After All?

The critics of Blanchard's theory of autogynephilic transsexualism have long been forced to concede that some MtF transsexuals believed the theory was valid and accurately described them. But avowedly autogynephilic transsexuals have historically been few in number. This has allowed some critics to get away with suggesting that autogynephilic transsexualism is rare or even "exotic." I don't expect the critics to change their stance any time soon; but with the publication of this book, the number of admittedly autogynephilic transsexuals described in the academic literature has probably increased by two orders of magnitude. As one who values diversity, I consider this a positive sign.

A.A. Lawrence, *Men Trapped in Men's Bodies: Narratives of Autogynephilic Transsexualism*, Focus on Sexuality Research, DOI 10.1007/978-1-4614-5182-2_12,

I should quickly add that not all of the 249 MtF transsexual informants who admitted to experiencing autogynephilic arousal agreed with Blanchard's ideas or mine on every point. Roughly 30 of them—about 12%—believed that the autogynephilic arousal they experienced was unimportant, was a manifestation of normal female sexuality, or was an effect rather than a cause of their gender dysphoria. Overall, however, the informants' narratives were strongly supportive of Blanchard's ideas.

What Do Autogynephilic Transsexuals Say About Their Condition?

Many of the informants considered the concept of autogynephilia to be a revelation: They reported that it was the first theory they had encountered that actually seemed to describe them. Often they were grateful to have learned about the theory, and they stated that it had improved their understanding of themselves. Many were relieved to discover that other transsexuals shared similar feelings. A few, however, found that recognizing themselves in the theory was disconcerting, as though their comfortable illusions about themselves had been shattered. Several informants reported that their autogynephilic feelings had previously made them doubt that they were really transsexual. Many had been reluctant to admit their feelings to their therapists or had lied to or misled their therapists concerning their feelings—perhaps yet another reason for the widespread but mistaken belief that autogynephilic transsexualism is rare.

Several informants began cross-dressing or having cross-gender fantasies in early childhood, long before puberty. Sometimes these early childhood behaviors and fantasies were accompanied by penile erections, masturbation, or feelings of intense excitement that informants identified as erotic. The erotic feelings associated with cross-dressing or cross-gender fantasies sometimes receded for a few years but typically reappeared at puberty. Autogynephilic erotic feelings commonly, but not invariably, continued throughout the informants' lives, including after SRS. In spite of their desire to be female, most of the informants denied that they had been feminine boys: Except for their autogynephilic fantasies and behaviors, they usually described themselves as having been unremarkably masculine. Those who mentioned their adult occupations usually reported male-typical ones.

The informants were invariably sexually attracted to women, for whom they felt a confusing mixture of lust and envy. Although they found women's bodies sexually arousing, many were never able to reach orgasm during heterosexual intercourse without engaging in autogynephilic fantasy: They discovered that the fantasy of being female themselves was more exciting than an actual female partner. Many fantasized about or engaged in sex with men, but only when they imagined themselves to be women; at other times, they found the idea of sex with men unappealing or repugnant.

Some informants found autogynephilic arousal unpleasant. Others were confused or distressed by the rapid but temporary remission of their cross-gender wishes that often occurred immediately following orgasm. Many valued the ability of hormone therapy to reduce their gender dysphoria, but a few experienced an unexpected weakening or disappearance of their cross-gender wishes and desire to pursue sex reassignment after beginning hormone therapy. A significant number of informants reported other co-occurring paraphilic interests. Finally, as noted earlier, some informants offered explanations that attempted to reconcile their autogynephilic feelings and behaviors with traditional theories and beliefs about MtF transsexualism.

How Can Understanding Autogynephilic Transsexualism Inform Clinical Care?

Most clinicians will probably regard the narratives in the previous chapters as fascinating, revealing, and a source of greater knowledge and understanding. Some may wonder, however, how to use this knowledge in their clinical practices with gender dysphoric autogynephilic clients. I believe that a clear understanding of the concept of autogynephilic transsexualism and its clinical manifestations can help practitioners with case conceptualization, formulation of prognostic information for clients, and treatment planning. Clinicians who are interested in a more detailed examination of these issues may wish to consult one of my review articles (Lawrence, 2009b).

The concept of autogynephilic transsexualism provides a useful model for conceptualizing the etiology and development of the most common form of MtF transsexualism in Western countries. In particular, it convincingly explains why some men who are not naturally feminine and who are sexually attracted to women experience the overpowering desire to turn their bodies into facsimiles of women's bodies and live as women. Traditional explanations of this phenomenon—ones that do not include the concept of autogynephilia—are inevitably circular and self-referential, as I explained in Chap. 10. Autogynephilia is a sexual orientation, and men are willing to risk a great deal to express their sexual orientations and attempt to unite themselves with the persons or things they love, lust after, admire, and regard as beautiful.

The concept of autogynephilic transsexualism can also help clinicians account for the elevated prevalence of other paraphilias in nonhomosexual MtF transsexuals. If one theorizes that these transsexuals have something resembling women's brains in their male bodies, the prevalence of their coexisting paraphilias makes no sense: With the exception of sexual masochism, paraphilias are almost nonexistent in women. But if one theorizes that these transsexuals are, in fact, men with a paraphilic sexual orientation that makes them want to become women, the prevalence of their coexisting paraphilias makes perfect sense. As a few informants observed, co-occurring paraphilias may in some cases be even more powerful and consequential than autogynephilia itself; clinicians who work with autogynephilic transsexual clients should keep this possibility in mind.

Because men's sexual orientations are believed to be essentially unchangeable in adulthood, clinicians may be puzzled by the tendency of many formerly heterosexual MtF transsexuals to fantasize about engaging in sex with men or, more rarely, to actually do so. The explanation of this phenomenon becomes obvious if clinicians understand that autogynephilic transsexuals may be sexually aroused by the prospect of enacting the traditional female sexual role in relation to male partners, even though they are not sexually attracted to men's bodies. Autogynephilic transsexuals do not experience a genuine change in their sexual orientations: Their fantasies and behaviors involving male partners are simply manifestations of their autogynephilic sexual orientations.

Moreover, because sexual orientations appear to be immutable in adult men, the autogynephilic sexual orientations of these transsexuals almost certainly cannot be changed, any more than the sexual orientations of ordinary heterosexual or homosexual men can be changed. In my opinion, clinicians should clearly advise their gender dysphoric autogynephilic patients that their condition is not curable: They will be dealing with their autogynephilic feelings, in one form or another, as long as they live. Fortunately, the severe gender dysphoria associated with autogynephilic transsexualism is manageable—and sex reassignment is often a good way of managing it.

The concept of autogynephilic transsexualism can also help clinicians understand the value and potential limitations of feminizing hormone therapy. Cross-sex hormones can help autogynephilic transsexuals more closely approximate the female appearance they desire and can also help control ego-dystonic autogynephilic arousal, which many autogynephilic transsexuals experience. For this reason, most severely gender dysphoric autogynephilic patients are very satisfied with feminizing hormone therapy. However, hormone therapy reduces testosterone levels and thereby reduces the intensity of autogynephilic erotic feelings; this can cause some gender dysphoric autogynephilic men to lose their motivation to continue using hormones. The deciding factors in an individual patient may be intensity of gender dysphoria and strength of cross-gender identity; both of these are outgrowths of autogynephilia, but cross-gender identity usually takes time and experience to consolidate. Patients with more intense gender dysphoria and stronger, better established cross-gender identities usually welcome both the feminization and libido reduction associated with hormone therapy. Patients with less intense gender dysphoria or less well established cross-gender identities often seem to do better on lower doses of hormones, which produce some feminization but are less likely to completely eliminate the autogynephilic erotic feelings that drive the patients' desire for feminization.

Can Autogynephilic Transsexualism Ever Feel Less Shameful?

Even though I have been one of the most outspoken advocates for Blanchard's theory of autogynephilic transsexualism, I have never been able to get over my shame about being an autogynephilic transsexual. I regard Blanchard's theory as brilliant and revelatory. As a clinician and researcher, I appreciate its descriptive, predictive, and heuristic value. I could never have completed sex reassignment without the insight it provided me, and for that I'm very grateful. But I'm not delighted by what the theory tells me about myself, and I doubt that I ever will be. I still feel deeply ashamed: not just about being a transsexual, which feels shameful enough, but about being an autogynephilic transsexual, which feels more shameful still. Sometimes I can put aside my shame for days or weeks, but it always returns, and it always feels agonizing when it does.

Why does the realization that one is a paraphilic man with an erotic motivation for wanting to become a woman feel so shameful? This is the rhetorical question that Meana (2008) so innocently but subversively posed:

> Why is being a "woman trapped inside a man's body" any more respectable than being a man who loves womanhood so much he yearns to become the object of his own desire? Why is an erotic motivation any less worthy than an identity performative one? (p. 470)

I think the answer is obvious: The theory of autogynephilic transsexualism forces us to confront the fact that both our essential natures and our motives seem to directly contradict our desired ends. We autogynephilic transsexuals want to be women; but the theory tells us that we are not women and that we don't even resemble women—not in the least. We would like to believe that our desire to be women springs from our need to express some internal feminine essence; but the theory tells us that we have no internal feminine essence and that our desire to be women actually springs from our paraphilic male sexuality. Many of us—I'm a rare exception—want to be recognizably "normal" women with respect to our sexual orientations, which implies sexual attraction to men; but the theory tells us that we are not really sexually attracted to men and never can be—that any attraction to men we seem to feel is illusory and merely another paraphilic fantasy. All of this is in addition to the shame we would inevitably feel even if we accepted some *other* theory of MtF transsexualism (such as the feminine essence theory; see Blanchard, 2008)—shame about our masculinized bodies, our life histories as men, and our inability to experience so many aspects of normal womanhood.

When we autogynephilic transsexuals become aware of the theory of autogynephilic transsexualism and recognize that it describes us, we have several options for attempting to manage our inevitable shame. We can try to face our shame directly, by acknowledging our sadness and our constant vulnerability to humiliation and despair and by pushing our feelings out of consciousness when they threaten to become overwhelming; this is the strategy I've tried to adopt. Or we can embrace one or more explanatory beliefs that acknowledge the fact of our autogynephilic arousal but deny its meaning and significance: for example, that autogynephilic arousal is an effect rather than a cause of our cross-gender wishes, is an epiphenomenon, or is a manifestation of normal female sexuality. Or we can simply engage in denial—the most primitive and most effective defense mechanism of all—by convincing ourselves that the theory *must* be invalid because it is so offensive to our sensibilities: Following the example of Winters (2008), we can reject the theory because it promotes "stigmatizing and dehumanizing false stereotypes" (para. 7) and is "an affront to human legitimacy and dignity" (para. 10). We can even go farther still and set about the emotionally satisfying business of trying to destroy anyone who dares to speak or write in favor of the theory, which manifests as narcissistic rage (Lawrence, 2008; see also Dreger, 2008). None of these strategies works terribly well, and some of them cause great harm to other people, but all of them are perfectly understandable responses to our overwhelming shame.

Would there be any way to make autogynephilic transsexualism feel less shameful, or at least make the shame of it easier to bear? I have a few suggestions: First, it might be beneficial if more personal narratives by self-described autogynephilic transsexuals were to become available. Knowing that one is not alone can potentially reduce shame, or at least make it easier to deal with. This book is a modest step in that direction. Second, it might be helpful if a few charismatic, appealing, or eminent MtF transsexuals were to come out as unapologetically autogynephilic and act as role models for the rest of us. Someone of the stature of Kate Bornstein would be perfect in such a capacity, although I have no idea whether Bornstein identifies as autogynephilic. I will say more about unapologetic autogynephilic transsexualism later in this chapter. Third, it might be useful if autogynephilic transsexuals were to create peer support groups—ideally in the real world, but perhaps first in the virtual world—in which autogynephilic persons could share their experiences. Fourth, publication of educational and self-help resources for autogynephilic children and adolescents and their parents would probably be extremely valuable; I will say more about this later in the chapter. Finally, I believe it would be beneficial if those of us who accept the theory of autogynephilic transsexualism were to more consistently describe autogynephilia as a sexual orientation. This would make it easier to talk about autogynephilic transsexualism in a way that might feel less shameful and that others might find more acceptable or recognizable.

Presenting Autogynephilia as a Sexual Orientation

Explaining autogynephilic transsexualism as a paraphilic phenomenon is factually correct, but this approach is not likely to be easily understandable or especially palatable to most audiences. The concept of *paraphilia* will be unfamiliar to many people and will sound vaguely psychopathological to many others; once it has been explained, associations with illegal paraphilias will probably be unavoidable. Attempting to explain autogynephilic transsexualism using the trope of "women trapped in men's bodies" is an even worse approach: Not only is the explanation inaccurate—autogynephilic transsexuals do not closely resemble women—but the trope is probably not genuinely comprehensible to most people, even though it enjoys some cultural currency. People may recognize the words "woman trapped in a man's body," but they arguably can't really grasp the concept; I know I can't really grasp it.

Almost all adults in Western countries, however, recognize the concept of *sexual orientation*, and many know some basic facts: Sexual orientations exist in more than one variety. Sexual orientations are not chosen and are not modifiable—at least not in men. Sexual orientations determine who (or what) we lust after, but also who (or what) we love and want to unite with in long-term relationships (hence the concept of gay marriage, which is generally comprehensible, if not yet generally accepted). Moreover, it is widely understood that people naturally feel strong desires to express their sexual orientations—to act on them.

Autogynephilia has long been conceptualized as a sexual orientation (e.g., Blanchard, 1989a, 1993a), but its advocates, myself among them, have not sufficiently emphasized this point. We should arguably use every opportunity to do so. Autogynephilia, we should explain, is another variety of sexual orientation: It is an unusual variant form of heterosexuality. Like other sexual orientations, it is something we autogynephilic transsexuals did not choose and something we cannot change. It certainly determines what we lust after, but it also determines what we love and want to unite with. And we autogynephilic transsexuals understandably feel strong pressure to express and act on our autogynephilic sexual orientations. Could an explanatory model emphasizing sexual orientation really lead to better understanding and greater acceptance of autogynephilic transsexualism? I believe we should attempt to find out.

Am I Really a Transsexual? Or Just a Transvestite?

The question autogynephilic clients in my practice most often want to have answered, whether they express it directly or indirectly, is: "Am I really a transsexual? Or am I just a transvestite?" Usually they hope that receiving a diagnosis could help them decide how to manage their gender dysphoria. In most cases, they have been thinking for some time about undergoing sex reassignment and living as women, but the prospect is daunting, and they remain hesitant. Often they believe that an authoritative diagnosis might decide the issue for them—not an unreasonable idea, given the established principle of Western medicine that diagnosis informs and sometimes dictates treatment. Usually their reasoning goes something like this: "If I'm really a transsexual, then I could—or should, or must—undergo sex reassignment. But if I'm really just a transvestite, then I shouldn't—it wouldn't be appropriate. If I'm just a transvestite, I should try to suppress or otherwise manage my desire to live as a woman." These clients hope that by receiving a diagnosis, they can avoid having to make this difficult decision themselves: The clinician will, in effect, make the decision for them.

I usually try to convey two messages to such clients, neither of which they are typically pleased to receive. First, it is often very difficult, if not impossible, to draw a clear dividing line between transsexualism and less severe forms of gender dysphoria. Usually it is more useful to try to characterize the nature and severity of the gender problem than to try to decide whether a client is transsexual or not transsexual, except in the most obvious cases. Second, even if one were to make a diagnosis of transsexualism, this would not necessarily dictate a particular treatment plan. Some clearly transsexual, severely gender dysphoric autogynephilic men decide not to undergo sex reassignment and are confident that their decisions are correct, given their particular circumstances. Some less clearly transsexual, less severely gender dysphoric autogynephilic men decide to undergo sex reassignment and are very satisfied with their decisions. Autogynephilic gender dysphoric men must confront and answer the existential question: How do I want to live, given that I have an unchangeable paraphilic sexual orientation? Experienced clinicians can help clients reach their decisions, but ultimately the clients themselves must decide. Often the decision is a very difficult one, in part because none of the available options are genuinely satisfactory.

The Existential Dilemma of the Gender Dysphoric Autogynephile

Consider the plight of the man who experiences anatomic autogynephilia and severe gender dysphoria. Since early childhood, he has secretly wished to be a female. He is erotically aroused by women and is also erotically aroused by the idea of being a woman himself. In both cases, however, his feelings go far beyond simple erotic arousal: He admires women, finds them beautiful, adores their bodies, and habitually falls in love with them. He also envies them and wants to have—wants to *embody*—all the admirable, beautiful features he loves in them. He wants to live in a body like theirs and lead a life like theirs.

At the same time, he knows that he is not naturally feminine. When he considers the adjectives that describe the women he habitually falls in love with—agreeable, affiliative, cooperative, empathetic, gentle, graceful, nurturant, pliant, tactful, tender—he realizes that most of these adjectives do not describe him. He tends to be competitive, dominant, independent, linear, logical, and tough-minded. He might wish he were more feminine, but his personality is not naturally feminine. When he is honest with himself, he also realizes that he never falls in love with men and only feels attracted to men when he is in the midst of an autogynephilic reverie. He has cross-dressed for years and still does at times, but he finds that it offers him limited satisfaction: Even wearing sexy women's attire, he still inhabits his unwanted male body and still has his ugly, embarrassing male genitalia. Falling in love with a woman or having sex with a woman sometimes makes his autogynephilic desires go into remission for a time, but these remissions are always temporary: His autogynephilic feelings always return. And every time he has an orgasm, he is reminded of two facts: Having a woman's body is the most erotic thing he can imagine—and he doesn't have one.

His circumstances force him to consider the existential question: Could he live a happier, more meaningful, more rewarding life as a woman—as a transsexual woman? Or would he be better off continuing to live as a man? This is a genuine dilemma, because neither option is really satisfactory. Continuing to live as a man would be the easier, less expensive, and safer option: That way he could keep his job, his reputation, his friends, and perhaps his marriage, if he has one.

Continuing to live as a man wouldn't kill him; he has, after all, done it for years. He could continue to live a life of quiet desperation. But he would still experience significant and often severe gender dysphoria, perhaps every day of his life. Eventually he would become an old man who had never tried to live his dream. He knows that what older adults invariably regret is not what they have done but what they failed to do when they had the opportunity. The thought of wasting the only life he will ever have is sad and frightening.

Alternatively, he could pursue sex reassignment. That way, he could at least tell himself that he had tried to live his dream. And, if he were to succeed in some measure, how great would that be? How many people can say that they achieved, in some measure, what they wanted most? If he successfully transitioned, he would finally be playing on the right team, the women's team; and those awful male genitalia would be gone forever. But he also knows that he would never have a normal life as a woman: He would always be an oddity, albeit perhaps a fascinating or even admirable oddity. And he could easily lose any of the things that currently make his life comfortable and safe: his job, his reputation, his friends, his family. Moreover, the kind of womanhood he could achieve would inevitably be shoddy and inadequate: He would never be able to completely erase the masculinizing effects of testosterone on his body and brain, nor the masculinizing effects of decades of living in society as a man. For an autogynephilic gender dysphoric man to be willing to try to rebuild his life around his paraphilia by pursuing sex reassignment, despite the genuine risks and inevitable limitations involved, he usually needs to be both very brave and very desperate.

The Value of Devaluing Autogynephilia

Probably it is also easier for an autogynephilic gender dysphoric man to pursue sex reassignment if he doesn't believe in the concept of autogynephilia—or, more accurately, if he holds one or more explanatory beliefs that make his autogynephilic arousal or the autogynephilic underpinnings of his wish for sex reassignment seem more conventional or acceptable. These beliefs function to reassure him and others that his autogynephilic erotic desire to have a woman's body isn't the whole story—and isn't even an important part of the story. What kinds of explanatory beliefs might be reassuring in this way?

One such belief would be that he really has a "woman's brain" in his male body. Another would be that autogynephilia is not a paraphilia at all but merely a normal element of female sexuality. Yet another would be that he really had been destined to be attracted to men all along, but that his natural inclinations were suppressed by social conditioning and homophobia. Still another would be that the cross-gender fantasies that he found so exciting earlier in life no longer hold any erotic interest for him, but were merely a temporary mechanism for coping with his gender dysphoria. A final such belief would be that autogynephilia is merely an effect of his cross-gender identification, not the cause of that identification.

Personally, I consider such explanatory beliefs to be implausible at best, but I understand their appeal. I remember looking carefully at an MRI scan of my own brain in 1995, hoping to find a feature I could declare to be female-typical—at that time, the splenium of the corpus callosum was still a focus of interest (see Emory, Williams, Cole, Amparo, & Meyer, 1991)—and therefore use to justify my desire for sex reassignment. I also remember with chagrin a few weeks during which I tried to convince my therapist and myself that I was actually sexually attracted to men. Explanatory beliefs of this kind function to justify or excuse the autogynephilic erotic desire that both animates and seems to discredit our wish to be women. These explanations make us seem to more closely resemble the "classic" MtF transsexual stereotype: feminine from earliest childhood, never sexually aroused by women's apparel, and romantically inclined toward men. If we embrace these explanatory beliefs, we can say to ourselves and others, "It may be true that I have experienced autogynephilic erotic arousal, but I have other characteristics that make me a recognizable and somewhat more acceptable kind of MtF transsexual: I have a woman's brain/only get aroused the same way natal women do/was meant to be attracted to men/no longer experience (much) autogynephilic arousal/had a cross-gender identity that preceded my autogynephilic arousal." In my clinical practice, I rarely see an autogynephilic gender dysphoric man—whether he identifies as autogynephilic or not—who has decided to pursue SRS and doesn't hold one or more explanatory beliefs of this kind. As the narratives in Chap. 10 demonstrate, even MtF transsexuals who clearly recognize themselves to be autogynephilic often hold these beliefs.

I'm not ordinarily an advocate for self-deception, but if explanatory beliefs like these make it easier for autogynephilic men who are good candidates for sex reassignment to move forward, I'm willing to condone them. Sex reassignment is often a very effective treatment for severe, persistent gender dysphoria in autogynephilic men. Hormone therapy and SRS usually significantly reduce gender dysphoria; satisfaction following MtF sex reassignment is high and regrets are rare (Gijs & Brewaeys, 2007; Lawrence, 2003; Muirhead-Allwood et al., 1999). But many autogynephilic gender dysphoric men who would probably benefit from sex reassignment decide not to pursue it because they fear that their autogynephilic feelings disqualify them. If implausible explanatory beliefs make it easier for these transsexuals to justify sex reassignment to themselves or others, I'm not inclined to argue too strenuously.

Unapologetic Autogynephilic Transsexualism?

But what about autogynephilic gender dysphoric men who see themselves more clearly and can't deceive themselves so easily—who know that they are men with a powerful paraphilic wish to become women and cannot pretend otherwise? They are in a more difficult position: They not only have to grapple with their own shame and sadness about being paraphilic men, but they also have to face the potential disapproval of others without being able to pretend to be different than they truly are. It is still not entirely respectable, even in "transgender friendly" settings, to appear to deviate too far from being a classic MtF transsexual. Although I'm not aware of any formal surveys, I suspect that neither the transgender community nor its professional caregivers, much less the general public, would be completely comfortable with the idea of avowedly, unapologetically paraphilic men undergoing sex reassignment and living as women. Thirty or 40 years ago, mental health professionals who specialized in treating gender identity problems used to argue that paraphilic men—autogynephiles—who sought sex reassignment were not acceptable candidates because they were not genuinely transsexual. Nowadays, their successors seemingly want to argue that paraphilic men—autogynephiles—who seek sex reassignment have become acceptable candidates because they are not genuinely paraphilic! Perhaps this is a measure of progress, but the message remains the same: We do not willingly offer sex reassignment to mere paraphilic men.

Some autogynephilic gender dysphoric men, however, cannot deny the uncomfortable truth that our very best gender specialists seem to insist on denying—that they are, without a doubt, paraphilic men. But autogynephilic gender dysphoric men would have to be very brave to pursue sex reassignment while saying openly, without apology: "We are not women trapped in men's bodies, nor do we bear any close resemblance to women. We are nothing more or less than men who experience a paraphilic desire to become women. Nevertheless, we are committed to becoming the best possible facsimiles of the women we love and admire, despite the fact that we have the minds and bodies of men. We believe that this path offers us our best hope of overcoming our gender dysphoria and achieving the bodies and social roles in which we can live satisfying, fulfilling lives."

Call me a romantic, but I think this kind of unapologetic autogynephilic transsexualism sounds both courageous and admirable; I hope that it eventually becomes more prevalent. It seems to me entirely consistent with what Person (1999) identified as one of the important trends in contemporary Western societies that serve to legitimize what she called "the shared cultural fantasy of transsexualism" (p. 363). Person called this phenomenon:

> Self-Realization as a Cultural Ideal. Once upon a time, an individual accepted certain external realities as unalterable. These realities determined his place in society. As historical changes, both technological and social, accelerated, the individual began to believe more in the alterability of his circumstances and ultimately of his person. The question was not whether to adjust to or rebel against reality but how to discriminate between those realities that needed to be recognized as unalterable and those one might change. We now assume that little of external reality is unalterable, an assumption derived in part from our increasingly astonishing scientific advances. (p. 364)

If the existence and meaning of autogynephilic transsexualism were to become more widely recognized and better understood, then this kind of unapologetic autogynephilic transsexualism might eventually become commonplace. I believe that this would be a very good thing.

Solutions Short of Complete Sex Reassignment

There are several different types of autogynephilia, as described in Chap. 6, but these types usually tend to co-occur: For example, most men who experience anatomic autogynephilia also experience transvestic and behavioral autogynephilia. Moreover, individuals who experience the anatomic form of autogynephilia usually desire to possess all the elements of female anatomy, not just one or two of them. In some cases, however, individuals with anatomic autogynephilia experience little transvestic or behavioral autogynephilia: They are aroused by the idea of having a female body but not by the idea of dressing or behaving like women. And some are aroused by the idea of having women's breasts or a vulva but are indifferent to having other female anatomic features. Blanchard (1993b) called this latter phenomenon partial autogynephilia; narratives by informants who experienced it were included in Chap. 11.

Moreover, even men who experience anatomic autogynephilia accompanied by behavioral and transvestic autogynephilia sometimes conclude that undertaking complete sex reassignment and living as women would be impossible or impractical. Some of these men have physical characteristics, such as extreme height, that would not only make it impossible for them to move easily through the world as women—even openly transsexual women—but would not allow them to meet their own minimal standards for an acceptable female appearance. Others have familial or social responsibilities that they would be unable to satisfy if they underwent complete sex reassignment and lived as women. Some of these men nevertheless suffer from severe gender dysphoria and believe that making their bodies more closely resemble women's bodies would ameliorate it.

Autogynephilic men who want to have women's breasts but do not want to live in a female-typical gender role usually have no difficulty obtaining what they desire. The current Standards of Care (WPATH, 2011) make it easy for individuals to qualify for and receive feminizing hormone therapy and surgical breast augmentation, even if they continue to live as men. But autogynephilic gender dysphoric men who want to undergo SRS but do not want to live in a female-typical gender role usually have a harder time qualifying for what they desire under the Standards of Care, which specify that having "lived continuously for at least 12 months in the gender role that is congruent with [one's] gender identity" (WPATH, 2011, p. 21) is an eligibility requirement for SRS. The vagueness of the language—what does it mean to live in a gender role that is congruent with one's gender identity if one identifies as a man but desires to have a woman's genitals?—potentially allows for some flexibility, of course. But, in the absence of a more explicit imprimatur, I doubt that most clinicians would be comfortable recommending SRS for autogynephilic men who want to live as men or feel that they have no choice but to do so. Some narratives in Chap. 6 demonstrate that it is possible to obtain SRS even if one has spent little or no time living in something resembling a female-typical gender role. Nevertheless, there is no unambiguous language in the Standards of Care that explicitly uncouples eligibility for SRS from the obligation to enact any particular gender role.

For most autogynephilic men, living in a female-typical gender role is the most difficult and daunting aspect of the sex reassignment process and is, in my clinical experience, the one most likely to be associated with severe social or economic losses. If some autogynephilic gender dysphoric men would be content to undergo SRS without living in a female-typical gender role—or were to conclude that this would offer the best compromise between managing their gender dysphoria on the one hand and dealing with the external reality demands imposed by their unsuitable male bodies, their obligations to their families, or their need to earn a living on the other—then I believe they should be allowed and even encouraged to do so, assuming they had been carefully evaluated and were able to give informed consent.

Needless to say, this solution is not what most autogynephilic gender dysphoric men really want; it would appeal to only a minority of individuals. But it would arguably do much to help relieve the gender dysphoria of men who experience severe anatomic autogynephilia but are unwilling or unable to live as women. I hope that the Standards of Care will eventually be modified to state explicitly that individuals can qualify for SRS without changing their gender role or gender presentation. If the autogynephilic motivation behind many requests for SRS were more widely recognized, such an outcome might occur more quickly.

Better Treatment for Severely Gender Dysphoric Autogynephiles?

We autogynephilic transsexuals would probably undertake sex reassignment more readily, and surely with greater success, if treatments to help us achieve facsimiles of female bodies were not so mediocre. The inadequacies of existing treatments result from the fact that exposure of our bodies to high levels of testosterone during puberty produces irreversible physical masculinization, primarily involving the bony skeleton but also other anatomic features. Exposure to testosterone results in the development of male-typical facial and body hair, greater muscularity, increased height, increased size of the shoulders, hands, feet, jaw, and parts of the skull (especially the supraorbital ridge), male-pattern scalp hair loss, deepening of the voice and enlargement of the laryngeal cartilage (Adam's apple), failure to develop a female-typical pelvic shape, and a variety of more subtle changes affecting body habitus. All of these effects of testosterone combine to create an impression of physical maleness.

It is a little-recognized fact that gender attribution is based primarily on the presence or absence of male-typical anatomic characteristics. To decide whether a person is male or female, we look for signs of masculinization, which are almost always signs of exposure to testosterone. If we observe several signs of masculinization—occasionally one sign is enough—we make a male gender attribution. If we observe few or no signs of masculinization, we make a female gender attribution. Signs of femaleness don't matter much; signs of maleness are what matter. Kessler and McKenna (1978) explained:

> In order for a female gender attribution to be made, there must be an absence of anything which can be construed as a "male only" characteristic. In order for a male gender attribution to be made, the presence of at least one "male" sign must be noticed, and one sign may be enough, especially if it is a penis. It is rare to see a person that one thinks is a man

> and then wonder if one has made a "mistake." However, it is not uncommon to wonder if someone is "really" a woman. The relative ease with which female-to-male transsexuals "pass" as compared to male-to-female transsexuals underscores this point. It is symbolized by the male-to-female transsexual needing to cover or remove her facial hair in order to be seen as a woman and the female-to-male transsexual having the option of growing a beard or being clean shaven. The female may not have any "male" signs. (pp. 158–159).

Consequently, if we MtF transsexuals want to make our bodies appear more like women's bodies, most of our efforts must be directed toward erasing the signs of masculinization caused by testosterone exposure during puberty.

Unfortunately, it is impossible to completely erase the masculinizing effects of testosterone, and achieving even partial erasure is very expensive and time-consuming. We MtF transsexuals often spend tens of thousands—occasionally hundreds of thousands—of dollars for facial and body hair removal and for reshaping of our hairlines, foreheads, noses, jaws, laryngeal cartilages, and even our vocal cords. All of this is in addition to the expense of SRS. But there is little we can do about our height, our broad shoulders, our narrow pelvises, and our outsized hands and feet. Even our best attempts at reversing pubertal masculinization are inadequate.

In the past two decades, treatment to prevent irreversible masculinization by testosterone has been offered to a few gender dysphoric adolescent boys, mostly those whose gender dysphoria was initially diagnosed in childhood and had persisted into adolescence. This treatment involves the administration of injectable hormones called *gonadotropin-releasing hormone agonists* (GnRH agonists), which prevent the pituitary gland from releasing the hormones (gonadotropins) that stimulate the testes to produce testosterone. GnRH agonists have also been offered to gender dysphoric adolescent girls with similar histories, but this discussion will emphasize the treatment of gender dysphoric boys. Treatment of selected gender dysphoric adolescents with GnRH agonists was pioneered in the Netherlands in the mid-1990s, largely due to the efforts of Dr. Peggy Cohen-Kettenis. Eligibility criteria, treatment protocols, and outcomes of treatment have been described in several recent publications (e.g., de Vries et al., 2011; Hembree et al., 2009; Kreukels & Cohen-Kettenis, 2011; Zucker et al., 2011).

Treatment with GnRH agonists blocks or delays the physical changes of puberty. The goal of treatment is to buy time for consideration of further treatment options. If the patient's gender dysphoria continues and the patient wants to undergo MtF sex reassignment in young adulthood, feminizing hormones can be administered and female-typical pubertal development will occur. This results in a young MtF transsexual whose appearance is female-typical, with minimal or no male secondary sex characteristics. If the patient's gender dysphoria desists and the patient wants to live as a member of his birth sex, GnRH agonists can be withdrawn and a male-typical puberty will result; but no patients treated in the Netherlands have ever chosen this option (de Vries et al., 2011).

In the Netherlands, where clinical experience with puberty-blocking hormones is greatest, treatment is currently offered only to children in whom there has been "presence of gender dysphoria from early childhood on" (Cohen-Kettenis, Delemarre-van de Waal, & Gooren, 2008, p. 1894) or "persistent gender dysphoria since childhood" (de Vries et al., 2011, p. 2277). A few years earlier, Cohen-Kettenis and Pfäfflin (2003) had further advocated that puberty suppressing treatment be limited to adolescents who "throughout childhood ... had demonstrated an intense pattern of cross-gender behavior and identity" (p. 145). These requirements—particularly the requirement of intense cross-gender behavior throughout childhood—imply that few, if any, autogynephilic gender dysphoric adolescents would be eligible for puberty-blocking hormones, based on the Dutch criteria. In fact, almost all of the adolescent boys who have recently received puberty-blocking hormones in the Netherlands have been homosexual (de Vries et al., 2011) and thus presumably not autogynephilic.

Recently, Zucker et al. (2011) reported the Toronto experience in evaluating adolescents with GID for a recommendation for puberty-blocking hormones. Zucker et al. observed that

> one criterion used by the Dutch group is a history of gender dysphoria from early childhood on. Yet in clinics such as ours, we see some adolescents with GID who show little or absolutely no evidence of GID in early childhood. ... The gender dysphoria appears to emerge, at least in the eyes of significant others (e.g., parents, therapists who have known the patient since childhood) only after the onset of puberty. It is not clear if this late-onset group should be deemed ineligible for early [puberty-blocking] hormonal therapy. (p. 63)

The Toronto group was, in fact, willing to recommend puberty-blocking hormones for some adolescent boys with adolescent-onset GID and a nonhomosexual orientation (K. J. Zucker, personal communication, May 23, 2012). It appears, then, that autogynephilic gender dysphoric adolescents might in some cases be eligible for treatment under the Toronto criteria (which unfortunately were never explicitly set forth), although Zucker et al. noted that a favorable recommendation was more likely "when parent-report indicated more concurrent cross-gender behavior, [and] when patients ... recalled more cross-gender behavior in childhood" (p. 71). It is notable, however, that the Toronto patients were evaluated at a mean age of about 17, which is quite late. The adolescent boys in the Netherlands, in contrast, were evaluated at a mean age of about 13 and began treatment at a mean age of about 14. It is possible that autogynephilic gender dysphoric adolescents experience a significant intensification of gender dysphoria and a consolidation of cross-gender identification between the ages of 13 and 17, which would make them appear to be more suitable candidates for treatment at age 17 than they would have appeared at age 13.

Puberty-Blocking Hormones for Autogynephilic Gender Dysphoric Adolescents?

Could autogynephilic adolescents ever obtain approval for and receive the puberty-blocking hormones that would make their lives so much easier if they eventually decided to transition and live as women? Could they obtain approval early enough to make a real difference—at age 13, rather than at age 17? I would like to hope that the answers would be yes, but I'm far from certain.

What would be necessary for an autogynephilic gender dysphoric adolescent to be approved for and receive puberty-blocking hormones? I can think of three obvious preconditions. First, the adolescent would have to come to clinical attention in early puberty. Ideally this would be facilitated by perceptive, well informed parents who would notice and understand the meaning of their son's cross-dressing—including the absence of any other signs of overt femininity—and arrange for a clinical evaluation in a non-shaming, non-stigmatizing way. Realistically, however, the adolescent himself would probably need to develop some understanding of his problem and overcome his shame and confusion sufficiently to seek clinical attention on his own. At present, neither of these possibilities could be expected to happen very often, given the complete absence of educational and self-help materials for autogynephilic children and adolescents and their parents. On a more positive note, finding a knowledgeable professional to conduct such an evaluation would be much easier than it used to be, at least in major urban areas.

Second, the adolescent would need to display sufficiently intense gender dysphoria. He might also need to report a credible history of significant gender dysphoria or overt cross-gender behavior in early childhood, depending on the criteria used in the evaluation. Intense *current* gender dysphoria presumably would not usually be an issue; the fact of the referral would imply this. Documentation of significant gender dysphoria or overt cross-gender behavior in early childhood might be more problematic; often these will not have been present. Consequently, a typical autogynephilic gender dysphoric adolescent probably would have a better chance of being approved under the Toronto criteria (whatever they turn out to be) than under the Dutch criteria.

Finally, the adolescent would have to agree to undergo—and continue to undergo— treatment with puberty-blocking hormones. In some ways, this might be the biggest obstacle of all. Even intensely gender dysphoric autogynephilic adolescents would probably feel some ambivalence about the prospect of future gender transition, which might preclude or at least render more problematic many of the male-typical behaviors and activities they genuinely enjoy, including heterosexual contact. Some of these adolescents might even hold out hope that their autogynephilic orientation might be curable, which would allow them to live as normal men—a vain hope, I believe, but an understandable one.

Moreover, puberty-blocking hormones would inevitably decrease whatever level of testosterone was already present during early puberty, reducing gender dysphoria but perhaps also reducing much of the adolescent's desire to continue treatment. Recall that some informants in Chap. 9 reported that they lost the desire to continue feminizing hormone therapy after losing their sex drive as a result of testosterone reduction. Of course, many adult autogynephilic transsexuals who begin feminizing hormone therapy do continue treatment, even after complete loss of their sex drives; but these transsexuals have probably developed strong, persistent cross-gender identities that provide an ongoing impetus to gender transition. Docter's (1988) research suggests that such cross-gender identities take years if not decades to develop. Could autogynephilic adolescents develop strong and persistent cross-gender identities more quickly, given the right circumstances—if, for example, they were given the opportunity to cross-dress freely and openly in a supportive, protective home environment? At present, one can only speculate about this possibility.

I'll briefly share my own experience: I was intensely gender dysphoric at age 14 (this was in 1965), so much so that I overcame my shame and told my parents about my desire to be a girl. I underwent psychiatric evaluation but was offered no real help. At age 16, I began trying to obtain feminizing hormones on my own. I finally succeeded at age 18—too late to prevent male puberty. If I had been offered puberty-blocking hormones at age 14, I might well have started treatment; but would I have continued? Perhaps, if I had had the knowledge and experience I have now; but quite possibly not, given how little knowledge and experience I had then. In 1965, at age 14, I had too much ignorance, too much shame—and too little experience in cross-gender presentation to have developed a strong, persistent cross-gender identity. I imagine that many intensely gender dysphoric autogynephilic 14-year-olds are in much the same position today, despite the passage of nearly 50 years.

Investigating the Developmental History of Autogynephilic Gender Dysphoria

Although sex reassignment is no panacea, it is arguably the treatment of choice for some intensely gender dysphoric autogynephilic adults. If these individuals could be identified before puberty, helped to understand their autogynephilic feelings, and encouraged to take the steps that might make them eligible for puberty-blocking hormones, their adult outcomes might be significantly improved. Whether such improved outcomes would occur is, of course, unknown. Conducting investigations that could help decide the issue would not be easy; investigators would need to address many challenging practical and ethical issues. Before such investigations could even be considered, however, it would be important to know much more than is currently known about the natural developmental history of autogynephilic gender dysphoria in childhood and adolescence.

According to retrospective self-reports, some boys who later become gender dysphoric autogynephilic men remember wanting to be girls or cross-dressing during early childhood; this was described by several informants in Chap. 5. Sometimes these cross-gender wishes and behaviors were recalled as having been explicitly erotic, sometimes not. Often these feelings and behaviors were never revealed to parents or caregivers, however. If there existed contemporaneous parental reports of the cross-gender feelings and behaviors of autogynephilic boys in early childhood or adolescence—and if there existed self-reports written by autogynephilic boys during middle childhood or adolescence—then researchers would be in a much better position to understand the developmental history of autogynephilic gender dysphoria and to design possible investigational treatment protocols involving puberty-blocking hormones. If such parental reports and self-reports were supplemented by observations by mental health professionals who had evaluated these autogynephilic boys, our understanding would be even greater.

I believe that the key to accumulating such parental reports, self-reports, and clinical case reports would be the availability of educational and self-help resources for autogynephilic children and adolescents and their parents. These resources could play a crucial role in stimulating and informing the process of data collection. Parents of autogynephilic boys need to know what to look for and how to interpret what they see; they also need to know when to seek professional evaluations for their children. Bright, self-aware autogynephilic boys in middle childhood and adolescence need resources to help them understand what they are feeling and what their feelings mean or might mean; they would also benefit from encouragement to write about their feelings and behaviors or document them in audio or video recordings.

Unfortunately, I have been unable to locate any useful educational or self-help resources designed for autogynephilic children or adolescents or their parents. I am forced to conclude that such resources probably don't yet exist. There are, of course, books written for the parents of overtly feminine gender-dysphoric male children and adolescents (e.g., Brill & Pepper, 2008; Krieger, 2011) and even books that contain advice for overtly feminine adolescent males themselves (e.g., Huegel, 2011). These books are sensitively written and probably helpful to many overtly feminine boys and male adolescents and their parents. These books do not, however, address the circumstances and needs of autogynephilic children or adolescents or their parents. These books never discuss the furtive cross-dressing in the absence of pervasive cross-gender behavior that most autogynephilic children and adolescents display, much less the erotic arousal that usually accompanies cross-dressing and cross-gender fantasies in these children and adolescents. Needless to say, the terms autogynephilia and transvestic fetishism appear nowhere in these books.

I believe there is a serious unmet need for educational resources that provide honest, forthright explanations of the cross-dressing and cross-gender fantasies that autogynephilic children and adolescents engage in and that explicitly discuss the erotic arousal that accompanies these behaviors and fantasies. I understand that it will not be easy to craft language that sensitively but accurately explains to parents what it might mean if their otherwise masculine 6-year-old son likes to put on his older sister's panties and gets an erection every time he does so, or that explains to 14-year-old boys what it might mean when they masturbate to fantasies of having bodies like those of the attractive girls in their school or wearing their clothes, rather than (or in addition to) fantasies of caressing those girls' bodies. But, if someone makes the effort and succeeds in creating such educational resources, autogynephilic children and adolescents and their parents will finally have access to information that can help them appreciate the nature and significance of autogynephilia and understand what can and cannot be done about it. Moreover, such resources could eventually result in the acquisition of a great deal of important data about the natural developmental history of autogynephilia in childhood and adolescence. These data could inform investigations that might eventually give selected autogynephilic adolescents access to treatment that could make their later lives as transsexual women much easier and much more satisfying.

Embracing Life as an Autogynephilic Transsexual Woman

Notwithstanding my earlier description of unapologetic autogynephilic transsexualism as a courageous and admirable stance, I've painted a rather grim picture of autogynephilic transsexualism overall. I don't want to minimize how difficult and painful our condition is. We autogynephilic transsexuals have a paraphilic sexual orientation that affects nearly everything about our lives—and usually not in a good way. Although sex reassignment is often the best solution to our problem and sometimes a life-saving one, it is a mediocre solution at best. Our efforts to create the kinds of bodies we want to live in are painful, expensive, and unsatisfactory. We often suffer terrible losses when we undergo sex reassignment and live as women. Once we have done so, we will never again live normal lives. I invariably tell my patients: Do not undergo sex reassignment if you can find happiness and peace in any other way.

If we do decide to undergo sex reassignment, at least we can console ourselves that our lives as transsexual women will probably be easier than those of our predecessors. Before the phenomenon of transsexualism became widely recognized, it used to be that autogynephilic gender dysphoric men who underwent sex reassignment either passed as natal women (if they were very somatically gifted) or were regarded as men pretending to be women. Nowadays, it is also possible to pass as a "good" or "sincere" transsexual woman: as someone who is known or suspected to have once lived as a man but who conducts herself as an appropriate and recognizable social woman. Few if any MtF transsexuals pass perfectly as natal women, but passing as a sincere transsexual woman is not a bad alternative and is an increasingly viable one in many urban areas of the USA and other Western countries.

When we autogynephilic transsexuals decide to undergo sex reassignment, we make the choice to rebuild our lives around our paraphilia—around the strongest feelings we know. Although this is not an easy path, it does offer some rewards. In one of my favorite "guilty pleasure" films from the 1980s, *Heartbreakers* (Roth & Weis, 1984), Peter Coyote portrays a photorealist artist who paints "pin-ups": depictions of women in fetish gear, with black leather, garter belts, whips and chains, etc. At first his paintings are not commercially successful, but eventually he finds his muse and his works begin to sell. In one scene, he talks about his interest in fetish depiction with a woman friend, explaining with relish, "Ever since I was a little kid I was into it. I found this magazine in my dad's closet. It was dirty. Forbidden." His friend scoffs: "That's not art. It's fetish." He replies, somewhat indignantly, "What's art? Those are the strongest feelings I know. Those are the most powerful images I know. That's my art."

In our postmodern world, with no God above and no hell below, many of us believe that the only meanings our lives can have are the meanings we create ourselves. Some of us might even start to think about our lives as extended works of performance art: unrehearsed, largely improvised, site-specific, one performance only. If we adopt this perspective, I think it makes sense to do what Peter Coyote's character did in the film I discussed: build our art—our lives—around the strongest feelings we know and the most powerful images we know. For most of us autogynephilic transsexuals, the strongest feelings we know and the most powerful images we know involve ourselves as women. We honor those feelings and images and give them a central place in our lives when we choose to undergo sex reassignment and live as women.

It is also possible to think about the transsexual journey as a kind of spiritual path. We autogynephilic transsexuals strive to become womanly in our bodies, but we can also strive to become womanly in our personalities. The feminine personas we create in the process of sex reassignment function as integral elements of the extended works of performance art that are our lives. We create our feminine personas by trying to express and embody the feminine virtues, whatever we think these are. For me, they include gentleness, nurturance, empathy, agreeableness, cooperation, friendliness, and grace. These qualities do not describe how I am naturally, but they describe the way I want to be and try to be; as such, they define a spiritual path that I attempt to follow. To try to express and embody these feminine virtues in our everyday lives makes us better people—especially if we have spent most of our lives expressing the kind of nerdy masculinity that values things over people, emphasizes competition over cooperation, and sometimes alienates us from our emotions and from other people. The transsexual journey is, in this case, less about finding our "true selves" than our best selves. Autogynephilia is a paraphilic sexual orientation, but it is possible to build a satisfying, passionate, spiritually fulfilling life around it—a life very much worth living.

Appendix
Transsexual Informants

This appendix lists the 249 transsexual (TS) informants by the three-digit numbers used to identify them in the text, along with the inclusion criterion that each satisfied in order to be classified as transsexual and the narrative information that indicated satisfaction of the criterion.

- Criterion a: identifies as TS, experiences gender dysphoria, or has a cross-gender identity.
- Criterion b: using hormones, living full time in female role, or approved for SRS.
- Criterion c: completed SRS.

No.	Criterion	Relevant narrative information
001	b	Has lived as a woman for 1 year; has used hormones for many years
002	a	Wants to be a woman and have a female body
003	a	Has gender dysphoria; has decided to transition
004	a	Wants to be female; experiences gender dysphoria
005	b	Experiences gender dysphoria; has used hormones, wants SRS
006	a	Envies women's bodies, wants to become female
007	a	Wants to be female
008	a	Want to become feminine and be a woman
009	b	Wants to become a woman; using hormone therapy
010	b	Experiences gender dysphoria; has been using hormones
011	a	Wants to undergo SRS
012	a	Identifies as TS
013	a	Identifies as TS
014	a	Wants to have a female body
015	a	Wants physical feminization
016	a	Has experienced life-long gender dysphoria
017	a	Identifies as TS
018	a	Identifies as a woman; wants to undergo SRS
019	a	Identifies as TS; feels the need to transition
020	b	Identifies as TS, wants a woman's body; has been using estradiol

(continued)

A.A. Lawrence, *Men Trapped in Men's Bodies: Narratives of Autogynephilic Transsexualism*, Focus on Sexuality Research, DOI 10.1007/978-1-4614-5182-2,

No.	Criterion	Relevant narrative information
021	b	Identifies as TS; has used hormones for about 2 years
022	b	Wants to be a woman; has been using hormones
023	a	Wants to have a female body
024	c	Completed SRS about 3 years earlier
025	b	Identifies as TS, has transitioned to live as a woman
026	a	Identifies as TS
027	a	Identifies as TS
028	b	Identifies as TS; has used hormones for about 2 years
029	a	Identifies as TS
030	b	Approved for SRS
031	a	Identifies as TS; wants to be female
032	a	Identifies as TS
033	a	Identifies as TS
034	a	Wants to be female; about to start hormone therapy
035	a	Identifies as TS
036	a	Experiences gender dysphoria
037	a	Identifies as TS
038	b	Identifies as TS; has been using estrogen
039	a	Wants to transition and live as a woman
040	a	Identifies as TS
041	a	Identifies as TS
042	b	Identifies as TS; using hormone therapy
043	a	Identifies as TS; approved for hormone therapy
044	a	Experiences gender dysphoria, wants to be a woman
045	a	Identifies as TS
046	a	Identifies as TS, determined to go through transition
047	b	Identifies as TS; using hormones for about 1 year
048	a	Identifies as TS
049	b	Approved and scheduled for SRS
050	c	Completed SRS about 3 years earlier
051	b	Identifies as TS; has used hormone therapy for years
052	a	Identifies as TS; wants to have SRS
053	b	Identifies as TS; has been using hormones for about 6 months
054	a	Identifies as TS
055	c	Completed SRS
056	a	Identifies as TS; wants to transition
057	a	Identifies as TS; about to begin hormone therapy
058	b	Living full time in female role for 3 years; approved for SRS
059	c	Completed SRS
060	a	Identifies as TS; wants to undergo SRS
061	c	Completed SRS
062	b	Identifies as TS; has used hormones
063	b	Has lived full time in female role for about 2 years
064	b	Lives full time in female role; approved for SRS
065	c	Completed SRS about 4 years earlier
066	b	Identifies as TS; has used hormone therapy for 18 months
067	a	Identifies as TS

(continued)

No.	Criterion	Relevant narrative information
068	b	Identifies as TS; has used hormones for about 2 months
069	c	Completed SRS about 2 years earlier
070	b	Approved for SRS; has lived full time in female role for 1 year
071	c	Completed SRS
072	c	Completed SRS
073	b	Identifies as TS; using hormone therapy, expects approval for SRS
074	a	Identifies as TS; wants to undergo SRS
075	a	Identifies as TS
076	a	Identifies as TS; wants to have a female body
077	b	Receiving hormone injections; living full time as a woman
078	a	Wants to be a woman
079	c	Completed SRS about 4 years earlier
080	a	Identifies as a woman at all times; expects to undergo SRS
081	a	Wants a female body; wants to undergo SRS
082	b	Wants to be a woman; has been using hormones
083	b	Has been using hormones for 2 years; wants to undergo SRS
084	b	Living full time as a woman for 4 years; scheduled for SRS
085	a	Wants to be a woman; has been approved for hormone therapy
086	c	Completed SRS
087	b	Using hormone therapy, has transitioned to live as a woman
088	a	Identifies as a woman; wants to have a female body
089	b	Lives full time in female role; has been using hormones
090	a	Identifies as TS, wants to undergo SRS
091	b	Has lived full time in female role for 1 year; approved for SRS
092	b	Has transitioned to live as a woman; using hormone therapy
093	a	Identifies as TS
094	a	Identifies as a woman
095	a	Identifies as TS; feels trapped in the wrong body
096	c	Completed SRS
097	a	Wants to be a woman; wants to have female genitals
098	b	Wants to be female; used hormones for 2 years
099	c	Completed SRS
100	a	Identifies as a woman; wants to become a woman
101	a	Experiences gender dysphoria; wants to have a female body
102	a	Would like to undergo SRS
103	a	Wants to be a woman
104	a	Wants to become a woman and undergo SRS
105	a	Has always wanted to be female; wants to have female genitals
106	a	Wants to become a woman and live as a woman
107	a	Would like to be a woman and have a female body
108	b	Identifies as TS; has used hormone therapy
109	a	Wants to be a woman; identifies as a woman
110	b	Identifies as TS; has used hormone therapy for about 1 year
111	a	Identifies as a woman; lives almost full time as a woman
112	a	Has always wanted to be female; hated physical changes of puberty
113	b	Undergoing hormone therapy; will have SRS soon
114	b	Identifies as female; has been using hormones for about 6 months

(continued)

No.	Criterion	Relevant narrative information
115	c	Completed SRS about 1 year earlier
116	a	Identifies as TS, plans to transition eventually
117	b	Identifies as TS; has used hormones several times
118	c	Completed SRS
119	b	Identifies as TS; using hormone therapy
120	b	Identifies as TS; has used hormone therapy
121	b	Identifies as TS, has transitioned to live as a woman
122	a	Identifies as TS
123	b	Identifies as TS; living full time as a woman
124	b	Identifies as TS; approved for SRS
125	a	Identifies as TS; experiences gender dysphoria
126	a	Wants to live full time as a woman
127	a	Identifies as TS; wants to transition
128	a	Identifies as TS; wants to have a female body
129	b	Identifies as TS; has used hormone therapy
130	b	Identifies as TS; has used hormone therapy
131	a	Has a strong desire to be a woman and have female genitals
132	c	Completed SRS about 6 months earlier
133	a	Identifies as TS
134	b	Identifies as TS; has been using hormones
135	a	Identifies as TS
136	c	Completed SRS about 6 months earlier
137	c	Completed SRS about 22 years earlier
138	c	Completed SRS about 20 years earlier
139	c	Completed SRS about 1 month earlier
140	b	Identifies as a woman; using hormone therapy
141	b	Identifies as TS; using hormone therapy
142	a	Identifies as TS; approved for hormone therapy
143	a	Identifies as TS
144	b	Identifies as a woman; has been using hormones for about 6 years
145	a	Wants to transition and have a woman's body
146	a	Is gender dysphoric; wants to have a female body
147	b	Wants to be female; used hormones before orchiectomy
148	a	Would like to have breasts and a vagina
149	b	Wants to have a female body; is using hormones
150	b	Would like to transition; has been using hormones
151	b	Has used hormones for 2 years; has lived in female role for 1 year
152	a	Experiences gender dysphoria; wants to be a woman
153	a	Wants to undergo SRS
154	b	Identifies as TS; has used hormones
155	a	Identifies as TS; wants to become a woman
156	b	Has used hormone therapy for about 2 years, scheduled for SRS
157	a	Wants to have a female body, hates male genitals
158	b	Identifies as a woman; is using hormones
159	b	Identifies as TS; has used hormones for about 4 years
160	b	Wants to have SRS; has used hormones for several years

(continued)

No.	Criterion	Relevant narrative information
161	b	Identifies as a woman; using hormones; wants SRS
162	b	Wants to be female and to undergo SRS; using hormone therapy
163	a	Wants to have a female body and female genitals
164	a	Wants to have female genitals
165	b	Wants to be female; has been using hormones for about 12 years
166	a	Wants to have female genitals
167	c	Completed SRS about 1 year earlier
168	c	Completed SRS less than 1 year earlier
169	b	Using hormones for about 20 months; approved for SRS
170	b	Using estrogen for feminization for about 4 years
171	b	Wants to have a female body; using hormones for about 7 years
172	a	Feels that her body is wrong; feels she should have been a woman
173	b	Approved for SRS
174	a	Identifies as TS
175	a	Identifies as TS
176	a	Identifies as TS; wants to have female genitals
177	a	Identifies as TS
178	a	Identifies as a woman, wants to have a female body
179	a	Wants to be female and undergo SRS
180	a	Identifies as TS; wants to become a woman
181	b	Identifies as TS; has used transdermal estrogen for 9 years
182	b	Has used hormones for 5 years; has lived in female role for 4 years
183	a	Would like to be a woman and undergo SRS
184	b	Identifies as TS; living full time in female role
185	b	Desires to be a woman; using transdermal estrogen
186	b	Has lived full time in female role for about 2 years
187	b	Wants to have a female body; has used hormones for about 1 year
188	a	Wants to transition; finds male genitals repulsive
189	a	Identifies as TS; wants to have a female body
190	c	Completed SRS
191	a	Identifies as TS
192	b	Identifies as TS; using hormone therapy
193	b	Wants to transition; has been using hormone therapy
194	a	Identifies as TS
195	b	Identifies as TS; has used hormones
196	a	Identifies as TS
197	a	States that her goal is SRS
198	a	Has felt she was a woman since early childhood
199	a	Identifies as female
200	a	Identifies as TS
201	b	Identifies as TS; using hormone therapy; approved for SRS
202	b	Identifies as TS; using hormone therapy
203	a	Wants to undergo SRS
204	a	Identifies as TS
205	b	Identifies as TS; has used hormones for about 3 months
206	a	Identifies as TS; wants to transition to live as a woman

(continued)

No.	Criterion	Relevant narrative information
207	a	Identifies as TS
208	c	Completed SRS
209	a	Wants to have a female body and be accepted as a woman
210	a	Feels a strong desire to be female
211	a	Identifies as TS
212	a	Experiences gender dysphoria, wants to have a woman's body
213	b	Identifies as TS; using hormone therapy, wants to have SRS
214	a	Identifies as TS; wants to have female genitals
215	b	Wants to have a female body; has used hormones
216	c	Completed SRS about 8 months earlier
217	b	Has a female gender identity; has used hormones
218	b	Lives full time as a woman
219	a	Feels an urgent need to transition and become a woman
220	a	Wants to become a woman; wants to start hormone therapy
221	c	Completed SRS about 10 years earlier
222	b	Identifies as TS; is using hormones; is living full time as a woman
223	a	Wants to be female; wants to begin hormone therapy
224	a	Wants to be a woman
225	a	Identifies as TS; wants to undergo SRS
226	b	Wants to be a woman; has used hormones
227	b	Has used hormones for 10 months; has lived in female role for 5 months
228	b	Wants to be a woman; has been using hormones
229	a	Wants to be a woman; wants to have a vagina
230	b	Identifies as TS; has used hormones for about 4 years
231	b	Has been using hormones; living full time in female role
232	b	Is using hormone therapy for gender transition
233	a	Identifies as a woman; wants to undergo SRS
234	b	Experiences gender dysphoria; using hormone therapy
235	a	Identifies as TS
236	c	Completed SRS
237	b	Identifies as TS; has used hormones for about 6 months
238	a	Identifies as TS
239	c	Completed SRS
240	b	Has lived full time as a woman for about 1 year
241	a	Experiences gender dysphoria
242	a	Experiences cross-gender identity; wishes she had been born a girl
243	a	Identifies as TS
244	a	Wants to live as a woman and undergo sex reassignment
245	a	Identifies as TS
246	a	Experiences gender dysphoria; wants to have a female body
247	a	Identifies as TS
248	a	Identifies as TS; is in the process of transition
249	a	Identifies as a woman; experiences gender dysphoria

References

Abel, G. G., & Osborn, C. (1992). The paraphilias. The extent and nature of sexually deviant and criminal behavior. *The Psychiatric Clinics of North America, 15*, 675–687.

American Psychiatric Association. (1987). *Diagnostic and statistical manual of mental disorders* (3rd ed., revised). Washington, DC: American Psychiatric Association.

American Psychiatric Association. (1994). *Diagnostic and statistical manual of mental disorders* (4th ed.). Washington, DC: American Psychiatric Association.

American Psychiatric Association. (2000). *Diagnostic and statistical manual of mental disorders* (4th ed., text rev.). Washington, DC: American Psychiatric Association.

Bailey, J. M. (2003). *The man who would be queen: The science of gender-bending and transsexualism*. Washington, DC: Joseph Henry Press.

Bakker, A., van Kesteren, P. J., Gooren, L. J. G., & Bezemer, P. D. (1993). The prevalence of transsexualism in The Netherlands. *Acta Psychiatrica Scandinavica, 87*, 237–238.

Bancroft, J. (1972). The relationship between gender identity and sexual behaviour: Some clinical aspects. In C. Ounsted & D. C. Taylor (Eds.), *Gender differences: Their ontogeny and significance* (pp. 57–72). Edinburgh: Churchill Livingstone.

Barnes, K. (2001). Some observations on autogynephilia. *Transgender Tapestry, 1*(93), 24–25,62.

Barrett, J. (2007). *Transsexual and other disorders of gender identity*. Oxford: Radcliffe Publishing.

Bartlett, N. H., & Vasey, P. L. (2006). A retrospective study of childhood gender-atypical behavior in Samoan fa'afafine. *Archives of Sexual Behavior, 35*, 659–666.

Beetz, A. M. (2004). Bestiality/zoophilia: A scarcely investigated phenomenon between crime, paraphilia, and love. *Journal of Forensic Psychology Practice, 4*(2), 1–36.

Beigel, H. G., & Feldman, R. (1963). The male transvestite's motivation in fiction, research, and reality. *Advances in Sex Research, 1*, 198–210.

Bell, S. (1902). A preliminary study of the emotion of love between the sexes. *The American Journal of Psychology, 13*, 325–354.

Benjamin, H. (1966). *The transsexual phenomenon*. New York: Julian Press.

Bivona, J. M., & Critelli, J. W. (2009). The nature of women's rape fantasies: An analysis of prevalence, frequency, and contents. *Journal of Sex Research, 46*, 33–45.

Blanchard, R. (1985a). Research methods for the typological study of gender disorders in males. In B. W. Steiner (Ed.), *Gender dysphoria: Development, research, management* (pp. 227–257). New York: Plenum.

Blanchard, R. (1985b). Typology of male-to-female transsexualism. *Archives of Sexual Behavior, 14*, 247–261.

A.A. Lawrence, *Men Trapped in Men's Bodies: Narratives of Autogynephilic Transsexualism*, Focus on Sexuality Research, DOI 10.1007/978-1-4614-5182-2,

Blanchard, R. (1988). Nonhomosexual gender dysphoria. *Journal of Sex Research, 24*, 188–193.

Blanchard, R. (1989a). The classification and labeling of nonhomosexual gender dysphorias. *Archives of Sexual Behavior, 18*, 315–334.

Blanchard, R. (1989b). The concept of autogynephilia and the typology of male gender dysphoria. *The Journal of Nervous and Mental Disease, 177*, 616–623.

Blanchard, R. (1990). Gender identity disorders in adult men. In R. Blanchard & B. Steiner (Eds.), *Clinical management of gender identity disorders in children and adults* (pp. 49–76). Washington, DC: American Psychiatric Press.

Blanchard, R. (1991). Clinical observations and systematic studies of autogynephilia. *Journal of Sex & Marital Therapy, 17*, 235–251.

Blanchard, R. (1992). Nonmonotonic relation of autogynephilia and heterosexual attraction. *Journal of Abnormal Psychology, 101*, 271–276.

Blanchard, R. (1993a). Partial versus complete autogynephilia and gender dysphoria. *Journal of Sex & Marital Therapy, 19*, 301–307.

Blanchard, R. (1993b). The she-male phenomenon and the concept of partial autogynephilia. *Journal of Sex & Marital Therapy, 19*, 69–76.

Blanchard, R. (1993c). Varieties of autogynephilia and their relationship to gender dysphoria. *Archives of Sexual Behavior, 22*, 241–251.

Blanchard, R. (2005). Early history of the concept of autogynephilia. *Archives of Sexual Behavior, 34*, 439–446.

Blanchard, R. (2008). Deconstructing the feminine essence narrative [Commentary]. *Archives of Sexual Behavior, 37*, 434–438.

Blanchard, R., & Clemmensen, L. H. (1988). A test of the DSM-III-R's implicit assumption that fetishistic arousal and gender dysphoria are mutually exclusive. *Journal of Sex Research, 25*, 426–432.

Blanchard, R., Clemmensen, L. H., & Steiner, B. W. (1985). Social desirability response set and systematic distortion in the self-report of adult male gender patients. *Archives of Sexual Behavior, 14*, 505–516.

Blanchard, R., Clemmensen, L. H., & Steiner, B. W. (1987). Heterosexual and homosexual gender dysphoria. *Archives of Sexual Behavior, 16*, 139–152.

Blanchard, R., & Collins, P. I. (1993). Men with sexual interest in transvestites, transsexuals, and she-males. *The Journal of Nervous and Mental Disease, 181*, 570–575.

Blanchard, R., Racansky, I. G., & Steiner, B. W. (1986). Phallometric detection of fetishistic arousal in heterosexual male cross-dressers. *Journal of Sex Research, 22*, 452–462.

Blanchard, R., Steiner, B. W., & Clemmensen, L. H. (1985). Gender dysphoria, gender reorientation, and the clinical management of transsexualism. *Journal of Consulting and Clinical Psychology, 53*, 295–304.

Bloom, A. (2002). *Normal: Transsexual CEOs, crossdressing cops, and hermaphrodites with attitude*. New York: Random House.

Bolin, A. (1988). *In search of Eve: Transsexual rites of passage*. New York: Bergin & Garvey.

Bornstein, K. (1995). *Gender outlaw: On men, women, and the rest of us*. New York: Vintage Books.

Brill, S. A., & Pepper, R. (2008). *The transgender child: A handbook for families and professionals*. San Francisco, CA: Cleiss Press.

Brotto, L. A., Heiman, J. R., & Tolman, D. (2009). Narratives of desire in mid-age women with and without desire difficulties. *Journal of Sex Research, 46*, 387–398.

Brown, G. R. (1988). Transsexuals in the military: Flight into hypermasculinity. *Archives of Sexual Behavior, 17*, 527–537.

Bruno, R. L. (1997). Devotees, pretenders, and wannabes: Two cases of factitious disability disorder. *Sexuality and Disability, 15*, 243–260.

Buckner, H. T. (1970). The transvestic career path. *Psychiatry, 33*, 381–389.

Buhrich, N. (1978). Motivations for cross-dressing in heterosexual transvestism. *Acta Psychiatrica Scandinavica, 57*, 145–152.

Buhrich, N., & Beaumont, T. (1981). Comparison of transvestism in Australia and America. *Archives of Sexual Behavior, 10*, 269–279.

Buhrich, N., & McConaghy, N. (1976). Transvestite fiction. *The Journal of Nervous and Mental Disease, 163*, 420–427.

Buhrich, N., & McConaghy, N. (1977a). Can fetishism occur in transsexuals? *Archives of Sexual Behavior, 6*, 223–235.

Buhrich, N., & McConaghy, N. (1977b). The discrete syndromes of transvestism and transsexualism. *Archives of Sexual Behavior, 6*, 483–495.

Christ, C. P. (1980). *Diving deep and surfacing: Women writers on spiritual quest*. Boston: Beacon Press.

Church, K. (1995). *Forbidden narratives: Critical autobiography as social science*. Amsterdam: Gordon and Breach.

Cohen-Kettenis, P. T., Delemarre-van de Waal, H. A., & Gooren, L. J. (2008). The treatment of adolescent transsexuals: Changing insights. *The Journal of Sexual Medicine, 5*, 1892–1897.

Cohen-Kettenis, P. T., & Pfäfflin, F. (2003). *Transgenderism and intersexuality in childhood and adolescence: Making choices*. Thousand Oaks, CA: Sage.

Cohen-Kettenis, P. T., & Pfäfflin, F. (2010). The DSM diagnostic criteria for gender identity disorder in adolescents and adults. *Archives of Sexual Behavior, 39*, 499–513.

Critelli, J. W., & Bivona, J. M. (2008). Women's erotic rape fantasies: An evaluation of theory and research. *Journal of Sex Research, 45*, 57–70.

Cummings, K. (1992). *Katherine's diary: The story of a transsexual*. Port Melbourne, Australia: William Heinemann Australia.

Daskalos, C. T. (1998). Changes in sexual orientation of six heterosexual male-to-female transsexuals. *Archives of Sexual Behavior, 27*, 605–613.

De Cuypere, G., T'Sjoen, G., Beerten, R., Selvaggi, G., De Sutter, P., Hoebeke, P., et al. (2005). Sexual and physical health after sex reassignment surgery. *Archives of Sexual Behavior, 34*, 679–690.

De Cuypere, G., Van Hemelrijck, M., Michel, A., Carael, B., Heylens, G., Rubens, R., et al. (2007). Prevalence and demography of transsexualism in Belgium. *European Psychiatry, 22*, 137–141.

de Vries, A. L., Steensma, T. D., Doreleijers, T. A., & Cohen-Kettenis, P. T. (2011). Puberty suppression in adolescents with gender identity disorder: A prospective follow-up study. *The Journal of Sexual Medicine, 8*, 2276–2283.

de Vries, G. J., & Södersten, P. (2009). Sex differences in the brain: The relation between structure and function. *Hormones and Behavior, 55*, 589–596.

Deogracias, J. J., Johnson, L. L., Meyer-Bahlburg, H. F. L., Kessler, S. J., Schober, J. M., & Zucker, K. J. (2007). The gender identity/gender dysphoria questionnaire for adolescents and adults. *Journal of Sex Research, 44*, 370–379.

Docter, R. F. (1988). *Transvestites and transsexuals: Toward a theory of cross-gender behavior*. New York: Plenum.

Docter, R. F., & Fleming, J. S. (2001). Measures of transgender behavior. *Archives of Sexual Behavior, 30*, 255–271.

Dolan, J. D. (1987). Transsexualism: Syndrome or symptom? *Canadian Journal of Psychiatry, 32*, 666–673.

Doorn, C. D., Poortinga, J., & Verschoor, A. M. (1994). Cross-gender identity in transvestites and male transsexuals. *Archives of Sexual Behavior, 23*, 185–201.

Dreger, A. (2008). The controversy surrounding the man who would be queen: A case history of the politics of science, identity, and sex in the internet age. *Archives of Sexual Behavior, 37*, 366–421.

Duisin, D., Barisić, J., & Nikolić-Balkoski, G. (2009). Case report of autogynophillia [sic]: Family, ethical and surgical implications. *Psychiatria Danubina, 21*, 242–245.

Ekins, R., & King, D. (2001). Transgendering, migrating and love of oneself as a woman: A contribution to a sociology of autogynephilia. *International Journal of Transgenderism, 5*(3). Available at http://www.wpath.org/journal/www.iiav.nl/ezines/web/IJT/97-03/numbers/symposion/ijtvo05no03_01.htm

Emory, L. E., Williams, D. H., Cole, C. M., Amparo, E. G., & Meyer, W. J. (1991). Anatomic variation of the corpus callosum in persons with gender dysphoria. *Archives of Sexual Behavior, 20*, 409–417.

Feinbloom, D. H., Fleming, M., Kijewski, V., & Schulter, M. P. (1976). Lesbian/feminist orientation among male-to-female transsexuals. *Journal of Homosexuality, 2*(1), 59–71.

Fine, M. (1988). Sexuality, schooling, and adolescent females: The missing discourse of desire. *Harvard Educational Review, 58*, 29–54.

Fisher, A. D., Bandini, E., Ricca, V., Ferruccio, N., Corona, G., Meriggiola, M. C., et al. (2010). Dimensional profiles of male to female gender identity disorder: An exploratory research. *The Journal of Sexual Medicine, 7*, 2487–2498.

Fisk, N. (1974). Gender dysphoria syndrome (the how, what, and why of a disease). In D. R. Laub & P. Gandy (Eds.), *Proceedings of the Second Interdisciplinary Symposium on Gender Dysphoria Syndrome*. Stanford, CA: Stanford University Press.

Freud, S. (1957). On the universal tendency to debasement in the sphere of love. In J. Strachey (Ed. and Trans.), *The standard edition of the complete psychological works of Sigmund Freud* (Vol. 11, pp. 177–190). London: Hogarth Press. (Original work published 1912)

Freund, K., & Blanchard, R. (1993). Erotic target location errors in male gender dysphorics, paedophiles, and fetishists. *The British Journal of Psychiatry, 162*, 558–563.

Freund, K., Steiner, B. W., & Chan, S. (1982). Two types of cross-gender identity. *Archives of Sexual Behavior, 11*, 47–63.

Friedrich, W. N., Fisher, J., Broughton, D., Houston, M., & Shafran, C. R. (1998). Normative sexual behavior in children: A contemporary sample. *Pediatrics, 101*, E9.

Friedrich, W. N., Grambsch, P., Broughton, D., Kuiper, J., & Beilke, R. L. (1991). Normative sexual behavior in children. *Pediatrics, 88*, 456–464.

Friedrich, W. N., Sandfort, T. G. M., Oostveen, J., & Cohen-Kettenis, P. T. (2000). Cultural differences in sexual behavior: 2–6 year old Dutch and American children. *Journal of Psychology and Human Sexuality, 12*(1/2), 117–129.

Gijs, L., & Brewaeys, A. (2007). Surgical treatment of gender dysphoria in adults and adolescents: Recent developments, effectiveness, and challenges. *Annual Review of Sex Research, 18*, 178–224.

Glaser, B. G., & Strauss, A. L. (1967). *The discovery of grounded theory: Strategies for qualitative research*. Chicago: Aldine.

Goldman, R., & Goldman, J. (1982). *Children's sexual thinking: A comparative study of children aged 5 to 15 years in Australia, North America, Britain, and Sweden*. London: Routledge & Kegan Paul.

Gosselin, C. (1979). Personality attributes of the average rubber fetishist. In M. Cook & G. Wilson (Eds.), *Love and attraction: An international conference* (pp. 395–400). London: Pergamon.

Gosselin, C., & Wilson, G. (1980). *Sexual variations: Fetishism, sadomasochism, transvestism*. New York: Simon and Schuster.

Govier, E., & Feldman, J. (1999). Occupational choice and patterns of cognitive abilities. *British Journal of Psychology, 90*, 99–108.

Green, R. (2008). Potholes in the interview road with gender dysphoric patients: Contentious areas in clinical practice. *Sexologies, 17*, 245–257.

Griggs, C. (1998). *S/he: Changing sex and changing clothes*. Oxford: Berg.

Griggs, C. (2004). *Journal of a sex change: Passage through Trinidad*. Oxford: Berg.

Guze, H. (1969). Psychosocial adjustment of transsexuals: An evaluation and theoretical formulation. In R. Green & J. Money (Eds.), *Transsexualism and sex reassignment* (pp. 171–188). Baltimore, MD: Johns Hopkins Press.

Hatfield, E., Schmitz, E., Cornelius, J., & Rapson, R. L. (1988). Passionate love: How early does it begin? *Journal of Psychology and Human Sexuality, 1*(1), 35–51.

Hembree, W. C., Cohen-Kettenis, P., Delemarre-van de Waal, H. A., Gooren, L. J., Meyer, W. J., Spack, N. P., et al. (2009). Endocrine treatment of transsexual persons: An Endocrine Society clinical practice guideline. *Journal of Clinical Endocrinology and Metabolism, 94*, 3132–3154.

Hirschfeld, M. (1918). *Sexualpathologie [Sexual pathology]*. Bonn, Germany: Marcus and Weber.

Hirschfeld, M. (1991). *Transvestites: The erotic drive to cross-dress* (M. A. Lombardi-Nash, Trans.). Buffalo, NY: Prometheus Books. (Original work published 1910)

Huegel, K. (2011). *GLBTQ: The survival guide for gay, lesbian, bisexual, transgender, and questioning teens* (2nd ed.). Minneapolis, MN: Free Spirit.

Humphreys, L. (1976). *Tearoom trade: Impersonal sex in public places*. Chicago: Aldine.

Hunt, N. (1978). *Mirror image: The odyssey of a male-to-female transsexual*. New York: Holt, Rinehart, and Winston.

Isay, R. A. (2009). *Being homosexual: Gay men and their development*. New York: Vintage Books.

Janssen, E. (2011). Sexual arousal in men: A review and conceptual analysis. *Hormones and Behavior, 59*, 708–716.

Jorgensen, C. (1967). *Christine Jorgensen: A personal autobiography*. New York: Paul S. Eriksson.

Kessler, S. J., & McKenna, W. (1978). *Gender: An ethnomethodological approach*. Chicago: University of Chicago Press.

Kise, K., & Nguyen, M. (2011). Adult baby syndrome and gender identity disorder [Letter to the editor]. *Archives of Sexual Behavior, 40*, 857–859.

Kreukels, B. P. C., & Cohen-Kettenis, P. T. (2011). Puberty suppression in gender identity disorder: The Amsterdam experience. *Nature Reviews. Endocrinology, 7*, 466–472.

Krieger, I. (2011). *Helping your transgender teen: A guide for parents*. New Haven, CT: Genderwise Press.

Kulick, D. (1998). *Travesti: Sex, gender, and culture among Brazilian transgendered prostitutes*. Chicago: University of Chicago Press.

Långström, N., & Zucker, K. J. (2005). Transvestic fetishism in the general population: Prevalence and correlates. *Journal of Sex & Marital Therapy, 31*, 87–95.

Lawrence, A. A. (1997, June). *Life after surgery: Questions and answers from the 1996 New Woman Conference*. Paper presented at the Second International Conference on Sex and Gender, King of Prussia, PA. Available at http://www.annelawrence.com/1997sicsg.html

Lawrence, A. A. (1998). Men trapped in men's bodies: An introduction to the concept of autogynephilia. *Transgender Tapestry, 1*(85), 65–68.

Lawrence, A. A. (1999a, August). *Lessons from autogynephiles: Eroticism, motivation, and the Standards of Care*. Paper presented at the Harry Benjamin International Gender Dysphoria Association XVI Biennial Symposium, London, UK. Available at http://www.annelawrence.com/1999hbigda1.html

Lawrence, A. A. (1999b, August). *Men trapped in men's bodies: Autogynephilic eroticism as a motive for seeking sex reassignment*. Paper presented at the Harry Benjamin International Gender Dysphoria Association XVI Biennial Symposium, London, UK. Available at http://www.annelawrence.com/1999hbigda2.html

Lawrence, A. A. (1999c). *Thirty-one new narratives about autogynephilia*. Available at http://www.annelawrence.com/31narratives.html

Lawrence, A. A. (1999d). *Twenty-eight narratives about autogynephilia*. Available at http://www.annelawrence.com/28narratives.html

Lawrence, A. A. (2000). Sexuality and transsexuality: A new introduction to autogynephilia. *Transgender Tapestry, 1*(92), 17–23, 29–30.

Lawrence, A. A. (2003). Factors associated with satisfaction or regret following male-to-female sex reassignment surgery. *Archives of Sexual Behavior, 32*, 299–315.

Lawrence, A. A. (2004). Autogynephilia: A paraphilic model of gender identity disorder. *Journal of Gay & Lesbian Psychotherapy, 8*(1/2), 69–87.

Lawrence, A. A. (2005). Sexuality before and after male-to-female sex reassignment surgery. *Archives of Sexual Behavior, 34*, 147–166.

Lawrence, A. A. (2006). Clinical and theoretical parallels between desire for limb amputation and gender identity disorder. *Archives of Sexual Behavior, 35*, 263–278.

Lawrence, A. A. (2007). Becoming what we love: Autogynephilic transsexualism conceptualized as an expression of romantic love. *Perspectives in Biology and Medicine, 50*, 506–520.

Lawrence, A. A. (2008). Shame and narcissistic rage in autogynephilic transsexualism [Commentary]. *Archives of Sexual Behavior, 37*, 457–461.

Lawrence, A. A. (2009a). Erotic target location errors: An underappreciated paraphilic dimension. *Journal of Sex Research, 46*, 194–215.

Lawrence, A. A. (2009b). Transgenderism in nonhomosexual males as a paraphilic phenomenon: Implications for case conceptualization and treatment. *Sexual and Relationship Therapy, 24*, 188–206.

Lawrence, A. A. (2010a). A validation of Blanchard's typology: Comment on Nuttbrock et al. (2010) [Letter to the editor]. *Archives of Sexual Behavior, 39*, 1011–1015.

Lawrence, A. A. (2010b). Sexual orientation versus age of onset as bases for typologies (subtypes) of gender identity disorder in adolescents and adults. *Archives of Sexual Behavior, 39*, 514–545.

Lawrence, A. A. (2010c). Societal individualism predicts prevalence of nonhomosexual orientation in male-to-female transsexualism. *Archives of Sexual Behavior, 39*, 573–583.

Lawrence, A. A. (2010d). Something resembling autogynephilia in women: Comment on Moser (2009) [Letter to the Editor]. *Journal of Homosexuality, 57*, 1–4.

Lawrence, A. A. (2011a). Autogynephilia: An underappreciated paraphilia. *Advances in Psychosomatic Medicine, 31*, 135–148.

Lawrence, A. A. (2011b). Further validation of Blanchard's typology: A reply to Nuttbrock, Bockting, Rosenblum, Mason, and Hwahng (2010) [Letter to the editor]. *Archives of Sexual Behavior, 40*, 1089–1091.

Lawrence, A. A., & Bailey, J. M. (2009). Transsexual groups in Veale et al. (2008) are "autogynephilic" and "even more autogynephilic" [Letter to the editor]. *Archives of Sexual Behavior, 38*, 173–175.

Lawrence, A. A., Latty, E. M., Chivers, M., & Bailey, J. M. (2005). Measurement of sexual arousal in postoperative male-to-female transsexuals using vaginal photoplethysmography. *Archives of Sexual Behavior, 34*, 135–145.

Lawrence, A. A., & Zucker, K. J. (2012). Gender identity disorders. In M. Hersen & D. C. Beidel (Eds.), *Adult psychopathology and diagnosis* (6th ed., pp. 601–635). Hoboken, NJ: John Wiley & Sons.

Levine, S. B. (1993). Gender-disturbed males. *Journal of Sex & Marital Therapy, 19*, 131–141.

Levine, S. B., Risen, C. B., & Althof, S. E. (1990). Essay on the diagnosis and nature of paraphilia. *Journal of Sex & Marital Therapy, 16*, 89–102.

Lippa, R. (2002). Gender-related traits of heterosexual and homosexual men and women. *Archives of Sexual Behavior, 31*, 83–98.

Lukianowicz, N. (1959). Survey of various aspects of transvestism in the light of our present knowledge. *The Journal of Nervous and Mental Disease, 128*, 36–64.

Lundström, B., Pauly, I., & Wålinder, J. (1984). Outcomes of sex reassignment surgery. *Acta Psychiatrica Scandinavica, 70*, 289–294.

Marks, I., Green, R., & Mataix-Cols, D. (2000). Adult gender identity disorder can remit. *Comprehensive Psychiatry, 41*, 273–275.

Martinson, F. M. (1976). Eroticism in infancy and childhood. *Journal of Sex Research, 12*, 251–262.

Martinson, F. M. (1994). *The sexual life of children*. Westport, CT: Bergin & Garvey.

McCloskey, D. N. (1999). *Crossing: A memoir*. Chicago: University of Chicago Press.

McCloskey, D. (2003, November). Queer science: A data-bending psychologist confirms what he already knew about gays and transsexuals [Book review]. *Reason Online*. Available at http://reason.com/archives/2003/11/01/queer-science

McCloskey, D. (2008). Politics in scholarly drag: Dreger's assault on the critics of Bailey [Commentary]. *Archives of Sexual Behavior, 37*, 466–468.

Meana, M. (2008). The drama of sex, identity, and the "*Queen*" [Commentary]. *Archives of Sexual Behavior, 37*, 469–471.

Meyer, W., III, Bockting, W. O., Cohen-Kettenis, P., Coleman, E., DiCeglie, D., Devor, H., et al. (2001). *The standards of care for gender identity disorders, sixth version*. Düsseldorf: Symposion.

Meyer-Bahlburg, H. F. (2010). From mental disorder to iatrogenic hypogonadism: Dilemmas in conceptualizing gender identity variants as psychiatric conditions. *Archives of Sexual Behavior, 39*, 461–476.

Miletski, H. (2005). Is zoophilia a sexual orientation? A study. In A. M. Beetz & A. L. Podberscek (Eds.), *Bestiality and zoophilia: Sexual relations with animals* (pp. 82–97). West Lafayette, IN: Purdue University Press.

Money, J. (1986). *Lovemaps: Clinical concepts of sexual/erotic health and pathology, paraphilia, and gender transposition in childhood, adolescence, and maturity*. New York: Irvington.

Money, J. (1988). *Gay, straight, and in-between: The sexology of erotic orientation*. New York: Oxford University Press.

Money, J. (1990). Paraphilia in females: Fixation on amputation and lameness; two personal accounts. *Journal of Psychology and Human Sexuality, 3*(2), 165–172.

Money, J., & Gaskin, R. J. (1970–1971). Sex reassignment. *International Journal of Psychiatry, 9*, 249–269.

Money, J., Jobaris, R., & Furth, G. (1977). Apotemnophilia: Two cases of self-demand amputation as a paraphilia. *Journal of Sex Research, 13*, 115–125.

Money, J., & Lamacz, M. (1984). Gynemimesis and gynemimetophilia: Individual and cross-cultural manifestations of a gender-coping strategy hitherto unnamed. *Comprehensive Psychiatry, 25*, 392–403.

Moser, C. (2009). Autogynephilia in women. *Journal of Homosexuality, 56*, 539–547.

Moser, C. (2010). Blanchard's autogynephilia theory: A critique. *Journal of Homosexuality, 57*, 790–809.

Muirhead-Allwood, S. K., Royle, M. G., & Young, R. (1999, September). Sexuality and satisfaction with surgical results in male-to-female transsexuals. Poster session presented at the Harry Benjamin International Gender Dysphoria Association XVI Biennial Symposium, London.

Multhaup, K. S., Johnson, M. D., & Tetirick, J. C. (2005). The wane of childhood amnesia for autobiographical and public event memories. *Memory, 13*, 161–173.

Nanda, S. (1994). Hijras: An alternative sex and gender role in India. In G. Herdt (Ed.), *Third sex, third gender: Beyond sexual dimorphism in culture and history* (pp. 373–417). New York: Zone Books.

Nieder, T. O., Herff, M., Cerwenka, S., Preuss, W. F., Cohen-Kettenis, P. T., De Cuypere, G., et al. (2011). Age of onset and sexual orientation in transsexual males and females. *The Journal of Sexual Medicine, 8*, 783–791.

Nuttbrock, L., Bockting, W., Mason, M., Hwahng, S., Rosenblum, A., Macri, M., et al. (2011). A further assessment of Blanchard's typology of homosexual versus non-homosexual or autogynephilic gender dysphoria. *Archives of Sexual Behavior, 40*, 247–257.

Nuttbrock, L., Bockting, W., Rosenblum, A., Mason, M., & Hwahng, S. (2010). The limitations of Blanchard's typology: A response to Lawrence (2010) [Letter to the Editor]. *Archives of Sexual Behavior, 39*, 1017–1020.

Nuttbrock, L., Bockting, W., Rosenblum, A., Mason, M., & Hwahng, S. (2011). Sexual arousal associated with private as compared to public feminine dressing among male-to-female transgender persons: A further response to Lawrence (2011) [Letter to the Editor]. *Archives of Sexual Behavior, 40*, 1093–1096.

Ovesey, L., & Person, E. (1973). Gender identity and sexual psychopathology in men: A psychodynamic analysis of homosexuality, transsexualism, and transvestism. *The Journal of the American Academy of Psychoanalysis, 1*, 53–72.

Ovesey, L., & Person, E. (1976). Transvestism: A disorder of the sense of self. *International Journal of Psychoanalytic Psychotherapy, 5*, 219–236.

Paulhus, D. L. (1984). Two-component models of socially desirable responding. *Journal of Personality and Social Psychology, 46*, 598–609.
Person, E. S. (1980). Sexuality as the mainstay of identity: Psychoanalytic perspectives. In C.R. Stimpson & E. S. Person (Eds.), *Women: Sex and sexuality* (pp. 36–61). Chicago: University of Chicago Press.
Person, E. S. (1995). *By force of fantasy: How we make our lives*. New York: Basic Books.
Person, E. S. (1999). Harry Benjamin and the birth of a shared cultural fantasy. In *The sexual century* (pp. 347–366). New Haven, CT: Yale University Press.
Person, E., & Ovesey, L. (1974a). The transsexual syndrome in males. I. Primary transsexualism. *American Journal of Psychotherapy, 28*, 4–20.
Person, E., & Ovesey, L. (1974b). The transsexual syndrome in males. II. Secondary transsexualism. *American Journal of Psychotherapy, 28*, 174–193.
Person, E., & Ovesey, L. (1978). Transvestism: New perspectives. *The Journal of the American Academy of Psychoanalysis, 6*, 301–323.
Prosser, J. (1998). *Second skins: The body narratives of transsexuality*. New York: Columbia University Press.
Richards, R., & Ames, J. (1983). *Second serve*. New York: Stein and Day.
Roth, B. (Producer/Writer/Director), & Weis, B. (Producer) (1984). *Heartbreakers* [Motion picture]. United States: Orion Pictures.
Roughgarden, J. (2004). *Evolution's rainbow: Diversity, gender, and sexuality in nature and people*. Los Angeles, CA: University of California Press.
Sandfort, T. G. M., & Cohen-Kettenis, P. T. (2000). Sexual behavior in Dutch and Belgian children as observed by their mothers. *Journal of Psychology and Human Sexuality, 12*(1/2), 105–115.
Savin-Williams, R. C., & Diamond, L. M. (2000). Sexual identity trajectories among sexual-minority youths: Gender comparisons. *Archives of Sexual Behavior, 29*, 607–627.
Schrock, D. P., & Reid, L. L. (2006). Transsexuals' sexual stories. *Archives of Sexual Behavior, 35*, 75–86.
Selvaggi, G., Ceulemans, P., De Cuypere, G., VanLanduyt, K., Blondeel, P., Hamdi, M., et al. (2005). Gender identity disorder: General overview and surgical treatment for vaginoplasty in male-to-female transsexuals. *Plastic and Reconstructive Surgery, 116*, 135e–145e.
Serano, J. M. (2010). The case against autogynephilia. *International Journal of Transgenderism, 12*, 176–187.
Seto, M. C. (2012). Is pedophilia a sexual orientation? *Archives of Sexual Behavior, 41*, 231–236.
Shore, E. S. (1984). The former transsexual: A case study. *Archives of Sexual Behavior, 13*, 277–285.
Singh, D., Deogracias, J. J., Johnson, L. L., Bradley, S. J., Kibblewhite, S. J., Owen-Anderson, A., et al. (2010). The gender identity/gender dysphoria questionnaire for adolescents and adults: Further validity evidence. *Journal of Sex Research, 47*, 49–58.
Sørensen, T., & Hertoft, P. (1980). Transsexualism as a nosological unity in men and women. *Acta Psychiatrica Scandinavica, 61*, 135–151.
Spada, J. (1979). *The Spada report: The newest survey of gay male sexuality*. New York: New American Library.
Steensma, T. D., Biemond, R., de Boer, F., & Cohen-Kettenis, P. T. (2011). Desisting and persisting gender dysphoria after childhood: A qualitative follow-up study. *Clinical Child Psychology and Psychiatry, 16*, 499–516.
Steiner, B. W. (1985). Transsexuals, transvestites, and their partners. In B. W. Steiner (Ed.), *Gender dysphoria: Development, research, management* (pp. 351–364). New York: Plenum.
Stoller, R. J. (1968). *Sex and gender: On the development of masculinity and femininity*. New York: Science House.
Stoller, R. J. (1975). *Perversion: The erotic form of hatred*. New York: Pantheon.
Stoller, R. J. (1985). A child fetishist. In *Presentations of gender* (pp. 93–136). New Haven: Yale University Press.

Strauss, A., & Corbin, J. (1998). *Basics of qualitative research: Techniques and procedures for developing grounded theory*. Thousand Oaks, CA: Sage.

Swaab, D. F. (2007). Sexual differentiation of the brain and behavior. *Best Practice & Research. Clinical Endocrinology & Metabolism, 21*, 431–444.

Teh, Y. K. (2001). Mak nyahs (male transsexuals) in Malaysia: The influence of culture and religion on their identity. *International Journal of Transgenderism, 5*(3). Available at http://www.wpath.org/journal/www.iiav.nl/ezines/web/IJT/97-03/numbers/symposion/ijtvo05no03_04.htm

Updike, J. (1991). Venus and others. In L. Goldstein (Ed.), *The female body: Figures, styles, speculations* (pp. 5–8). Ann Arbor, MI: University of Michigan Press.

Veale, J. F. (2008). Prevalence of transsexualism among New Zealand passport holders. *The Australian and New Zealand Journal of Psychiatry, 42*, 887–889.

Veale, J. F., Clarke, D. E., & Lomax, T. C. (2008). Sexuality of male-to-female transsexuals. *Archives of Sexual Behavior, 37*, 586–597.

Wallien, M. S., & Cohen-Kettenis, P. T. (2008). Psychosexual outcome of gender-dysphoric children. *Journal of the American Academy of Child and Adolescent Psychiatry, 47*, 1413–1423.

Walworth, J. R. (1997). Sex-reassignment surgery in male-to-female transsexuals: Client satisfaction in relation to selection criteria. In B. Bullough, V. L. Bullough, & J. Elias (Eds.), *Gender blending* (pp. 352–369). Amherst, NY: Prometheus Books.

Whitam, F. L. (1987). A cross-cultural perspective on homosexuality, transvestism, and transsexualism. In G. D. Wilson (Ed.), *Variant sexuality: Research and theory* (pp. 176–201). Baltimore, MD: Johns Hopkins University Press.

Whitam, F. L. (1997). Culturally universal aspects of male homosexual transvestites and transsexuals. In B. Bullough, V. L. Bullough, & J. Elias (Eds.), *Gender blending* (pp. 189–203). Amherst, NY: Prometheus Books.

Wilson, G. D., & Gosselin, C. (1980). Personality characteristics of fetishists, transvestites, and masochists. *Personality and Individual Differences, 1*, 289–295.

Wilson, P., Sharp, C., & Carr, S. (1999). The prevalence of gender dysphoria in Scotland: A primary care study. *The British Journal of General Practice, 49*, 991–992.

Winter, S. (2006). Thai transgenders in focus: Demographics, transitions, and identities. *International Journal of Transgenderism, 9*(1), 15–27.

Winters, K. (2008). *Autogynephilia: The infallible derogatory hypothesis, part 2*. Retrieved from http://gidreform.wordpress.com/2008/11/19/autogynephilia-the-infallible-derogatory-hypothesis-part-2/

World Health Organization. (1992). *International statistical classification of diseases and related health problems* (10th rev., Vol. 1). Geneva, Switzerland: World Health Organization.

World Professional Association for Transgender Health. (2011). *Standards of care for the health of transsexual, transgender, and gender nonconforming people*. Available at http://www.wpath.org/documents/Standards%20of%20Care_FullBook_1g-1.pdf

Yates, A. (2004). Biologic perspectives on early erotic development. *Child and Adolescent Psychiatric Clinics of North America, 13*, 479–496.

Zander, E. (2003). *TransActions*. Stockholm, Sweden: Periskop Förlag.

Zucker, K. J., & Blanchard, R. (1997). Transvestic fetishism: Psychopathology and theory. In D.R. Laws & W. O'Donohue (Eds.), *Sexual deviance: Theory, assessment, and treatment* (pp. 253–279). New York: Guilford Press.

Zucker, K. J., Bradley, S., Owen-Anderson, A., Kibblewhite, S. J., Wood, H., Singh, D., et al. (2012). Demographics, behavior problems, and psychosexual characteristics of adolescents with gender identity disorder or transvestic fetishism. *Journal of Sex & Marital Therapy, 38*, 151–189.

Zucker, K. J., Bradley, S. J., Owen-Anderson, A., Singh, D., Blanchard, R., & Bain, D. (2011). Puberty-blocking hormonal therapy for adolescents with gender identity disorder: A descriptive clinical study. *Journal of Gay & Lesbian Mental Health, 15*, 58–82.

Author Index

A.A. Lawrence, *Men Trapped in Men's Bodies: Narratives of Autogynephilic Transsexualism*, Focus on Sexuality Research, DOI 10.1007/978-1-4614-5182-2,

Subject Index

A.A. Lawrence, *Men Trapped in Men's Bodies: Narratives of Autogynephilic Transsexualism*, Focus on Sexuality Research, DOI 10.1007/978-1-4614-5182-2,

MIX
Papier aus verantwortungsvollen Quellen
Paper from responsible sources
FSC® C105338

If you have any concerns about our products,
you can contact us on
ProductSafety@springernature.com

In case Publisher is established outside the EU,
the EU authorized representative is:
Springer Nature Customer Service Center GmbH
Europaplatz 3, 69115 Heidelberg, Germany

Printed by Libri Plureos GmbH
in Hamburg, Germany